IS MANAGER'S GUIDE TO
Implementing
and Managing
Internet
Technology

RICHARD BARRETT CLEMENTS

PRENTICE HALL

Library of Congress Cataloging-in-Publication Data

Clements, Richard Barrett
    IS manager's guide to implementing and managing
  internet technology / Richard B. Clements.
        p.   cm.
      Includes index.
      ISBN 0-13-974890-3
      1. High technology industries—Management. 2. Industrial
  management—Computer network resources. 3. Management information
  systems. 4. Business enterprises—Computer networks—Management.
  5. Internet (Computer network) I. Title.
  HD62.37C62 1999
  658'.054678—dc21   98-50419
                                                               CIP

© 1999 by Prentice Hall

This publication is designed to provide accurate and authoritative information in regard to the subject matter covered. It is sold with the understanding that the publisher is not engaged in rendering legal, accounting, or other professional services. If legal advice or other expert assistance is required, the services of a competent professional person should be sought.

—From a Declaration of Principles jointly adopted by a Committee of the American Bar Association and a committee of Publishers and Associations.

Printed in the United States of America

10 9 8 7 6 5 4 3

ISBN 0-13-974890-3

ATTENTION: CORPORATIONS AND SCHOOLS
Prentice Hall books are available at quantity discounts with bulk purchase for educational, business, or sales promotional use. For information, please write to: Prentice Hall Special Sales, 240 Frisch Court, Paramus, New Jersey 07652. Please supply: title of book, ISBN, quantity, how the book will be used, and date needed.

PRENTICE HALL
Paramus, NJ 07652

On the World Wide Web at http://www.phdirect.com

Preface

The Information Systems Manager/Internet Crisis

There is a growing crisis in the information technology field. The number of companies wishing to connect to the internet is growing at an astounding rate. At the same time, the number of people qualified to take a company onto the internet is far fewer than the demand.

This situation creates several problems that this book is designed to solve. Because of the shortage of knowledgeable people, technicians are quickly promoted into management positions or take on management responsibilities without adequate training or experience to carry out these duties.

The explosion in hardware and software products for the internet makes it nearly impossible for one person to find the perfect combinations for maximum efficiency and effectiveness. At the same time, IS managers need to find the right people to install and maintain software and hardware. Again, because of the shortage of such people, the IS manager is forced to train people to fill the need.

Meanwhile, successful IS managers who have installed and maintained networks within a company are now being asked to implement internet services. Top management sees this as a small project when, in most cases, it is a major undertaking. Top management has to be made aware of the competitive opportunities on the internet. The IS manager also has to quiet fears about the internet with both management and employees.

At the same time, the IS manager has to evaluate the true internet needs of the organization and accurately predict future needs. These predictions must be converted into a plan of implementation that accounts for all needed resources, such as software, hardware, support, personnel, time, money, and politics. Adding to the problem is the growing use of intranets—private, in-house versions of the internet. Intranets can be used to increase the efficiency of a company and to develop communication systems that were never possible before.

Therefore, introducing your company or organization to the internet will be a high-profile project. Success will bring praises from management; failure will be a disaster to your career. The stakes are high. Careful planning and hard work by the IS manager are required for a successful implementation.

This book introduces you to the standard management techniques used to successfully complete any major project. The projects discussed in the text involve making internet connections and building intranets. The emphasis is on proper management techniques over hardware and software features. My goal is to make you a better manager through the experience of introducing the internet to your company.

As fate would have it, I had already installed a local area network at our company, Solution Specialists, and a web hosting site on the internet, when I was asked to write this book. Solution Specialists specializes in management consulting, specifically new techniques and technologies. We currently maintain several sites on the internet and own the domain "9000.net." We also have an intranet running our ISO 9000 documentation system for the office. A wide area network and extranet help us to keep in contact with both customers and contractors around the world.

As you read this book you will occasionally note the stories of frustration. These are based on our experiences with implementing our own systems and those at customer locations. The internet and its related technologies are both new and dynamic, leading to many situations where literally no one knows the solution to a problem. Advancing technology also leads to compatibility problems, lack of technical support, incorrect information, and other situations that make work life fun.

Such a situation can be a nightmare for the unprepared manager. However, the properly prepared manager will sift through these problems and offer appropriate solutions without much trouble. As one manager we interviewed stated, "I would rather have complete unpredictability. With that I can use almost any method to solve a problem."

In other words, fluid situations give you more flexibility. Rigid systems present too many barriers. The internet is a very fluid situation. Therefore, you need to understand the nature of the internet and how it is properly managed. The secret is that there are no final answers. Your solutions must be as fluid as the environment. This is why we discuss "best practices" and not "standard procedures." This is why policies must be written to allow for rapid change. This is why we plan with contingencies in mind and constant testing scheduled.

In short, if you are assigned the role of introducing the internet to your company, prepare for one of the more interesting experiences in your life. The opportunities and pitfalls are both endless. This book will be your guide around the pitfalls toward the opportunities.

Richard Clements
Alto, Michigan

How This Book Will Help You

This book is designed to guide you through the process of introducing the internet to your company or organization. At the same time, we will accomplish the following goals:

1. Teach you management techniques that improve the performance and professionalism of any IS manager.
2. Give you policy and procedural templates to jump start your internet management system development.
3. Show you how to prepare evaluation checksheets for selecting hardware, software, support, and personnel for your IS/IT projects.
4. Warn you of the management and technology pitfalls bundled with internet usage.
5. Show you how to train your own people.
6. Explain how to get support for your implementation project and how to get people to be enthusiastic users of the internet and your own intranet.
7. Illustrate the power of continuous improvement and preventive actions to create a nearly crash-free system.

In short, implementing internet connections and corporate intranets will be a considerable learning experience for you.

Problems We Will Avoid

Pick up almost any book on how to connect a company to the internet or how to conduct business on the internet and you will discover that the majority of text is spent discussing hardware and software. The installation of hardware and software will be about 20% or less of your involvement time in introducing your company to the internet. Also, by the time a computer product is mentioned in a book, the information is already partially or completely obsolete.

How This Book Works

At the heart of this book will be four different implementation projects. These examples, taken from real organizations, represent the range of possible situations the IS manager might encounter when required to introduce the internet to his or her company. The four examples vary by the size of the company involved and the extent to which the internet will be used. They are:

1. Dickerson County Public Schools—a suburban county school system located outside a major U.S. city. The 50 employees currently use a single local area network. They feel that internet access could bring the parents and students closer to the process of education. Budgets are limited, however, and politics are running against the idea of ever using the internet.

2. Avix Manufacturing—a medium sized automotive supplier with 500 employees at three manufacturing sites. Management here wants the company catalog on the internet to help promote new sales and speed communications with existing customers. The company is also pursuing ISO 9000 registration and wants an internal system of document control on an intranet.

3. The Law Firm—a large law firm that badly needs to coordinate communications with an intranet while providing limited internet access for legal research. The current local area networks in-house also carry audio and video conferencing to the seven regional offices.

4. Megalith, Inc.—a large corporation employing over 20,000 people in offices around the world. The headquarters building alone has 5,000 employees using several local area networks and a mainframe network. Management feels there is a need for internet presence, but is divided on how to proceed.

Although these do not represent all possible scenarios, they do contain enough of the elements of implementation that you can read through these examples and create the action plan that best fits your company's needs.

There are several methods we will be using throughout this book. You should be aware of them and their purpose to reap the maximum benefits from this book. They are:

1. *Discovery exercises.* You will be asked to complete a series of exercises as part of the process of preparing an internet management system. The exercises are designed to help you discover important facts that must be kept in mind when introducing the internet to your company.

For example, it is easy to say that you need a policy restricting which sites employees may access on the internet. The discovery exercise for this issue will make you aware of some of the difficulties you might have deciding which areas to restrict. You will discover by going through a checklist of possible sites to restrict that many could be both beneficial and harmful to your company. Don't worry; the text will show you how to resolve such conflicts.

2. *Stories from the real world.* Years of training experience have taught me that the number one thing people want to learn is what other people are doing to cope with a problem. One of the big problems for companies today is how to use the internet to increase their sales, to enhance their competitive position, or to provide new services for customers. How other companies have accomplished these objectives is explained in this book.

3. *Our own web page.* What would a book about the internet be without its own web page? To keep you up to date on the latest developments and to discuss what other companies are doing, a web page was established at:

www.9000.net

You can also help write the next edition of the book by telling us your experiences, sharing solutions, and responding to questions from the authors.

4. *Lists of further resources.* At the end of each chapter is a list of other books and software packages you can use to further your understanding of the topics discussed. Many times the text may talk briefly about a topic that interests you. For example, this book discusses the process of project management. A complete understanding of project management techniques takes additional study and training. The list will tell you where you can find these resources.

5. *Web links.* One of the best sources of information on the internet is the internet itself. Of all of the topics available on the internet, web technology and related products seem to dominate. Therefore, the book includes lists of resource-rich sites you can go to for further information and discussion.

6. *Search strategies.* The internet is armed with many search engines that can ferret out information on a particular topic. Because internet sites can change, move, or vanish overnight, it is best to run a search on particular topics to find the most recent information. Search strategies require an exact description of what you want that won't return an overwhelming list of possibilities or fail to find what you are looking for. Therefore, each chapter includes the successful search terms we used to research many of the topics in that chapter.

Most of all, this book uses a straightforward approach to discuss the complete project of implementing internet connections. About 80% of your time will be spent planning, preparing, training, recruiting, evaluating, testing, and validating your system. Hardware and software will be the least of your problems.

Several things will be accomplished at the same time within the chapters of this book. For example, Chapter 1 is a discussion of the terms and technologies related to the internet. It also contains the recipes for making connections to the internet. At the same time, the chapter can serve as a training package to educate management and employees on what the internet is and what it can do for them and for the company.

What You Will Need Before You Start

The most important item to have before you start the process of introducing the internet to your company is your own dial-up account with access to the internet. You will need this account to search the internet for information, to communicate with suppliers, to test your internal systems, and a host of other critical tasks. Having a dial-up account will also introduce you to the companies that can supply internet access to your company. The independent service providers (ISPs) of the internet have a wide range of capabilities and qualities. By experiencing these firsthand you will quickly learn which companies are not good choices for providing access to your entire company. Finding the right company will take extra investigation.

Next, you will need a spiral-bound notebook and pen. Carry this with you always as you implement the internet management system. This will be used to write down your experiences, both successful and not so successful. At the end of your implementation project, this log book will be summarized to help you learn from the experience and to share with others so that they will not make the same mistakes on related projects.

Finally, you need time. The implementation of internet connections is a time-consuming process. If you take the time to do it right the first time, you will prevent hundreds of hours of wasted time later trying to fix preventable problems.

Contents

Phase One:
Planning the Internet Project
1

Chapter 1

Chapter 2

Creating a Successful Action Plan   27

Chapter 3

Taking Inventory of Existing Resources   55

Chapter 4

Getting a Handle on Security, Virus Protection, Encryption, Access, and Privacy Issues

71

Chapter 5

Creating the Corporate Internet Policy

107

Chapter 6

Finding, Evaluating, and Contracting Vendor Assistance

125

Phase Two:
Implementation of the Project
149

Chapter 7

Selecting Hardware   151

Chapter 8

Selecting Software   175

Chapter 9

Establishing an Internet Connection   201

Chapter 10

Understanding HTML   225

Phase Three:
Running the Network
319

Chapter 14

The Internet and the Law 321

Chapter 15

Auditing the Internet or Intranet System 339

Introduction

Your Chance to Shine as the IS Manager

This book will teach you how to introduce your company to the internet. At the same time, we'll also talk about forming an intranet within your company. Internet technology is the use of common browsers and networks to connect widely dispersed computers for a common purpose. This would include intranets. Your job is to introduce internet technology to your company. The purpose of this book is to show you how to do this effectively and efficiently, using the techniques described in the preface.

The introduction of internet technology into a company represents a high-profile project. This is your opportunity to demonstrate your effectiveness as an IS manager. It is also an opportunity to stumble badly and come off looking incompetent to management. Therefore, we shall take pains to avoid the pitfalls and trouble spots. This book emphasizes professional management techniques. What you'll discover is that common and widely applied management techniques are very effective at implementing internet technologies.

To understand how all of this is accomplished, we must first work through some discovery exercises. As mentioned previously, we will use a series of exercises and examples so that you may fully discover why certain techniques are used and what opportunities lie before you.

Discovery: What's Wrong with This Picture?

Let's begin with our first exercise. Figure I–1 is a diagram of a typical local area network. There are 16 computers linked together on an ethernet. Each com-

Figure I-1. What is wrong with this picture?

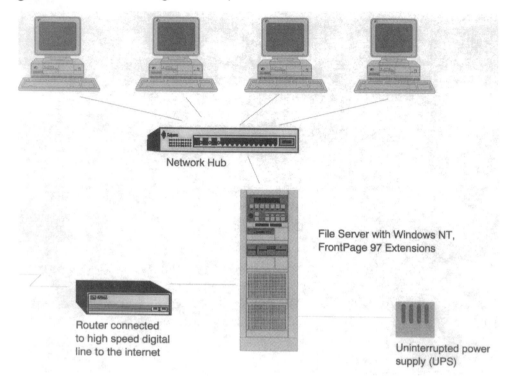

Network Hub

File Server with Windows NT,
FrontPage 97 Extensions

Router connected
to high speed digital
line to the internet

Uninterrupted power
supply (UPS)

puter is running Windows 95. Novell NetWare is being used to run the local area network. The IS manager has placed a file server onto the local area network to serve as the web server to the internet. This server is running Windows NT 4.0. The extensions for FrontPage 97 have been loaded into the web server. FrontPage 97 has been used to design a discussion group that is placed on the internet so that customers can ask questions about the products your company makes.

Question: What is the probability that this system will work without a single problem for an entire day?

The answer is zero. This system will not work. Although this is the textbook example of a local area network and has been featured in several internet technology books, the fact is, it just will not work. Several problems are encased in this type of design of an information system.

As we work through this book you'll discover many of the problems in this design. The first one that we will point out is that discussion groups in FrontPage 97 never did work with the extensions for web servers. In other words, even though it is implied that anything created on a piece of software will work with other compatible pieces of software, this is not always the case.

Therefore, the first problem to discover in the system's design is that the IS manager did not prototype the system to see if the software packages were all compatible to the mission. As we shall see, there are other problems inherent in the system.

Hardware/Software Seduction

Another common theme that we will talk about in this book is the seduction of hardware and software. If you pick up most books on how to connect your company to the internet, you'll discover that over 90% of their content deals with the hardware and software required. This is a major mistake for most IS managers. Although the selection of proper hardware and software is one of the critical goals of introducing internet technology to your company, it should only occupy about 20% of your time.

Now let's try our second discovery exercise. Following is a common job description for an IS manager. Read through the ad and see if this accurately describes your job.

> "Network manager—responsible for the overall operation of the local area network, must find and negotiate deals with the outside vendors, must deal with down networks and possible loss of data, must know how to handle security breaches and anticipate future needs, must anticipate and implement new technologies, must know how to take advantage of the internet, and must know how to develop systems compatible with company's strategic needs."

Question: What is wrong with this description?

Did you read through the job description and say to yourself, "Yes, that sounds just like my job?" This is exactly what should happen to the majority of IS managers currently on the job. The company's primary focus is keeping the network up and running and supplied with hardware and software.

What is missing from this job description is anything to do with management. A professional manager is responsible for the planning, coordination, implementation, and continuous improvement of systems. This includes the recruitment, training, and development of personnel. A manager is responsible for setting the policies and writing the procedures for departments. Now, does any of that sound like the previous description?

The answer is no. Today's IS manager is in high demand by companies that require local area networks and internet technology. The number of people that can actually work with internet technologies and local area networks is less than the demand. This leads to two anomalies. The first is a very high salary for some of these people. The second, which is more important to our discussion, is the fact that these people are being thrown into a situation known as "firefighting."

Firefighting is where a manager spends the entire day solving immediate problems within a system. Now look at the job description again. Everything here is a discussion of firefighting. It is firefighting that we must get away from. The professional manager has people on the staff to fight fires. The professional manager plans strategies that prevent problems instead of spending all of his/her time correcting the results of those problems. Therefore, this book emphasizes management techniques that will help you not only prevent problems, but expose opportunities you'll find within the implementation of web technologies.

The Special Techniques

The bulk of this book will be a straightforward discussion of how to implement internet technology within your company. However, we'll introduce to you three management techniques that are not widely practiced in the information technology field. These techniques are used effectively by managers in other departments. Our experience with implementing the same techniques within the IS department has met with great success. Let's look briefly at these techniques to see why they are so important.

1. **Failure Mode and Effects Analysis (FMEA).** Successful implementation of internet technology depends on a well-designed system. FMEA is a complement to the design process. It is a systematic group of activities intended to do the three following things.

- Recognize and evaluate potential failure points in the design.
- Identify actions that could eliminate or reduce the chance of potential failure points.
- Document the process so that future design work can benefit from the analysis.

We will be using FMEA to anticipate where the system might fail. Figure I–1 actually has several potential failure points. Later in the book we will look at where those points are and how to prevent the failures.

2. **Continuous Improvement.** This is the idea of each day implementing a slight improvement in the system. In other words, all people are encouraged to look for better ways to perform their jobs and to make the system run a little bit better. We discuss continuous improvement throughout this book.

One of the techniques we emphasize is something called "best practices." This is the idea of having procedures as living documents. This means that people can find newer and better ways to perform the procedures and suggest these to management. As the IS manager, it will be your job to coordinate the continuous improvement of these procedures.

3. **ISO 9000.** The ISO 9000 standard is a voluntary standard for management systems. The emphasis of the standard is on quality assurance, but it provides your company with an internationally recognized model of management. As we shall see, this model will be invaluable to the development of the management system for the IS department.

The other advantage of the standard is that many companies are pursuing certification to this particular model. Therefore, one of the examples we use for managing an intranet involves establishing ISO 9000-style documentation. Using this example, you will be able to instantly show the advantage of having an intranet to solve one of your corporation's primary business goals.

Besides these three primary techniques that are new to information technology, we also talk about some other common concepts that managers should always be aware of. This includes the nurturing of your personnel, the continuous maintenance of your system, the setting of specific numeric goals for the performance of your system, and the auditing of your system to ensure that the plans you made are being followed. Therefore, as you discover how to implement internet technology within your company you'll also be expanding your knowledge of professional management techniques.

Some of the Problems You Can Anticipate

As soon as you use the word internet in a company setting, several red flags will go up in management's heads. Because of the wide-scale media treatment of the internet and the fact that millions of people have experienced internet technology, you are entering an emotionally charged area. This always has to be kept in mind when implementing internet technology into your company. Unlike a new software package that has never been seen before, there will be political baggage attached to the implementation of internet technology. This will include both prejudices and mistaken beliefs on how web technology is used.

Let's begin by looking at a couple of examples that will probably occur during your implementation phase.

The instant internet presence

Senior management comes to you and says they have decided they need a web presence on the internet for the company. They don't care if it takes all afternoon, just "put our company on the internet."

This is a common problem that you will encounter with internet technology. Managers and employees are frequently under the impression that getting on the internet means simply opening a Web page. For a very small company or companies with a very small objective of using the internet, this might be true. However, in most cases you'll need an interactive presence on the World Wide Web to establish a competitive position. You'll definitely need a dynamic presence on the web to be able to garner the maximum benefits of internet commerce. Therefore, early in the process you need to educate both management and employees about the amount of effort it will take to put a dynamic presence on the internet.

The evil internet

You are in the middle of a meeting suggesting that the company establish an internet presence. The president of the company stops in mid-sentence saying "Isn't the internet that place with all the pornography?" Again, there are many mistaken beliefs about the internet. Although you may see this as a petty prejudice—the idea that the internet is somehow a setting of pornography, dissent, and crime—the fact is, such opinions among top management will create a hurdle too high to cross to successfully implement internet technology. What happens when key personnel decide that they do not like the internet? Now you have factions working against you during the implementation phase of internet technology. This can delay or even destroy the best laid plans.

Therefore, you have to work with these people to educate them on the potential of the internet. We will show how you can integrate this type of activity into both the proposal stage and the training phase of your implementation. For example, if you enter the word "sex" into Yahoo!, you will get a list of 1922 sites (as of this writing). However, if you enter the word "Christian," you get 6001 sites. It is this type of education that will be critical for clearing a path for your implementation plans.

Summary

If today you look at your job as a living hell, a day-to-day existence of solving petty problems that occur all day long, you need to implement many of the techniques we describe in this book. If, on the other hand, you're one of those lucky IS managers who has a firm grasp of your job and have your system under complete control, you'll need to pay more attention on how to implement internet technologies. Whatever system you are currently using in your management role, continue to use it. For you, this book can be used as a straightforward recipe for introducing internet technology to your company.

For everyone else, you'll need to work through all the exercises and do a considerable amount of planning and thinking before the introduction of internet technology to your company. The good news here is that by taking the steps recommended in this book, you can implement the internet technologies successfully with a minimal number of problems. You will look good to your management and you'll avoid annoying the majority of people in your company. At the same time, your list of technical skills will grow. In short, when implemented correctly, internet technologies benefit everyone.

Read This First

This book requires you to read several chapters before you can begin the implementation process, so read this section first. What follows is the normal sequence for introducing the internet, an intranet, or both to your company. Mark this page and remember it well. This section describes the sequence that we refer to throughout this book.

First, you will either be assigned by top management the task of introducing the internet to your company, or you will need to convince the company that the connection to the internet is needed. If the top managers want the connection, spend your first hours with them making sure they understand what the internet is, what potential it has for the company, and the goals they need to set. All members of top management must agree on the purpose of the project before you proceed. If one manager thinks the internet is "evil" this will lead to tremendous problems down the line.

If you want to introduce the internet to your company, you need to lobby the top managers to secure permission for the project. Again, the top managers must be educated to the point where they can make an informed decision on how much internet your company needs. Either way, you start with step one.

Step One: Get top management committed to the project. Without this, you face nothing but problems ahead. The commitment is needed to assure that management-level implementation problems can be solved. Also, top management must establish the objectives and goals for the internet system. Later you will evaluate your success based on these benchmarks.

Step Two: Do Research, Make a Plan, Create a Budget and Timeline. You must study the options and prepare a plan carefully. You will use simple project management techniques to create and follow the plan.

Step Three: Gather Your Resources. People have to be signed on to assist you, suppliers located, software purchased, contracts made, and other preparations.

Step Four: Set Up the Prototype and Test. Once the hardware and software is available, it should be tested in a prototype mode. Knowledge gained from prototyping is used to prevent wide-scale problems during the full roll out.

Step Five: Establish Policies and Best Practices. Starting in step one, you begin to draft the policies for internet management. By this point the policies should be in place and best practice procedures available for distribution.

Step Six: Educate the Employees on What is Coming. Using the plan for the system, along with your policies and procedures, prepare the employees for the new service.

Step Seven: Roll Out the Hardware and Software, Test Again. Full-scale roll out is done to complete hardware and software installation. The full system is tested and then made available to your company.

Step Eight: Install Content, Test Again. Employees provide the content for your internet/intranet system with management approval. Content is tested before its release to the public.

Step Nine: Establish Maintenance System, Audit, Test Again. Now you implement the system that will maintain and monitor the system. Audits assure that your policies and procedures are being followed and that system usage and availability meets demand.

Step Ten: Evaluation and Continuous Improvement. At regular intervals, you and management review the success of your system against your original goals and current needs. Improvements are made.

Your particular situation may require modification of the steps or rearrangement of their sequence. You may also have to conduct two or more steps at the same time. You will be able to make these decisions when you finish reading this book.

A word of warning is also due. Many companies want the internet connection and the creation of an intranet carried out as a single project. In most cases they should be carried out as two separate projects.

Good luck!

phase one
Planning the Internet Project

Chapter 1
Getting Started on the Net

Your job is to introduce your company to the internet. On the surface, this is easy to do. You call the phone company and have a 128K bps ISDN line laid into your company. You buy an ISDN modem and router combination to hook at your end. This is then connected to the network interface card in a computer that will serve as your web server, gateway, mail server, or whatever else you may need. Configure the system and you are done.

Many people from the internet side can now see web pages you post. Several people at a time from your local area network can access the internet. Will this meet all of your needs? Probably not. Will this be the best possible system? Maybe.

On the surface, connecting to the internet sounds like a simple task. In some cases it is. In most corporate circumstances, however, to introduce the internet successfully, to have it work the first time and every time, is a very difficult task. Before you can prepare to implement the internet in your company, there two things you must do first.

Understanding the Size, Power, and Potential of Internet Basics

The first thing you must do is learn and understand the terms and technologies involved with the internet. Even if you already understand the terms and technologies, you still need the ability to teach management and employees the basics of the internet. This chapter will provide you with tools you need to perform that task. We will look at definitions of common terms as we examine examples of how companies might connect to the internet.

Your second task is to understand the potential that is contained within the internet. The internet presents you with several competitive advantages that your company can profit from. At the same time, it has the potential to embarrass you in front of upper management. The internet is so vast and powerful it takes careful planning, control, and maintenance to ensure the successful use of its potential.

Later, we will look at what can be done on the internet. This information is provided so that you may begin to plan what you want to do once your company is connected to the internet.

Understanding Packets Is the Key to Understanding the Internet

Before you ever discuss the internet, before you ever consider the technology that has been spawned by networks and the internet, you must understand the concept of a packet. Put simply, a packet is a bundle of data sent over networks.

To understand why this is so important, we must talk about a couple of other concepts. The first is the use of telephones over analog lines. With an analog system any message you are sending is transmitted in one piece. You can talk to a person at the other end of the telephone and that person can talk back to you. Not much else can take place.

However, when we talk about the world of computers and how they can be tied together using networks, we're talking about digital communication. Digital communication is much more flexible than analog communication. With digital communication you can break the message up into small pieces and label who is sending what and who should receive it. That way you can accommodate several people trying to send messages at once. The messages can be sent to several destinations at the same time. Each destination will pull out the message that is addressed to its site.

The small pieces of the message are called packets. The ability to divide messages into packets that can be identified is a very powerful technology. It makes possible many forms of networking including the internet. As we shall see later, almost all technology related to the internet comes down to the use of packets.

Packets come in many different sizes. The type of network being used, the software involved, bandwidth limitations, and other factors will determine the size of packets. The largest packet that can be thrown around on the internet is around 128K bps. As we shall see in later chapters on communications, knowing about packets and how they are handled will help us determine what type of communication lines to install.

The most important concept to remember about packets is that this technology gives a single computer the ability to communicate with hundreds of other computers at the same time. A steady flow of data packets from many computers can be flowing down one wire into one machine. The receiving computer is able to retrieve packets addressed to its site and reassemble them into the information being sent.

The TCP/IP Protocol and its Massive Importance to the Internet

As mentioned above, data packets can be bundled with additional information that identifies who sent the packet and where the packet is destined to arrive. This is known as addressing the packets. This ensures that each packet is sent and successfully reaches its destination and will be reassembled into the correct order to recreate the data file that was transmitted. Several standards have been proposed on how to address data packets. The hands down winner in the contest for which standard would be used is IP addressing.

IP stands for internet protocol. The internet protocol is a communication protocol that is used to send packets to the destination without first establishing the communications link. Packets are given a destination and sent on their way. If they are successfully received at the correct destination, they are then re-assembled into the necessary data.

This is all well and good if you assume that all connections are successful. However, the internet is a tricky place to communicate. Therefore, you need a second communications protocol to ensure that the data will arrive successfully. On the internet this is known as the transmission control protocol, or TCP. TCP establishes communications between two computers on a network. The communication allows data to flow in both directions.

What happens with TCP is that the two computers connect and perform a series of handshakes in which they exchange information on what type of communication is going to take place. As the destination computer receives data from the sending computer, it sends acknowledgements back to confirm that it has received the packets. It also checks to make sure that the packets arrive safely with the information still intact. Should the destination computer miss a packet or find corruption within a packet it will ask the sending computer to resend the information.

When these communications function together, you get what is called the TCP/IP protocol. This system is the heart and soul of how the internet works. It is the protocol that establishes how packets are sent across the network. It has the following advantages:

- It can set how much data goes into each packet.
- It establishes a standard for how the packets are addressed.
- It makes it possible for packets to be directed to destinations even when there is equipment failure somewhere along the route.
- It performs several error detection methods to ensure that data is received accurately and completely.

TCP/IP is the revolution that created the internet as we know it today. Originally the internet was created by the Department of Defense. The intention was to make a web of interconnected computer networks so that the destruction of some of the sites would not bring down the entire network.

Around the time the internet was created, local area networks (LANs) were being developed for personal computers. Manufacturers of networking hardware had their own ideas about how to address packets. Despite their best efforts to introduce more efficient addressing systems than the IP, they all fell victim to the internet. The TCP/IP method of packet delivery proved to be too popular with internet users. Local area network developers were forced to include TCP/IP in their networking capabilities. Therefore, when discussing the internet and intranets you'll find that TCP/IP will be the standard by which all communications are established.

An Analogy on How All of This Works

Many authors have struggled with finding an analogy that best describes how TCP/IP addressing works. The analogies of post offices and highways have frequently been used. For example, the post office analogy defines packet transmission as taking a single letter and cutting it up into sentences, then mailing each sentence to its destination, marking the sequence of each of the sentences. The receiver of your packages then reassembles the individual messages back into your original letter. In the highway example, parts of a message climb into different cars and get on the highway, each knowing where it needs to get off. The cars represent packets on the network.

Both of these analogies are easy to understand and explain. However, they are not completely correct. A better analogy is the delivery of a message across the country of France. Assume that you have never been to France. You are in the northern harbor town of Calais. You need to deliver a pile of documents to No. 13 Rue Dijon in Lyons. To ensure that the message will arrive safely, you divide it into several parts, handing each part to a driver. Each driver has a car but no map of the country of France. They have no idea where

Lyons is in France. Therefore, they drive to the first town and ask directions. The people in this first town know roughly where Lyons is in France. They route the first car south on Highway 22. Most of the cars you send out also take this route.

However, a couple of the cars drive to a different town and get different routing instructions. As each car arrives in a major city they ask further directions. Eventually they are all correctly routed to Lyons. From here they ask local people where to find No. 13 Rue Dijon. A short while later, all but one of the cars successfully arrive at their destination. The people at No. 13 call you in Calais and ask you to send another car with the missing piece of the documents. Eventually, that car finds its way to No. 13. The recipients call you to confirm that the message has been sent successfully.

Although this sounds strange and unusual, this is how the internet works. Understanding packets, TCP, and IP are critical to understanding both the internet and how to connect your company to the internet. As you go through the process of choosing communication lines, routers, bridges, file servers, software, and other internet components, you'll discover that you always will be coming back to the issue of packets and TCP/IP.

In later chapters we'll discuss the actual addressing methods used by TCP/IP. For right now, this is enough knowledge to discuss the internet intelligently.

What Is the Internet?

The three biggest questions you'll receive when discussing the internet are:

- What is the internet?
- Who owns the internet?
- Who controls the internet?

The answer to all three questions is "nobody knows."

The internet has become so large, so vast, and so dynamic it is impossible to describe what it is with a high degree of success. In fact, by the time someone could accurately describe the internet, the information would be obsolete. That is how fast the internet is growing and changing.

As we speak, there is a major project underway just to archive one small time section of the internet. Fifteen supercomputers are necessary just to look at all the content that's on the internet in a short period of time. In short, the scale of the internet is almost beyond comprehension.

However, your job is to successfully define and explain the internet to the management in your company. Here's how you can do it. First you begin by giving a brief history of the internet.

The History of the Internet

As we mentioned above, the internet originally started as a Department of Defense project in the United States. The idea was to establish a method for connecting computer networks at various defense sites and in universities, into a web that could not be completely destroyed by nuclear attack. The key to this plan is a device called a router.

A router is a physical device that is used to link different networks. Networks can also be linked using a device called a bridge. A bridge links to networks and passes information between the networks without any consideration to their contents. In contrast, a router will look at the packets coming through and direct them to the correct locations on the connected network.

The original internet was created by connecting the many different networks together with a series of routers. Within each router are alternative routes that data could take to reach the same destination. That way if several communication lines were destroyed during war the routers could still figure out a path for data to reach its intended destination.

The internet is best described, in simple terms, as the connection of many networks together into a large network. The advantage of using routers is that you can connect dissimilar networks to each other but still freely exchange information. Thus, a UNIX-based system of networks can be freely connected to a Windows-based networking system and in turn to a Novell network. As you can imagine, this opens up a huge opportunity to share data between the dissimilar computer systems. It is this single advantage that has accounted for the massive growth of the internet and the use of TCP/IP.

Eventually, the Cold War wound down in the 1980s. The Department of Defense slowly opened up the internet to private users. At first large-scale computer networks used by private corporations and universities attached themselves to the internet. With TCP/IP it was possible to share data files, E-mail, and not much else across the internet. These were valuable tools for people wishing to communicate over great distances at very little cost. However, it wasn't until around 1990 that the real revolution began.

The concept of the World Wide Web was born. This was the idea of developing a browser that could look at standard forms of data. In other words, you could create pages of information, illustrations, and later other characteristics that could be browsed by any computer connected to the internet. This would result in the massive decentralization of the publication of information. Put into simple terms, it means that any person can place information on the internet and share it with the entire community.

At this point, the number of terms that we have to discuss begins to expand rapidly. Therefore, we will explain these terms by working through actual examples of how a company would connect to the internet. These will be brief explanations of connection methods, or "recipes." Following each example will be a discussion of the terms related to the example. By the end of the chapter you will have a good working knowledge of the terminology used on the internet. If you are already familiar with these terms, then you will have ready-made examples and definitions to use when teaching others the basics of the internet.

Example: The Dickerson County School Board Decides to Establish a Web Site

To fully explain the nature of the internet, it is necessary to use a specific example. In our case we will use the Dickerson County school board. This is a small county school system comprised of six schools and 210 classrooms. It is a nonprofit organization of a fairly small size. In later chapters we will explain the issues involved in the decisions that were made on how the Dickerson County school board would establish an internet presence.

For right now, we will use the way they establish themselves on the internet as an example for explaining common internet terms. After some conversations and decision-making, the Dickerson County school board gave the network administrator the task of establishing a web site on the internet for the school system. The recommendation was that space would be rented from an independent service provider (ISP) to create the web pages needed for the school system.

We will start by looking at how they establish the internet presence. We will then explain the terminology being used. You can use the same example to help explain the internet to employees at your company.

The Dickerson County school board established their internet presence by using the following method:

1. They contacted an independent service provider (ISP) of internet resources.
2. The ISP sold them 40 MB of space and provided them with the tools to load web pages onto the ISP's web server computer (see Figure 1–1).

Figure 1-1. Dickerson County Schools' Internet Presence

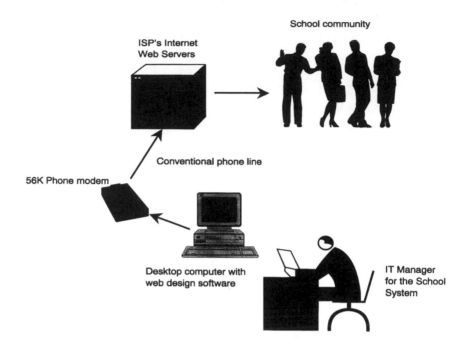

3. The ISP established a series of E-mail addresses for the staff of the school system.

4. The network administrator for the Dickerson County school board purchased web page creation software and web browsing software for the school system.

5. Seminars were given to teach staff and students how to create web content.

6. The network administrator created the standard web page for the entire school board system.

7. Staff and students from each school created additional web pages.

8. The URL of the web site was distributed to parents, staff, students, and state officials. Use of the web pages to get homework assignments, learn about school activities, and other public relations activities was encouraged.

The total cost to do this was about $70 a month for the school system plus the cost of software. The network administrator dedicated half of his work time for six months to create the initial system. On an average school day about 300 people visit the site. Teachers report improved communication with parents and other schools. The full potential of the internet is just being realized by this school system.

Understanding internet terminology

To fully understand what is going on here with the Dickerson County school board, we need to define several terms related to the internet.

Dial-up account Most individuals reach the internet by using a modem attached to their computer to call up and connect to an independent service provider. This is called a "dial-up" account because a phone line is being used to dial into an internet connection point. The actual connection requires your modem signals to be transformed into a data stream acceptable to a network of computers. The two ways of doing this are either a serial line internet protocol (SLIP) or point-to-point protocol (PPP). The difference between these two are not important at this point. You only need to know that you will have to configure your communication software at your end of the connection for either SLIP or PPP.

Independent service provider (ISP) Mistakenly called an internet service provider by many publications, the ISP is actually the *independent* distributor of access to the internet. An ISP is any company that buys direct access to the backbone communications of the internet. Several extremely high-speed fiber-optic lines connect key centers on the internet. Any company with communications equipment and the money to buy access to these bandwidth backbones can become an ISP. The ISP, in turn, then divides its share of the internet among individual users and businesses. In the case of the Dickerson County school board, they purchased a single dial-up account with a 40-meg piece of the internet.

Web pages Web pages present the information you have created to the internet audience. Basically, they are the window to the World Wide Web. The World Wide Web is a collection of standards and protocols that allow for universal viewing and usage of information. Figure 1–2 shows what a single web page looks like.

Some of the protocols that make web pages work are defined later in this section. These protocols are used by an internet software program called a web browser.

Figure 1-2. Single Web Page Example

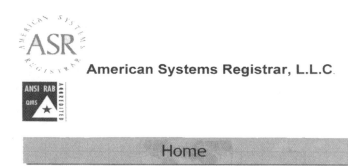

Web server   A computer with a capability to share files with other computers on a network is called a server. When files being shared are intended for internet content, we call that computer a web server. As we shall see later in this book, it is possible to have a web server inside other types of file servers. You can also have several web servers running on the same machine. However, that is not important right now. What is important is to realize that a special software program is running to present web-based material to the internet.

Web browser   The two most common web browsers now used on the internet are Microsoft Internet Explorer and Netscape Navigator. These are software programs that use the standards and protocols of the internet, especially the World Wide Web, to make it possible for any computer platform to connect with and utilize the internet.

Your browser makes you a *client* of the web server. The main reason the internet has such overwhelming power is that web browsers are able to work on several different computer operating systems and still present the same picture of information to the user. It is as though the entire world suddenly learned to speak English. If that happened there would be an overwhelming rush to translate all written works into the English language. That way all people can read the same information.

Essentially, that is exactly what happened on the internet. With the advent of web browsers, suddenly all computer users could access the information being presented by any other user of the internet. The protocols explained below demonstrate why this is such a powerful application. In fact, browsers have become so powerful that software installation is now done using a browser. Future operating systems for computers are considering using browsers as their main interface with the user.

Hypertext The concept of hypertext is a nonlinear way to present information. Specifically, it is text that can have embedded links. These links can take the reader to another point in the same text or jump to an entirely new text located somewhere else.

Later in this book we will be writing a procedure that will include definitions of common terms. Normally we would list the definitions as part of the procedure. With hypertext you don't need to do this. Instead, you create a single glossary for all procedures in your corporation. When a term is mentioned in a specific procedure, you can create a link to its definition. Readers can choose to jump to the definition to read about it and then jump back to the point where they left off in your document.

Another example would be the reading of a technical paper on the internet. Somewhere in the paper it mentions that someone is using the ISO 9000 standard. You wish to learn more about the standard before proceeding with the rest of the paper. By clicking on the link attached to the name ISO 9000, you are presented with a list of additional links that you can choose from to learn more about the standard. You can spend some time jumping from link to link to see the opinions of several different groups on the standard. When you've gotten enough information you can jump directly back to the technical paper you are reading.

HTTP: The hypertext transfer protocol To make hypertext work, the internet uses something called HTTP. This is the hypertext transfer protocol, the most basic protocol used on the internet and one of the most popular features of the internet. When you type in the address for a site of the internet you often began with "http://." This indicates that you are invoking the hypertext transfer protocol.

It is HTTP that calls up web pages and allows you to use hypertext. When the following internet address is entered on your web browser,

http://www.9000.net/index.html

you are asking for the index page of the domain 9000.net. The "html" on the end of the address indicates hypertext markup language. This is the programming language that allows you to build web pages. We will discuss it in greater detail later. The "www" in the address refers to the World Wide Web. We will discuss domains on the internet later in this chapter.

Uniform resource locators (URLs) The example address on the internet that we just discussed is called a uniform resource locator, or URL. A URL is a form of pointer that locates information on the internet. It begins with a protocol to tell your web browser what type of information is being retrieved. So far we have seen the hypertext transfer protocol for calling up Web pages. URLs can also call up different protocols and thus different types of information. The format for a URL is:

protocol://internet address/path/filename

We will look at different types of protocols below. We have already seen that an internet address involves a domain name. Once you reach a domain, the path tells your web browser where to go on the network and that you are now connected to find the file you are seeking. This is why the URL usually comes with the filename that you are seeking. If you do not list a filename most web servers will default to a file which will help direct you to what you might be looking for. We will discuss this concept later the book.

File transfer protocol (FTP) Another popular protocol of the internet is the file transfer protocol. This allows you to download files from other internet sites to your particular computer. These files can be data, illustrations, executable programs, and other computer applications. This allows for the rapid and efficient transfer of files between computers linked to the internet.

For example, if you need to upgrade a Microsoft product, you can go to their internet site and download the latest version of the software. As we shall see later in the book, this capability can be quite powerful for commercial sites—allowing companies to sell software, services, and other value-added products over the internet 24 hours a day, seven days a week.

Network news transport protocol (NNTP) The NNTP allows your browser to work with internet newsgroups. Internet newsgroups are discussion forums hosted on the internet. This allows a single person or organization to moderate a discussion on a particular topic. Although you can form discussion groups within web pages, newsgroups represent another alternative.

Other protocols The internet actually uses several different protocols. These include ones with names such as Gopher, WAIS, SMTP, and others. We will discuss each of these protocols as they are encountered in this book. Right now, the important thing to know is that new standards and protocols are continually being introduced for the internet. This means the flexibility and the power of the internet continue to grow each day.

What we have learned

The Dickerson County school board will be contacting the ISP to obtain a dial-up account. At the ISP there is a network of computers, many of which function as web servers. The dial-up account will be able to use the school board's computers, or the computers of parents and students, to connect into the network already located at the ISP. By typing in the following URL, they will connect to the web server holding the web pages for the Dickerson County school board.

http://www.dickerson.9000.net/index.html

This URL tells the Web browser to use the hypertext transfer protocol to contact the World Wide Web, and to look for a machine called "dickerson" at a domain named "9000.net." Once contact is made with this particular machine, the web page called "index" is to be downloaded to the browser. The index page for the Dickerson County school board will contain a list of links to the information from the various schools within the district. By following these links, students and parents can obtain the information about the school board, the schools, or any activities of the students (see Figure 1–2).

Example: Avix Installs a Web Server on Their LAN

Avix Manufacturing is a very interesting company. The first local area network they installed was for office workers. Engineering, quality assurance, purchasing, and the financial groups were all on the company's local area network. A total of 25 computers were on a single ethernet. Over the past few years the operating systems of the computers and the local area network have been steadily upgraded. The computers now all run Windows 95.

Novell's NetWare is used to run a local area network from a single powerful file server. Basically, the people in this local area network share only a few applications such as spreadsheets, databases, and word processing. A simple E-mail system allows people to send messages from one workstation to another. Figure 1–3 illustrates the layout of Avix Manufacturing's system.

Two years ago, Avix decided to automate the factory floor. Avix Manufacturing has only one manufacturing site located in a 50,000 square foot production facility. Down the center of this building was strung a backbone cable for networking. A powerful file server with factory automation software was connected to the backbone. The network serves only the factory. Each work cell was given a network hub into which each workgroup is connected to the backbone. Inventory control, machine control instructions, and other factory related information was loaded into the file server. Every machine operator in the plant was able to check inventory, research production schedules, and download setup instructions for their machines straight from the computer located next to the work station.

For the past several months, management at Avix Manufacturing has been discussing the idea of somehow using the internet to expand their business. The file server is cared for and monitored by a single network administrator and two technicians. They were brought into the conversation early. The feeling was that there were essentially two possibilities the company could pursue.

The first possibility was to make a web server to allow the sales force to present the catalog of goods traded by Avix Manufacturing to the internet world, specifically to customers and potential customers who already have internet connections. The network manager brought up the second possibility: using an intranet to share information, policies, and other communications within the company more efficiently. He was quick to point out that there was now no physical connection between the factory automation system and the office's local area network. The network manager strongly suggested that such a connection be made so communications could flow smoothly between the two groups. Thus, they're looking at the need for a network bridge, router, or gateway; a proxy server; and a web server.

A bridge is a connection device that will pass all communications from one network to another network. In the Avix example, it would "bridge" the two networks. A router, in contrast, will bridge the two networks but only pass through packets from the first network that are addressed for the second network. This reduces the flow and brings better order to the system. A gateway is a computer that handles this task. It can perform the router function while adding more security and capabilities. A common use for a gateway computer is to form the actual link between your local area network and the internet. Thus, people working at Avix that want to access the internet would send packets to the gateway computer that would, in turn, pass them along to the internet connection.

Figure 1-3. The Avix Manufacturing Network

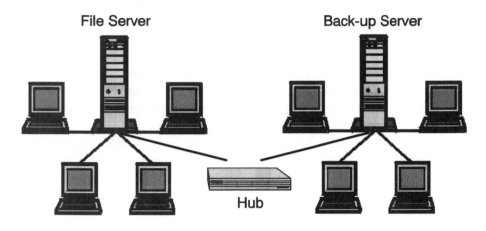

File Server

Back-up Server

Hub

Front Office's Local Area Network

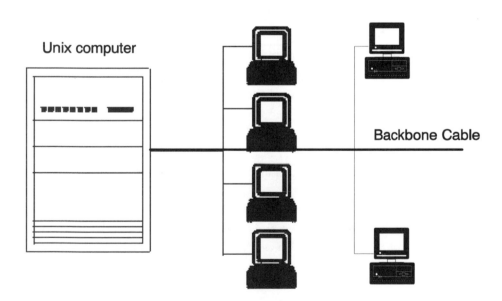

Unix computer

Backbone Cable

Factory Automation System

A proxy server is an interesting device. It is a computer that accesses the internet and gathers requested web pages into a cache memory. If a person in your company requests a page that was recently obtained by someone else, then a copy is sent to the requestor without the need to contact the internet. This saves on resources and time.

Proxies can also perform a variety of other functions, such as supporting a firewall. A firewall is a security system where incoming and outgoing internet traffic is stopped, examined, and then either sent to its destination, or turned back. If a request from an internal person does not meet the proxy's set of rules (i.e., a security breach) then the request is denied. If a request comes from an apparent authorized user from an unauthorized site, then this external request is turned away. We will talk more about this in Chapter Four when we discuss security issues.

Implementation of this plan will be broken down into two main tasks. The first is to install the web server and make a connection to the internet for the company's web page. The second is to connect the networks, purchase a proxy server, and then establish browsing and E-mail capabilities for a limited number of employees. The following steps will be involved:

1. A site survey will be conducted to confirm that the equipment is already in place, that IP addresses are set up, and to gather other relevant information. The IS manager will establish an internet policy.

2. A single, powerful desktop computer will be purchased and loaded with a web server software program and an E-mail server.

3. ISPs will be interviewed to find the best combination of service, quality, and price.

4. A dedicated digital phone line will make the link between the ISP and Avix.

5. The web system will be tested and problems resolved. The security policy will be established.

6. A selected group of office people will provide the web page content. Content will be tested before the web site is announced to the public. Management will establish the access policy.

For connecting the networks, the following steps are anticipated:

1. Locate a bridge device between the two internal networks. Introduce the factory to the internet policies.

2. Test the link between the networks and establish permissions for access to various resources on the two servers and the web server.

3. Purchase a second desktop computer to run the proxy server software. Make gateway connections to existing computers with internet access permission.

4. Upgrade the E-mail system to include internet E-mail capability. Distribute and test the E-mail accounts.

5. Begin maintenance of the new system and audit internet usage. Make adjustments where necessary.

To start with, Avix Manufacturing has a system based on local area networks. Unlike the Dickerson County school board, they will not be renting space at an ISP. Instead they will bring many of the capabilities of the ISP in house. That means they will make a physical connection between their local area networks and the internet.

In three of our examples, and with most corporations, the focus of the project is deciding how to make the physical link between the company and the internet. Unless you are engaging in a small internet project, such as the case with the Dickerson County School Board, you will need to have your own web server and internet E-mail system as a minimum. If more than a few people in the company want the ability to browse the internet, a proxy server might be needed. As we shall soon see, you can install a lot of internet technology in your company. However, you have to balance needs and wants against internal capabilities.

The Key to Understanding Server/Client Software and Hardware

Before our next example, we must pause to briefly discuss the idea of server and client. Understanding this concept is key to understanding the task that lies before the companies in our next two examples.

Remember, the internet is a network of networks. Chances are your local area network must be connected to the internet. What a server does is act as a site on the network that can "serve up" information requested by client computers that are also on the network.

The server tends to a be a high-speed, high-capacity computer dedicated to this task. It takes advantage of the communications system within your local area network to receive and send information requests. When it is receiving requests for HTML pages, the HTTP protocol, or other internet related requests, we call it a web server.

Clients are the computers being used by individuals at their desks and within your company. Laptop computers and personal digital assistants (PDAs) connected remotely through modems can also be clients. For internet technology, the most likely client software is the browser programs like Internet Explorer and Netscape Navigator, or E-mail programs. These programs send requests for information to an identified server (such as www.9000.net) and then assemble the information sent back into a usable form. The most common form is the web page.

When web servers are used inside of a local area network to service the browsers in that network, an intranet is created. An intranet is a captured version of the internet for use within a company.

When people are able to contact your local area network from a remote location and use it as if they were part of the network, we call that an extranet or wide area network. As we shall see later in this book, it is possible to connect to your local area network through the internet.

Example: A Law Firm Connects Employers, Clients, and Courts

A law firm is located in a downtown region of a medium-sized city in the midwest. It occupies the top five floors of the largest building in the town. Two hundred fifty attorneys and more than a hundred other assistants are connected to a local area network. A series of very powerful file servers are connected in redundancy to ensure the smooth operation of the network (see Figure 1–4).

The most widely shared applications software on the network is word processing. Thousands of legal documents and letters are traded every day using the system. Reliability of the system is paramount. The law firm also has branch offices in five smaller cities in the same state. Each of these offices has a 128K bps. ISDN telephone line connecting their small local area network to the central network at the law firm. In addition, telephone modems allow attorneys in the field to access databases and other documents by dialing into the central local area network.

The partners of this law firm have decided it is time to use internet technology. They have approached their network administrator about this idea. The administrator is supported by a staff of eight individuals, including technicians and trainers. It is their job to keep the system running and to teach people how to use it correctly. They also have a wide range of subcontractors that help maintain and expand the existing network.

The network administrator feels that the best first move would be to introduce intranets into the law firm. This allows the migration of their training and standard operating procedures across the entire law firm and its branch offices.

Figure 1-4. File Server Redundancy Connections

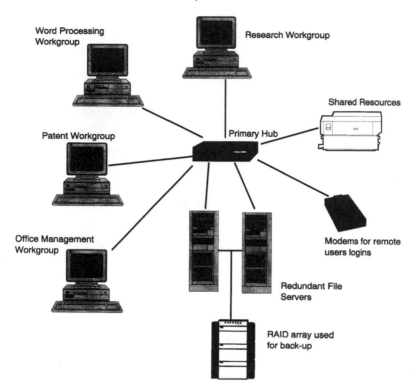

In addition, they wish to add audio and videoconferencing so people at different offices can meet without having to actually physically leave their offices.

Connecting the law office to the internet is seen as a second and later project. The internet part of the project is being visualized as some means of connecting the clients of the law firm to the information that is normally transmitted by letter or phone call. For example, one idea is to have a database of the current status of any legal actions the law firm is representing. The client could log on the internet, give a password, and learn the current status of the legal defense. This would save both time and manpower for the law office. Plus, there is the potential of becoming more competitive by being able to make law services available worldwide through the internet.

To accomplish this project, the following steps are anticipated:

1. Web server software and web page development software will be evaluated.

2. The internal policies and procedures will be reviewed for upgrading to cover the issues presented by an intranet.

3. Software will be loaded and tested on one of the existing file servers.

4. Access will be granted to a limited group for developing content. The database will be integrated into a web page by an outside consultant.

5. The word processing department will have three people trained on web page development. They will convert existing documentation for use on the intranet.

6. After testing the intranet, the browser software will be migrated and browser training will begin.

7. Once all users are comfortable with the intranet, the database will be made available and more training on how to use it will be placed on the intranet.

8. Video and audio conferencing will be implemented on a limited scale for further evaluation.

9. Connection to the internet will be determined based on the experiences of implementing the intranet.

Internal Domain Names Versus Internet Domain Names

One of the most confusing points in hooking a local area network to the internet is that many of the terms used for the local area network are also used on the internet. Both systems can use TCP/IP addresses. These have to be kept organized and apart.

Also, internal domains on the local area network have names that could be similar to domain names used on the internet. The sales department might be organized into a local area network domain called "Avix.Sales." At the same time, the web server connected to the internet might have an internet domain name of www.sales.Avix.com. Both administrators and users can become easily confused on which is which.

To expand the naming problem, workgroup names are typically assigned within the network. The network tree may breakout several workgroups. Once an intranet is set up, users will have to know which workgroup to contact with their browser to get the information they need. That would normally mean having to know specific network location names to get to the correct web pages. We will eliminate this problem by forming central tables of contents that make these links transparent.

Finally, firewalls and security software keep the right people in and the wrong people out. Because client information is so confidential, there is a critical need for the proper security within this law firm. Therefore, we should take a moment to introduce several terms used in the establishment of intranet and internet security. In Chapter Four we will examine these technologies in detail.

Example: Megalith Installs a Complete Set of Intranets with Internet Connections

Megalith is a very big corporation. The world headquarters building has 5,000 employees alone, with 23 manufacturing sites, a central research and development area, 50 distribution centers, and several other corporate properties spread out all over the world. The world headquarters building has all its computers connected through a mainframe-based network system.

The vice president of IS has a very large task to accomplish. Although supported by several network administrators, generally one for each of the sites, the vice president has to figure out a single and effective method for implementing internet connections throughout the corporation. At the same time, top management wants E-mail and databases to be freely shared across the corporation and through private access on the internet. The vice president of IS knows this will be a very difficult job.

To begin with, corporate headquarters has an E-mail system already in place which is quite antiquated. The new system will have to be put in place based on internet technology. That means the current E-mail will have to be migrated into the new system without the loss of a single message. Existing databases of messages will have to be preserved. The same is true of sharing information about other databases. The idea is to convert to a system where anybody with a web browser will be able to obtain data from the corporate databases. However, a major problem is that several of the departments are armed with only 3270 terminals that cannot run browser software. It is already felt that it will be too expensive to replace those with individual PCs (see Figure 1–5).

Another problem is known only to the vice president of IS and a couple of the network administrators. As part of the initial research for this project, they have looked closely at their local area networks. Besides the mainframe computer system within the company, several departments run their own local area networks which are the gateway into the corporate network system. However, it is known that there are some local area networks that have been set up by special workgroups. Buying their own ethernet hubs and using peer-to-peer networking available on Windows 95, some work teams

Figure 1-5. Existing Systems Layout

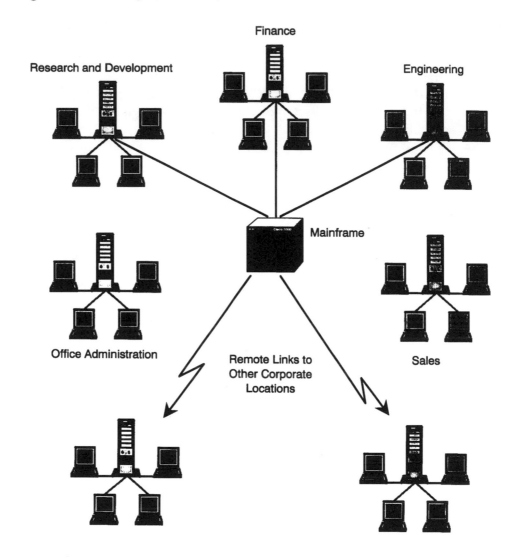

have built their own local area networks without the approval of the corporate IS staff.

Therefore, it becomes quickly obvious that the vice president of IS has to accomplish a monumental task. This will include the need for thorough planning, careful political maneuvering, and the need to convince many people to join into a unified system. Added to this is the demand that it be done on a specific budget within a particular time frame.

A complete project plan is not possible at this time. First, a full-scale audit of existing computer technologies at Megalith must be accomplished so that the vice-president of IS can get a grip on the scale of the project.

Second, this project will decentralize the use of web technology far more than our previous examples. Therefore, sites of authority will also have to be established where a web server or other central internet technology will be placed. For example, sales will have their own web server and they want no one outside of sales to have access to it over the local area network.

Third, several different operating systems and networks are already in place. In some areas there are 3270 terminals incapable of browsing. In some areas Unix is the chief operating system. Although one site might have a Novell Network, another is using token-ring.

Finally, politics are also playing a part. One of the executive vice-presidents used to work at MicroSoft and is insisting that BackOffice is the software of choice for this project. Thus, the vice president of IS has a long road ahead. As you proceed through this book, you will discover how our methods can untangle all of these problems and the ones in the previous examples.

Let's examine some of the technology that will be used by Megalith. To begin with, most internet technology for web pages includes something called open database connectivity or ODBC. This allows databases created in programs such as Excel, Oracle, Access, and the like to be linked to web pages. It opens up the possibility of having web browsing clients submit data, create reports, or browse through summaries via web pages. It is also how everyone can freely share data on, for example, a mainframe with users using several different types of personal computers.

SNA servers and SQL servers are also available to allow a local area network to distribute data from AS-400 and mainframe systems to personal computers. These types of servers add even more power and flexibility to the sharing of information on the internet or on an intranet.

Paramount to the success of Megalith's project will be the use of network administration software to hold the whole system together. Someone at one point in the system has to be able to monitor the use of all of the resources mentioned so far in this chapter. Typically, this is the system's administrator. As we will discover in the final chapters of this book, several packages are available to give you the information you need to know that your internet system is functioning properly and to its highest potential.

Summary

As we have seen in the examples described in this chapter, and the definitions of terms and technologies related to these examples, we have a wide variety of implementation problems presented. The use of a concrete example to explain terms and technologies is an effective tool for teaching others about the internet. It is also helpful to have the actual equipment you are talking about when discussing it with groups. This allows you to point to the equipment and explain how it operates within the system.

At the same time, you are beginning to see what we'll be discussing in the next chapter. Namely, internet technology gives you a wide variety of pieces, with each piece capable of assuming any one of several functions. Therefore, by the end of Chapter 2 you'll realize that internet technology is really a giant construction set with many different interesting pieces. Your main job is to decide which pieces to use, what function each piece will serve, and how to best integrate the pieces for the lowest cost, most highly efficient system possible.

Chapter 2
Creating a Successful Action Plan

You now have a specific goal: to connect your company to the internet. This requires careful planning including a detailed design of how the connections will be made and of the relationships that exist between the various users within the system. In the next few chapters we will focus on how to plan and design internet technology and connections to the internet.

In the simplest terms, we will be pursuing a method known as "plan unto policy." This means we will create a plan with enough information that when we are finished we will be able to write all our internet policies directly from our action plan. Another way to look at this is, the planning process will begin with a very simple goal, using internet technology, and will end when we start to draft the policies for that system.

Before we delve into the details of creating an effective action plan, we must touch upon two topics. The first will be the use of a structured management program to design and implement our system. The second topic will deal with internal politics.

Implementing a Management System for Quality

IS departments vary widely in their size, scope, and level of sophistication in management. We can make no safe assumption about the management structure that may exist at your company. Therefore, we shall introduce an internationally recognized standard for management systems, ISO 9000, as a common model that we can use to develop our internet system.

Management is the act of planning, deciding, implementing, maintaining, and continuously improving the system. ISO 9000 is a voluntary international standard that focuses on the minimal amount of management necessary to create a management system for quality assurance. In our situation, the quality assurance that we're setting up is to make sure the system we design will later be highly effective and cost efficient.

We must digress for just a moment. Throughout this book we'll make references to the standard. Discussion of the ISO 9000 standard and its implications have already filled several books. Therefore, if you take an interest in the standard, you might wish to pursue it further. It would benefit you to get one of the books that introduces the standard and study it carefully. In the meantime, we will we be using it as a standard model to design our management system for information technology, and in particular internet technology.

Understanding Internal Politics

Information is power. Whenever power is present so are politics. IS departments tend to be the focus of political struggles within most companies. Nonprofit organizations and service-based companies can also suffer similar problems with their information systems departments.

You must face up to this reality. When planning your system, securing permissions, gathering support, or selecting team members, you need to keep in mind the internal politics of your company. Throughout this book we will make reference to this where it applies. To have a successful project you must keep all of these realities in mind.

For example, it will only seem logical that the IS manager should lead the implementation project. However, if an IS manager has made enemies in several key departments, it may be wise to select someone who can get along with departments whose cooperation is badly needed. The IS manager can still lead the project, but an identified project leader will be the person who gets the support of other departments.

You cannot fully account for internal politics in creating a plan for new information technology. However, the successful handling of internal politics is paramount to the success of your project.

Developing the Design Process

When designing the system, it is recommended that you have a documented method of planning and review. We will use element 4.4 (Design Control) from ISO 9001. It is important that you assign qualified people equipped with adequate resources to conduct the planning and designing of the system. The design process for your system will include IS people, suppliers, future customers, and any other relevant personnel.

In a series of meetings and interviews with top management and future customers of your internet technology, you must gather what are called design inputs, along with several features and specifications that stakeholders in your proposed system feel that they need. This would include things such as the amount of hard disk space required, bandwidth for communications, types of software to be used, appearance of screens, levels of support that are expected, and so on. Your job as IS manager is to make sure that incomplete, ambiguous, or conflicting requirements are caught before a final list of design inputs is created. At the same time, you have to add to this list the items that everyone is assuming will be a part of the system. For example, everyone may assume that E-mail will be a part of your system. Your job is to make sure such assumptions are listed with the design inputs.

Your next job as IS manager is to develop a list of design outputs. The design outputs are the specifications that your internet technology team will deploy. These outputs will contain all specifications that you can later verify and validate, prototypes, and the final working system. Examples include the actual rate of flow of data across communication lines, percent usage of local area network resources, effectiveness of software deployed, accuracy from the help desk in securing support for users, and so on. Not only does this list of design outputs help you design the system, but it will help you evaluate the success of your system. For example, you may specify that you will have 99% of uptime for your file server. Later in this book we will discuss how you correctly evaluate the success of your system.

During the design process you will have to have a regular design review meeting. Representatives from all functions that are part of the design process will meet to review how well you are meeting the design outputs. You'll also discuss time lines, milestones, and objectives that you are attempting to achieve. The purpose of the design review is to keep the design project on track and to correct problems as they appear. Whenever possible you'll also attempt to prevent oncoming problems.

In the first chapter we introduced specific examples of organizations implementing internet technology. Each of these examples will have various levels of commitment for resources and time to the project. When the Megalith Corp. implements its project, it will have to be done in several stages. Therefore, part of the design process is to verify specific stages as being successfully completed. This is when you will perform various tests to ensure that the stated design outputs are being achieved.

You will also need to validate the design of your system against the needs of the user. This involves getting actual users of your system to test new components and new services. The success of the system in meeting the needs of the user is paramount to the overall success of your project. Make no mistake—launching an internet project within a company can lead to disastrous consequences for the IS manager. In contrast, a successful internet implementation with highly satisfied customers can promote the credibility and status of the IS manager.

You should also put in your design plan a method for changing the design at any time. You may discover that a particular piece of technology will simply not work with your system. Problems like that have to be corrected as soon as possible. A large-scale problem will usually require a change in the overall design of your internet technology systems. It is a wise precaution to have a procedure for the employees on how to make such a change and get the necessary approvals in a short amount of time.

A Worksheet That Will Take You from Design to Action Plan

The purpose of this chapter is to move from the concept of what you'd like to do with internet technology through the design phase to the point where you can create an action plan. In the next chapter we will look at how you account for the resources you have and see how well you can implement the action plan you create in this chapter. After a discussion of security issues you'll be ready to draft your first internet policies and begin the implementation of internet technology within your company. Let's begin by looking at the worksheet you can use to move through the design phase toward the action plan.

Completing this worksheet builds up the database of information you need to create the site designs, project time lines, personnel assignments, and other design functions. You should complete this worksheet to get a firm idea of what you want to achieve with your internet technology. Later in this chapter we will look at specific examples of how people use this form to refine the design of their system. You will also return to this worksheet at the end of this chapter to refine your system.

Forming a Planning Team Using the Best People

For any serious internet project, a team of people to do the planning and designing is required. These planning teams will work on a project basis. That is, they will treat the implementation of internet technology as a single project.

Planning Worksheet

The following worksheet should be used to develop a rough design of the internet technology you wish to deploy. Initially you should answer these questions fairly quickly. Later in this chapter will discuss the issues involved with each question. After you read this book you can go back and fill in the sheet with greater detail.

Step 1: Strategic goal. In the following space, state as clearly as possible the overall strategic goal of the internet technology you wish to deploy. What is it you hope to achieve by deploying internet technology and connectivity?

Step 2: Site map. If it does not already exist, create a site map of your current networks. This map should show the number of file servers, hubs, routers, and other system resources. Details about these resources and their connections are not needed at this time. In Chapter 3 we will examine this part of the site map in greater detail.

Step 3: Overall goals. This and the following step is an algorithm you will repeat for each of the overall goals you state for your project. Begin by stating one of the general goals for your system (i.e., "increase document control within the company.")

Step 4: State objectives for the goal listed previously. Using the goal you listed in step 3, list all objectives related to this goal. Objectives should be stated in a form that can be quantified. Fill out as many of the following as needed for the goal.

Objective 1:
- What benefits should this objective create?
- How will you evaluate the success of this objective?
- Who will ultimately be responsible for this objective?
- Who is assigned the task of completing this objective?
- When should the objective be completed?
- Will any special approvals be required? How long will these take?
- List any potential problems or obstacles you may encounter.
- Is training required to accomplish this objective?
- Will this objective require new personnel or equipment?

Objective 2:
- What benefits should this objective create?
- How will you evaluate the success of this objective?

- Who will ultimately be responsible for this objective?
- Who is assigned the task of completing this objective?
- When should the objective be completed?
- Will any special approvals be required? How long will these take?
- List any potential problems or obstacles you may encounter.
- Is training required to accomplish this objective?
- Will this objective require new personnel or equipment?

Objective 3:

- What benefits should this objective create?
- How will you evaluate the success of this objective?
- Who will ultimately be responsible for this objective?
- Who is assigned the task of completing this objective?
- When should the objective be completed?
- Will any special approvals be required? How long will these take?
- List any potential problems or obstacles you may encounter.
- Is training required to accomplish this objective?
- Will this objective require new personnel or equipment?

Objective 4:

- What benefits should this objective create?
- How will you evaluate the success of this objective?
- Who will ultimately be responsible for this objective?
- Who is assigned the task of completing this objective?
- When should the objective be completed?
- Will any special approvals be required? How long will these take?
- List any potential problems or obstacles you may encounter.
- Is training required to accomplish this objective?
- Will this objective require new personnel or equipment?

Repeat this entire step for each goal of your project. Worksheets and exercises in other chapters of this book will help you define the resources you need, the look and feel of sites you want to create, the type of connectivity you select, and other related issues. For right now the objective is to begin an overall definition of the design of your new system.

In cases where an elaborate system is being designed, you may want to break this down into several parallel projects. In the next chapter we will discuss project management in detail.

For right now, you need to consider who will sit on your planning team. The most important person will be the project leader. This is a person that has the communication skills and technical background to be able to lead a successful project. The project leader needs to go out and garner support, pay meticulous attention to details, and have the ability to convince people to complete their portion of the project on time.

You are looking for a person who has considerable experience in leading large-scale projects. Whenever possible it should be you, the IS manager. As we discussed earlier, there may be internal political reasons why this choice cannot be made. There could also be resource limitations, defined work scope, or other reasons why you, the information systems manager, cannot also be the project leader.

In most cases however, it is you, the IS manager, who will be looked upon to be the project leader. If you are selected for this role and feel that you are lacking any of the skills that a good project leader needs, then this would be a good time to develop such skills. For example, if you have never used project management software to keep a project on task, this would be a good time to take a course on how it is done properly.

In some cases top management selects who'll be on the planning team to help the project leader. More commonly, however, the project leader is able to pick people to work with. A good project leader will select people who represent the stakeholders in the finished system and who also possess the skills needed to complete the project.

The following worksheet can be used to help you select the appropriate people for your project team.

Let's look at our four examples to see how such a team would be put together in different circumstances. For example, the Dickerson County school board has just one person in charge of information technology. Obviously that person becomes the project leader. No other staff people are available to assist the IS manager. But there are other stakeholders in the system that need to be represented. Therefore, the IS manager at the Dickerson County school board selects two of their teachers, two parents, and one member of the school board to serve on the planning committee.

The parents will be able to provide a vision of what the web pages for the school district should look like. They will also discuss the type of information they need as parents. At the same time, the teachers will be able to talk about their needs for the new system. The school board representative will

Checksheet for Successful Project Team Members

This checksheet can be used to make sure that you select the proper people for your internet technology deployment team. The sheet is intended to complement your selection process. Whether you are connecting to the internet or developing an intranet, the particular needs of your specific project should be considered to help you modify this checksheet to your situation.

The following descriptions and check items can be used to select the proper people to fill these project team positions.

Project team leader

The project team leader has the overall responsibility of running the project team and making sure that assignments are accomplished on time. The project team leader will also bear the responsibility of successfully completing the project. The following qualifications should be looked for in the candidate for project team leader:

- ✓ Available full time for the project
- ✓ Has full management commitment
- ✓ Works well with people
- ✓ Can communicate verbally with clarity and persuasion
- ✓ Has demonstrated successful leadership in past projects of similar size
- ✓ Can clearly communicate in writing
- ✓ Is familiar with the technology of the internet
- ✓ Knows no fear

Technical expert

The technical expert is responsible for educating other project team members on the requirements of software and hardware. The technical expert will also be given assignments to evaluate software and hardware and its adequacy for the completion of the project's goals and objectives. Such a person, or a small group of people, must have the following qualities:

- ✓ Excellent verbal communication skills with the ability to discuss technical matters in simple language
- ✓ Works well with other people
- ✓ Has extensive experience with internet technologies
- ✓ Deals well with stress, especially tight timelines
- ✓ Can dedicate a majority of time to the project

Management representative

A good project team will have a management representative, who is a senior executive from your company who attends the project team meetings for informational purposes. This person is not given a task to complete under normal circumstances. Instead, the management representative's job is to assure that the commitment of management is carried out by people asked to assist the team; in other words, to clear political roadblocks from the path of the team. Therefore, this representative needs the following qualities:

- ✓ Has the respect of subordinate managers throughout the corporation
- ✓ Has a clear mandate from upper management to assist this project
- ✓ Can clearly communicate to all corporate personnel involved in the project
- ✓ Personally believes in the benefits of this project

Missionary

The missionary is a person who will go out to garner cooperation from other teams and departments whose cooperation is necessary for the completion of the project. In other words, this person sells people on the benefits of the project and the need for them to participate. In an ideal world, the project team leader would also be able to do the missionary work. However, in many IS departments the project leader, who is typically the IS manager, does not have the corporate history to hold this position. Another person is brought onto the team who does have a history of being able to garner such cooperation. This person should have the following qualities:

- ✓ Dynamic personality
- ✓ Has the respect of most employees at the corporation
- ✓ Is able to speak clearly and communicate effectively in writing
- ✓ Has several hours a week available to assist the team
- ✓ Is willing to take risks, be persistent, believe in the project, and act enthusiastic at all times

Recorder

The recorder is the person who will document all activities of the project team. Many project teams believe that all you need to do is drag in a secretary to take notes at the meetings. With an IS deployment project, much more is needed. The person brought in not only has to take detailed minutes of the meetings, but also has to control all documentation that the team creates. Another

Issue is the distribution of these documents to the right people at the right time. The recorder should have the following qualities:

✓ Is available full time to support the team

✓ Has extensive experience with document control

✓ Is willing to work hard

✓ Is able to take dictation at a rapid rate

✓ Shows strong people skills and can work on a tight schedule

Each candidate should be scored against the qualities that are needed for each position. It is very difficult to find a perfect match. Your objective is to find a person for your project who meets the critical needs and as many of the secondary needs as possible.

have the political clout to make sure that internal bickering or other political problems will not occur or hold up the project.

The Law Firm will have their IS manager serve as the project leader. Two of their attorneys, two of their legal secretaries, two of their largest clients, and one of the partners of the law firm will be selected for the project team. The representatives from the large clients will provide them with a list of services they will need from the law firm's databases. The development of an internal internet will consider these outside requirements for future planning and to help increase the services being delivered by the law firm. The lawyers will help define the type of information they've always needed to help improve their efficiency. The legal secretaries will know what type of input and output screens will be required. The law partner serves the role of political clout carrier who is on the committee to keep outside issues from blocking or stalling the project.

Avix Manufacturing will assign their IS manager as the project leader, who, in turn, will select representatives from the office and manufacturing departments to provide useful feedback for the design of their system. Because of the small size of the company and the clear mandate from top management, internal politics don't seem to be much of a problem at this point. In addition, the project leader is going to bring in sales representatives from internet technology companies to help in the planning process. Their expertise in the capabilities of the hardware and software will help foster a successful project.

Megalith will have several project management problems to overcome. First of all, the vice president of Information Technologies cannot be the project leader. He is too highly placed and too busy to engage in such a large-scale project. Therefore, he becomes an advising member on the planning team. If any political problems arise, it will be his job to correct or eliminate them.

One of the new local area network administrators with the best communication skills and experience with large-scale projects is selected as the project leader. Top management must make it clear that this project leader has their full backing, thus giving this person the ability to carry out the job. She will select the network administrators in the corporation to participate with the planning team. Each administrator will then use a full cadre of representatives of potential users of the future system. These smaller teams will show the central planning team how to plan the particular components of the system for their departments. They will also call upon technical experts from within the company, as well as outside consultants, to develop the information they need for proper planning.

As you can imagine, the Megalith project in particular requires a very skilled project manager and the use of elaborate software to keep everyone on target. The software used will involve both project management software and communications packages that will automatically update all team members on the current developments. Ironically, one of the systems to be developed is a project management system that will exist as an intranet feature for the new systems.

Each member of the project team should be instructed on his or her role as a team member. The expectations of team members and the scope of their activity should be clearly spelled out in manuals that are issued to these people when they are invited to join the team. At the first meeting, the planning team should talk about the overall goal that the proposed project is trying to achieve. The team should also spend time having each member meet and get to know all the other members. The rules of conduct and conflict resolution should be settled at this first meeting. The first meeting should also begin with a list of tasks for each member to perform before the next meeting.

Creating and Communicating Focused Objectives

Most projects begin with a list of goals to be achieved. These goals usually originate with top management and are passed on to the project team for implementation. In many cases it will be a simple, one-statement goal such as, "We want our company connected to the internet." One of the first jobs for the project leader is to break a single general goal down into a specific mission, then divide that into particular goals with objectives.

Goals should be clearly stated and quantify all terms. Some examples of the these include:

- Use of internet technology to reduce our time-to-market
- To increase our market share
- Expand our customer service
- Increase communications between departments

Each goal, in turn, is then broken down into a list of clearly defined objectives. Objectives are milestones you must achieve on the way to a major goal. It is the list of objectives you made previously that will help you plan the successful system. Some example objectives are listed here.

Goal: Increase in our customer support

- Objective: Survey our current customers, their level of satisfaction and expectation of services delivered.
- Objective: Install a World Wide Web server to facilitate customer support web pages.
- Objective: Develop, test, and improve the customer support web pages.
- Objective: Test the new customer service web page with selected clients and measure against previous customer satisfaction.
- Objective: Implement the new customer service through web pages, achieve at least 10,000 hits on the page per month within three months of implementation.

With a list of goals and objectives, you can examine the potential benefits of achieving each item. This helps you to put together a business case for the overall design of the proposed internet technology. Later we will look at how the goals and objectives in our four example companies are used to create action plans and make a business case.

As we discussed in Chapter 1, there are many potential benefits for using internet technology. At this point in the planning process, you'll need to sit down and focus on the specific benefits you wish to achieve. You should identify the potential benefits of reaching the objectives laid out in the plan. Where possible, you should also state the return on investment that will be achieved by meeting each of the objectives.

Following is a list of common benefits reported by companies already conducting business over the internet. Potential benefits from using the internet include:

- Increased access to data
- Increased communication with suppliers, subcontractors, vendors, and clients
- Reduction of travel time and expenses through the use of virtual teams
- Development of new methods of problem solving
- Increased market share
- Exposure to new marketplace
- Increased speed in handling of paperwork
- Increased research capability
- Increased speed at which internal personnel can access important information
- Flexible and adjustable training available 24 hours a day

These are just a few examples of the benefits that might be possible. What you should do is focus on each particular objective and find the most likely benefit that it will achieve. Be sure to build a case to discuss the return on the investment of achieving goals and objectives. Following is one such example you can use.

"Example: Currently each employee of our company is required to attend a two-hour training session on basic safety techniques in the factory. The cost of the instructor and materials averages out to $250 per participant. Our goal of making training available on the corporate intranet includes the objective of placing the safety training on the intranet. Part of the orientation for all new employees will be to participate in this training using the computer at their desktop. The cost per participant for a one-year period of time is calculated to be $60 using the intranet method. For each participant the savings will be approximately $190. With an average of 100 employees per year needing this training, the total savings will be $19,000. The cost of the file server and related software to support the training system is approximately $5,000. We can look at a return on our investment of roughly $14,000."

In summary, the creation of an internet technology plan involves the listing of goals and objectives followed by identification of the benefits of achieving those objectives. This information now leads to a business case study that can be submitted to upper management for approval of the final plan. But first, you'll need to complete the design phase of your proposed system.

Drafting the Layout of Your Proposed System

At this point you can begin to physically lay out a drawing of your proposed system. In the examples that will appear later in this chapter, we will look more intensely at how this is done. Basically, you want to create a visual interpretation of the proposed system. The reason for doing this is to create something on paper that is easily communicated to a wide variety of people. Typically, a picture or map of the proposed system aids greatly in the communication of your intentions.

Another way to express your intentions is to show mock-ups of the types of screens that people will see once the system is working. This is used in the case where internet technology will be focusing on the communication of information or data, more than on the physical layout of the equipment and software.

There are software packages that lay out proposed networks. Examples include Visio and Crane. Some CAD packages also have this capability. Not only can they allow you to use symbols to lay out your existing network and the proposed additions, but, some packages can evaluate whether the equipment you are specifying will function properly in the proposed layout.

Take the example of Avix Manufacturing. They would begin by mapping out the existing networks within their company. This would create an illustration similar to the figure in Chapter 1. As shown in Figure 2–1, they would then add the components for the proposed internet project. This is usually done by coloring the new components in a color different from the rest of the plan. Next, each component would show a few details of the software involved in the other network issues.

During this process, you would build up a considerable database of what it is you plan to accomplish. Next you will start to draft out ideas on how to assure the quality of the system once it is in place. After that you can begin to build the actual action plan to implement this project.

You should note at this point that hardware and software should only be described in general terms. Things become obsolete very quickly. You may find that it is only a few weeks before your plans for a particular software package may have to change because something better has been introduced. Therefore, try to arrange your design so that when it comes to the moment of purchasing hardware or software, you are buying the very best that is available at that time.

Figure 2-1. Added Internet Project Components

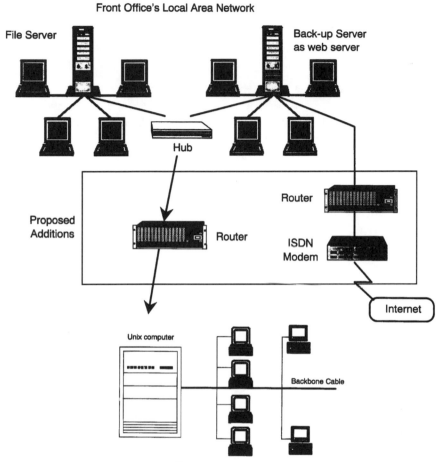

Front Office's Local Area Network

File Server

Back-up Server
as web server

Hub

Router

Proposed
Additions

Router

ISDN
Modem

Internet

Unix computer

Backbone Cable

Factory Automation System

Forming a Plan for Quality Control

You now have to think about the quality assurance system that will become part of the company's internet technology. This will take two basic forms. The first form will be the testing and assurance of the quality of the hardware and software you have purchased. In other words, there are certain expectations you'll have in the performance of these components. Design tests and verification methods will be used to make sure that they are performing to your expectations.

The second form of quality assurance involves the interface between your new internet technology and the people that have to use it. This will include people inside your company accessing information as well as clients outside your company looking at information. You'll have to come up with a method for assuring that:

- Accurate information exists on the internet technology databases you created.
- The transmission of such information is fast enough.
- The user is comfortable with its presentation.

For the testing of software or hardware you have to go back to your list of design outputs. Here you listed the specifications for the hardware and software. For each of these you can develop a specific test to assure that you are reaching the level of performance you expect.

For example, the web server you are planning to purchase and the type of communication line that will be opened are supposed to achieve a maximum of 6,000 hits per web page, per second, without problems. It would be very difficult to set up a test where 6,000 requests for the same web page would all come in at the same time. What should be done instead is to set up a loop of requests for a certain web page that runs for a specific amount of time. You then check the clock and the response time from the web server and try to assertain its true performance.

Another way to attack the same problem is to look at the size of web pages that would be placed onto this web server. You may have a design specification that says at the most you'll have 10,000 requests placed on the server for these web pages every single day. You can then create a particularly large web page and time how long it takes a remote user to download that page. From this you should be able to extract the actual performance data for the server.

The second form of the quality assurance system is far more interesting to set up. First you need to go back to the map of your network. You will need to identify where in that system users will make contact with your internet technology. This could be all the people that will want access to the internet through your company, web pages where clients will be obtaining data, remote access points where subcontractors can interface with your personnel, and the like.

At each of these points you need to define the type of interaction that will take place and list the qualities of interaction that are expected. This is called developing a service plan. A service plan defines how you deliver information technology services at the point of contact between the technology and the user.

For example, a single employee in your company may access the internet using a desktop computer. In your service plan you define the qualities that this user expects from the service. This includes items such as rapid response to a requested web site, filtering out pornographic sites, and the ability to send E-mail freely to outside web servers.

In the planning phase, you only need to come up with the quality that people are expecting from your internet technology. In later chapters you will see how you can develop the actual methods you need to test and evaluate each of these qualities. For example, the idea of being able to rapidly call up web pages from the internet is a difficult quality to quantify. You'll have to reach an agreement on how many seconds a person is willing to wait before the web page arrives at his or her screen. Let's say for illustration purposes, that you place a maximum of 10 seconds before the web page begins to assemble on someone's browser. You can then go around your company and test various outside web page responses and loading time at each browser in the various users' computers.

If top management has placed a high priority on filtering out pornographic sites from the internet, you can also test this by going to each browser and attempting to access known sites of adult material. As you'll see in later examples, we'll give you interesting sites that have adult material but don't necessarily advertise that fact until you are deep into their web pages.

Exercise: Drafting the Web Site Plan (Interactive Form)

We have done enough talking now in the abstract about how you design your internet technology and form your action plan. For the rest of this chapter we will look at our example companies and how they are going to complete the design phase. We'll also present you with exercises you can use to begin designing the internet technology for your own company. Let's begin with an exercise for drafting the web site plan.

In particular, let's look at the law firm. Top management has come up with two actual projects. The first is to create an intranet within the law firm. The second is to create internet connections, and in particular, connections to clients. For this discussion we'll look only at the first project right now.

This project began with top management deciding that adding the intranet would be a strategic move for the law firm. The IS manager was appointed the project leader. His first task is to go back to management to have them help with a list of goals for this project. The information technology manager begins by explaining that the project should have one central strategic goal. From this one central goal the list of secondary goals will be developed.

To help stimulate the thinking of top management, the IS manager presents a list of possible goals that all the partners are thinking about for the intranet. These include:

- Improved communications
- Reduction of paperwork
- Reduced cost of operations
- New lower costs and more efficient training presentation
- Making available standard operating procedures
- Making revisions and distribution of standard operating procedures more efficient

The IS manager now challenges management to select which of these stated goals are central to creating the intranet. After many minutes of discussion they jointly agree that the central goal is the improvement of communications within the law firm. From this central goal is formed a breakdown of specific goals they wish to achieve. Many are based on the original list the IS manager presented. A few objectives under each goal might also be listed by management.

The IS manager now goes back to his project team to start discussing the overall benefits that can be achieved and the particular objectives that will have to be met as part of achieving these goals. The result is a piece of paper like the one in the following form.

Now let's just take one of the objectives listed in the form and go through the questions from our worksheet. Let's look at the objective of purchasing training packages for intranet applications. To help illustrate this example, we will look at the objective of purchasing a word processing training package to be applied to the intranet.

The company is a heavy user of WordPerfect. In a typical month at least three new employees are brought aboard with the need to be proficient in WordPerfect. The expense in money and time to send them to seminars is seen as too costly. The objective is to put a WordPerfect training package on the intranet so people can learn at their own pace while still at their job.

On our worksheet we have a series of questions for each objective. By answering these, we begin to create our action plan. By using our example objective, we see how this is done.

- What benefits should this objective create?
- How will you evaluate the success of this objective?

Strategic Goal: *Improved internal communications through the introduction of an intranet*

Goal: Make available standard operating procedures while making the updating, distribution, and control of such procedures more efficient.

- Objective: Create central document approval authority.
- Objective: Create a master list of procedures accessible from any browser.
- Objective: Install a web server capable of handling up to 40,000 requests a day.
- Objective: Successfully migrate web browsers to all internal users.

Goal: Make basic employee training available on the intranet

- Objective: Install web server on LAN for delivery of training that includes video and audio.
- Objective: Assure that the web server can store and deliver up to 100 different training packages.
- Objective: Purchase training packages for Intranet application.
- Objective: Deliver and test intranet training before dissemination to the entire firm.

and so on...

- Who will ultimately be responsible for this objective?
- Who is assigned the task of completing this objective?
- When should the objective be completed?
- Will any special approvals be required? How long will these take?
- List any potential problems or obstacles you may encounter.
- Is training required to accomplish this objective?
- Will this objective require new personnel or equipment?

The benefit of this objective is the cost savings from doing the training in-house and preventing travel time. It also assures uniform training to all employees, and allows flexible schedules for taking the training.

The success of this objective will be evaluated by testing the people who take the training to see how proficient they have become with WordPerfect.

The director of human resources is the person ultimately responsible for making sure that this objective is completed successfully. The director of human resources assigns a training specialist to the task of completing the purchase, evaluation, and implementation of a WordPerfect training package.

The director of human resources estimates that it will take three months to complete this objective. Approvals will be required from the IS manager for the resources required to run the training package on the intranet, and from the supplier of the training package to secure a license to give the training on the intranet. Both of these permissions should be obtained within a few days. Potential problems could include issues such as no one having a training package effective enough for the task, the training package eats up too much bandwidth, or that people just don't like the look and feel of the training. These potential trouble spots will be evaluated closely by the training specialist.

To properly implement this objective, it will be necessary to develop a short instruction guide for employees on how to take training on the intranet. Guidelines will have to be set up so that employees know how much training they should participate in per day to be effectively taught the WordPerfect skills.

This particular objective does not require additional equipment. The training package will be loaded onto one of the file servers already in the local area network. There is also no need to hire new personnel to achieve this objective or to maintain it. However, the training personnel will have to spend a few hours every week checking to make sure that people are properly using the training package.

As we look back over the answers we have just given to our questions for this objective, we notice that we're gaining some valuable information. Now we know who has to do what, when it has to be done, and some of the issues that will be encountered. This type of information can naturally flow into an action plan. For example, our action plan may state that for these objectives, the human resources manager will assign a training specialist to achieve the objective within three months. It will also state that the specialist is to look at critical issues such as the compatibility of the training package with current equipment, and its accessibility to the potential customers, that is, the people seeking training within the company.

As we shall see, this breaking down of objectives into an identifiable task is the heart of the action plan and the essence of project management. Before we look at this more closely, another issue that comes up with internet technology is the look and feel of the internet at the point of interface with customers.

Planning the Look and Feel of the Web Site

One of the primary goals of using internet technology for most companies is to create a dynamic web presence. This means you will create a web site accessible to the http protocol. In other words, you will be doing web page design work.

The goal of a dynamic web presence means that you have to pay particular attention to the look and feel of your web pages. In Chapter 10 we will discuss this issue extensively. For right now you need a rough idea of what it is your web pages will do if it is part of your implementation plan to have a web site, or multiple web sites.

For example, your company may want to place a database onto the internet so that sales people and associates across the country can access the newest price and availability information. This will be a data warehousing project of considerable effort. Let this become part of your design phase and action plan.

If one of the goals of your internet technology project is to have effective web pages, then you need to draw up a list of objectives for those web pages. In addition to the questions asked for the objectives above, you'll have to ask the question of who supplies content, who will set the standard format for the content so the look and feel of your web sites are consistent, and who will have overall control of web page creation.

Obtaining Access to Necessary Data

We are assuming that you, as IS manager, are likely to be a project leader or significant participant on this project team. A key issue for you will be the acquiring of necessary data to complete the action plan. Much of the information you need about software and hardware can probably be obtained within the IS department. However, information about the type of data that exists, who actually controls it, where personnel will come from, and other non-technical issues will involve the cooperation of other departments. This is why it is very important to have good communications and relationships with other departments during the project phase.

Example: The planned Avix Manufacturing site

If we look at the Avix Manufacturing company, one of their primary goals is to put their product catalog onto the internet. The company has decided that this could be done by purchasing a web server for the office's local area network. This creates a design worksheet that starts to look like this:

Goal: Put company catalog on the internet
- Objective: Buy web server
- Objective: Buy web server software
- Objective: Create web pages that can draw information from company catalog database
- Objective: Test and implement the web pages

On the surface this looks like a fairly simple set of objectives for which to obtain information. However, as we look at it more closely we see that there will be some difficult points.

Under the objective of creating web pages that will draw information from the company's catalog database, you will need to talk to the manager of the database. In this case it is a professional sales staff member who helped design, and now maintains the database. This project is outside the IS manager's scope of responsibilities. You'll need to approach this person and convince him or her to give you free access to that database.

Because information is power, you may find it difficult to convince people to give free access to the information which has been making their jobs valuable for several years. Once the information is freely available and other people in the company can easily obtain it, the value of the person in control of it may diminish. You must approach this delicately to negotiate the level of access you need, against the level of job security this person may require.

At the same time, you may find that a person from a different department has volunteered to do the web design work. This will involve open database conductivity to the web page. If this person has some level of experience, you need to know exactly how much experience. You also need to know roughly how long it will take this person to complete the task. It may turn out that neither one of you actually knows what the timeline would be. The two of you will need to sit down and try to estimate as best as possible.

Example: Megalith's multiple sites

When we move to the size of project that the Megalith Corp. is pursuing, with its multiple sites and multiple goals, you can see that the task of obtaining the information you need becomes even more difficult. In fact, the task may become so large that you need to divide up the data-gathering phase across several members of the implementation team.

The vice president of IS at Megalith has local area networks located throughout the corporation and multiple sites around the world. It would be too much of a task for this vice president to chase down all the information needed for planning purposes from all the different sites. Still, the goal remains to make sure that all of these are somehow connected to the internet in the standard format.

It is only logical to have each of the local area network administrators begin the task of obtaining the planning information necessary to complete the action plan for Megalith. During this phase, the people seeking information inevitably will run into roadblocks that cannot be surmounted.

If one local area network manager reports that someone controlling particular information refuses to divulge it to the team, this must be noted. An alternative plan has to be drawn up or an estimate made based on what is known of the situation. Then a new objective is listed under the action plan. The new objective is to get over this obstacle. If the situation is critical enough, you call in upper management to break the deadlock. The timing and finesse used to break such deadlocks has to be exercised carefully. You need the cooperation of as many people as possible to successfully pull off an internet project of this magnitude.

Using Failure Mode and Effects Analysis to Avoid Problems

So far we have been talking about a positive approach to planning the implementation of internet technology. In other words, we have talked about the goals and objectives we wish to reach. Once your rough plan is laid out on paper, it is time to do some negative thinking. What could go wrong?

Under current systems of management, such as ISO 9000, QS-9000, and common sense, the emphasis is on the prevention of problems. This would include prevention of problems with your product or processes. One tool of choice is a Failure Mode and Effects Analysis (FMEA) which is used to evaluate the potential for a failure.

When an engineer sits down to design a product, he has to go through several mental processes. He has to think about the type of product to produce, the material at hand, the need of the customers, and the capabilities of the production process.

FMEA is a kind of stream-of-consciousness method used to document what might happen to a particular product or process. The intention of a FMEA is to brainstorm out a list of potential failure points and then examine the likelihood of them happening. After that, you would also analyze the potential effect that each failure point could cause. This allows you to convert your internal thinking about a product, or process, into a tangible table of possibilities and probabilities. This, in essence, builds a database of information about potential failures. You can then sort through your potential failures by the risk they present and take corrective actions based on objective information.

You can go through a similar process with the design of a system that uses internet technology. When you finish the action plan, you should have a map of the actual system to be put in place and a list of goals and objectives to create. This type of systems design will have many points of potential failure. The goal of FMEA is to identify these potential failure points and quantify the risk. Then you can rank order these potential failure points and take actions to assure that they will never happen or that the chance of them happening is greatly reduced.

Exercise: What is wrong with this picture?

Returning to the first illustration we presented in the introduction, we must once again ask, What is wrong with this picture? Using Failure Mode and Effects analysis we can begin to see where the problem lies in this illustration (see Figure 2–2).

To successfully place a web page on the internet we are depending on all components of the web server to work correctly. When we do an FMEA we first break down the system into its basic components. In our illustration, we have the following four components:

- Uninterrupted power supply
- Web serving hardware
- Web server software
- Connection to the internet

Failure in any of these components results in an inability to deliver web pages to the internet. For each component we break it down into potential failure points. For example, in the software we have several potential failure points. Three of these are as follows:

- Incompatibility of web page with FrontPage extensions
- Incompatibility of FrontPage with Windows NT system
- Failure of internet information server to present web page

Figure 2-2. Analyzing Problem Using Failure Mode and Effects Analysis

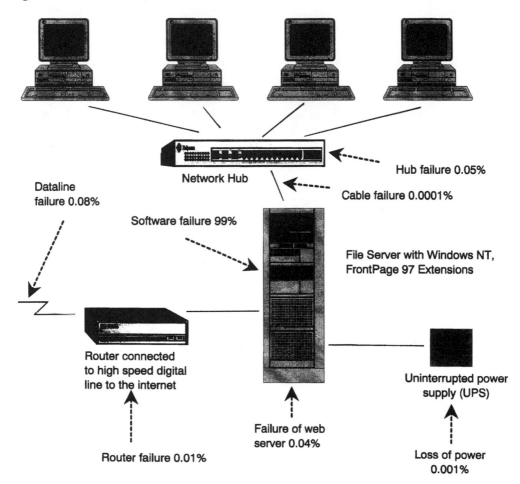

Network Hub

Hub failure 0.05%

Dataline
failure 0.08%

Cable failure 0.0001%

Software failure 99%

File Server with Windows NT,
FrontPage 97 Extensions

Router connected
to high speed digital
line to the internet

Uninterrupted power
supply (UPS)

Router failure 0.01%

Failure of web
server 0.04%

Loss of power
0.001%

This is only a short list used as an example. In a full FMEA, you would list all potential failure points. For each failure point, you would then estimate the probability of that failure occurring. You would also rank the severity of the failure and your capability to detect that failure. Combining this information you get an overall score for the potential failure. Usually a 1 to 10 scale is used to write each of these three quantities.

In the example, the system is using FrontPage 97, FrontPage 97 server extensions, and internet information server version 3.0. The three potential failures listed above are all ranked as being potentially high in severity because they would stop the users from presenting web pages to the internet. The ability to detect these problems is also high because they would become quickly obvious.

At this point I should tell you that these failure points are based on actual experience at customer sites where my associates and I were asked to implement internet access. Only discovered with testing was that the probability of one of these failures occurring was nearly 100 percent. The reason for this is that we found out when creating discussion groups, FrontPage 97 extensions have bugs that cause failures. Even though all three pieces of software came from the same company, it was not wise to assume they would all be compatible.

What our FMEA told us was that our planned system simply would not work. Luckily, we discovered this before we attempted to implement it. Hours of troubleshooting and frustration were prevented. We could now return to the positive aspect of design work. We looked at the best way to prevent this problem from occurring. We quickly learned that we needed to update our software to FrontPage 98 edition, install a patch on the web server, and all would be well.

Issues to Consider to Avoid Problems

The actual list of problems that can occur during implementation is too long to discuss at this point. However, several areas will be a great concern throughout the implementation of your internet technology, including:

- Security
- Corporate-wide buy-in
- Time management
- Quality control
- Ongoing maintenance
- Continuous improvement

Security concerns include who has accessed your system and how they are using the system. By carefully planning your security system in advance, you can avoid many of the problems from unauthorized access, unintentional uses, and potential loss of data. At the same time, your security policy must not be so tight that people are hesitant to use the internet technology. You want to promote corporate-wide acceptance of the new internet technology. We'll show you how to encourage this type of acceptance through proper policies, training, and maintenance of the system.

While you are implementing your internet technology project, you'll find that time will be one of your chief enemies. The best way to prevent problems related to the amount of time you have to complete your task is to have a strict system of project management. Part of project management is to be a good time manager. In the next chapter we will look at some of the issues involved in scheduling your implementation.

Internet technology requires quality control for both content and operation of the system. Inaccurate information or resources that are not available when needed can cause serious problems for the customers of your system. The focus throughout this book will be to satisfy the needs and requirements of your customers. A few formal quality control procedures will be introduced as part of the system.

Once the system is in place, you need to continually maintain the high level of quality you have designed. One of the largest problems that IS managers experience with internet technology is that after establishment of the service, quality slowly degrades. This is the effect of resources getting heavier usage over time and people forgetting to follow their procedures. Therefore, later chapters will show you methods to keep your system operating as well as you planned.

Related to this is the concept of continuous improvement. This is the idea that every day, you should think about incremental ways of improving the existing system. To have this work effectively, you must encourage all users of your internet technology to think about better ways to perform daily operations. In later chapters we will look at the concept known as "best practices." You will begin the system by designing the procedures and work instructions employees will use. If the internal personnel of your company can come up with better ways of performing the same tasks, these are then incorporated into a new version of the procedures and work instructions. In short, they continually document the best practices they have found to date to finish specific jobs. Each of these topics will be covered in depth in subsequent chapters.

Further References

Intranet Web Development by John Desborough, New Riders Publishing, 1996, ISBN 1-56205-618-2.

Virtually any book on Project Management.

Web Sites to Visit for Further Information

Many internet sites exist to guide you in designing and planning your internet access or corporate intranet. You can begin with the makers of the equipment you will use (i.e. 3com) and then move to specialized sites such as:

www.cio.com

www.wordmark.com

www.intranetjournal.com

www.changedynamics.com

Internet Search Strings

Search the most recent resources through Yahoo!, HotBot, or other large-scale search engine using keywords such as:

Project management

Planning designing intranet

Internet connectivity plan

Internet case studies

Teamwork dynamics

Chapter 3
Taking Inventory of Existing Resources

The IS manager at Avix Manufacturing was having a pretty good day. Before launching the implementation of internet technology at Avix, he had decided to look over the existing resources. His first step was to look at the computer hardware and software that the company already possessed.

Because all purchases of computers had to have his approval, he had a list of all computer equipment that should be onsite. The list said there were 34 PCs located somewhere in the plant. He had found all 34 computers. A random audit of six of these computers revealed that the software loaded in them was company approved software that had been purchased with his okay. There were no games, betting pools, or other nonproductive software on any these machines.

The local area network in the front office was configured exactly as stated on the site map. The Unix machine running the factory automation system was in place and working well. The map of the backbone network cable matched the actual location of cables in the factory. The right people were using the right software at their jobs. All was going well.

Megalith was another story. Although she was armed with a good audit schedule and excellent checklist, the network administrator for the corporate office realized she was living in the middle of a nightmare. The existing site plans for local area networks indicated there should be five local area networks within the corporate office. So far she had found seven.

In the marketing department, she discovered a pirate network. It had been set up by two women who had taken a local area networking class. What were supposed to be stand-alone computers in this department was a collection of machines with networking cards from various manufacturers strung together with inferior cable.

The story of the sales department was worse. Not only had this department set up their own local area network without informing anyone else, they had purchased a file server. Examining the file server closely revealed a high-speed modem connected to a telephone line. When the network administrator examined the software on the machine she was greeted by a dial-up monitoring software package. The display indicated this line had been opened to the outside world for over a week. In fact it was connected to the internet. There was no security on the sales data.

Megalith Corp. has not yet implemented an official policy on internet conductivity. Yet the network administrator discovered that one department had already been serving up web pages to the internet under the name Megalith. This was being done without any formal policies or procedures, or for that matter, any oversight of the process.

Resources Needed for Success

In the previous chapter we showed how to develop a database of the goals and objectives you wish to achieve by implementing internet technology. From this you are able to break out specific tasks to be performed by particular people within certain time lines. The next step is to determine whether you have the resources needed to successfully complete this project.

The following types of resources are required for a successful project:

1. Human capital
2. Money
3. Hardware
4. Software
5. Time

Naturally, this is assuming you already have full management commitment.

Human capital represents the people with the expertise to actually install, implement, monitor, and continuously improve your internet technology. Depending on the objectives of your specific project, you will need the personnel who can perform tasks such as successfully installing new software, stringing cables, making data line communication connections, troubleshooting problems, removing political barriers, and so forth.

Money is required in any project. One problem with most projects is how to implement new technology without throwing money at the obstacles you encounter. Therefore one of your objectives is to spend money as efficiently as possible to achieve at least 100 percent of your objectives.

For example, you can cobble together a file server using existing components from several computers. You would save a few thousand dollars by not buying a name-brand file server. However, it is likely to create more problems than it is worth. You would spend far more in your time and human resources than the amount of money that would have been saved. This is why you want to spend your money where it will do the most good.

Hardware purchase provides an excellent example of how money has to be spent correctly. It is not always the low bid that is the best idea when it comes to hardware. File servers, modems, routers, bridges, and other critical components of internet technology should all be name-brand goods. You want to buy products with a demonstrated history of reliability and durability. High quality is a must.

In the same way, you need to select software that will successfully implement your projects and objectives. Unix and Windows NT are popular operating systems for internet software for good reason. These two operating systems have demonstrated that they have the durability and reliability necessary for a high percentage of up-time. The careful selection of software is paramount to the success of your project. Take the example of the SMS Manager from Microsoft. This is a powerful software package to control almost every aspect of your intranet, internet, and local area network activities. However, it takes an incredibly skilled person to operate the system. The convenience of the package can easily be offset by the frustration of trying to find the right person to control it.

Finally, time is a critical factor for the success of a project. The number of people you can use will be limited by the amount of time they can dedicate to the project. Always consider time as one of your most reliable resources and spend it wisely.

Checklist of Implementation Resources

You should take a moment to look at a checklist that breaks these five basic resources down into individual components. You should use this checklist to jog your memory of which resources you have internally. The list is comprehensive and would be used in whole by Megalith or by the law firm. The Dickerson County School Board would mostly be interested in human capital. Avix Manufacturing would focus more on software than on human capital.

Checklist of Resources

1. Human capital—list the names of the people in each category partici-
   pating in this project.
   - Project leader
   - Network administrator
   - Web designers
   - Database designers
   - Database entry personnel
   - Cable layers
   - Communication installation specialists
   - Technical support
2. Money
   - Budget for hardware
   - Budget for software
   - Budget for support
   - Budget for new personnel
   - Budget for subcontractors
   - Research budget
3. Hardware—indicate which equipment and how many pieces are
   required for each category
   - Servers (file, web, news, mail, etc.)
   - Proxy machines
   - Gateways, routers, bridges, and switches
   - Modems
   - Workstations
   - Firewalls and other security equipment
   - Extra hard drives, memory and other components
   - Network hubs
   - Network interface cards and cabling
4. Software
   - Servers (file, web, news, mail, etc.)
   - Proxy software
   - Browsers
   - Operating systems (NT, Unix, etc.)

- Security
- Communications packages
- Administration
- Database
- Data back-up
- Groupware
- Web design
- File transfer
- Videoconferencing
- Audio
- Programming (Perl, Java, etc.)

5. Time—for the people listed in item 1, please indicate the amount of time each person can dedicate to this project on a weekly basis.

In short, you will be using this checksheet to determine the amount of resources you have in-house. You will then compare your available resources against the amount of resources you'll need to successfully complete your project. Any discrepancy between the two lists will indicate whether you'll need additional help or resources.

Before you do that, however, you should take some time to audit your existing resources. Auditing is the process of comparing what you think you have against what you really have. In this case you should have some idea of what hardware, software, people, and time are available in your current system. The amount of money that will be available will be set in the project budget by top management. Your job at this point in the project is to confirm what you think you have on your system and what you need to add.

Preparing to Audit

The process of auditing is fairly simple. You must go out and gather evidence to confirm the amount of resources that you have. You must do this as simply as possible. You should not be out looking for problems or reasons to discipline anyone. Instead, you need to adopt a positive attitude toward the problems at hand. You'll need to talk to people and look at the hardware located near where they work. Therefore, you must use good judgment and courtesy with all auditing.

This is accomplished by letting everyone know that you are coming around to inventory existing resources. In a short memo you should explain to everyone that they will come in contact with you, what you are doing, and the purpose of your audit. There's really no reason to mention the word audit. You can explain that a large project is about to launch and you need to count the existing resources to make sure that all contingencies have been accounted for. Be sure to mention that by cooperating with you, everyone will help make this a successful project.

Next you'll need an audit schedule to let people know when they can expect you to arrive. This doesn't have to be an elaborate document, just a quick schedule of when you will be in certain departments looking around. The manager of each of those departments should be aware that you are coming. Good political sense should be applied when making the schedule. Make sure that you won't be conflicting with activities going on the department.

You can then put together a list of what are believed to be the current resources in your system. Someone should have a map of the local area networks. There should be a list of the hardware and software on site at the company. The names of the people that will participate in the implementation of the internet technology should be on a list along with short job descriptions of what these people normally do.

Conducting the Audit

The actual audit process involves you and a small team going into each department to confirm the existing resources. You should take careful notes on what you observe. It will be necessary to talk to several people as part of the audit process. Information you learn by observation, interview, random sampling, and other methods should all be noted.

Step 1: Confirm the existence of hardware

Start with the site map for the local area network. Lay this out on a table in the department where the local area network is located. Starting from the file server, trace back the connections to hubs. From the hubs trace back connections to the actual machines. Does this match the site map you are holding? If this does not, note what is different. These discrepancies can be used to create a more up-to-date site map.

Next, use the list of hardware that is supposed to be in this department. Confirm the presence of all machines that are supposed to be here. Note any machines that are missing or additional equipment that is not on your list. For the machinery that will be involved in the implementation of internet technology, such as file servers and routers, note the existing capabilities of that equipment. Pay particular attention to the apparent amount of usage already being applied to that hardware. For example, your planning team may believe that the file server in marketing is only using 20 percent of its capability. They feel that this is enough of a resource to locate a Web serving package on this machine. Your audit reveals that 75 percent of the file server's capacity is being used by the department. Obviously, this information will be critical for changing the plan to insure success.

Step 2: Confirm the presence of software

The first part of this task is to confirm that the software believed to be in this department is indeed present. For example, your project teammates believe that the Engineering department is using Windows NT version 3.5, in fact to discover they are using version 4.0 and also have Unix available.

You then have to check to see if any software is missing. For example, you may believe that all computers are ready to receive browser software. Instead, you discover that out of 18 PC workstations in this department, three of them are using a mosaic browser, two have Netscape Navigator, and one is using Internet Explorer. The team should make notes on what is currently in existence on these machines. The project team has to decide which standard browser will be migrated to all of these machines and whether existing hardware can handle the software.

Step 3: Interview the people

Finally, you need to talk to the people who will be involved in the implementation of the internet technology, and particularly to the customers of the new technology.

For example, the director of the marketing department is expecting to be able to post web pages on the internet. In talking to this person you find that he has several pre-conceived notions on how this will be done. He believes that Windows NT is the right operating system and that Microsoft's FrontPage 98 is the package to use to create web pages. You find that he already has experience with these two packages. Even though you noted that the team is thinking about using Net Objects Fusion for the web design, do not bring this up in your review. Your job is only to collect information, not to begin the implementation process.

Interviewing is a delicate process that must be handled carefully. You must get a rough idea of how much time critical people are able to dedicate to this project. You must make a judgment call on how committed they are personally to the project's success. All this must be handled with tact and courtesy.

Reporting to the Project Committee

The result of this audit of resources should be summarized in a report to the project team. The report should list what was audited, what was found, and who was interviewed. At no time should you try to interpret your own results. Instead, you are to report your findings. For example:

> "Site map indicated that 18 workstations were in Engineering Department. Found 18 machines, 16 Pentium based PC and two Macs."

What your audit report is designed to do is provide raw information to the project team. It is up to the team to interpret this information and make the appropriate changes to the implementation plan.

Items off of the list

Outside of the formal reports and records you keep should be an accounting of the political and emotional issues involved in your project. These can be noted in your reports in very polite and business-correct format. You should actively consider how you will get the resources needed to make sure that emotions stay calm and politics are kept to a minimum.

One example of a political issue is the need for a top manager that can clear away resistance from line managers. Take the situation where a manager controls a database of vital information. It will be necessary to make this person an active participant of your project, yet he insists that he is "too busy" to participate. It will be necessary to placate this person by arranging for free time so that he can participate in the project. Other top-level management maneuvers could also be used to get this person's cooperation.

What is important here is that you must have a close working relationship with the top managers that support your project. You want to use the authority they have as little as possible. You need to work out an agreement by which you can seek out their cooperation in correcting a major problem. At all costs you must keep top managers as enthusiastic members of your team. This will include not interrupting them constantly with problems coming from your project.

In-house versus Leased Server

The Dickerson County school board faces a decision about whether they want the web server to be in-house or leased from an independent service provider. In their case, they've decided to lease space. This is based on the results of a checklist like the ones above. They looked at the maximum amount of web usage and space that they will need, and found that the amount is far too small to justify owning their own web server. It is clearly cost-effective to lease the space they need.

For the law firm and Avix Manufacturing, the decision was not so clear. The law firm anticipates some need for web presence in the near future, with more later on. Working through the anticipated demand for the intranet they find there might be enough resources left over to use the same server for internet presence. However, this makes the project team leader nervous. If they underestimated the amount of resources that will be required, one or both of their systems will suffer. Therefore, they decide they will lease server space for the short-term until demand justifies a separate web server at the law firm. Avix Manufacturing will be using an extensive set of databases and web pages to communicate with suppliers and customers. After some discussion among the project team, it is decided that they will bring the web server in-house. They lack the ability to set up databases without the restrictions that may be applied by an independent service provider. At the same time, they take full control of where the information is located and who can access it. This is an issue we will discuss in the next chapter.

Megalith has an easy decision. It is clear that they will need their web server in-house for all of the tasks that they have laid out on their checksheet for their internet system.

Understanding and Anticipating Customer/User Needs

One of most common problems we see with project teams setting up internet technology, and other similar projects, is their failure to anticipate needs of the customer. The customer is the end-user of the system the company will develop. It could be the person in the marketing department accessing pricing information on the internet or a member of the general public browsing through literature about your company on the internet. A customer is any person, whether internal or external, who comes in contact with the output from your internet technology.

The success of using internet technology hinges on your ability to present information successfully to these customers. Success means that the information is presented in an easily understandable format, is very practical, can be quickly searched and used, and adds value to the experience of coming in contact with your internet technology.

However, it is not always easy to judge the needs of your customers. To begin with, many customers are not sure what it is they want to obtain from the internet. For example, a person shopping for a new automobile might use the internet to go to the web sites of major manufacturers. Here they can read all of the usual sales literature and learn how great each one of the cars are. Sometimes they can fill out forms to get exact price quotes on what the cost would be on the exact car they want. But does the customer want to take a three-dimensional tour of the car? Will such a presentation sell the car or merely bog down the web browser at the customer's location? Does the customer want to find the nearest dealer? Is the customer more interested in being able to bid between several dealers to get the best price?

The point here is that customers are not always sure what it is they want. You need to take several steps to create a presence on the internet that will result in the customer's belief that it was well worth the time to experience your sites.

The best way to do this is to begin by making sure that customers are part of your project team. Let's take the example of Avix Manufacturing. The manager at one of the companies wants to put the catalog of products on the internet to help promote new sales and speed communications with existing customers. It would then be a good idea to have at least two existing customers be active participants in your project team. They do not need to attend every meeting of the project team. Instead, the project team would call them to discuss their information needs from a customer's perspective. They would also give final approval to the look and feel of your web pages, and the presentation of information.

The next thing would be to have a marketing group or research group look into the potential needs of new customers. Contacts made during the past year would define who would be the potential clients or customers, what is the best way to let them know there's information on the internet, and how are they likely to respond to the proposed look and feel of your web site. Focus groups, questionnaires, and testing of prototype web pages can be valuable tools for gathering information on what a customer likes to see at your site. This type of feedback can be invaluable to the overall planning of your internet technology.

For example, Avix Manufacturing was originally considering the idea that the customer can click on a part item number and see either a schematic drawing or a picture of the component. A little bit of research uncovers an interesting fact. Most of the potential new customers will be engineers at other corporations that use components built by Avix. Interviewing several of these engineers reveals that they want more than just a schematic drawing. They also want the engineering specifications and performance information. Therefore, the Avix project team decides to change the design of the web sites. Along with the schematic drawing there will also be the option to download a file on engineering information. They'll also want a page which will allow engineers to enter the engineering performance data they need to achieve. At that time active portions of the web site will choose possible components that will fit their need. This saves the potential customers time and effort in their own jobs. Thus the Avix web site becomes a valuable resource and a good marketing tool.

Finally, you need to hold interviews with customers who will be working internally. These are the people at your company who will be actively accessing information that you are going to place on your intranet. Take the example of the law firm. One of their major projects is to present training over the internet. Employees recently hired into the firm should be interviewed to determine what form of training they like best. It should also be determined how they want to seek support when they have questions that the training package does not answer. You should also look at their potential work schedules and see how large a block of training courses should be presented at one time.

All of those types of information assist the project team in designing internet technology that will be successful and warmly welcomed by the people who use it. You should make every effort to design sites that are easy to use, pleasant to look at, and responsive.

Computing Time and Monetary Commitments

The computation of costs for projects can be complicated. The easiest way to approach this task is to look at both tangible and intangible costs.

Tangible costs are those that you can quickly identify, such as purchasing hardware or software. Intangible costs are estimates of how much money will be required to complete tasks that have no identifiable boundaries. An example of this is the troubleshooting of web servers once they are installed. It is almost impossible to estimate how long it will take in both time and money to make sure the web server has been configured correctly and will cope with the type of load that will be placed upon it.

To help in calculating the intangible cost of a project, it is very helpful to have information from former projects. If you have an existing local area network then hopefully you have people that remember how long it took to collect and set up different components. File servers, for example, are about as difficult to install and troubleshoot as are web servers. Tapping into the written records and memories of the people involved with the project of setting up the local area network will help you begin to better estimate the intangible cost. Another way of obtaining this information is to prototype parts of your system.

Prototyping means setting up a stand-alone version of a small component of the overall system and testing it thoroughly. For example, Megalith will have to set up several web servers. They may elect to pick a single web server, set it up as a stand-alone server, and load simulated web pages onto it to see if it can handle the load successfully. They hope to also uncover many of the problems they may encounter when they install the other web servers.

Tangible costs can be broken down using standard accounting forms. If your company has a standard format they want you to use to report these types of cost, then by all means use that system. As an alternative you can always itemized things by standard categories such as:

- Hardware cost
- Software cost
- Labor
- Service contracts
- Maintenance
- Insurance
- Miscellaneous

Let's look at the law firm to see how this list would be used. The initial request for the project is to buy two web servers, a router, several software packages, a service agreement, hiring of a new computer technologist, and some other miscellaneous costs. As project team leader, you want to present this in a format that management finds acceptable. Here's one possibility.

Reporting the projected cost in this format helps top management to make key decisions. They will be able to see where the money is going to be

Intranet Project

Hardware Costs:	2 - Server computers @ $3,495 each
	1 - Cisco router @ $1,500
	6 sets of CAT5 cables @ $8 each
	2 - ISDN Modems @ $295 each

Total Hardware Cost: $ 8,833 plus sales tax

Software Costs:	Windows NT @ $699
	Net Objects Fusion @ $295
	Java Programming @ $250
	Security Add-ons @ $195
	Back-up @ $499

Total Software Cost: $1,938 plus sales tax

Labor:	estimated at 100 man-days; $20,000
Training Items	Law practice and formalities, $1299
	How to file a brief, $899
	Phone procedures, $1200
Service Contract	$2500 per year for up to 125 hours of service and $45 an hour after that
Misc.	Back-up tapes, copying costs, media, etc; $500

Projected Project Cost: $37,285

spent on specific items. This allows them to ask specific questions about each item. Do not be surprised to find top management modifying your project plans. You must be ready at all times to justify any of the items on such a list.

How to Ask Management for Additional Resources

The purpose of this chapter is to encourage you to sit down and take an accounting of the resources you have at hand. You can then hold this list up/against the resources you'll need to successfully complete your project. There's always the possibility of a difference between the two amounts.

If you have more than enough resources to complete your project, then you can comfortably proceed with implementation. In many situations you'll discover that you have a shortfall in resources to complete the project. That means part of your project will involve approaching top management to get permission to secure further resources.

Already you have to approach them to buy new hardware and software, as well as other services, to complete your project. Working through the exercises in this chapter may reveal that you need additional resources that were not anticipated. For example, you may need more time, additional personnel, additional training, the help of outsiders, or other such resources. This will have to be requested at the same time you are requesting a budget for your project.

This means you have to prepare a business case study that will be presented to top management. Business case studies are justifications of the task list you wish to carry out. Many corporations have a standard format they want to follow when filling out a business case study. There are important points and facts that must be covered in any of these. If you work in a company where a standard format exists, follow that format.

However, if your company has not already developed a formal format, the following one may be used as a guide:

- Proposed
- Justification
- Implementation
- Budget
- Actions Required of Management

Proposed Using one short paragraph, describe the project you are proposing. The idea here is to quickly communicate to your audience the intention of the project. Let's use the Avix Manufacturing example as an illustration. The opening paragraph in the written proposal might look something like this:

> "It is proposed that an Internet connection be established to our local area network. This will enable the company to present its price information and parts catalog to the general public and to existing customers."

Justification In the justification section, spell out the benefits to be achieved through the successful completion of the project. This should list the obvious benefits to internal productivity, but should also discuss the return on investment. Typically, the justification section is short and focuses only on the key benefits. Continuing with the Avix example, it might look something like this:

> "Currently a new customer requesting price information or parts cata-log can wait up to three days until one can be delivered. The cost of preparing and mailing a single set of catalogs to one customer is cur-rently estimated at twelve dollars. By converting the catalogs to an internet format, delivery will become almost instantaneous, and the cost of delivery will drop to nearly 0. The estimated cost savings per year will be approximately $19,000."

As you can see, the justification segment is written in language that man-agement understands—money!

Implementation   In the implementation sections you describe how the project will be carried out in general terms. It is usually not appropriate to pre-sent your entire project management plan to top management. Instead,a rough outline of the number of people involved, the time lines, and the way the pro-ject will be conducted should be presented. For example,

> "The implementation of the internet project will be the sole responsibili-ty of the IS manager. One member of the computer technology staff, three people from the office staff, and one outside supplier shall form a project team to implement the project. The three office team members will also be responsible for converting the catalogs into the form of web pages. This will take an estimated three months. It is estimated that the internet connection will take 30 days to install and properly configure. At the same time, we have been told, it will include at least 21 days to have the dedicated line installed."

This is only a partial sample of what the implementation section might read like. The idea is to quickly communicate to management the amount of commitment that will be required by different people to complete the project. This is also the area where you mention any activities that top management must engage in to insure a successful project.

Budget   The actual cost for hardware, software, new personnel, sup-port, and other budget items should be listed on a spreadsheet and presented at this part of the proposal. This would be extremely similar to the budget that was prepared earlier in this chapter.

Actions Required of Management   A business case study should conclude with a list of the decisions management must now make. Typically, this will include approval of the budget, the time lines, and authorizing the requested personnel to participate in the project.

During the presentation of the business case study to top management, you must make sure that any questions or hesitation by top management are addressed at this time. Members of the management team may request alterations to the plan. You must be ready to give responses to such requests. If the request is reasonable you should attempt to adjust your overall plan then and there. That way, approval can be obtained at the same meeting as the presentation.

Summary

At this point, you have accomplished two things. First, you developed a list of the resources at hand. You also created the overall design of the internet technology system you wish to install. The difference between these two are now resolved and have been taken to management for approval. The goal here is to ensure that adequate resources will be available for the successful completion of the project.

In the next chapter, we will discuss the issue of security at length. This will introduce a whole new set of concerns that will also require, in most cases, additional hardware, software, time, and human resources. Once that issue has been addressed, we will be ready to start the implementation phase.

Chapter 4

Getting a Handle on Security, Virus Protection, Encryption, Access, and Privacy Issues

Security is one of the famous weak points in information technology management. Most IS managers pay too little attention to security issues. Many totally misunderstand the concept of security. Some others pay way too much attention to the topic.

This can be quickly illustrated through a simple exercise. Take a moment and picture when it is you think about computer security. Perhaps you think about the day that you come in and find a new and unexpected page on your web site. It is a message from a hacker stating that your system has been hacked. Furthermore, the hacker has now planted a virus bomb within your operating system for the entire network. If you ignore this, and do not pay fifty thousand dollars immediately to the specified Swiss bank account, the virus bomb will go off in a few days to bring down your entire network. You have visions of 17-year-old kid in a copy shop with a ring in his nose laughing to himself.

Most discussions of computer security come back to examples somewhat like this one. Perhaps this is a vision you have in your head when you think about security. In reality, this is the totally incorrect way to think about security matters. This type of attack is incredibly rare. You have a long list of real dangers you need to worry about and we will discuss them in this chapter.

How to Think About Security

Let me provide you with another version of security. You are in charge of the security of medieval walled city. This city has seven entrances; you have a limited number of guards. How many guards do you position at each entrance? Where else do you place guards?

The local area network you control is going to be connected to the internet. This type of connection might be taking place in several locations. Therefore it is the equivalent of the wall of the city with entrances out into the wide world. You can control security within the city easily. The security activities outside of your city are much more difficult to judge and control. Your range of options go from tearing down walls and allowing anyone into or out of the city, to placing entire companies on guard at each entrance, questioning anyone who tries to enter the city.

The same is true of your internal systems when exposed to the internet. You can leave your system wide open and let anyone come in and go out. Or at the other extreme, you can provide so many security measures that no one can get in or go out. Therefore, obviously, security is a balance between the needs of the users within your community versus the threats against your system. You need to find the right number of guards to place at the entrance so that threatening people are kept out and the people that have legitimate business with your city are allowed to pass freely and not feel like they are under constant scrutiny.

When you design the security measures for internet connections you need to have three policies in place. The first is a general statement of policy about security and the internet. Second is a statement on how the internet will be used. The third part covers what type of access will be offered between your company and the internet. These three parts make the triangle of security—intention, usage, and access.

What this chapter will do is look at the three parts of the security triangle. You'll go through a series of exercises that will help you draft the initial policy statements for security. These will be presented along with your general plans for implementing internet technology. The draft policy statements will be approved when the implementation plan is approved. The issuing of these policies constitute the beginning of the implementation of internet technology.

Security Policies and Procedures

Before we draft our security policies, let's begin with two simple exercises that will help you frame your thinking for developing the written security statements.

First exercise

Which of the following internet sites would you want to prevent people in your company from accessing?

- Joke of the day
- Bagel recipe site
- Yahoo's classified ads
- JenniCam where a photo of Jenni's life is transmitted every three minutes
- Stock quotation site
- The Mercedes-Benz page
- Adult material site
- Pedophile discussion group
- Off-shore child pornography site
- Information page of notorious terrorist group

Second exercise

Which of the following people within your company should access the Internet?

- The IS manager
- Network administrator
- Marketing representatives
- Sales associates
- The company president
- Engineering staff
- Training specialists
- The librarian
- The janitor
- Temporary workers
- Visitors
- Spouses of employees

Answers to both exercises: There is no correct answer and every answer could be correct. You may be horrified by the idea of allowing access to a child pornography site, but if you are the FBI you would want to find this site and track who was running it. The classified ads may seem like a harmless location until you realize that many employees are wasting hours looking for a better job using your equipment and company time. At the same time, you may want to allow one employee from human resources to look through classified ads to see how well company requests are being placed. The lesson learned here is that you should always think about security as a productivity issue and state your policy in positive terms!

This chapter will show you a couple of security policies you can use for your own organization. Instead of working through exercises and checklists to have you form a security policy, we will start with the finished policies and then examine how they were created. The reason for doing this is because the policy you will write at this point in time will only be a draft. It will be a well thought-out draft that will play a critical role in the next chapter.

In the next chapter you need to write the policies for the internet technologies. By starting with an existing security policy, you will have a strong base upon which to write other policies and procedures. Also, you don't want a security policy written by a committee. You will want feedback from the community that will be affected by the policy, but you still need the "single vision" to keep the policy effective.

Sample Security Policy

Let's begin with an internet security policy and look at what makes it unique. A policy statement is a general description of a company or other organization's position on a specific topic. It could be the overall approach to quality assurance, environmental responsibility, handicap access, and the like. In our situation, it is a statement of the approach used to keep internet technology secure. Here is one such policy:

> "The Dickerson County School system provides internet access to its community of students, faculty, staff, and administrators. It also provides web pages to the community of students, parents, and other interested parties. The existing policies and guidelines of the school system regulate both of these activities. These technologies are almost entirely funded by tax dollars and as such should not be used for questionable or objectionable activities. We ask that the users of the Dickerson County School system Internet technologies create, maintain, and promote a positive environment conducive to learning by students of all ages. The school's staff works toward the development of our internet technology to enhance the exchange of ideas, coordinate learning activities, expand the learning process, and enable the community to express creativity while providing valuable feedback to our continuous improvement of the educational system."

Now let's examine this policy from several different levels and see how it works. At the superficial level it sounds like a "mom and apple pie" type of statement, asserting that the internet can be used for good. That sort of language is used to keep the statement fairly light, positive, and easy to understand. This is critical to the success of a policy. The affected community cannot feel threatened by the statement or they won't obey its intentions.

Obviously, this statement comes from the Dickerson County School example. The IS manager had to sit down and think very carefully about the use of internet technology in an educational setting. He developed a list of objectives the policy should achieve. Then he carefully studied other policies at other schools to find a way to express the general security intentions in a positive light.

The approach here was to say that there is a clear intended use for the web pages and internet connections, namely to promote better communications between the schools and the community. Then it justifies the need for security by showing that tax dollars are at work and there are already existing policies in place for similar activities.

Therefore, at this level, the policy statement is establishing its authority. Just issuing a policy statement isn't effective unless you tie it to a mandate for authority. With a school system you have two obvious sources of authority. Tax dollars imply that state and federal laws are involved. The other source of authority is that the school board already has established rules of conduct for students and staff members. These have to be mirrored by your security policy. The Bill of Rights may guarantee freedom of speech, but the school board can restrict speech when their equipment and resources are being used.

The lesson to learn here is that you should examine your company's existing policies related to employee behavior and general security first. Your internet security statement should reflect the corporate culture and policies. For example, the doors to your office are locked every night and important files are locked away so the information is available only to those with permission. You can set up the internet equivalent of this same philosophy.

Next, the Dickerson policy statement makes it clear that abuse of the system will not be tolerated. This enables you to punish violators because you have stated that specific behaviors are not allowed. Without a statement that there are restrictions and that top management can determine punishment, you will find it nearly impossible to enforce any rules.

At the same time, this is not the place to get very specific about the behavior that is not allowed. It is stated in general terms in the policy. The security procedures you develop later will get more specific.

Finally, the whole policy is completed with a statement on the type of behavior that is expected on the internet. This is a critical issue often overlooked by IS managers. To get people to move to a desired spot you must lead them. You need to state the way you expect the system to be used. When this is done in a positive tone, people will understand how to use the system correctly and won't be tempted as often to "play" with the system.

Exercise: Emphasize the positive

We can illustrate just how important the positive approach to policy statements is with a simple example you can try at work or at home. Get a small box and mount a red button switch on the top. Inside the box hook up any device that will count how many times the button is pressed.

Now, paint on the outside of the box a large warning label that says, "Do not push this button!" Place the box in a public place at the office or at home and leave the room. About once a day, open the box and see how many times the button was pushed.

What you will discover is that human nature is unusual. When confronted with a sign telling us what not to do, the first instinct is to investigate further why we shouldn't be doing this activity. If you issue an internet policy that says, "You cannot access the stock quotes at work" you will soon find an underground chain of E-mail reporting stock quotes to employees. Keeping in mind that practically no one was interested in stock prices before the policy statement, you get the picture of how small communities (like businesses) actually behave.

Another Policy Statement

Now let's examine the policy statement for the Megalith Corporation. Here we will see a statement tightly associated with the existing culture of the corporation.

"Megalith strives to find new avenues of competition and continuous improvement. Our expanding Internet technology system is just one such system. Just like sales presentations, business letters, recruiting, and other forms of interfacing with customers, suppliers, and the general public, the internet is another form of business communications. As such the same rules of conduct for employees and management apply to internet communications as we would expect for any other form of business communications. You are representing Megalith. Be sure to use the same positive, clearly expressed methods of communications you normally use every day. The internet is a valuable resource that must be used wisely and efficiently. Network administrators are available to grant you the access and permissions you need to accomplish your tasks on the internet."

The first thing to notice at this point is how short in length these policy statements are. At the policy level you want to keep things short and to the point. These are general statements of intent. You are explaining why things are being done. The issues of who, what, where, when, and with what equipment is left for the standard operating procedures.

Next, you should again note that this is being said in a very positive way even though a big threat is hidden in the statement. The policy talks about everyone following the same codes of ethics and rules of conduct for other office activities and contact with the public. That means that there are existing rules and methods of punishment already in place that will now be expanded to include the internet technology system.

An employee caught stealing an office chair can be dismissed. The same employee caught stealing a computer file from a secured area of a file server faces similar punishment.

Another key point is that corporations in the United States already have permission to listen to your phone calls and read your memos. That means they can also look at your E-mail and read your web browsing logs. The Megalith policy opens this door as well by making the connection between normal business activities and internet activities.

Finally, the policy statement ends with the interesting statement that network administrators can issue access and permissions. What that means is that Megalith plans to lock down access and permissions for most users from the start. Individuals and workgroups will have to justify specific access and permission requirements before they can have them. This allows the IS personnel greater control in restricting access to avoid problems. At the same time, IS management will have to work hard to ensure that the restricted access will not slow down or interfere with ongoing projects.

As discussed below, there are several aspects of security you will have to consider to get a positive and friendly policy statement that also assures an effective internet system.

The Three Steps to an Effective Security Policy

There are three basic steps you should take to draft an effective security policy. They are an evaluation of the risks, the security of the physical system, and the security of the people using the system. Remember you are only creating a draft with a well thought-out line of justification. This draft will be used in the next chapter when you need to guide the management committee on the correct overall internet policy.

Step One: Evaluate your risks

An individual with a personal web page doesn't usually run much, if any, security risk. A large, multi-national corporation will have a variety of risks. The reason is simple; the more interfaces you have with the internet, and the more people involved with your internet technology, the greater your risk tends to be.

Let's return to our opening exercises to see where risk can originate. Which of the following people represent a security risk to your internet system that you would consider "critical" or "very high"?

- The company president
- The average users of your system
- A dedicated gang of hackers
- The janitor
- Temporary employees
- Visitors to your web site
- Visitors to your company
- Spouses of employees
- Computer service technicians from your supplier of such services
- A disgruntled employee

Any of these people could be a massive security concern or no threat at all. In most cases they will land somewhere between these two extremes. By carefully thinking through your company's situation, you can accurately evaluate these security risks and plan a system to prevent problems. Let's go through this list of "people risks" first. Later we will look at other sources of risks.

Who is the threat to your security?   In most cases, people constitute the greatest threat to an internet technology system. Whether intentional or not, they can cause problems that range from annoyances to destruction of equipment and records. Therefore, go through our short list, add any other groups at your company, and indicate the level of risk each group presents.

The company president is a good example of someone most people don't think about when designing a security system. If your company president is also the very visible leader of an extreme conservative political group, several opposition groups could decide to target your internet sites.

The average users of your system can also be a big problem for security. The most notorious of these problems is password security. Let me take a moment to defeat your current local area network security system. I walk into the average employee's cubicle and lift the mat under the keyboard or look in the center drawer of the desk. Most times I will find the employee's network password written down. A few keystrokes later and I am inside your network. Because of the size of this problem, the security of the people that use your system will be covered in the next step.

Outside hackers are always seen as a threat to internet technology. The connections your company makes to the outside world might allow a hacker into the system. However, hackers tend to enjoy challenging sites. Avix Manufacturing would not tend to be a hacker's target. Megalith would because of its size. The Dickerson County School district would also be a hacker's target. This comes from a different source; talented computer students in the system would see it as the closest target at hand.

A recent example of this occurred in a school system where a student brought in a virus to deliberately load into the learning lab's computers at his high school. What he didn't know was that the lab was part of the entire school system's local area network. The result of having no virus protection at the main file server was the mass destruction of data files. It was a huge mistake to let a high school lab have a direct connection to the rest of the network. If E-mail connectivity was needed, it should have been routed out to the Internet and then back to the school's local area network.

Surprising to many IS managers is the idea that most benign people in the organization have to also be considered. The janitor may need to order supplies directly from a supplier using an internet web page. This would speed delivery and cut costs. At the same time, the janitor is not regularly monitored by a supervisor. Therefore, you would restrict the janitor's total internet access to just the supplier.

Temporary employees can be a great security risk to most companies. They may be working for you this week, but your competitors next week. Because of recent labor shortages, they rarely worry about losing their current job. This creates a situation where they will not be afraid of using web browsers to visit their favorite sites for hours on end or sending hate E-mail to an ex-spouse. So when temporary employees need to use the internet technology as part of their job duties, you will want to create special access accounts that audit their usage and restrict services. This makes it clear to them that nonbusiness activities are strongly discouraged.

The design of web sites has to be open and friendly. However, it also has to be secured against web visitors who might accidentally or deliberately upset your site. The classic example of this is a situation that occurred with Windows NT. In the past, you could enter just the right number of characters in the URL request and crash the server. Thus, a security problem was created through a software flaw.

Similar to the problem with people leaving their passwords written down by their computers, visitors to your company can be tempted by lapses in security. Visiting sales representatives from a company trying to close a big contract with your company will be strongly tempted if they realize they have been left alone with a computer already logged on to the system.

Another common security problem is that employee spouses visit. They have not been through the education about your computer security policies. At the same time, many of them see themselves as very computer knowledgeable. What happens is that they either log on or use a terminal already logged on to the system to "look around." Your security system must attempt to keep them out, or prevent damage by notifying someone when they do get in. This is especially critical for workers who have remote access privileges. They have to be made aware that any abuse carried out with their account from home is their responsibility.

One great source of viruses and computer spies are the technicians that come in to fix your computers. They can use disks contaminated by viruses from other locations. These people can be underpaid and looking for extra sources of income, such as selling your company secrets. That is why you will need a procedure just for making sure that technicians are properly escorted at all times and no viruses are introduced.

And, finally, we end with another true story. An ISP employee decided one evening that he had had enough with his current employer. He knew he would end his shift at midnight and never come back. As a parting gift he took the central hub for the network running the ISP's internet services. This $80 piece of equipment took down the entire system for a day while a replacement was found. The ISP suffered a full day of very dissatisfied customers. The police would not arrest the offender because the value of the theft was so small. Disgruntled employees, especially those working for the IS manager, can be a very serious threat. Later in this book we will discuss how you find people you can trust and how to keep them honest.

Step Two: Secure the physical system

Your company locks doors, bolts valuable equipment to the floor, requires tools to be checked in and out, and takes other standard precautions for physical objects. Your internet technology system will be composed of many pieces of physical equipment. How you keep the equipment secure should be a reflection of your current system of keeping the local area network equipment secure. After all, some of this equipment will be doing double duty as both network and internet equipment.

Physical Security The physical location of equipment will help with its security. If you already use locked wiring closets and controlled file server rooms, then continue to do so. A person determined to gain access to your internet services can do it best from the servers. Therefore, lock them away and restrict access to trusted members of your staff.

Network hubs, routers, bridges, gateways, and other similar equipment should be in locations where they will not be tampered with or damaged accidentally. The ISP that had the employee steal the central hub suffered this problem because the hub was in the central wiring closet where all employees had access. It should have been in a locked cabinet where the employee needed permission to open the door.

Cables should be secured where possible by running them under the floor, in the wall panels, into cable runs, or up above the suspended ceiling. This prevents many accidents caused by people stepping on or tripping over a cable. It also keeps the curious at bay because they are unaware of the cable's presence. In short, you need to add to your security policy a supporting procedure for how equipment is to be secured.

The Dickerson County School system has a particular security worry: the level of physical security at the ISP. Since the web server belongs to the ISP and is located in their facility it makes it almost impossible for the Dickerson IS manager to assure that the site is secure.

Avix Manufacturing will have to add a web server to the IS room to keep it away from employees and visitors. Access should be restricted to vital IS personnel only. People supplying content can do it remotely over the existing local area network. The Law Firm will have to take similar measures.

Megalith will have to expand its current local area network security procedure to include the new internet equipment. New cables and routers will have to be installed with the same security concerns for physical equipment that any critical computer component now receives.

Security within the Network Once the physical equipment is secured, then you must go down your list of risks and begin to design the internal security for your local area network with internet capabilities. If you originally had a local area network operating solely within your company, then only some of the security risks listed earlier would apply.

However, when you add internet capabilities you are making a physical connection to the outside world where you cannot fully control who comes into your system. While trying to keep undesirable people out, you need to make access for acceptable people as free and open as possible. This can be a tricky balancing act.

To keep your network secure while attached to the internet, there are several layers of defenses you can employ. We will review these shortly, but keep in mind that any defense can be overcome and defeated. What you need to do is deploy as many defenses as your resources allow without noticeably interfering with the operation of the system. This will keep out most accidental intrusions and discourage all but the most determined attacker.

Returning to our example of the walled city, the network can be entered without permission by methods similar to defeating a walled city with guards. Attackers can disguise themselves and slip in, blow a hole into a wall and walk in, attack in great numbers and overwhelm your defenses, or use any other siege techniques.

When security is a vital corporate concern, you should do as much as you can and then hire outside security experts to improve the system as far as possible. If you know your system will be a target of attacks, then also use the convoy defense strategy. That is, if you know that the attackers are coming after your system, patrol it all the time, detect the attack, and chase down the attackers.

For most situations, a well-planned software-based security system will be adequate. This will include setting permissions, controlling access, installing software security programs, and enforcing stringent application of passwords, audits, logs, and other techniques.

Setting permissions and access levels Local area network software and operating systems allow you to set the permissions each user has within your system. For example, in Windows NT you can establish a "Guest" account that allows a user to read files that are not password protected, print output, and run a few applications. Nothing else is allowed.

Your network administrators should be given permission levels that allow them to do everything short of changing the security system. They can issue passwords, create new accounts, move files, make backups, and the like, but they cannot change the existing permissions within accounts or other security set ups. To do that, they will need your permission. Only the IS manager should have full control of the system with a trusted second person able to perform these tasks if the IS manager is not available. This prevents a disgruntled network administrator from deliberately arranging a "back door" for tampering with the system. It also lets you know who is doing the most system-wide manipulation (see Figure 4–1).

Figure 4-1. Sample Access Levels

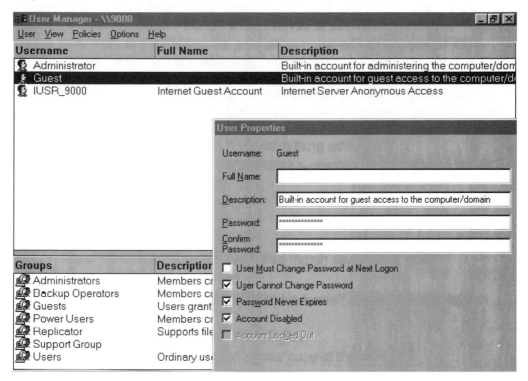

Access levels are different from permissions. They represent general access rules for selected portions of the network. Take the example of a web server being attached to the local area network in the Marketing group at Megalith. You want to prevent anyone from the internet getting into the general corporation network. Thus, you place a gateway server and router at the connection point between Marketing and the rest of the network. The internet connection also has a firewall. If the firewall is breached, then the second level of defense at the gateway machine will keep outsiders from vital files.

Now we pause for another true story. One day an engineer is logging off the Unix based network running off of a DEC minicomputer. The check for new E-mail command is placed after the logoff command for all accounts. This frustrates the engineer because you get a message that you have mail but you are now logged off the system.

Out of curiosity, he looks for the logoff sequence file and finds it on a root directory. Opening it in a text editor he moves the "check E-mail" command to a line before the logoff. For good measure he adds an alert message of "Dude, you got mail." He finishes and logs off for the day. Sure enough the "dude" message comes up and he can check the mail before the logoff is completed. Unfortunately, and unknown to the engineer, the same message is now appearing corporate wide. The next morning, the VP of MIS and two security officers are waiting in his cubicle.

The lesson to be learned here is that a real danger exists from people unaware of what they are doing within the system. The root directories should be protected at all times from access by all but the top administration accounts. Also, if a work group in your company has no reason to be accessing the web server, then exclude them from access at the operating system level.

In Windows NT, for example, you do this by setting ranges of IP addresses that are excluded from access. Although a knowledgeable person can spoof the server into thinking the IP address is allowed, this will keep out accidental intrusions (see Figure 4–2).

Firewalls and other connectivity defenses   In our example of the walled city we placed guards at each gate. A wiser precaution would have

Figure 4–2. Excluding IP Addresses from Access

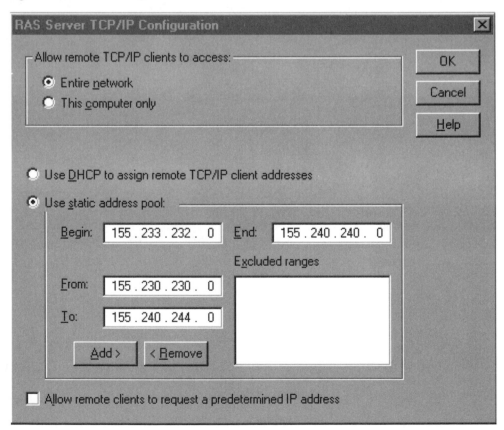

been to add guards to critical points within the city. For example, we want to have guards at our armory. This is how a firewall works for network security.

There are two different types of basic firewalls. The first controls access between networks. The second is an application-specific firewall. Network level firewalls operate as a gatekeeping function of the connection to another network. For the purposes of this book, we're talking about your connections to the internet. A firewall stands between your network and the internet connection. It examines IP packet headers and decides whether or not the addresses involved and the ports being used meet security requirements. If they do not, they are rejected. This helps you to keep people out who you don't want on your system while still allowing approved personnel in. Figure 4–3 shows what a typical firewall setup looks like.

This is not the only way a firewall can be set up. For example, you can place the computer between your web server and internet with two network interface cards. Each network interface card gets a different IP address. For packets to pass from the internet through the first computer to the second network interface card, which is connected to your network, it must meet the security rules in the firewall software.

For example, World Wide Web pages are served to the internet typically under port 80. If someone from the internet is attempting to get your web server on something other than port 80, the firewall will stop them. Attempting access by using a different port number is a common trick used by intruders to gain access to your system.

Figure 4–3. Typical Network Firewall Setup

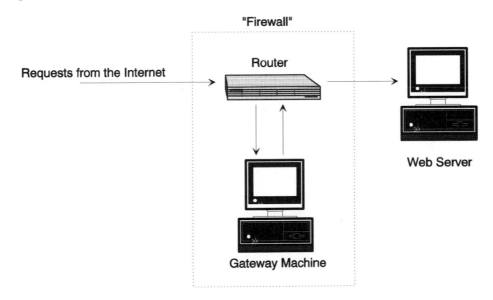

The nice thing about network level firewalls is that they work very fast and they're transparent to the people using your system. However, they are not foolproof. If an intruder learns the type of firewall security you have put in place, it becomes possible to design the solutions to go around the security protocols. Therefore, you place application level firewalls at the point where applications are being served under the network.

Application level firewalls are usually more elaborate than the network level firewalls. Not only do they look at the IP addresses and the ports being called for, but they also look at the commands that are being requested of the file server. For example, if someone coming in from the internet makes a request of Telnet connection, the firewall can refuse this. The use of the Telnet command, FTP, and other file transferring applications allows outsiders to tamper with your system.

Firewall software also logs all activities that they are monitoring. This is very helpful when you have found intruders in your system. You can document how they came in and what they were doing. Therefore, for any business it is highly recommended that the firewall software and firewall devices be placed in all connections between your network and internet. However, keep in mind that to use this equipment and software properly your internal networks must be using valid IP addresses.

Uninterrupted power supplies Although it seems obvious to have an uninterrupted power supply to all of your computers, it is still surprising to find web servers, file servers, and other critical components of networks without this power backup. The result of the sudden loss of power to the computer can cause more than just lost data. Line surges, folded spikes, excessive voltage noise, and other threats can potentially damage data files and the physical equipment.

Especially important for internet connections is to have another uninterrupted power supply that can protect the telecommunications lines as well. My one experience with lined voltage came from a direct hit by a lightning bolt on my company's telecommunications line. The surge of electricity followed our twisted-pair cables and destroyed every communication device attached to the telecommunications system. Computers were surprisingly unharmed. Minimal voltage protection was in place on the telecommunication line. Damages were over $60,000.

The lesson to learn here is that the minimal amount of lightning protection that the Telephone Company installs is not enough. For super-critical applications, you need to get the highest level of voltage protection available.

It is also a good idea to have an uninterrupted power supply that has network intelligence built in. This way the backup power source can communicate across your network to the administrator's computer. Information on power losses or systems that are now running on battery power can be sent immediately to a central location. This will alert network administrators that they have only a certain amount of time to shut down critical systems or find an alternative power source.

Backup for Data and Equipment At this point, I would like you to pause and engage in another discovery exercise. If you are at work, put this book down and go to your nearest wiring cabin or the location where your file servers are located. Look around the room where these critical computers are housed. Now imagine you are holding a lighted match. If you were to drop the match and start a fire in this room destroying everything, how long would it take you to recover your data and place it into new equipment?

In the next section we will talk about disaster recovery in some detail. For now we want to talk about the issue of backup data. The following is a true story. The network administrator used an array of hard disks to store all the information from the file servers. Each day he was to backup onto a streaming tape. At least this is what was supposed to be happening.

One day he suffered a statistically improbable situation. Two of the hard drives in his RAID array locked up at the same time. That meant that he suffered a loss of the data in the entire array. Already nervous, he reached for his backup tape. Quickly he discovered that the daily backups had only been done on a weekly basis. The one he found was already three days old. Inserting in the tape backup drive and requesting a restoration of all data, he discovered the tape was unable to restore the data to the machine.

Looking around frantically, he found the next backup tape that was already two weeks old. It too failed. The only tape that would successfully backup was a month old. The entire month of information created by a large company was lost. However, we're quite sure that he did find another job.

In your security policy, you should cite that you have a data backup procedure. Typically, you should be making at least daily backups. Each Friday you make the second backup for the week. This tape is retained for a month. The daily tapes are rotated each week. For super-critical applications, two backups should be made twice each day.

It is not enough to make tape backups of your system's data. These backups should be tested on a separate platform to ensure that they are actually functioning properly. To test your backup system, take a computer, set it up as a file server, and read your last backup tape to its hard drive. Next, test the system thoroughly to make sure that all applications were completely restored and that all data was successfully retrieved.

Auditing of the backup procedure should be done on a monthly basis, at the least. The testing of backup aids should also be done at the same time. The loss of data is one of the most critical problems the network administrator faces. Therefore, devote the appropriate amount of attention to your backup procedures.

Disaster Recovery   Returning to our example above, what would happen if your critical equipment were destroyed? The answer is, you would be in big trouble, unless you had practiced an aggressive disaster recovery plan. The mark of a good disaster recovery plan is that you can restore your system so fast, practically no one notices that anything happened. This is especially true for internet connections. If you are conducting commerce over the internet, loss of the connection and the supporting equipment costs your company money.

Disasters come in many forms. When preparing a disaster recovery procedure, it is wise to consider all possible kinds of disasters. Following is a partial list of what can happen to destroy part or all of your system:

- Earthquake
- Flood
- Tornado
- Theft
- Fire
- Sabotage
- Software lock up
- Electronic pulse
- Loss of systems administrator
- Loss of telecommunications line
- Your ISP goes out of business

These are just a few of the disasters that can take place in your company. The likelihood of these depends on your location and your particular situation. For example, earthquakes are not a worry in the Midwest. Companies in California constantly have to worry about earthquakes. At the same time, Californians rarely worry about tornado damage.

Basically, the disaster recovery plan is a script for who does what to make sure that equipment and software are quickly replaced if you should suffer a loss. The idea is to have a list of what needs to be replaced, where to go to get the replacements, who gets replacements, who installs the replacements, where the replacements are put, and other details that allow you to completely reconstruct the damaged or missing portions of your system.

Critical to your disaster recovery plan is to identify a single person that will coordinate efforts. This person should regularly review the plan against the existing equipment and software in use. The same person should also make sure that suppliers are standing by to replace critically needed equipment. Extremely critical situations that involve vitally important pieces of your network must be kept nearby at a separate site.

For example, part of your normal backup procedure should be to keep copies of all the applications software in a locked and secured location at a different site, yet close to your company. One way to do this is to rent space in a bank vault. Here you would store copies of your critically needed software. However, if you feel it may be necessary to retrieve these copies outside of banking hours, another location would have to be found.

Critical pieces of your system's hardware should be available from local suppliers at all times. The disaster recovery plan should list several known suppliers of the components that feature express delivery. As an alternative you can also look at other local area networks within your system that can take over the function of a different local area network. For example, you may have a local area network file server that, in an emergency, can fill in for the corporate web server.

Much like the backup procedure, you should practice your disaster recovery. Weekends make typically good times to do this. You can select the network supporting your web server and ultimately shut down for a few hours. If it is critical to keep contact with the internet, perhaps you could just pretend that you lost all internet connection capabilities. The IS manager can even write a scenario such as, telecommunications line loss, one of three web servers shut down at the same time, how do you recover?

Technical staff then has a set number of hours to create a replacement for the lost communication line and equipment. The success of the emergency crew is then evaluated against the disaster plan. These types of exercises are invaluable for creating a good disaster recovery plan.

Step Three: Securing the people portion of the equation

Finally, we have to discuss the human side of the security equation. No matter how well you design the physical security system, whether for a computer network, an office building, or a walled city, someone working within that system can easily defeat the security measures. In an office building, someone can leave a door unlocked when it should be secured. In the walled city, someone might be bribed into revealing a secret passage open to invaders.

With a computer system, the user could leave a workstation logged on but unattended.

Therefore, you need to spend a considerable amount of time making sure the people within your system all operate within the intentions of your security policy. The best way to do this is to make them fairly unaware that they are cooperating with the security policy. For example, you can automatically encrypt E-mail messages that are being sent both within and outside your system. Your system users do not even need to worry about security of the E-mail. The security system is nearly transparent.

Password management   One place where your computer security system will be blindingly obvious to users is the management of passwords. Most modern security systems come down to a moment when the user has to enter a password. The most common occurrence of this is when one user logs on to another workstation. As mentioned earlier, this is one of the easiest ways to determine if an intruder was in your system. People tend the leave their passwords where they are easily discovered, or use password names that are easy to guess.

As we shall see later, education and training are critical to the success of your security system. Password management is an excellent example. It is no longer considered adequate to merely assign passwords to particular user accounts.

Instead, you need to assign to each user a password that is only good for a limited amount of time. At regular intervals the user needs to change the password. The user also has to be educated on the proper type of password to use for the account when it is changed. The idea is to make users responsible for password management on their own accounts. This allows accounts to have their passwords changed frequently without overwhelming the resources and personnel of the information technology department.

An example can illustrate how this should work. To support your general security policy, you would write a password management procedure. In this document, you would establish that each new user to the system is given an account name and a password. The policy would also set up guidelines for what type of passwords would be used, and how often the passwords would be changed.

The Law Firm is planning to do this by educating all of their employees that they will have to change their passwords each month. Each employee is then given a memo explaining the importance of protecting their passwords. They are given tips and techniques for hiding their passwords. One of the examples given is to bury the passwords in what appears to be a note to yourself somewhere on your desk. The password has to be at least six characters long and not a single word.

Janice at The Law Firm is given the user name "LawSec12" which means she is the 12th account for a legal secretary. Her password is "392Fish." This combination of a random number and easy to remember word will discourage most password hacking programs. At the same time Janice is able to hide her password in plain sight using a note posted among many notes on her bulletin board which says,

"Congratulate Ed for his haul of 392 fish during his vacation."

Feel free to use your imagination to come up with more clever tricks like this to teach people how to properly hide their password. Since they are changing their password every 30 days at The Law Firm you also want to educate them not to use obvious passwords. For example, the following words would not be allowed:

- January
- February
- March
- April

Employees should also be discouraged from using the names of their children, their phone numbers, or any other piece of information that an outsider could easily obtain. Instead they should use memorable phrases, names, or numbers that are important in their life that other people would not be aware of. For example, the 1994 academy award winning best picture title could be one example. This could be the employee's favorite movie but other people would not be aware of this.

You would also make sure that Human Resources helps you to have joint policies on punishment for people who are lax with their passwords. The largest security threat that you usually face is people leaving their workstations to go to lunch while still logged on to the system. This allows anyone passing by to gain access to the system. This is why you must have a strict policy that will punish workers for this practice.

Extremely important is that administrative accounts are never left unattended. Your system wide management computers should be locked away in a separate room and stay that way as often as possible. The person using that computer should be locked in the room to prevent the odd passer-by from drifting in to talk. A single trip to the bathroom could leave open the possibility of someone setting up an illegal account to later gain access to the entire system.

Developing a strict system of password management is not enough. At least twice a year there should be an audit of existing passwords being used by employees and your administrative staff. In the nicest way possible you should talk to people using inappropriate passwords or other breaches of security to convince them to follow your security policy. The supervisor of the person violating the policy should also be notified. Punishment is not required for this type of incident. Instead, your job is to encourage people to maintain the security system.

This will be particularly difficult when members of top management are some of the most frequent violators of the policy. It is not unusual to have the president of a company giving his or her password to several systems so others can perform tasks that the president is too busy to accomplish. If that becomes a situation within your company, you'll need to modify your security procedures to maintain the integrity of your system for these top managers. This could include the distribution of limited access accounts for the assistance of the president.

Encryption   Encryption is the process of converting a message into a code that only selected people can read. The coding is the process of converting the code back to a readable message.

For thousands of years there has been an interest in coded messages that prevent other people from reading them. Thanks to computers there are now thousands of ways to encode messages and thousands of ways for people to crack that code. For the purposes of communicating with the internet, encryption can be an important tool for business competitiveness.

From Chapter 1 we learned that all messages on the internet are sent with IP addresses attached. Anyone who has access to one of the routers used on the internet can use software to look for messages from particular IP addresses. This is known as "sniffing out" a message. Even if the messages are broken into several pieces they can be found and reassembled. This allows the staff to read the correspondence or data files you are sending over the internet.

As you can imagine, this would be disastrous if you are transmitting information about your pricing structure, competitive strategy, a list of key customers, or any other piece of information that would normally be under heavy security.

At the same time there are major obstacles blocking the use of coded encryption on the internet. The most famous of these is the fact that you cannot export encryption technology outside the United States. Encryption technology is seen as weapons technology under import/export laws. As the

"Enigma" code demonstrated in World War II, encryption technology can be critical to the success of warfare. The major concern is that enemy countries, terrorists, drug dealers, or (heaven forbid) tax evaders can use encryption to carry out their business. They would then be free from the threat of active monitoring by law enforcement or military officials.

However, at the same time, business requires the same high level of encryption capabilities to be able to use the internet for secure business transactions. Leading the pack of business applications that need encryption are electronic data interchange and financial transactions. It is one thing to worry about someone on the internet intercepting your Visa number, but it is quite another concern to have someone gain access to the purchase order for a multimillion dollar contract.

As IS manager, you'll have to talk to the people that are thinking of communicating over the internet about the level of security they require. Anything more than casual messages back and forth with customers and suppliers will require encryption.

Keys and how they work   Encryption technology is a massive field of study. The controversies and potentials of encryption technology on the internet is a very popular topic within the internet. Thus, it is actually beyond the scope of this book. This is why this discussion is limited to a general overview of what is possible in just one type of encryption.

To help to fully understand all of the possibilities, you should also consult the following two sites on the internet:

www.rsa.com
www.commerce.net

These two sites are seen as the internet leaders in the discussion of encryption technologies.

The trick to encoding a message is to develop an encoding key. The key is a mathematical algorithm that scrambles the original message into a form that is impossible to read without knowing the key that created the message.

Traditionally encoding keys were kept to a minimum and used from a central location. People that were given authority to read encoded messages were given a decoding key. The decoding key was physically carried to the person who would use it, and then secured to prevent others from using it. This is why you see such an emphasis in spy movies on breaking into embassies and other locations to get their decoding machine.

Unfortunately, the internet community is so large that is not practical to send a key to each person you want to receive your coded messages. The number, type, and location of the people that send E-mail and data files varies wide-ly day by day. So, the public key method was developed. In this scheme, the decoding key is made public on your server. A person wishing to send you a coded message, would use this public key and then send you the message. A second key that is not made available to the public is used to decode the mes-sage. Only a person with this private key can read the messages.

This enables many people to encode the messages that are being sent to you with a relatively high degree of security. Central to this concept is the idea of a certification authority. The certification authority issues both the public and the private keys to qualifying businesses. The role of the certification authority is to confirm the legitimacy of the business, verify its location, make certain that people need encryption, and other such details. In this way other businesses that want to communicate with you using encryption can go to the certification authority to make sure that you are indeed who you say you are.

Encryption alone is not enough to secure a system such as E-mail on the internet. Because it is very likely that your business wishes to engage in com-merce on the internet, you are in need of another level of security.

Digital signatures and receipts   Just because a person picked up your public key and encoded a message to a business does not authenticate the person sending the message. What is also required is a method to know who has sent the message and that the message was received. This problem is solved by two additional technologies.

The first of these is the digital signature. This again is a mathematical algorithm that is used by the person sending the message. It is not part of the encryption scheme. Therefore it is possible to attach a digital signature to the message but still have the message encoded. It is highly recommended that whenever two digital signatures are used, the message also be encoded.

The digital signature comes from a separate key that the person gets from a certification authority. Again, the certification authority is verifying that this person actually exists, has a business location, and other details. This vouch-es for the authenticity of the signature. The person receiving the message can use a public key for the signature to confirm that the message did indeed come from the person claiming to have sent it. It also confirms that the message was not tampered with during transmission.

The second piece of technology in the encoding of a message is a receipt, which is sent back to the person sending the message. This is a critical piece of technology because it confirms the message reached its destination with full integrity. The originator of the message uses his private key to confirm the receipt's digital signature. Now the person who sent the message knows that it had not been tampered with and that it was received.

Luckily, your software handles most of this activity in a transparent fashion. This enables businesses to carry out many forms of commerce safely. A person can place an order, attach payment information, and digitally sign a message before sending it to your company. If the buyer encodes the entire message, this information is not likely to fall into the wrong hands. Digital signatures and receipt messages help you to document that the order had actually been placed by the person whose name appears on the form. Disputes about the order are settled because electronic receipts confirm that the message was both sent and received.

The role of the IS manager To make this system of encryption, two digital signatures, and receipt messages work, the IS manager has to administer the keys. Web serving software typically comes in a package with key management software. This allows you to log in to a certification authority and order both private and public keys.

The private key is then placed into a secure location within your network. The public keys are made available on each of your web servers accessible to internet customers. For internal communications a second private key can be placed in a secure location with a public key made available to the intranet. You must then enable the encryption and the digital signature capabilities of the E-mail system and data file transfer software used internally. This is no small task.

It is highly recommended that you first research which certification authority you wish to use. Then you'll have to decide whether any of your messages will be traveling outside of United States or Canada. If they do travel overseas then you face export restrictions on the size of the public key you can use. In other words, the public key that you can use on your web server will be strong enough for most applications, though weak enough for the U.S. government to be capable of cracking it to read your messages. The keys that you use internally or with your wide area network within the United States can use a stronger encryption key.

Your web serving software can guide you on how to load both public and private keys. They should be thoroughly tested before you release their use to your systems users. You need to regularly audit the use of encryption to make sure it matches your security policies. You'll also need to keep up-to-date on developments of public and private key technologies. This is best found by regularly checking the web site of your certification authority.

Access control It is one thing to lock a door, but quite another to keep it locked. So it is with access control. You can design strict access control for your network and connections to the internet, but holes in the system eventually begin to appear. Therefore, constant vigilance is required.

Luckily, some of the newer operating systems on internet serving software allow you to write security policies directly to the system. Figure 4–4 illustrates such a feature on the internet server running under Windows NT.

This feature of the software allows you to lock out access for specific user accounts. You can create a general users account for, say the local database creators, and then designate where they can go, what they can do, and where they are not allowed according to your security policy. This is a very handy feature that allows you to establish security access for groups of people at the same time instead of having to set up each user's account separately.

Figure 4–4. Writing Security Policies Directly to the System

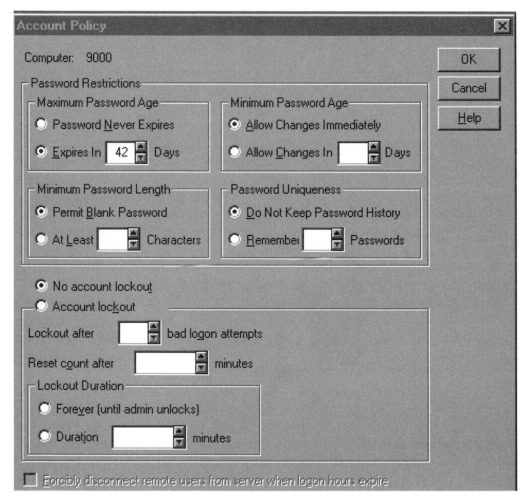

Your password administration can also be handled inside the software level policy. You can allow users to have only a few attempts of entering their password, require them to change passwords every 30 days, and set the minimal links for passwords at six characters, for example. That gives you the flexibility to apply the middle level of security to the general users that lead to a much higher degree of security to special users.

For example, the person responsible for loading web pages into your web server needs special access privileges to read and write from the web server's hard drive. The ability to write or edit data on the web server should be restricted for all other users except development people and administrators. Any access to the web server that involves operations such as editing, writing, file transfers, and other potentially dangerous activities for data security should be carefully logged in and regularly audited for appropriateness.

Returning again to our example of the walled city, access control is a lot like establishing one-way streets within the town. You can force traffic to pass through certain points in your city no matter where they are traveling. This allows you to position a security person at that point to watch for trouble. The same is true of your network system and your internet connection. There will be critical points everywhere from the internet coming into your system. Likewise there will be points where people in your system who try to get out onto the internet must also pass. These are the points where you put your heaviest security.

The best example of one of these critical points is the dial-out modem. When talking about connecting your network to the internet, we generally talk about focusing everyone's access to the internet on a central computer that has the single connection to your ISP. However, many local area networks also have modems that can both place and accept telephone calls. Thus, a user in your system only needs their own private ISP account to be connected to the internet from work.

This presents the need to strictly control who dials out and who can dial in to your network. People at work who want to use their own internet accounts to contact the internet should be required to go through the same security system used for your network at large. There is really no need for individuals to use their own accounts to contact the internet when a freely available corporate account is in place. If it becomes necessary for individuals to contact the internet, security measures should be placed on their modem, computer and operating software. This would also include firewall security.

The other half of this equation is also dangerous. Modems allow people to dial in and gain some sort of access to your network computers. At a minimum, you should use callback modems. Thus, a person dialing and connecting to the modem who does not provide proper authorization, will have the line disconnected. The modem then calls back the number where this person is supposed to be located, for example at home. This prevents someone from using a stolen user account to access your computer from a remote and unknown location.

Proper Utilization of the Internet

As we will see in the next chapter, one of the critical issues for the overall internet policy statement is the usage and application of the internet for your company. As stated earlier, it is best to avoid negative language when writing security policies. The security policy you create will be used as one of the key documents in creating a statement of rules and usage for internet access within your company. The type of access control and security measures you have set up, along with how passwords are generated and used, will frame the rules for using the internet.

As shown in one of our earlier policy statements, the intention is to encourage productive use of the internet for business related matters. This includes assuring that people act professionally while on the internet. The policy on the usage of the internet will also mention the efficient use of resources within the company to access the internet. There will be some need to discourage people from "parking" on a web site while they go to lunch, downloading huge files that are available through other means, conducting teleconferencing over the internet when a phone call would accomplish the same thing, and other practices that use up much of the bandwidth setup for the internet.

Education and Training

Let us emphasize again that a positive approach to security is far more effective than sets of rules telling people what they cannot do. An educational program for the users is critical in this positive approach. Once your security policies and procedures are established you can directly create training for the users to educate them on effective ways to utilize the internet.

It is far more effective to tell people that there are several ways to gain valuable information from the internet. For example, The Law Firm users can be shown the access URL for the Library of Congress. Here, while in the classroom, they can learn how to access valuable research tools. Your in-house instructor can show the benefits of using the internet. Then, instead of going over the things people should not do, the instructor might walk the students through several exercises.

One exercise might be a simulation of students who are accessing a discussion group to pick up information about the company they are investigating for a lawsuit. Inside a chat room, someone begins to describe personal experiences at the company using inappropriate language and racial slurs. The instructor stops the class and asks them how they should respond to this person. Obviously the information they have may be valuable for the lawsuit. At the same time, the instructor points out that the language and tone of the conversation is inappropriate for the law firm's professionalism. The students are actually doing a discovery exercise. The instructor should attempt to have the students discover that the normal procedure used when taking a deposition from a hostile witness should also be applied in this situation.

Another example of a possible exercise would be used in the Megalith Corp. Students would begin the assignment by going to another student's workstation to see if they can find a poorly hidden password. Points are awarded on how quickly one student finds another student's password. A discussion afterward will involve the importance of protecting passwords.

As you can see, when properly applied, training and education can be extremely effective for making people aware of the security policies and making them active, enthusiastic supporters of the way the internet connections are used.

Special Circumstances Require Special Precautions

Finally, there will be special circumstances where the security policy will be exempt and other precautions applied. There will always be special projects and special circumstances that will require greater security or a great reduction in security.

For example, the special projects sales team may have to go to potential customers' sites to close the deal of a million-dollar contract. The easiest way for them to get continuous access to the information they need is to use the internet and their dedicated modem line to access the database at the corporate headquarters. They have set up a "war room" in a local hotel and are coming and going constantly. This means the chance of one of the laptop computers being left logged on to the system with the password already given, is very high. Even a well-meaning hotel employee might accidentally cause problems within your network.

Instead of coming up with extra security precautions just before the team leaves, it would be better to have a special circumstances procedure already in place. This would include a checklist of the extra risks that will be taken, the types of hazards that may be encountered, the value of the data being accessed, and other critical issues. Based on the outcome of filling out that checklist, guidance will begin as to the proper security measures to put in place. This allows someone like the off-shift systems administrator to begin implementing special security measures immediately instead of waiting until the IS manager is back at work the following day.

The special circumstances procedure allows a company to be very flexible and cope with emergency changes in the way people access the internet or use the internet to access your network. Once again, you are preventing problems before they occur.

In summary

Security is a massive topic in and of itself. Hopefully, by reading this chapter you realize the magnitude of the task of establishing security for your internet connectivity. In most cases you'll have to consult outside security experts for any critical situation in your company. As a minimum you, as high key manager, will need to be very well educated about the different security systems that are possible for your network.

Understanding Viruses and How to Combat Them

Viruses are a unique and special threat to any security system. Therefore you need to have a separate procedure and policy for dealing with the threat that viruses pose to your system. If you are already operating a local area network or any other set of computers, virus protection should be part of your normal operations. By connecting to the internet you open up a few new avenues of possible infection.

What is a virus?

Essentially, a virus is a portion of code or small programming package that can copy itself onto other programming code. Viruses come in a wide variety of types with colorful names. Their ability to replicate themselves from one program to another is what makes them such a large threat to computer systems.

They also present a wide variety of possible dangers. They can alter data, erase information, obtain confidential information, use up valuable resources, and a host of other damaging effects. Some viruses are fairly benign. They do things such as make interesting comments appear on screens at random or post a one time message that your system has been compromised.

If we take a moment to look at a few examples of types of viruses, we can see the scope of the threat. There is the *logic bomb,* a program that copies itself into your system and waits for a particular moment in time or an event within your system to launch its destructive tendencies. There is the *rabbit,* a program that continues to reproduce and copy itself within your system until it has exhausted all of the resources available. There are programs such as the *Trojan horse,* one form of which simulates your login screen so that when you enter your user ID and password, it is saved and sent to the malicious spread of the virus. Thus, unknowingly when you logged onto your system, you just compromised the password security you are using.

What to do about viruses

The first thing to understand about viruses is that they can affect virtually any computer. The more connections a computer has to the outside world, the greater the threat. People bringing in infected diskettes and using them on their office computer, downloading an infected program from the internet, or copying an infected program off the network can spread viruses. Therefore, for a company attempting to implement internet conductivity the threat from viruses rises in proportion.

The best defense against viruses is to prevent their introduction and spread as much as possible while being constantly vigilant for their presence. This begins by mentioning your virus protection scheme within your security policy. Then you'll need a separate virus control procedure that supplements the security policy. In later chapters we will examine such a procedure in detail. You should be aware that the critical elements to put into such a procedure are as follows:

- A statement about the threat from viruses
- The method that will be used to make employees aware of health viruses that are introduced and spread through a computer system
- A list of the general security practices to be followed
- Regular backup of critical data and programs
- Constant review of backups to ensure they are not already infected

- Strict control of user accessibility to the system, especially allowing people to bring in outside software
- Testing of new software for virus threats
- Use of virus detection software
- Instructions for how to eliminate an existing virus
- The methods to be used to assess the damage done by the virus
- The method used to assure the virus has been completely eliminated
- A review process to determine the prevention of a similar infection

The critical element here is to develop a strong plan for how to deal with a virus before the problem arises. This will include arming each workstation with virus detection software. This will also involve active programs of virus detection software at the server sites along with manual examination of the server's existing software.

Once a virus gets into your system it usually will create symptoms. Typically, you'll see the file length of critical portions of the operating system programs changing. Also, you may notice a change in the use of resources for the system. In the event logs that are kept by servers, you will notice that some operations involve copying files to places where they do not belong. These are symptoms of a virus, but not necessarily an indication that one is present.

You should also educate the information systems staff on how to keep an open eye for virus infection. They should be well versed in the preventive methods being used to keep viruses away from your system. You should spend some time designing access controls to the internet to prevent employees from downloading executable files into your system. A person who wants to download an executable file should seek permission from the local network administrator. That program can be downloaded to a safe location, where it will be tested for viruses before being allowed into the system.

One of the interesting techniques used to prevent viruses is what's called a virgin machine. This is a computer completely detached from your network or any outside connection. Locked away safely in a room, software is only introduced to it under controlled conditions. This allows new programs that have been purchased for your servers to be tested for viruses. If an infection is found, it is controlled inside the single machine. Therefore an infection into your system is not possible. Although not fail safe, it is a good way to screen all software and executable programs before they are introduced into your system.

When possible, use many lines of defense against viruses without intruding into the productivity of the company. Part of this defense is an education program for the users of your system. They should be taught what viruses are, how they are spread, common sources of viruses, and what to do if they suspect a virus has entered their computer. This will include a reaction plan that is available at each workstation. Once a virus is suspected, the user can reach for the reaction plan and follow the steps to ensure that any spread of the virus is well controlled. That way removing the virus and clearing up the damage can be done more quickly.

You'll also need a reaction plan for the information systems people. They need to be armed with proper software to both detect and remove viruses. However, software that says it will disinfected your system of a virus is not always 100 percent successful. Therefore, there should be plans for manually checking the system to ensure that the virus infection has been completely eliminated. Sections of your system may have to be quarantined and observed for a short period of time to ensure the viruses are really gone.

One of the instinctive reactions to a virus infection is to erase the infected portions and install your backup files. This should only be done with great caution because you don't know if the virus was already in your system and is now part of the backup files as well. Therefore, before doing any backing up you should clearly examine the backup files for infection. Only once you're assured that the backup files are completely free of the virus should you use them as part of the damage control.

One of the great advantages of web servers and file servers is that you can centrally locate the software that everyone uses. This allows you to put extra protection around these few critical points. You can also appoint information technology specialists to watch these critical software repositories. With strict access control you can keep employees from accidentally or intentionally loading their own programming codes into the servers. If users want to add their own executable files to the server, you should have a short procedure for them to follow to ensure that the files are not infected with a virus or other security threats before loading.

As we shall see later in this book, we encourage the use of production centers for web content. These are small workgroups that develop parts of the web content or databases used by the web and then copy it to all users within your system. Because much of the work they do will be copied to the servers and many user systems, these are critical points to watch for viruses. Once infected, their own programming network can rapidly spread a virus.

Again, we want to emphasize to you the importance of detecting viruses as early as possible and responding as quickly as possible. Given time, a virus will replicate itself many times and create exponentially larger amounts of damage. Even the most benign of viruses will prove annoying to business operations.

How to select the proper virus detection software

The number of viruses being created in the world grows daily. At the same time, a wide variety of programs to counter the viruses are also being developed. Because the number and nature of viruses keep changing, the type of software to use also keeps changing. This is why you have to find a software package with deep technical support and ongoing updates that are easy to obtain.

Your first job is to narrow the field to programs that are very active and aggressive at finding new viruses and updating you on the threats. Some computer operating systems now come equipped with viral detection software already installed. In most cases, this will not be adequate to counter the threat. You'll need specialized software that can be updated regularly to look for the newest forms of viruses.

You'll also need the type of software that can alert you to a virus that is detected but not identifiable. In other words, the software should be able to find a new form of virus and alert you to its presence. This will allow you to work with the software in finding a way to eliminate the virus.

Because you have a connection to the internet, you need a software package that can scan information being sent into your system for the presence of viruses. This will include scanning of E-mail containing file attachments, downloaded executable files, programming code attached to web pages, and the like.

Finally, you'll need a software package to inoculate your system. Inoculation of your system involves the removal of the virus and repairs to any damage the virus may have caused. It is rare to find a single software package that can both scan and inoculate your system. Typically, you'll need one package to scan for viruses and a second one to perform a thorough inoculation. I recommend those packages which include the creation of a log that lists what parts of your system were corrected. In that way you can double check to make sure that all possible sources of damage were removed.

Further References

As mentioned before, the two best sites to look through on the internet are:

www.rsa.com

www.commerce.net

The best reference books on security are also found on the internet. For example, the NIST's special publication on Internet Security Policy: A Technical Guide.

Csrc.nist.gov/isptg

There are also organizations such as the Network Security International Association:

http://www.netsec-intl.com/

Use the search engines of the internet to find a wealth of information. Use search terms such as:

"Encryption"

"Network Security"

"Computer Security" + organizations + associations

Chapter 5
Creating the Corporate Internet Policy

So far, we have planned out the internet system for your company and discussed security issues. Then we drafted the first security policies. Now it is time to set the tone and direction of your internet technology usage within your company by writing the internet policy statement.

This chapter will walk you through the process of writing and deploying such a policy. The companywide internet policy will be the basis of the establishment, maintenance, and continuous improvement of your internet technology. It will give the employees direction in using internet technology to achieve specific corporate strategic goals. As such, the internet policy is an integrated part of the overall policies that operate within your company.

ISO 9001 Quality Systems Model for Quality Assurance in Design, Development, Production, Installation, and Servicing, contains an interesting statement about policies. One of the central requirements of this international standard is that the companywide policy is understood, implemented, and maintained at all levels in the organization. This is the sole responsibility of the top managers including the IS manager. This is also a key point during an ISO 9001 audit. Likewise, it is a key point for the IS manager during any system-wide audits.

Overview of the Internet Policy Creation Process

Let's begin with another discovery exercise. Let me pose the following three questions. Write down your answers.

1. How many paragraphs should be in the corporatewide internet policy?

2. How many procedures that result from the corporate internet policy should be present at each user's desk?

3. How many pages of work instructions should be on the user's desk related to the policies?

The answer to all three questions is one. Before we discuss how to create corporatewide policies, it is important to remember that you must keep in mind the final form and size of the policy document you will create. How will this guide work with a system that has a target of creating a single page of information that will be with every computer in your corporation? It will be printed on cardboard stock, folded, and attached to the top of each monitor. It will briefly explain the corporation's policy for using the internet. It will contain a corrective action procedure that will give brief instructions on what a person is supposed to do if anything goes wrong. It will also have brief instructions on how to properly maintain passwords.

This single small document will prevent the vast majority of problems people usually have with using the internet. It will help you maintain your security and correct problems without involving your help desk, and it will make clear to the users what they need to accomplish with internet technology to make your business more competitive. All of this can happen only if the corporation's top management sets a clear policy for the use, intention, and overall goals of your internet technology.

Where to Begin Writing Your Policy

The first thing we should make clear is the different types of documentation that are required to operate information technology systems. This book will be focusing on the use of internet technology as part of the information system.

Your company should already have an overall corporate policy. This is usually a policy that states the intention of the company, its mission, its stand on quality assurance, its position on environmental issues, and other related topics at a strategic level. For example, the Dickerson County School System would have an overall operating philosophy that serves as its school-wide policy. The Law Firm should have an overall operating policy related to the relationship between the law firm and its clients, services to be rendered, and quality objectives to meet. Avix Manufacturing might have a corporatewide strategic policy that explains the competitive position of the company, its emphasis on the use of work teams, its conformance with known quality standards, and its objective to be a responsible environmental citizen. Megalith might have a corporatewide policy emphasizing its need to be a world-class leader in several different fields.

These companywide policies are based on the overall strategic plan of each organization. Inside your company there should be an operations manual that begins with the overall corporate policy. The first section of this manual should describe both the companywide policy and the policies related to the departmental level operations. For the information systems department, you will need policies on issues such as audits, documentation, programming, general administration, and other related issues.

These policies are general statements that explain the overall objectives for your particular system and who has ultimate authority to ensure that the system is running correctly. These are known as level one documents. Figure 5–1 shows the various levels of documentation used in the IS department.

Policy statements explain why something is going to be done. The second level of documentation, the level two documents, are known as standard operating procedures. Inside any company are many systems. Each system is described by the policy statement. Any system is made up of processes. For each process there should be a procedure. For example, the process of making regular backups of all system data requires a procedure. A procedure tells who is going to do what, when it will be done, how it will be done, and what equipment will be used to complete the task. Later in this book we will look at how to write the proper procedure.

Within each process are a series of tasks to be completed. Many of these tasks require written work instructions. These represent the third level of documentation. Work instructions tell an individual how to complete a single task. For example, the process of documenting a system's failure is one task. Thus, you would likely have a form to fill out with an attached set of work instructions on how to complete the form properly. (See Table 5–1.)

Table 5-1. Levels of Documentation

UNIT	DOCUMENT	LEVEL
System	Policy	I
Process	Procedure	II
Task	Work Instruction	III

The fourth level of documentation includes the records created by the procedures and work instructions from levels two and three. Written records are your evidence that the procedures and work instructions are being followed properly. During audits, it is the written records that are most often examined.

Figure 5-1. Levels of Documentation

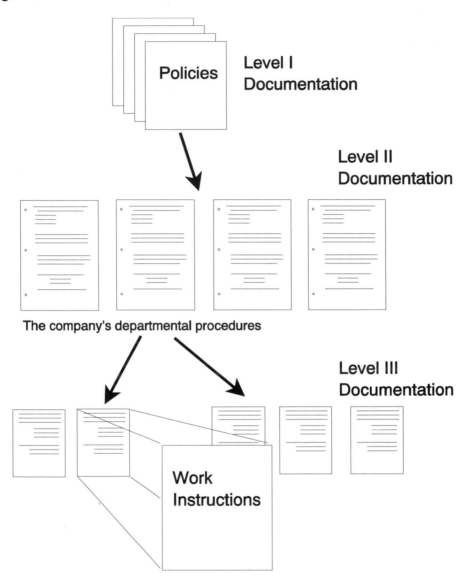

Your job as IS manager is to use this type of documentation to successfully establish and maintain your internet technology system with a minimal number of policies, procedures, and work instructions. The idea is not to create a paperwork blizzard. Instead, you have to determine the critical points that will require documentation.

What a Properly Formatted Policy Looks Like

Later in this book we will look at the proper way to create and present standard operating procedures and work instructions. In this chapter our interest lies with policy statements. We're building an operations manual that is easy to use, clearly understood, and frequently used by the IS personnel. Small portions of this manual will also be placed with each computer user.

Figure 5–2 illustrates the format of a procedure. By examining this illustration you can see several points that must be included in any policy statement. First of all, there has to be a title for the policy. This is followed by information on what number policy this is, the areas of the company that are affected, the revision level, the date of origin, and a signature of authorization.

At the bottom of the page, there should be a page numbering scheme that indicates which page this is, out of how many; for example, "Page 2 of 3." Not only does this inform the readers which page they are on, but it will quickly indicate whether a page is missing from the policy statements. This can prove especially helpful during audits.

Figure 5–2. Policy Statement Avix Manufacturing

Policy Statement-Avix Manufacturing		
PLY-003 Internet Usage	Approved by: JPL	Effective Date: January 12, 1998

1.0 Policy
 	
  Blah, blah, blah,.. ..
 	
    1.1 Access
 	
    1.2 Security		

Application: All Departments		Controlled Document
Revision Date: July 4, 1998	Revision B .04	Page 1 of 1

When writing policies, procedures, and work instructions, you need to use a paragraph numbering scheme to indicate the level of importance and organization of the information. Typically, the following scheme is used:

> Chapter
>   Section
>   Sub-Section
>   Item

An example of this would be the overall policy for a particular system that would be a section under a chapter heading. It might look something like this:

> 1.0 Management Responsibility
> 1.1 Policy - It is the intention of Avix that...

For most policy statements, the first two levels of the numbering scheme are used. As we shall see with procedures, deeper numbering schemes will be deployed.

When we put this all together we have the overall format for any policy statement. In this chapter we will be establishing the content that will be placed into this format. The results will be the first section of our operations manual, a series of policy statements outlining the general intention of the internet technology. Wherever possible you need to use existing policies and procedures for information technology, human resources, corporate security, or any other documents that already apply to systems similar to internet technology. Remember, we're avoiding the creation of extra paperwork wherever possible.

Mission, Goals, and Access

Back in Chapter 2, you completed exercises to find the goals and objectives of using internet technology. Now we will use that information to create the overall mission statement that lists the most basic goals. These will be placed in the corporatewide internet policy. Let's look at one set of those example goals.

- Goal: Increase our customer support
- Goal: Increase market share
- Goal: Improve internal communications
- Goal: Encourage additional training

If these were the strategic goals of The Law Firm, they would be combined with its overall mission to be the world-class leader in delivering legal services. All of this would then be reflected in the internet policy. It might look something like this:

> "In our quest to become the world-class leader in legal services we utilize internet technology. This technology is part of our overall focus on customer satisfaction, quality service, and promotion of the professionalism of our employees. As such, we expect all employees to utilize this type of technology to its maximum advantage."

This policy statement would be followed by the goals and objectives The Law Firm expects to achieve through the use of internet technology. Again, the goals and objectives we first listed in Chapter 2 would be used to create this follow-up document. It would appear right after the overall internet goal. It should also make references to the strategic plan for the firm.

In the case of the Dickerson County School System, the internet policy would also be based on the internet goals and objectives they would have already listed. Their policy statement might look something like this:

> "The Dickerson County school district is dedicated to the continuous improvement in the delivery of educational services to our community. Internet technology represents one of the newest ways to deliver traditional and innovative educational services. Like any educational tool it works best when applied properly. Thus, our use of internet technology to promote education and learning experiences is tempered by the standards of the community and the regulations of our profession."

Most school systems will have an extensive strategic plan, loaded with various educational goals and objectives. The best way to proceed in this situation is to select some representative goals and objectives of which the internet technology will be an integral part. This list of goals and objectives would be followed by the rules of conduct and the levels of access that will be allowed into the Dickerson County web sites. This explanation of the rules and levels of access is distributed to all potential users.

It is completely possible that every parent in the school district would receive a copy of the policy and the access rules with the code of conduct for the internet. Within these rules would be pointers on how to control the children's access while using internet accounts from home. This special concern about children using internet accounts is then addressed upfront in the policy, mission, and access statements.

What If Our Company Doesn't Have Policy Statements?

In the case with Avix Manufacturing, the IS manager discovers that there really are no policy statements for the operation of the company. There is a collection of standard operating procedures. In this situation, the IS manager will need to talk to top management about putting the internet policy into a couple of overall corporate policy statements that will be released to all employees.

For example, the company really should begin at its strategic plan. From this point the top managers should issue an overall corporate policy statement about operations. This might read something like this:

> "Avix manufacturing provides world-class metal stamped parts to the automotive industry and other select clients. Our high level of quality parts results from continuous improvement by management personnel and proactive teams of employees. We also see ourselves as responsible environmental citizens."

The issuing of an overall operational policy accomplishes two things. First, it lets all employees know that policy statements set the tone and direction for the company. Second, it spells out particular targets the company is trying to achieve. In our example, that would be the highest quality metal stamped parts. It also informs people on how these targets are to be achieved. As the above statement indicates, aggressive, proactive use of teams and management personnel are the primary method. This also paves the way for you, as the IS manager, to release your own policy statements on the use of internet technology. As we'll see in later chapters, we follow this up with operational procedures and work instructions.

If your company does not have policy statements about operations, the following checklist shows some of the areas that would normally be covered under the ISO 9000 model of management:

- Management responsibility
- Quality system
- Contract review
- Design control
- Document and data control
- Purchasing

- Control of customer supplied product
- Product identification and traceability
- Process control
- Inspection and testing
- Control of inspection, measuring, and test equipment
- Inspection and test status
- Control of nonconforming product
- Corrective and preventive action
- Handling, storage, packaging, preservation, and delivery
- Control of quality records
- Internal audits
- Servicing of products
- Statistical techniques

The ISO 9000 model of management says that each of these 20 points, if they apply to your company, should be addressed by a short policy statement. The management standard spells out the requirements to be addressed in these policy statements. Thus, if your company does not have any policy statements this is one possible model to use for developing them.

When Your Company Already Has Existing Policy Statements

In the situation where your company is already using operational policy statements, such as in the case of a company registered to ISO 9000, you need to carefully integrate your internet policies and procedures into the existing system of documentation.

When a company is large enough that the IS department can create its own set of internal policies and procedures, the following topics are usually addressed:

- Management responsibility
- Documentation process
- Systems analysis and software design
- Configuration management
- Support operations

- Asset management
- Workgroup operations
- .The use of freestanding personal computers
- Internal audits
- Training
- Project management
- Vendor relations
- Forms management

These would be the policies and procedures for use only within the IS department. As you can see, there is some overlap with the overall management model presented by ISO 9000. Where these overlaps occur, you can either use the existing policies and procedures, or make reference to them in a specialized version of the policy or procedure for IS operations. At the same time, your internet technology will be an integral part of your IS department. Therefore, your goal is to create the fewest number of policies and procedures that really effectively document how internet technology will be used.

Internet technology will need to be mentioned in the following policies:

- Management responsibility
- Control of documentation and data
- Internal audits
- Training
- Design control
- Purchasing
- Process control
- Corrective and preventive action
- Control of records

Management responsibility will have to also spell out who's in charge of the internet technology and its various components. These would be the managers who are ultimately responsible for assuring that each component of the internet technology operates correctly. For example, the operation of the web servers may be the ultimate responsibility of the network administrator. Be sure to list the person responsible by title only, do not use a name. This way when personnel is moved around, the policy does not have to be updated.

The amount of documentation and data created by internet technology is usually quite large. Web pages, support documents, and the like should all be considered controlled documentation. Controlled documentation means that you know where the document is located, you can determine its most recent revision, and you know that it has been approved for use. Control of data would include your backup procedures.

Training is used to ensure that the personnel know how to use the internet technology properly. Internal audits confirm that it is being used properly and that the equipment is performing to expectations. Internal audits also check to make sure that the policies and procedures that you have written are being followed.

When services are introduced using internet technology, design control is applied. Services would include web pages, online training, intranet controlled documentation, and so on. Design control is the planned and scheduled creation of the services that makes use of regular design reviews to check that the needs of the customers are being met by the product being designed.

All companies purchase products and services. Internet technology will require you to buy hardware, software, and follow-up support. The existing policy and procedures for purchasing at your company might have to be modified slightly to account for the unique nature of buying software and follow-up support. You may want to draft a short policy statement saying that in the case of information systems or internet technology, a representative from the IS department will work alongside a purchasing agent to secure the materials and services needed.

The day-to-day maintenance of the internet technology and the delivery of the services it can produce are part of process control. Process control looks at the day-to-day operation of your internet technology. It establishes the criteria for the successful delivery of internet technology services to your company. It also calls for work instructions for each person involved in that delivery of services. We will discuss these ideas throughout the book.

Problems are bound to occur with internet technology. Corrective actions are taken to fix a problem that has been experienced. You'll need a procedure on how people are to react when a problem occurs. At the same time, you'll need an aggressive stance on preventing as many problems as possible. Throughout this book we have discussed the importance of prevention as a competitive position. The cost of preventing a problem is far lower than the cost of fixing the impact of that problem.

Finally, your internet technology system will create records of activities. These records are critical for letting management know the success of the internet technology. Therefore, they should be strictly controlled and stored in places where they will not be lost.

As you can see, there is a need to establish an overall vision of how the internet technology will operate. This is the purpose of policy statements. They tell people why certain things will be done. Standard operating procedures will explain who is going to do what, when it will happen, how it will be done, and what equipment will be involved.

Publishing the Policy and Getting Corporatewide Buy-in

The magic moment comes when top management has approved your internet technology policy and it is time to publish the policy. Writing a policy is one thing; getting people to follow the intentions of the policy is quite another. However, you can take several steps to make sure that the policy is adhered to by employees and effectively deployed.

The best way to ensure that you'll get corporate buy-in to your new policy is to take three basic steps:

- Tell people the policy is coming.
- Tell them about the policy.
- Tell them when they have just received the policy.

In other words, explain to everyone what will be coming in the policy, and when the policies are released, explain it to them again. After the policy is put into force, take any occasion, where appropriate, to review the policy again.

For example, Megalith Inc. is an excellent example of a company where introducing a new policy could be difficult. The employees of the corporation may already be operating under several policy guidelines. The IS policy will be seen as just one more policy statement.

What the IS manager should do at Megalith is to issue a memo to all employees explaining that internet technology is about to be introduced into the corporation. When each affected department receives the new internet technology, another memo is sent out to those department employees. This time, when the new technology is announced again, the difference will be that the specific technology for that department is mentioned and names of the people responsible for both using and maintaining the system are listed. This should be followed with an orientation session for all employees that will be involved with the new internet technology in the department. As part of this training, the overall IS policy is reviewed, the specific effect of that policy on the employees is discussed, and questions about the policy are answered.

After the internet technology has been introduced into a department, the IS manager should return with an auditor in six weeks to hold a review session with the same employees. At this time, the policy is again reviewed and comments are solicited on how successfully the policy is working in comparison to the objectives and normal work habits of the department.

Thus, each department receives an advance notice of the policy statement; each department receives an orientation session to explain the policy and answer questions; and then each department receives a follow-up visit. Any problem or resistance encountered in any of these three steps are dealt with at that time. One of the important things you can do with a policy statement is to support its procedures that make specific managers responsible for ensuring the policy is carried out. For example, the financial department may be resistant in following the rules for E-mail. The director of finance is given the responsibility of enforcing the internet policy for E-mail. The director of finance then confronts the employees one at a time to explain the proper use of E-mail.

Another good tool for ensuring that policies are followed is to spell out the consequences of violations. As we mentioned earlier, you try the keep policy statements as positively worded as possible. Eventually, however, you will Have to mention that there is punishment for deliberate violations. This would include the guideline on how the punishments are to be deployed and the appeal process that the employee can activate.

Enforcing the Policy

In all four of our example companies, the most difficult part about the policy statement will be enforcing its intentions.

Exercise #1: Dickerson County school board

Let's begin with Dickerson County school board. We will assume they have now adopted an internet policy for the school district stating that the existing web site and its related E-mail shall not contain any hateful language. Yet, despite the clear warnings repeated throughout the Web page, and the information sent home to the parents, two students have begun to use their E-mail accounts to call each other names such as "booger face" and "fancy pants."

This raises an interesting problem for the school board. Several of the parents complain that the web page has a discussion group littered with this type of name calling by these two students. Is this a clear violation of the policy?

Chances are this is not a clear violation of the policy against hateful, obscene, or racial language. At the same time, this is not an appropriate use of the web site. Luckily, the Dickerson County school board has established an internet policy. As you may recall, we said the policy was supported by rules of conduct. Those rules would prohibit the nonproductive use of the web technology. Because they accompany the policy, they can be used in this situation. The offending students should be reprimanded and given instructions on the proper use of the web technology. A written record would be created so that if there were any further misuse by the same two students, stricter punishment will be dealt.

Exercise #2: Avix Manufacturing

Avix Manufacturing discovers a group of employees downloading jokes from the internet and distributing them by E-mail to other employees. The Avix policy on internet technology says that it is to be used for productive means to support the competitive position of the company. Again, the activities of this group of employees seems to violate the policy. What is the appropriate response?

With the case of a minor infraction against the internet policy, the IS manager needs to make a judgment call. Was this a deliberate attempt to violate the policy, or just human nature raising its head? If it is determined that malice is not part of the violation, the idea is to encourage the employees to use the internet technology properly through the most positive route available.

In this case, that might be a special orientation session for the affected employees. The internet policy and the rules of conduct discouraging nonproductive use of the internet would be reviewed. This would be reinforced by working through examples of the proper way to use the internet technology available. If this message is too subtle for the employees, their supervisor can end the session by explaining that if there is another violation, it will go into their personnel records, with appropriate response by human resources.

Exercise #3: The Law Firm

The Law Firm has a clearly written policy encouraging the professional use of all internet resources including E-mail. Because their system is mainly intranets, there is very little contact to the internet. However, two of the attorneys within the firm are having an extramarital affair. One of them scans a revealing photograph of them together and sends an explicit invitation to the other partner via internet E-mail. Because the sender slightly missed clicking the correct E-mail address it was intended for, it was transmitted instead to an entire workgroup. That is, about 50 different people received the message. What would be your response to this situation?

Here we have an interesting case. Not only do we have a clear violation of the internet policy, we also have a violation of the code of professional conduct within the office, and a high level of punishment already being generated from the sheer embarrassment of the incident. Therefore, you need to use a very imaginative approach to address this situation.

There would be an overwhelming need for professional response by the Law Firm. It would be highly recommended that the human resources manager and the IS manager handle this problem together. In all likelihood, you would end up trying to control a situation that is going to resolve itself. Specifically, at least one of the parties would probably want to resign immediately. Again, both the office policies and your internet policy will help guide you in your decision-making and whether to approve contingencies such as the resignation of one of the affected parties.

Exercise #4: Megalith

Late one night at Megalith, the security guard finds an employee working feverishly at a computer terminal. It is many hours after the closing of that area. This observation is brought to the attention of a supervisor who passes it along to the IS manager. An audit of the particular terminal finds that he has been probing for company secrets. Continued investigation reveals that this employee has been lifting patent information from the research and development department and selling it to a competitor. Human resources fires this individual immediately. What is your next course of action?

This time you would have to move beyond the policy toward one of your procedures. Specifically, we're now talking about corrective action. A severe breach of the internet policy calls for immediate corrective action. This is laid out in a three-step process. First, you must determine how long the damage has been taking place. In this case you need to know how long the employee has been able to get into the research and development computers. You must do a thorough examination of data files over that time period to find if there is any undiscovered damage or theft. This is information that might be of use in a possible lawsuit. Also you may discover accomplices.

The second step is to stop the problem from occurring. Naturally, the employee's user account and password and any other accounts used to perform the break-in would be erased from the system's security system. Next, you would check to see if the employee still had any method for getting into your computer network. If the employee ever had any capability of using an outside modem or other device to reach your system remotely, that must be scrubbed from the system.

Finally, you must update your security system to ensure that this type of problem does not occur again. This will take an investigation, to find where the weakness was in the security that allowed this employee in. Basically you need to know how much effort it was for him to reach out of his workgroup and into one where he had no authorized access. Most likely you'll discover a failure in the security system that the employee exploited. You need to set up an interim security system to prevent another employee from using the same tactic. Then the design of your system and security measures must be changed to prevent this type of break-in from occurring again.

As a final note on this exercise, without written policies and security procedures that spell out who has access to what, your company would find it very difficult to prosecute this industrial spy. Most of the evidence of deliberate tampering will not be allowed in court because you had nothing saying that this person was not allowed into the area where he was found. Instead, you need to prove that he sold the secrets to a competitor. This is usually nothing short of very difficult.

Updating the Policy

Policies are living documents. That means they have to stay flexible and able to change with the evolution of your company. This requires you to have a procedure for updating policies once they've been put into force.

For example, the Dickerson County school district may decide to upgrade their internet technology to include wide area networking between the schools. This would now open up the possibility of passing data and E-mail between classrooms. The existing policy would have to be updated to address this issue. Also, rules of conduct and access would have to be updated as well.

Basically, you would go through the same process you went through to develop the original policy. The original policy would be sent to a small committee for review. The IS manager would brief the committee on what was changing with the technology and would also make recommendations of how the policy should be changed. Working together, the IS manager and the committee would draft a new version of the internet technology policy. Once again the school board would have to approve the new policy. The document control procedure would be invoked to remove the existing copies of the policy that are under document control and replace them with the new updated policy. A letter would be sent to the parents and students that would explain the new policy and a memorandum sent to all staff members to update them on the changes. Orientation sessions would likely be held for staff members who are active internet users. This same sequence of events would take place in practically any organization when a policy is updated.

Making Specific Exceptions

At this point you have established policies that delineate the purpose of your internet technology, limits to access, and other security measures. Inevitably you will encounter a situation where you need to make an exception to the policy.

One of the best ways to be prepared for a case in which an exception is required is to include flexibility in your policy statement. For example, you can state:

> "Our security policies and procedures will be strictly followed unless an exceptional situation exists and the IS manager declares that limited exemptions and changes to the security policies can be made on a temporary basis."

What this statement does is leave in place a method for people or workgroups to appeal their current security settings. Let's take the example of a large contract being bid on by Megalith and a joint venture partner. This requires engineers from the two companies to freely exchange E-mail and information about the project. At the same time, other projects at Megalith must be protected from examination by the partner company.

As IS manager you would issue a memorandum outlining the purpose of the joint venture and the cooperation between the two companies. This brief memo would mention the scope of cooperation that can exist between the two companies and how this will be facilitated by the existing internet technology. Basically, engineers on project teams will have a new type of access account with additional security measures to keep all of their joint project activities within an isolated area of your system.

For example, you can set up in the new user account an area called the "joint project." This account would be positioned on an isolated web server within the engineering department. Firewall security would be set up on both sides of the connection to the web server, that is, the connection leading to the internet and the one leading back to the local area network of the engineering department. Such stringent security would ensure that only members of the Megalith engineering department could pass information through the web server.

At the same time, messages and data coming from the joint venture partner would be encrypted and only accepted from the IP address of their web server. For a long-term project, you may want to consider a dedicated high-speed digital phone line between the two companies. This would provide greater security than using the internet as the connection medium.

As our example illustrates, there can be exceptions to the policies and procedures you will put in place. Common sense should dictate whether an exception is granted. At least one person at management level should be responsible for granting such exceptions. Any exceptions should be a rarity in your system. If you find you are granting exceptions more than a few times a year, you should consider an examination of your security design or operational procedures.

IS Manager's Role in Corporate Policy Statements

In conclusion, the discussions within this chapter should make it obvious that the IS manager plays a critical role in the establishment of policy statements. It is not required that the IS manager actually write the policy, although it is crucial that the IS manager review and approve any policy statement involving internet technology.

In some companies you may find that the top management team wishes to create the internet technology policy. When this occurs the IS manager should serve as a key adviser to the management committee. Part of this process is to educate the top managers about internet technology and the issues related to internet connectivity.

Smaller companies will require the IS manager to not only write but also publish, enforce, and constantly review policy statements related in any way to the internet. At the same time, the IS manager has to carefully balance the need for a policy statement for internet technology against any existing policies already in the company. Some corporations operate with dozens of policy statements on many different topics. It is already a difficult task to keep employees aware of the policy statements that apply to their jobs.

Therefore, IS managers must practice minimalism in the creation of policies and procedures. This is equally true for any policy, procedure, or written work instruction for use within the department, or for all departments in the company.

Chapter 6
Finding, Evaluating, and Contracting Vendor Assistance

In the following chapters we are going to look at the process of issuing a bid to purchase hardware, software, and services. Before you reach that stage, however, you need to establish the features you want in the product you're about purchase.

There are four different areas within the use of internet technology that could possibly require you to contract an outside vendor. They are:

1. Software

2. Hardware

3. Technical support

4. Connectivity (including the ISP)

Each of these require one or more suppliers. This means that as IS manager you'll have a very strong say in which companies will supply your company with these products and services. Therefore, you should be aware of the aspects of finding, evaluating, and contracting vendors for maximum efficiency.

This will also include the issue of getting suppliers that can work within your schedule and meet your quality requirements within cost guidelines. The task is usually difficult, but persistence can make its success very profitable. For example, for years we used to use a software distribution company that could obtain for us virtually any software in less than 24 hours. Thus, when a client would ask us to develop training for a particular type of software, we would have the software in-house, loaded on a machine, and being discussed by the project team the next day. The cost of this rapid response service was the same or less than any other supplier of software.

Developing a Relationship with a Supplier

Most IS managers are not aware of the elaborate relationship that must exist between vendors and the company. Not only must you find vendors willing to make adjustments for your time schedule, they also must be able to take great amounts of stress to help you correct problems in a timely manner. Take the example of the network hub going down at midnight. A vendor that can be contacted at 1:00 in the morning and can have a new hub delivered before the office opens the next day is far more important than any price discount.

Later in this chapter we will look at four different evaluation checklists for each of the four primary types of vendors you'll have to deal with. What we want to examine now are the different activities that might take place between the information systems department and the potential vendors.

1. *Define the requirements of products and services, including quality requirements.* Before you purchase software, hardware, connectivity, or services, you should evaluate the exact needs of the internet technology system. Take the example of purchasing a web server. You can include the processor speed, make of hard drive, amount of RAM, and so on, on a specification list. This should be supplemented with the level of quality expected of components, when they are to be delivered, installation to be performed by the vendor, and follow-up support that is expected.

2. *Select and rate your suppliers.* The checklists presented later will help you in the selection process. Basically, you are looking for suppliers that share the vision you have for your internet technology. You want vendors that can be active partners in the creation of your internet system. That means you have to establish performance criteria that are shared with the vendors. You then evaluate the performance of each vendor against these criteria and report the results to both the management and the vendor. What you're looking for is continuous improvement in an already good vendor.

3. *Finding and evaluating alternative sources of supply.* You can have the world's best source for computer components but that will not stop that company from having a labor strike, burning down, or suffering some other catastrophe that will cut off your flow of supplies. One of the biggest threats a company faces today with suppliers is the sudden change in personnel or ownership of the supply company. You can suddenly discover that a supplier that used to cooperate with you closely has, overnight, lost the knowledgeable personnel required to complete your project. Therefore, you always need a list of alternative suppliers you can turn to in such crises. You might want to give partial contracts to some of these alternative companies to constantly test their performance.

4. *Conduct joint planning with the supplier.* Even the best IS manager does not have all the answers for what is possible with internet technology. If you have existing software and hardware suppliers who have successfully worked with your company before, you may want to include them in your internet technology planning project. Even during implementation of the internet technology, you could also turn to your vendors for ideas and suggestions for correcting any problems that you may encounter along the way.

5. *Confirmation of conformance by the supplier to your stated requirements.* When software or hardware is installed, telecommunications lines are connected, or other services are rendered for technical support, the need is to assure that all expectations by the company have been met. In other words, you do not pay a supplier until all products and services have been delivered as expected. Therefore, you'll need to work with the purchasing department for conflict resolution, contract initiation, payment schedules, and other related issues. (Also see Chapter 14.)

Evaluating a Connectivity Service

To establish internet connectivity you need to have dedicated telecommunication lines, a contract with an ISP, or both. In the case of Dickerson County School Board, the contract with the ISP will be the most vital vendor relationship. The ISP will provide internet access and host their web pages.

The following checklist is provided to guide you in the selection and rating of ISPs:

Supplier's Name:

Address:

City, State, Zip:

Contact People:

Phone:

FAX:

E-mail:

Web site:

Services Provided (check those that apply):

__ web hosting

__ dial-up access

__ E-mail

__ secure server with credit card processing

__ online training

__ 24 hour support

__ router set-up

__ dedicated lines   _ 56K _ 128K _ 386K _ T1 _ T3 _ Other

__ national access POP lines

__ autoresponders for E-mail

__ security or restricted access

__ multiple web sites on one account

__ domain name registration

__ supporting software provided   _ FTP _ page creation _ E-mail reader _other

__ access filtering

What amount of disk space does the account provide? ___ megs

How much bandwidth? ___ megs of monthly transfer

Type of connection the ISP has with the internet?

Do they have back-up communication lines? Which kind?

Is there a minimum of daily data backup?

What is their disaster recovery plan?

Which web programming languages are supported? _ HTML _ CGI _ Perl _Java _ Other

Are statistics of web site usage available?

Do they have other traffic analysis tools available?

Does the ISP allow your servers to be located at their office?

Is 24-hour technical service available? Test the service.

What are the terms of billing the account?

Description of services offered and pricing:

- Describe web hosting prices
- Describe dedicated line services and charges
- Describe charges for using your servers at their site
- Describe charges for adding on memory to your site or additional features

For each ISP interviewed, one of these forms should be completed. Some of the questions will not apply because they are outside the scope of your current project. Get answers to these questions anyway in case you later decide to expand your internet system. Knowing all of these answers will assure you that you can comfortably expand with this supplier.

Let's review why you should ask many of the questions on this form. The list of services provided will allow you to judge the scope and depth of both services and support talent at the ISP. You may be like the Dickerson County school board and only be looking for a web site and some E-mail accounts. In the end you know that the school board will look at the lowest bids that can fulfill their needs. However, if you find that most of the bidders already have low prices, then you can narrow the list to those that provide the most services and the best connectivity.

In a few years the Dickerson County school district may decide that they need dedicated telecommunication lines with the ability to put a database online connected to their existing web pages. If the ISP they selected always had these types of capabilities, then such upgrading can proceed without the need to change the web hosting vendor. Not only does this save time and money, but if the Dickerson County school district did not get their own domain name, they would need to inform all users of the new addresses and URLs if they choose to switch ISPs.

For web hosting services there are several critical issues that the purchaser should keep in mind. One is how much disk space on their server they give for the type of account you need. The monthly cost of the ISP must always be evaluated against the cost of building and using your own web server in your company. For companies that need very little web presence or few E-mail accounts, renting web space makes economic sense. If you rent, be sure they are giving you enough disk space to go with the account. Likewise, if you have 50 employees, you should be able to add up to 50 E-mail accounts for an amenable amount of money.

Another issue is bandwidth. For business applications you want an ISP with at least a T3 connection to the internet. Better still is an ISP with multiple links to the internet where if one link fails others can still be used.

Even though you should always keep a backup of any information you send to an ISP, you'll still need to know what their backup procedure is at the ISP. It is much quicker and far more economical to have the ISP back up your critical data for web presentation at their site. If you are choosing to place your server at their site to be connected to the internet, then you'll need to know whether their personnel will back up your data or if you need to send someone to the ISP to perform this function.

Before you approach an ISP you should have a good idea of the types of internet related software you will be using. If you plan to do a job of programming, CGI work, or use software products that have their own active components, you need to make sure the ISP can support these functions. For example, Microsoft's FrontPage 98 requires that a set of server extensions be loaded on the server at the ISP. If the ISP does not support these server extensions, then your web creation package will be crippled.

With any ISP you should also test several of the promises that they may make. For example, they may say that technical support is available 24 hours a day. Try calling at three in the morning to see how long it takes someone to answer the phone. Then, try the same test at three o'clock in the afternoon to see if it's impossible to get hold of anyone. You should not have to make more than two attempts to reach an ISP technical support person. If the line is constantly busy, or the answering machine seems to always pick up the calls, you should look for a better ISP.

You may recall that at the beginning of this book, we strongly encouraged you to have your own personal internet account. The ISP selected for this account should not be a casual decision. You should try to get an account and an ISP that seems to be well-suited for your company. Then place your own personal web page under this account and use E-mail heavily. Whenever you have the slightest problem with your account, contact their technical support and ask for help. Take notes of the type of response you receive.

The sign of a good technical support department is that the person who answers your phone call is also the technical expert. This person will respond immediately to your call and when the problem can't be corrected immediately, he or she will inform you how long it should be before someone calls you back to tell you what the fix was. A good technical support department member never lets a problem last more than a few hours. If the problem is serious and requires major corrections to their system they should inform you that they are investigating an estimated time of correction.

In most cases, you'll need an ISP as your link between your network and the internet. That means that the ISP will be installed on a dedicated data line to your company and can provide you with a router to connect your network. What you're looking for from a good ISP is a package where the router is already pre-programmed to work with the system at the ISP. You also want to know how quickly they can bring in dedicated data lines. Companies that can do this quickly and effectively are the vendors you seek.

If you are a major corporation and using data lines of T1 or larger for internet access, then you should consider contracting directly with backbone links to the internet. These are companies such as UUnet, Sprint, AT&T, and so on. Essentially, you are bypassing the ISPs and buying your time directly from the internet. Any company that has very heavy traffic to and from the internet should consider this option. It requires more technical support to insure continuous operation. However, you will receive special attention from the select few providers of direct backbone access.

Evaluating a Telecommunications Company

In some situations you may want to have the telecommunications company provide you with the dedicated data lines and routers between your site and the ISP. This could occur for a variety of reasons, such as discounts you could receive from existing telephone service contracts. Another possibility is that you really like services provided by an ISP, but you're uncertain of their ability to correctly install dedicated data lines.

In Chapter 9 we will examine the types of dedicated data lines you should consider for making your internet connection. Most telecommunications companies offer all of the types of connections we will discuss. Therefore you'll need to select two or three strong candidates to be potential vendors of conductivity.

The following checklist is provided to guide you in the selection and rating of telecommunication companies:

Supplier's Name:

Address:

City, State, Zip:

Contact People:

Phone:

FAX:

E-mail:

Web site:

Services Provided (check those that apply):
 __ dedicated data lines
 __ frame relay
 __ full ISDN service, including teleconferencing

__ data line installation

__ technical support and repair services

__ router set-up, sales, and installation

__ modem set-up and sales

__ internet E-mail accounts

__ web hosting

__ PBX phone switching service, sales, repairs, etc.

- What are the limits of the company's services?
- Can they lay cable in your office or only up to the service point of your buildings?
- What surge and backup protection do they offer for their communications lines?
- How long is the delay from applying for ISDN and getting service?
- How long is the delay for T1 or T3 service?
- What other telephone companies will have to be contacted to complete the installation of service?
- Which long distance services can be attached to these communications lines?
- How much of the work can be done by your own personnel?
- Is 24-hour technical service available?
- What are the terms of billing the account?

Describe the costs of the services being provided:

List the costs for repairs by the hour, technical support, and other add-ons:

Again, fill out one of these forms for each of the telecommunications companies you are thinking of using. You should always get at least three quotes. Do not be afraid to look for companies outside of your local area. Many international companies can easily compete with local providers. One of our first calls for a telecommunication T1 line bid was answered by British Telecom.

Besides the dedicated data lines we have been discussing, there are other communication options which can be part of your internet technologies system. Or, you may choose to integrate your internet technologies system into the network of existing communications lines within your company. Either way, the telecommunications companies you are currently using can become involved. If a separate person is responsible for the phone system within your company, that person should be consulted in this evaluation process.

Especially important are questions about what will be involved in the installation of any dedicated data lines. Personal experience was a good teacher in this particular issue. When we ordered our first T1 line the company we contracted said that all we needed to do was to provide a three-inch diameter hole coming into the building where the cable could be laid. We knew that this type of line came off of a fiber-optic cable and would be translated eventually into a copper line about the size of the networking cable for a local area network.

We went ahead and drilled in an access three inches across to the outside of the building from our wiring closet. When the crew arrived to install the T1, they began by digging an eight-foot-deep trench across the parking lot of the building. Unfortunately, we were only leasing space at this building and were not the actual owners of the parking lot. This was followed by the laying in of a one-inch wide copper cable into our offices. For the next two weeks we met several different union workers that came in to perform each of the functions necessary to splice, connect, install, and eventually provide data service.

The lesson learned here is that the extent of impact of installation can be understated by the telecommunications company. You should press them on the exact details: how will lines be brought in, at what point do you take over in the connection, and any other details that might apply.

As we mentioned back in Chapter 4, our T1 also suffered a direct hit by lightning. This was made possible by the fact that the connection to the fiber cable was done in an above-ground box. The resulting surge passed through the surge protection equipment and destroyed the telecommunication equipment. This is why you ask vendors about surge protection and data line redundancy so that if one portion of your data line goes down, other portions are available to take over. This capability varies by the type of data line you install, but still, this is a good question to ask the telecommunications company.

Although it sounds silly, always ask whether the service you desire is actually available in your location. Our current office is located in a small rural community. However, this rural community also has full ISDN services available from the local telephone company. This is because a major corporation is located just a few miles down the road. However, the next town just a few miles away, cannot get any form of ISDN communication. Our telecommunication company tells us ISDN and other dedicated data services are usually only available where there is a demand.

You also want to make sure the data line service you request will be fully installed by the telecommunications company. What you're trying to avoid is the situation where two or more companies have to work together to complete the installation. For example, one company may provide the routers and internal cabling, while the telecommunication company brings the service up to the wiring closet. This requires both companies to be able to coordinate their schedules successfully.

You should also ask questions, especially with ISDN service, about the long distance charges that may apply. If your company and the ISP you have selected are both on the same local exchange, long distance should not be an issue. However, when connecting distant offices using your network and dedicated data lines, long distance charges become very important.

Many IS managers are not aware that you do not have to use the long distance services of the company that installs your data line. If Ameritech provides you with ISDN service you can still get your long distance service from Sprint. This ability to shop around is vital for keeping the efficiency of your internet connections high. This is also a good reason to consult the telephone administrator in your company. An existing third party telephone service provider may also be able to provide some of the services you need for internet connectivity. Because of your company's already existing business with this third party, you can negotiate deep discounts.

Perhaps the most difficult thing to obtain from the telecommunications company is a final fixed price for the delivery of services. Things have been improving lately, but there are still many instances where there are charges not mentioned during the negotiations process. For example, if you're using ISDN solely for data transmission you can have the telecommunications company drop the charge for the phone channel bundled in the ISDN package.

Evaluation of your telecommunications company and ISP should take place at the same time and usually by the same committee. In the end you may find you need to closely coordinate these two services and their installation. You would also have to carefully evaluate whether their technical services will overlap or leave gaps. These are all issues the selection committee should consider carefully before making their final choices.

Purchasing Software

Software comes from three basic sources. There is off-the-shelf software like MicroSoft Office 98, Windows NT, Lotus Notes, Lotus Approach, Eudora Pro, and Netscape Navigator. The second common source is custom designed, vertical applications that are already written and available to a limited market.

These are the specialized software packages for situations such as heavy security of your web server, specialized database engines, add-ons for your network mail system, and the like. Finally, there is the customized software written specifically for your company. These are the custom web pages, java applets, database warehouse applications, one-of-a-kind order entry systems, and so forth.

Each of these three software choices require a different approach for purchasing. They will also share some common characteristics, such as the use of purchase orders and the need for written approval before purchase. Let's look at these three situations in detail before discussing the checklist to be used when purchasing software.

Commercial software

Typically, you can establish a corporate account with a software distribution house to obtain commercial software. When you need a new software package, you call the company and provide them with a purchase order number so the product will ship almost immediately. The authorization is usually nothing more than the IS manager's signature or even the signature of one of the system administrators.

For example, the people at Avix Manufacturing may be training personnel about web pages using a shareware HTML editor. Someone suggests that they should purchase two copies of Net Objects Fusion to speed the development process. The IS manager signs off on the request and calls the purchasing manager to secure a purchase order number. This is then handed to the secretary of the information technology manager who phones in the order. Using the corporate account number or having the purchase order number can get delivery within 24 hours.

As you can see, commercial software is typically fairly inexpensive, easy to obtain, and easy to ship. Its availability is almost immediate. In fact the internet allows you to download directly many popular software packages and pay for them online. A simple operating procedure can be used for either type of purchasing.

Specialized software

Software designed for vertical applications are different in several ways. Typically they will cost more, take longer to deliver, and require more careful consideration by your company before purchasing. The level of authorization required will probably include a signature by the purchasing manager.

Let's take the example of an application package that allows your web site to collect resumes from people interested in working for your company. This is a database application written to be used with your web server. The originator of the software is a small software company that typically sells fewer than 300 copies of the software every year.

When you want to order a copy of the software, one of the company's representatives comes to your site, evaluates your needs, and goes back to custom-design the software to fit your system. The representative also can negotiate technical support for the product and decide how updates will be handled. Because of the large expense involved, typically over five thousand dollars, your company is interested in closely evaluating the software before purchase. This means additional agreements have to be reached on how a test version of the software can be installed in your system for full evaluation.

As you can see, the purchasing process is no longer a one-step activity. Instead, several steps are taken until final purchase is achieved.

Custom or in-house software

Even more complex is the situation where you are going to contract someone to write a specific application for your system alone. This is where your company wishes to develop a "proprietary" system. This can be accomplished either by an outside software programming firm, or by a group of programmers already on staff in your company.

In either case, a long series of meetings will occur as the people in need of the software discuss the characteristics they desire with the developers. Typically, these projects are so large and complex a series of tests have to take place as each module is completed.

For the purchasing process, it means you have more than just a single point of purchase. Instead, you have a series of milestones. As each objective is achieved, expenses incurred are then reimbursed. Essentially, you pay the people as services are rendered.

Another common characteristic of complex projects such as these is that your company changes its mind from time to time on what the final product should be. Thus, changes need to be made to the programming that is ongoing. The cost of making these changes late in the project have to be spelled out as part of the purchasing agreement.

Now you can see that the project is so complex several people will be signing off on different aspects of software creation, installation, and ongoing support. A series of tests will have to be performed using a quality control plan. The time between the realization of the need and the fulfillment of that need could stretch out for months or even years. Therefore, you can quickly see why it is so important to carefully evaluate a software vendor.

Checklist to Use Before Selecting a Software Vendor

There are actually two considerations to be taken into account before the purchase of software. The first one is to find a vendor that works well with your corporate culture and the objectives of your internet technology project. In the case of custom-designed software, you would be evaluating the depth and strength of their programming staff as well. The second consideration is to actually test and evaluate different software options to find the best match to your mission.

In this chapter you are shown how to examine and find a proper software vendor. In the following chapters, especially Chapter 8, we will discuss how to test software.

Supplier's Name:

Address:

City, State, Zip:

Contact People:

Phone:

FAX:

E-mail:

Web site:

Services Provided (check those that apply):
__ Overnight delivery
__ Rebates
__ Corporate discounts
__ Corporate accounts
__ Do they take purchase orders?

___ Notification of updates

___ Installation by vendor?

1. Will the vendor offer support for the software they are selling? If not, who does provide the support?
2. How rapidly will support be delivered? Will support be delivered by telephone, E-mail, or will a person be available onsite from the vendor?
3. Describe the fee structure this vendor offers for support and shipping, special situations, updating of software, and return of goods.
4. Provide each potential vendor with a sample request for a proposal. How well does each vendor responded to your list of needs?
5. Interview the three vendors with the best combination of features listed above. Rank each of them on the following three characteristics:
- Ability to communicate with your organization
- Technical capabilities
- Interpersonal communication skills

Additional comments:

Complete one copy of this form for each vendor that you are considering for software purchase. Feel free to add or delete items as you feel necessary.

As mentioned earlier, there are different forms of software to consider when evaluating a software vendor. For example, commercial software can be purchased via mail-order with very little trouble. You want prices low, delivery quick, and customer support provided by the company that produced the software (not the distribution company).

With commercial software, your concerns include quick replacement of damaged disks, obtaining multiple media, and other related issues. You would not be able to audit the creators of the software. It is very likely that the software producer is a company actually larger than yours.

One of the major problems with mail-order is that you are unable to test different software packages before purchase. It is best to find a local retailer that allows testing of different packages before purchase and can match the price of the mail-order houses. With this ideal situation, you purchase most of your software from the retailer and only use mail-order when the retailer is unable to immediately deliver a needed package.

One of the great advantages of commercial software is that thousands of other companies have been using the product. Typically this creates user groups, discussion groups on the internet, and other forms of feedback that allows the software producer to continually improve its product. It also supplies you with a large database of information on how well the product actually works.

It is one thing to sit down and read through the product literature for the software package. It is quite another to log on to the internet and read through discussion groups supporting that package. You are likely to get an entirely different picture on how the software works. This is where you learn that even though the product can run under a 486 processor, you really want to use a Pentium. This is also where you read about the bugs it has and where to locate software patches to keep the program running smoothly.

Almost all of these advantages are lost when you get into vertical market and specialized software. Take the example of an order entry package that works with your web server. Let's assume this package was written to meet the EDI requirements of the automotive industry and is widely used by automotive suppliers. Avix Manufacturing wants to purchase such a piece of software. Even though the package is widely used in the supplier community, the company that produces the software still only sells about 500 copies a year.

What this does is keep the community of users so small that it is unlikely you can find third party sources of information about the software. Therefore, you'll need to use stringent evaluation methods to determine the quality of the software and whether it has functionality that suits your internal needs. What you would need to do in this situation is ask for references from the software producer. Then a site visit and an interview would be required at a minimum of two sites using the software.

The checklist provided above would be expanded and modified to ask the particular functionality questions that your staff would have. You would also ask these questions while observing the software as it runs on your equipment, if possible, or on similar equipment. You'll want to closely evaluate the user interface and the overall quality of the software. You will also want to check on systems resources required to support the software.

Technical support for the software would typically come from only a few sources. The original software producer would most likely provide technical support. A handful of consultants who are experts with the software also might be able to help you. Each of these will have to be evaluated for their effectiveness, efficiency, and dedication to customer service.

For custom software, the need for evaluation becomes critical. Now you will be solely dependent on one group that both produces and supports the software being created. Chances are, your company will be the only user of the custom-designed software. This eliminates any possibility of evaluating the performance and functionality of the software until it is actually installed under your system.

What you need to do is take a proactive, preventive stance in evaluating the vendor of the software. The depth and strength of the programming staff should be closely evaluated. You should look at the success of similar projects carried out by this company. You should ask for least three references and check them closely.

The checklist provided above will be used and greatly expanded for the evaluation of the ability of the software programming company to communicate with members of your organization. The interpersonal communication skills of critical people from the programming company should also be considered. As with most custom software programming jobs there will be personal conflicts. The ability of the people involved to professionally resolve such conflicts will prevent needless misunderstanding. Thus, your checklist for evaluation will extend beyond just the functionality of the software and capabilities of the producer.

Checklist to Use Before Selecting a Hardware Vendor

As with software vendors, you need evaluate a hardware vendor thoroughly. Many of the same questions will be asked. However, the hardware vendor is more likely to require an onsite visit. The onsite visit allows you to see how well they organize their company, whether their procedures are documented, and other standard concerns any company would have with any supplier.

Supplier's Name:

Address:

City, State, Zip:

Contact People:

Phone:

FAX:

E-mail:

Web site:

Services Provided (check those that apply):

__ Stock is immediately available

__ Able to build a customer system

__ Overnight delivery

__ Rebates

__ Corporate discounts

__ Corporate accounts

__ Do they take purchase orders?

__ Notification of updates

1. Will the vendor offer support for the hardware they are selling? If not, who does provide the support?

2. How rapidly will support be delivered? Will support be delivered by telephone, by E-mail, or will a person be available onsite from the vendor? Will troublesome components have to be shipped to the vendor's location for repair?

3. Describe the fee structure this vendor offers for support and shipping, special situations, updating of software, and return of goods.

4. Provide each potential vendor with a sample request for a proposal. How well does each vendor respond to your list of needs?

5. Interview the three vendors with the best combination of features listed above. Rank each of them on the following three characteristics:

   • Ability to communicate with your organization

   • Technical capabilities

   • Interpersonal communication skills

Additional comments:

Complete one copy of this form for each vendor that you are considering for hardware purchase. Feel free to add or delete items as you feel necessary.

Selecting and Evaluating Technical Support and Outside Contractors

Finally, we come to the category of selecting technical support and outside contractors. Basically, this involves the evaluation and selection of people for the knowledge they possess. In many situations, you are looking for people outside your company to assist with your internet technology and the custom resources you possess within the company that are already deployed. So, before we can begin to discuss how to evaluate these types of people, we have to pause and discuss how you can realize when it's time to seek outside help.

How to know when you need outside help

The issue of contracting technical support or outside consultants begins when you determine that you need help beyond the resources available within your company. The decision to seek outside help can be difficult and should be done with caution to assure that you don't bring in outside help when it really isn't needed. Another problem to avoid is bringing in help long after it was needed, thus wasting extra money clearing up the problems created from too little support being available at critical moments.

As IS manager you must be able to determine if and when outside help is needed and how much will be needed. If you followed our advice to use project management techniques to plan for implementation, then your time charts should begin to indicate where outside help will be needed.

The following questions should be asked continuously during the planning and implementation phase of your project to determine if outside help is required.

1. Does your production staff find they are redoing major portions of web pages, server settings, or other configuration tasks?
2. Is your help desk already used to almost full capacity?
3. Are the milestones in your project consistently missed or late?
4. Are computer network system resources being used up more than 20% faster than you predicted?
5. Are you experiencing long log-ins or server crashes that occur more than once a month?
6. Are responses to user requests for help taking longer than one day?
7. Does it take your staff longer than a day or two to load in and test a new software package?
8. Have you experienced a large number of user reported problems with any part of your internet system?
9. Has a major security breech been detected?

If the answer to any of these questions is "yes" then you should consider seeking outside assistance. All of these questions are based on the symptoms of a system not being implemented as efficiently as possible.

When it takes a person several days to get a new software package loaded and working properly, chances are the person does not have the experience and knowledge for efficient installation. An outside consultant may charge you several hundred dollars for a quick and efficient installation. This could be a considerable savings over a system that is late in installation and fails after full ramp-up.

When you get symptoms of system problems such as committed resources being used, security breaches, or long delays in response to requests, these could be an indication that the configuration is not working properly. Sometimes an outside opinion is a good way to discover better ways to configure your system. This is assuming that the person brought in to examine your system has the expertise to make beneficial suggestions. Therefore, you need to closely check references from companies and individuals that claim they can help you with your problems.

How to Negotiate the Contract

Once you have successfully located a consultant, programmer, technical support organization, or other outside help, you need to negotiate a contractual relationship. Although it would be easy to say that you want to negotiate your contract so that your company receives all of the benefits, this is not realistic in today's environment. Technical troubleshooters that are very good at their job are in high demand and well paid. Therefore you'll need to both give and take during the negotiation of the contract for services.

One point you want to make sure of is that you always succeed in securing a performance-based contract. This means that the person or company delivering technical services to your company will be held accountable for how well they perform their job. Let's look at a typical example of a performance-based contract.

Megalith purchases its personal computers directly from a famous manufacturer of computer systems. As part of the purchasing agreement, they also buy technical support for keeping their system properly configured and for repairing hardware problems. Because of the size of Megalith the contracted company keeps at least three of their technical people onsite at all times.

Under the terms of the contract that was negotiated, these three technical people have to be approved by Megalith. That means that if a substitute is sent in, the IS manager must approve the credentials of this person. Also, all work performed by these three individuals is carefully logged and reported to the IS manager. In turn, the manager can regularly survey the satisfaction the users have with the services delivered.

The terms of the contract allow the IS manager to share these results with the technicians and their manager. Should the IS manager be dissatisfied with the services being delivered, several corrective action steps are available. These are spelled out under the contract. One such step is to insist that if sub-standard work is done, (i.e. not to the level of quality expected) there will be no charge. Another contractual corrective action is that the IS manager can assign an in-house person to correct the problem. Finally, Megalith has the option of canceling the technical support contract at any time.

These may seem like harsh terms, but they are critical to assuring the successful use of outside experts. It must be made clear to the people being contracted exactly what it is they need to accomplish. As IS manager you should draw up a list of expectations for any person being contracted to support your department. This should be reviewed with the person in the contract. This contract should also specify payment according to proper performance. Performance goals and measures should be spelled out and regularly monitored by both contractor and IS manager.

There are also some other points to keep in mind in your contractual obligations. One is that you always leave open your option to inspect the products and services being delivered with an outside technical expert. For example, if you hire a Windows NT expert to configure your web servers, you should make clear the performance criteria that will be used to inspect his work. This will include the responsiveness of the system, the amount of resources consumed, and the capabilities that will be made available.

It is also a good idea to have one of your technical people escort the outside consultant. This involves more than just meeting a consultant at the door. An escort also sits somewhere nearby offering to bring to the expert any needed assistance. At the same time, your technical person should watch to make sure that the outside expert does not take any drastic actions against your company.

Here is one example of a situation that might occur at your company. A technician is brought in to solve a web server problem. It was decided that it lay in the formatting of the hard drive. The technician begins to remove the hard drive from the web server to do a low-level reformatting of the drive. Because one of your technical people is there, you are able to stop this process and let the technician know you have no interest in going that far backward to try to fix the problem. As it turns out, a simple reconfiguration of the operating system solved the root problem.

One of the most difficult items in maintaining the contractual agreements is the delivery of services and goods. Expertise is an unusual product. It is very difficult for most experts to determine how long it will take to solve the problem when they do not know the extent of the situation. Therefore, you should set up a schedule that is flexible—with goals and clearly stated milestones that have to be achieved.

For example, if the Law Firm detected a security breach in one of the web servers, they may hire an outside security expert to see if the same problem exists on other points in their system. It would be easy to say that such a person has seven days to discover how many security breaches occur and where the weaknesses are in your system. However, the expert has no idea on how your system is exactly configured or where the weaknesses may occur. It may be necessary to completely audit the entire configuration of the internet technology system. This could take weeks.

To get around this problem, you may want to write a schedule into the contract that says the first seven days will be spent auditing for discovered security breaches and analyzing the breach that did occur. The outside security expert will then meet with the IS manager to review the seriousness of the problem and up to seven more days can be allocated to correcting the situation. If the problem is more serious than expected, a second round of contractual negotiations can take place. This gives you the option of stopping work, modifying the contract, or figuring out a solution to the security problem.

In contrast, if you had signed a contract saying this person will stay onsite until the problems are completely fixed, you may have just obligated your company to tens of thousands of dollars of work. The actual security problem could turn out to be much larger than you or the expert ever expected. Yet, in your contract you are obligated to pay the expert until the problem is fixed. Chapter 15 will discuss legal matters in greater detail.

Finally, you should be clear on how payment will occur. Typically, technical experts are hired with the agreement that they will be paid as services are rendered. In cases where you contract your help desk, or like our example at Megalith, where people were contracted to be onsite at all times, you have a fixed annual payment schedule.

Establishing Proper Relationships with Suppliers

As we mentioned earlier, technical experts with talent are a very rare commodity. The demand for technical expertise far outstrips the supply. Therefore, you are in a supplier relationship situation very different from the one most companies experience. The supplier has considerable leverage.

As a comparison, Avix Manufacturing contracts with hundreds of suppliers for small parts and raw materials. For the items they need, there is at least a dozen companies that can supply them. Therefore, they have the advantage of forcing their suppliers to compete among themselves for the best terms, conditions, and price. In this situation, companies frequently engage in adversarial type relationships with their suppliers. Basically, this is the "give us what we want or we'll cancel your contract" mentality.

For the IS manager, the situation is quite different. While hardware and software suppliers are plentiful, technical experts are scarce. Therefore, you need to engage in a partnership arrangement with the technical experts. You need to work closely with these people and make them feel that they're part of your organization. Information is freely exchanged with them so they are constantly aware of your mission and what needs to be accomplished.

Surprisingly, even the manufacturing companies that can choose among dozens of suppliers are discovering that this cooperative type of relationship is actually beneficial overall to both parties. Because of new technologies such as just-in-time delivery, total quality, and concurrent engineering, companies are discovering that they need to work more closely with their suppliers. Even in your situation with a multiple number of hardware and software suppliers, you'll discover that this closeness is also required. Price alone is no longer the determination of a good supplier.

A few chapters back, you completed exercises to determine your goals and objectives in connecting your technology system. As you'll discover reading this book, these experiences will be used repeatedly to assist you in the implementation of your system. This is one of the early points where they are used. Once you locate a properly qualified supplier, bring them in-house to share your goals and objectives. The supplier should be made very aware of what it is you are trying to accomplish. They should also be made very aware that failure to help you with these goals and objectives will result in the termination of their contract.

The message you are trying to send the supplier is that the person who can cooperate with you successfully and offer a low price will get this contract and possibly future contracts. In the next chapter, we will look at the issue of competitive bidding in greater detail. We will be paying particular attention to the idea of the total value being offered by the supplier.

Further References

The Purchasing Manager's Handbook and other standard purchasing reference guides are of great assistance for this topic.

Internet Search Strings

"purchasing management"

"supplier relation"

"vendor relation"

"just-in-time"

phase two
Implementation of the Project

Chapter 7
Selecting Hardware

The time has finally come to implement your internet technologies system. You have created major plans, listed goals, established objectives, and you have evaluated the risks. Now it is time to begin by purchasing the hardware and software you need to build your system. In this chapter we will begin by examining how you select, purchase, and install your hardware.

Constructing an Effective Web Server

The economics of selecting hardware for internet applications is constantly changing. The trend is faster, better equipment at lower costs over time. The changes are happening so fast that the very best equipment that is available as this is written will be obsolete when it's published.

Recently, the price on hardware has collapsed so far that balancing the cost of equipment versus its performance is an almost irrelevant argument. This means that in almost all applications, you should buy the very best equipment that is available at that time. Just a few years ago you would have spent tens of thousands of dollars for the hardware for the web server. Today you spend about $3,000 to obtain a competent web server. In fact, a couple of months ago we built our own web server and installed all the needed software, and the total bill was below $2,500!

It has reached a point that if the management objects to the cost of hardware, you have to seriously question their commitment to the project. For a few thousand dollars you can get a web server capable of serving thousands of web pages per second to the network or to the internet. As we shall see in Chapter 9, the bottleneck for internet communications is the connection to the internet. No longer will hardware or software slow down a system. We will begin by discussing the components you need to install a web server that is both efficient and effective.

Motherboards

In many computer catalogs you'll see desktop boxes that look a lot like personal computers advertised as "file servers." File servers and web servers are really the same machine performing two seemingly different functions. A file server is presenting files on request to local area network users. A web server is presenting web pages and related file links to internet clients. In both cases, files are being served up to a network-like connection.

Companies such as Avix, The Law Firm, and Megalith will be purchasing file servers to work as web servers. What makes a personal computer a file server is the nature of its motherboard. This is the base upon which the computer is built. It determines what type of processing chips, RAM, storage devices, communication lines, and other critical components can be used on this particular computer.

Dedicated file servers from companies such as IBM, Digital, and Hewlett-Packard, to name a few, are true file servers. The motherboards are designed for multiple processors, very large storage devices, and very fast communications. They also tend to have internally encoded software for maintaining network applications. In short, they are designed from the ground up to serve as file servers. Third-party file servers should be evaluated carefully for how well they have been designed for network applications.

Discovery exercise

Here is the configurations list of a file server built from scratch for about $1500 U.S. Please look over this list and see if you can spot the weaknesses in the design.

- 166 MHz Pentium Processor with MMX
- Third-party motherboard
- 64MB of SIMM RAM
- 4.5 gigabyte fast-IDE hard drive
- 24x CD-ROM
- 56K bps modem
- PCI video card with 2MB of RAM
- PCI network interface card baseT10/100

- 3 gigabyte back-up tape drive
- 14" VGA monitor

This machine was loaded with Windows NT 4.0 and the internet information server. It was set up as a primary domain controller area network and it was given simple web pages to serve up over a dedicated internet connection. Within days it was nearly dysfunctional.

The two primary weaknesses in this particular machine involve the use of a motherboard not designed for file serving applications, and the lack of systems resources, particularly memory. Let's walk through each of the basic components of the file server to see where strength is needed and where less than world-class products can be used successfully.

When evaluating motherboards, you want to make sure that the data buses connecting various components are extremely fast and wide. Fast means that the clock speed for communications across the motherboard is the highest possible. Wide refers to the width of the communications links on the motherboard. For example, the PCI slot is highly recommended on modern motherboards. This can provide you with up to 64 bits of data width for communications. Whenever possible you should look for motherboards that pass data between components at high speeds and provide a width of at least 64 bits.

Pentium chips   Pentium chips seem to be ruling the world of computers these days. Still, there's a wide variety of microprocessors that can be used in a file server. There are alpha chips that can be used at speeds in excess of 500 MHz. There are Pentium chips running at 333+ MHz. Competitors to the Pentium chip are constantly matching or exceeding the fastest speeds.

Surprisingly, the microprocessor is not the weak point in a file server. Because most of the duty of a file server is to find and retrieve files, and then make them available to users, it is the speed at which it can manipulate storage space that is critical. A good tactic with a file server is to buy one that can have at least two microprocessor chips installed. Start out by buying the fastest microprocessor chip appropriate for your application. For running commercial software the Pentium chip and its competitors are good choices. Unless you know that a particularly heavy load will be placed on a web server, start out with a single microprocessor and eventually upgrade to either a faster processor or two parallel running processors. Supporting the processor is a cache memory. You want this to be as large as possible. This helps to further speed up the microprocessor's activities.

RAM and other memory requirements   The first major weak point in the example presented earlier was the amount of memory that was installed—

64 megabytes (MB) of RAM. This amount of memory is only adequate for running light applications under Windows NT. The machine in the example was serving both web pages and trying to control a small local area network, where more than a half dozen programs were running simultaneously. This quickly consumed the memory.

Any web server should start with a minimum of 128 MB of RAM. Despite what you might read about software products, applications almost always demand more memory than you expect. The greater the demands you expect to place on your web server, the larger the amount of memory you'll want to install. When you select a file server make sure its motherboard can take up to at least 1 gigabyte (GB) of current memory technology.

In many applications related to internet technology, the computer will set up a swap file on the hard drive for handling large loads of data. If you put enough memory into your computer you can actually download the entire application and the swap file to RAM. This will represent a significant increase in performance.

Selecting appropriate high-speed hard drives The ability of your motherboard to pass data between components at high speed and through wide data channels becomes especially important with hard drives. In the past, standards such as the Integral Drive Electronics (IDE) disk system was the fastest available way to communicate between hard drives and other components. Today, even the fastest IDE is only adequate for the latest of internet applications.

The fast/wide and ultra SCSI disk drives are now considered minimal for file serving applications, including web servers. An ultra SCSI drive can hit speeds of 100 megabits (MB) of throughput per second and better. They can spin at 10,000 rpm and have 8 millisecond access times. This sounds fast and powerful, and it is. However, the hard drive can be quickly limited by slow communications, inferior motherboard, or inappropriate configurations.

Therefore, a few precautions should be taken to make sure that your hard drive's performance is fully utilized. You should start by making sure you have the dedicated SCSI drive controller for a PCI slot. This should create the maximum amount of throughput. Also, the disk cache memory should be as large as possible. At this time, it is very common to have a full megabyte of cache memory to serve the hard drive.

Another option for massive data storage is the RAID array (redundant arrays of inexpensive disks). This is a set of hard drives working together as if it were a single storage drive. Data being stored is broken down into individual bits that are then stored on separate drives in the array in a technique called "striping." Fault protection for the array is provided by writing parity information to the auxiliary drive. That way if a single drive fails, the other drives can reconstruct the missing data. You "hot swap" the drive, meaning to remove the drive while it is still on, and the missing data is automatically reconstructed onto the new device. Thus your storage system continues to work even though failures may occur.

Another form of data redundancy is called "mirroring." When you set up your operating system the web server then copies all of the data files being sent to the primary hard drive onto a secondary drive as well. In other words, a mirror copy of all the data is created. Thus, if the primary drive fails, operating systems such as Windows NT can automatically switch functionality to the backup drive. Once the defective drive is replaced you can copy the data from the secondary drive back to the new primary drive. Again, you continue to operate the web server even though failures have occurred.

Both of these fault tolerance methods are highly recommended for any critical web applications.

We should also take a moment to discuss an interesting concept that is occasionally brought up in the purchase of hard drives: Mean Time until Failure (MTTF). When selecting the hard drives to use in your system, you may see an advertising claim such as "250,000 hours MTTF." Normally, we would be left with the impression that the hard drives should last for one quarter of a million hours before you would expect a failure.

This is not true. What MTTF refers to is the average amount of time it takes for *half* of the drives in a sample to fail. For example, if you own 100 of these drives you expect that after a quarter of a million hours, about 50 of them would have failed. Now if you take out a calculator and enter one quarter of a million (250,000) divide by 24 hours each day, and then divide that by the 365 days in a year, you can see that a quarter of a million hours is about 28.5 years.

If you study the calculation of reliability you'll discover that some of the drives will probably fail early in their lifespan. Technically, a drive can fail at any time. You are really taking a chance that your drive will perform at least as well as the average. In our example, the chance of one of these drives failing in the first few years of its use is going to be incredibly small. The important thing to remember here is that the probability never drops to zero. Because hard drive failures always seem to occur at the worst possible time, you need to design your system to recover quickly from such a major problem.

The actual storage capacity of your hard drive will be determined by the type of software you are using and the type of demands you expect to put on your system. For example, a web server dedicated solely to processing the E-mail for your intranet for more than 100 users should have a hard drive of at least five gigabytes. The web server connected to the internet presenting your catalog of products and taking about 5,000 hits a day can get by nicely on one gigabyte.

Because the cost of hard drives is relatively inexpensive you should buy the largest amount you can afford. You never know when you may need to scale up your internet system to cope with new demands that are unexpectedly placed on the popularity of your service.

Software loading equipment (CD-ROMs)   Any web server should have a floppy drive. This can be used to load the odd utility program. However, in the majority of cases you'll need a CD-ROM drive to load software. Practically all serious internet software now comes on CD-ROMs.

Today the speed of the CD-ROM drive is ever increasing. Only a few years ago a quad speed CD-ROM drive was considered state-of-the-art. Today drives spin at 32 times the standard data read rate and faster. When you look for a CD-ROM drive for your server, make sure it also has cache memory. This speeds up the rate of the loading process and prevents long delays. In addition, you'll want to test your CD-ROM drive to make sure that it is constantly accessible by your system.

Where possible, it is important to have the maker of the web server also install the CD-ROM drive. Although you can install your own CD-ROM drive, in some cases you'll find it's not completely compatible with your system. Sometimes, when your operating system attempts to read the CD-ROM drive, the delay while it spins up to speed makes computers think there is no response. The result is the need to make several requests to read a file before it can be successfully located.

Tape backup systems   There are a variety of backup systems available for web servers. The most commonly used is the streaming tape backup drive. Other possibilities are the write-able CD-ROM, mirror backup disk, and removable hard disk.

The advantage of the streaming tape backup drive is the low cost to create a backup of all of your data. As with your hard drive, you will want the SCSI interface for the streaming tape backup. This will increase throughput and access time. The result is a shorter amount of time necessary for complete backup.

When you are selecting your tape backup system you should calculate the number of gigabytes of data that will be saved on a daily basis. Then you should look at the rate at which the tape backup can record this information. Ideally, you do not want to spend more than two or three hours a day making a backup. This includes your once a week total backup of the system.

Network interface cards (NICs) Sometimes servers are actually machines independent of your local area network. They are isolated in this fashion as a security measure. However, in most cases you'll have some sort of network connection to your web servers. This will allow personnel at your company to produce content for the web server and deliver it over your local area network. In a large corporation like Megalith, the networking of web servers allows the IS manager to centrally control several machines.

This makes the role of the network interface card critical to the mission's success of the web server. Today you can buy a 10M bps network interface card for about $20. For just over $100 you can purchase a 100M bps network interface card from a leading manufacturer, such as 3Com. These are all relatively inexpensive prices. Therefore, buy the best cards you can find.

You'll want to purchase the same network interface cards for all machines involved in your internet technologies system. It's possible to use the same network interface cards throughout your local area network. At a minimum they should be manufactured by the same people who supplied your other NICs. In this way you can preserve compatibility across your entire system. In most cases different NICs can work with each other, but if conflicts occur they will be difficult to correct.

Next you'll want to consult the compatibility list for the operating system you're using. Operating systems such as Windows NT and NetWare will tell you which network interface cards work with their system. This way, you can be sure that your operating system already handles the device drivers for your network interface card.

Again, you are looking for PCI cards. This will create the maximum throughput to the motherboard. The goal in seeking maximum throughput wherever possible is to avoid communication bottlenecks within the file server.

Modems In some cases you'll want to equip your web server with a modem. This will allow you to dial up the web server remotely and supply it with content for repair problems that are occurring. Programs such as Remote Access Service, PC Anywhere and CarbonCopy allow you to seize full control of the machine from a remote location. This allows the administrator of the web server to take care of problems even when on vacation.

At the same time, it opens up a massive security problem. By having a modem on a web server you create a back door into your system. In many cases this back door will be outside the normal security precautions that you designed into your internet services. Therefore, you need to look for modems that have dial back capabilities. Combined with security software that comes with the remote access services, you can establish a secure way to ensure that only the administrator is able to gain access to the web server using a modem.

There are basically two types of modems you should consider for use with a web server. The first is the 56K bps analog modem. These are high-speed modems that use conventional analog phone lines. They are widely available and extremely inexpensive. Although achieving the actual 56K bps connection speed is unlikely on most phone lines, it still gives you enough speed to be able to control the machine remotely without needless delays while your screen refreshes.

The unique thing about 56K bps modems is the fact that no one has settled on a single standard for the protocols. Thus you get two types of modems to choose between—Flex and X.2. Whichever of these two standards you select, you have to make sure that everyone connecting to the web server has the same standard in their modems.

The other modem choice is an ISDN modem. These use digital phone lines to make the connection. Their connection speed starts at 128K bps. This allows very fast and effective connections to web servers. Thanks to compression and error checking, 100% accuracy is achieved in transfers. The disadvantage is that the people who need to connect to the web server remotely have to have ISDN phone lines installed at their location.

This is typically done for the homes of administrators. By putting an ISDN phone line into his or her home, the administrator can have access to the web server during off hours to take care of small problems. Again, extra security measures are required.

Another interesting consideration for modems is whether you want to have the modem mounted internally or placed outside your machine. External modems are easier to monitor and replace if something goes wrong. The heat they create tends to go into the atmosphere instead of adding to the heat already inside your machine. The downside of an external modem is that it is dependent on the speed of your serial port. Machines that do not have special high-speed serial ports cannot successfully handle the throughput of today's faster modems.

Internal modems are more convenient and take up less space. They have no problem with high throughput speeds since they are connected directly to the motherboard. Again, you are looking for a PCI modem.

Other components to consider

Other equipment that may need to be added to your web server includes things such as advanced video devices, sound, and faxing capabilities. If a web server is going to be used by an operator for more than one hour a day, you should get at least a 17-inch monitor. This should be connected to a high-resolution video card with at least two megabytes of RAM.

This is also true in the situation where the web server is also the production machine. In a smaller company, you may find that the people creating content for the web server want to do so using the web server itself. This means they will be running the web page design software while the web server is connected to the internet. A larger video screen with high resolution helps reduce the eyestrain of the worker.

Some web servers will offer both audio and video content. Such machines should have a larger monitor with a high-resolution video card, as well as a sound card with external speakers. This allows the web server's administrator to directly monitor the audio and video files for quality, content, and clarity of presentation.

Additional hardware can be added to the web server to assist internet software programs. For example, there are internet web page programs that allow people looking at your web site to enter basic information and request quotes from your company for proposed projects. The information is used to create a rough quote automatically and fax the result to the requester's company. Therefore, you will need some sort of faxing capability within the web server. Most modern modems can easily fulfill this need.

Calculating the Amount of Hardware Needed

Now that we have reviewed the basic features you want to look for in hardware, it's time to think about how much hardware you'll need. In the previous chapters we took deliberate steps to carefully plan out the type of internet system we are developing. We also have a list of goals and objectives for the system. These now provide us with the benchmarks for estimating how much hardware will be required.

Most commercial software will include an estimate of the type of hardware and resources you'll need. For example, the Microsoft exchange server is an E-mail system that requires a large amount of system resources. Depending on the number of E-mail boxes that you set up for the system, you can make a rough estimate of the amount of RAM, hard disk space, and communication throughput you'll need to have the system run smoothly.

One rule of thumb for internet systems is that each major internet service should have its own server. In the case of Avix Manufacturing, they wish to have a web presence on the internet. Therefore, they will need a web server to fulfill this function. They would also like to integrate their E-mail system using internet technology. To keep the system simple, they will purchase a second separate E-mail server.

Each of our four example companies will need to spend some time looking at the list of services they wish to provide using internet technology. They should try to keep one major service to each server. Attempting to run web pages, news net, and E-mail for the internet on one server is asking for trouble. Keep in mind that a web server is already running a high-level operating system and probably two or three monitoring programs before the internet software is even loaded.

To the list of services to be provided you must add security concerns. The gateway computers and firewall computers need to be added into the requirements. In addition, routers and other network hardware may be required. Finally, there is the need for the equipment to allow connectivity to the internet. This will include the modems, multiplexers, switching equipment, and other communication devices.

Estimating Hardware Costs

At some point you will need to order your hardware. This will require a competitive bidding process, which will be discussed below. The first step is to develop an estimated budget that can be used for planning and negotiations.

Supplier catalogs and retail prices posted at web sites are good places to start to get the maximum cost of purchasing your equipment. You will also want to have installation expenses included in the price. Ongoing maintenance and technical support should be quoted as separate items since you can obtain these services from other suppliers, if necessary.

To help itemize the needed hardware, refer to the network map that you created at the beginning of this book. On this you have the existing network and the internet-related equipment you wish to add. The cost of the new equipment is itemized to form the estimated budget.

In smaller companies this process is fairly easy. In larger organizations you might need to get several groups to agree on what existing equipment should be used, to stay within a given budget. The example below will illustrate how to cope with both of these situations.

Example: Avix gets ready to bid for equipment

Figure 7–1 is the Avix map of their existing network and the equipment they wish to add. This is a fairly straightforward situation where the hardware needs are obvious and the itemized list will be short.

Figure 7-1. Avix Map of Existing Equipment

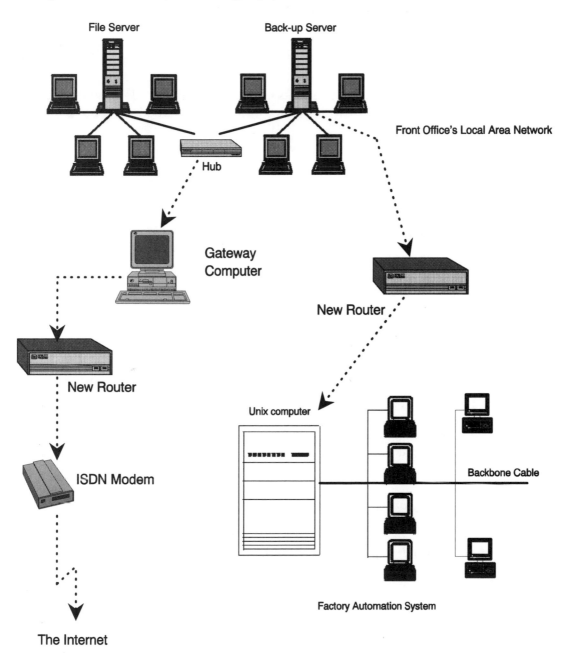

Here, Avix wishes to install two routers and an ISDN modem. One router and the modem will establish the connection to the internet. The other router will pass E-mail between the office network and the factory network.

The IS manager would take this map of the proposed additions to the people affected by the change. Here the administrator of the file server for the office can verify that there are indeed enough resources available for adding web-serving software to the office file server. However, the administrator may also point out that security calls for better protection between the internet and the office file server.

It is suggested that another network interface card be added to the file server so that internet traffic comes in on a different IP address than office traffic. Also, the administrator wants a gateway computer between the internet router and the file server. Extra firewall protection can be placed at that location. The IS manager agrees with these suggestions.

The list of equipment needed has grown to the following:

1 - 400 Mhz based gateway computer ($1500)

2 - routers ($1600)

1 - ISDN modem ($400)

3 - network interface cards ($300)

Total estimated cost of hardware is $3900. This is the number first reported to management with a note that a lower bid for the equipment will be sought. Later, when you get the lower bid, you can send another memo to management pointing out the savings.

At the same time, you would be preparing software and connectivity cost estimates for the purchasing process. As a taste of what is to come, the combined costs of hardware, software, and connectivity is typically a small fraction of the total cost of implementing internet technology. Labor, service, and technical support will dominate most budgets.

Exercise: Calculating what you will need

Megalith's IS manager has received approval for a $1 million budget for equipment to connect the corporation to the internet. The IS manager knows that the budget will not satisfy the desires of every department's needs related to internet technology. A million dollars can be spent quickly in a large corporation.

The IS manager's strategy is to meet with each of the affected departments and create the final list of equipment that they think they will need, using the network map for that department. This is posted in a large format on the wall of a departmental meeting room. The proposed internet connections are marked in a unique color.

Representatives from that department discuss their particular needs of the system and a consensus is reached on the equipment that will be required to meet those needs. The IS manager then explains the limited budget and the group checks to see how close their request is to the proportion of the budget set aside for their department.

If the department is at or below budget, they can be congratulated for working well as a team. In this way the departmental personnel feel that they have ownership of the project.

If the department's requests are well beyond the budget, then the IS manager can start a new conversation on how to cope with this problem. The representatives are then given a few days to think through some options brainstormed by the group. When they meet again, they will have to work out a way to stay in budget. Options include:

- Delay implementing some parts of their system
- Reduce power features of some equipment
- Reevaluate the capability of the equipment versus their needs
- Join other departments to share equipment

The possibilities are limited only by the imagination of the group. By working in teams, the IS manager helps the future users of the system feel that they have a very active role in implementation. This feeling of ownership will prevent many problems later in the project.

Now, let's look at the hardware requirements in one Megalith department—public relations.

1 - Digital web server with 6.0 GB hard drive, dual 233 MHz Pentiums, and 256 MB of RAM

2 - 233 MHz based personal computers for production work

2 - laptop computers with voice recognition capabilities

1 - network hub (100M bps)

4 - network interface cards (T-base-100)

1 - color laser jet printer

2 - ISDN modems

2 - PCMCIA ISDN modems

1 - transportable 3.0 GB tape backup unit

1 - color scanner

1 - digital camera

Public relations wants the capability to create multimedia web pages within their department. Not only can they scan in photos or create digital photos directly, they have all of the production and proofing equipment a good web development company would need.

Then they have also added laptop computers and ISDN modems so that their production people can work on the road or from home. In short, this would be a very well-equipped department. In total, they are looking at about $26,000 of equipment. The problem is that the budget for this department is only $20,000.

To handle this situation the IS manager needs to prepare to confront the department's director by looking up the mission, goals, and objectives for the public relations department in the internet project. Let's assume the IS manager discovers that their role is to create the promotional materials to be incorporated into the web pages being built by other departments.

Next, their existing collection of computer equipment is inventoried. Here it is discovered that their staff already has several laptop computers capable of working with web page creation software. The office services department already has a couple of color scanners and a good digital camera.

With this information the IS manager proposes that the requests for laptops, scanner, and digital camera can be dropped. In addition, one or two 56K modems are adequate for transmission of files to and from the department. The list of required equipment is thus pared down to below $20,000.

Getting Bids on Hardware

Competitive bidding is the process whereby you secure the best possible equipment of the highest quality at the lowest price you can negotiate. The basic rule here is to never pay retail price for anything.

Because of the large number of equipment suppliers in the computer world, competition is easy to encourage. In fact, once you have the best value in a bid you can frequently get the supplier to cut the price just a bit more or add a few more services. The larger your order, the more likely you are to have good leverage in negotiations.

This is also the most important aspect of competitive bidding; you need to remember that this is a process of negotiation. This will be a two-way communication with suppliers. You need to be open and honest in your dealings if you want good products, timely delivery, and excellent service. When you treat a supplier fairly, you should get the same treatment in return. If you don't get fair treatment, you will have easy reasons to drop the supplier.

The first step in this process of open communications is to meet with your purchasing department to discuss the format for a competitive bid being issued by your company. Generally, the purchasing department will want to issue the bid. They should also brief you on the legal and ethical rules of handling bids.

For example, your company may already have an ongoing purchasing relationship with a computer equipment supplier. The purchasing people would give them the information on the need for a quote early in the process, to get their feedback and to keep good relations. The existing supplier would be informed that other suppliers would be given an opportunity to bid on this job because that is the standard procedure for your company.

In this way the supplier is warned that they should think in competitive terms when preparing their response. At the same time, the supplier has its importance for your company confirmed by the fact that they are the first out-siders invited into the process. However, it is kept clear in communications that this job is not a "given" for this supplier.

Another problem you might encounter is the one that Megalith is encoun-tering. Microsoft is a large client and one of the vice-presidents is a former employee. As a result, the BackOffice suite of software will be used in the internet project. The decision making for software is taken away from the IS manager. All that is left is to follow along with the corporate tide.

Obtaining Requests for Quotes

The itemized list of equipment you need to purchase, and related costs, is used as the centerpiece of a document called the request for quote. This is the for-mal request to suppliers to prepare a formal bid for your project. Suppliers will respond to this request in writing.

You may want to include your site maps and proposed goals of imple-mentation. In this way suppliers can also make suggestions and propose alter-native equipment to better meet your needs. As discussed earlier, suppliers are often made members of your implementation team. You want their feedback, but you also want to retain the final say in layout of the internet technology system.

There are some common elements that go into requests for quotes. Many organizations, such as the U.S. government, have strict guidelines on what is included in a request for quote and how the quoting process is handled. You always want to stay inside any existing rules or regulations that apply to your request for quote. Let's take a look at some of these elements and how they are used in the quoting process.

1. *Qualification of bidders.* The minimal qualifications of suppliers wishing to bid should be spelled out early in the document. This helps suppliers to quickly identify whether they should proceed with the bid. For example, you may want a hardware supplier that is 3Com certified, experienced with your type of business, and can service Hewlett-Packard computers. A supplier that specializes in Apple computers would usually stay away from this request for quote.

2. *Summary of the work to be done.* A bullet point review of the hardware to be purchased and when it will be installed is presented, to give the bidders a feel for the size and scope of the project.

3. *Major goals of the project.* By listing the major goals, not the related objectives, you give bidders a feel for what you are trying to accomplish by installing the new equipment. This helps bidders to suggest better systems or less expensive hardware with the same capabilities.

4. *Time frame and rules for the bidding process.* Here you list the amount of time the bidders have to respond, who is the primary contact at your company, where bids should be sent, the form the bids should take, and other related information. Any regulations that apply should also be noted. For example, the Dickerson County School District would have to follow the open and competitive bidding practices of their state.

5. *Acceptance criteria.* Here you list how the bids will be evaluated and by which criteria they will be judged. For example, you can say that the bid will be evaluated publicly in an open meeting of the implementation committee using a combination of price, quality, and delivery times as major criteria. You will also want to evaluate the financial security of the supplier and its track record of delivering quality service.

There are dozens of other details that go into a standard request for quotes. These include:

- Disclaimers by your company (such as the fact that your maps may not be completely accurate)
- Leasing terms
- Rights of ownership

- Confidentiality statements to be signed by the bidder
- The need for bidders to list their subcontractors for this project
- Length of the bid validity in days (i.e., bid in effect for 60 days)
- How bids can be withdrawn
- Whether partial bids, joint venture, or other alternatives are acceptable
- How a bidder can ask questions
- Notification method if the request has to be changed before bids are received
- Warranty terms
- The number of copies of the bid required
- Whether a security bond needs to be posted
- The format to be used in presenting the bid

These details typically appear at the beginning of the request. A well-written request for proposal will use five or fewer pages for this part of the documents. It is then followed with a detailed list of what is required.

This section begins with a definition of the work to be performed. This is a detailed outline of the project, the equipment to be installed, and the connections to be made. Locations of new and existing equipment directly involved are listed.

Supplier Guarantees on Quality Components

During the planning phase of your internet project, you need to develop a control plan for quality assurance. This doesn't mean the creation of a new and complete quality assurance system in your company. Instead, a control plan for quality assurance is where you identify at which points in the process of implementing your internet project you need to check critical components and critical characteristics.

One of these early points will be the inspection of the quality of the components being delivered by the supplier. You begin by spelling out the quality requirements in your request for quote. Then you repeat these requirements in the actual purchase orders you use. The material coming into your company should be inspected against these requirements. Later, you will prototype your systems to assure that the level of quality you expected is achieved.

The following items should be noted on the request for quote.

1. Quantities of each item, including the brand names and model numbers.
2. Standards that apply to items.
3. Expected delivery times.
4. Condition of the components and systems at the time of delivery.
5. Warranties.
6. Return and replace agreements.
7. Performance parameters, where applicable.

By specifying the quantity of items by brand name and model number you are assisting the potential supplier by being as specific as possible. It is up to you whether you will allow the "or equivalent" option. If you do, then you need to break down the performance characteristics expected of the alternative equipment in greater detail.

Many computer components have to comply with national and international standards to be considered compatible with other system components. These standards come from organizations such as ISO, IEEE, ANSI, and the like. The specific standards that apply to particular items should be noted so that no misunderstandings exist between you and the bidder.

Delivery time is a quality of particular importance in computer equipment based projects. As we will discover in the next two chapters, your software, hardware, and connections to the internet have to be carefully coordinated to prevent wasting time and money. Suppliers should be evaluated partly on their ability to meet your scheduling needs.

When you order a web server, you must specify that the server is new, complete, and undamaged at the time of delivery. A major problem encountered in purchasing computer equipment is that some suppliers will attempt to sell you returned or refurbished equipment in place of factory-new equipment.

This can be the result of a simple misunderstanding or a deliberate attempt at fraud. What can happen is that a supplier receives, say, a web server from the factory. They configure it and send it to another customer. The customer attempts to use the system but finds that their software is not compatible. Within a day of the original delivery, the system is back at the supplier's warehouse. The hard drive is erased. A few days later, that system is sold to your company as new.

This may not cause any problems, but technically the unit is neither new nor unused. By insisting on new, unused equipment you can generally avoid problems from viruses and unintentional damage experienced at another site. It also reduces the amount of handling the unit receives.

Most equipment you buy comes with some form of a warranty on defective goods. You will be looking for offers to replace defective units immediately. The repair of a defective item is interesting but can take weeks when you are in the middle of the implementation of your system. You also want to know about any additional warranties added by the supplier and whether the factory or the supplier performs repairs and replacements.

The time limits on return of defective goods should be noted. You will also want to know the supplier's policy on replacing items that are found inadequate for the application you designed. This happens fairly frequently. For example, the literature on a modem says it works with your type of computer. The supplier says that it will work. All the research says that it should work. You install the modem and nothing will get your system to recognize its presence.

Normally, a lot of time could be spent hunting down the conflict causing the problem. A better tactic is to establish an agreement with the supplier that if something like this occurs you can replace the troublesome item with another brand for only the cost of shipping. The rapid replacement of the troublesome modem with one that works will save you time and frustration.

Point of inspection

Upon receipt of the computer equipment, you should have a list of items to check. This list will be based on the characteristics described above. You need to confirm the condition, quantity, and conformance of the equipment.

In your purchase order, you can include the note that you can reject equipment based on an inspection of internal components and construction dates. You may go so far as to specify this year's model of computers and other components.

Upon receipt you would open a computer and check several things.

- No sign of previous use
- Damage free
- Date of construction is within specifications
- Certifications of conformance to specified standards
- Internal components match your request (i.e. the make and model of hard drive)
- Proper configuration

Later we will talk about how to prototype and test the equipment in conjunction with software and your internet connection.

Cables are checked for bent pins, cracks in the casing, and other obvious defects. Uninterrupted power supplies are plugged in and charged overnight.

The next day, they are unplugged while running a server and checked for their length of battery support. Routers are hooked to communication diagnostic equipment to assure that all ports are operating.

The results of these inspections are noted and filed with the purchase order. Obvious defects should be flagged and the affected item sent back for replacement.

Basically, you are attempting to weed out major problems before they are installed. Once you start loading an operating system, install software, and connect different components, it becomes expensive to correct major problems.

Evaluating the Bids You Receive

Let's learn about buying computer equipment by going through an exercise based on an actual purchase. The Avix Manufacturing shopping list can be used for this example. It is simple and straightforward. Most likely, a single supplier can meet all of their needs. The question is, which supplier?

Background

The Avix Manufacturing company needs to add a gateway computer, two routers, and an ISDN modem to their existing system. They begin their purchasing process by preparing a request for quote. The first part of the request describes the goals and objectives of the project in general. Following is an abbreviated version of the request.

As you can see from this brief portion of the request, it is fairly easy for Avix to describe what they need, what it will be used for, and when they need delivery. This was sent out to six different hardware suppliers. Four were local and two were national retail units. One of the local stores is also an existing supplier for the company.

Example: Actual quotes received for equipment, which has the best value?

In response, three of the suppliers indicated that they did not wish to bid on the contracts or they did not respond. The other suppliers submitted the following three bids, which are summarized here for brevity.

The purpose of this exercise is to determine which of these bids serve you the best.

Request for Quote—Avix Manufacturing

Items Requested:

1 - 233 Mhz Pentium based computer with 2.5 gig hard drive, 64 megs of RAM memory, 4 PCI slots minimum, CD-ROM drive, 15-inch non-interlaced monitor, and video card with at least 2 megs of memory

3 - 10/100 3Com network interface cards

2 - Bay Network routers

1 - ISDN modem (128K bps)

Bids are due on May 23, 1999 at Avix Manufacturing, 123 Commerce Drive, Kentwood, MI 49508. Contact person is Richard Poor (616) 891-9114. This is a closed bidding process with the contract going to the company providing the best combination of components, service, and price.

Bids should give itemized prices and model numbers. Information on delivery, warranties, and quality assurance should be noted. We will also need three references from companies similar to our own that you have done business with in the past year.

A network map is provided noting where the new components are to be installed. The computer is to be used as a gateway machine for the internet connections and it must be capable of running the software noted earlier in the project description.

Supplier 1:

1 - 233 MHz Pentium machine with 64 megs RAM, 2.5 gig hard drive, video card and 15" monitor, CD-ROM drive - $2,595

3 - Fast EtherLink cards - $270

1 - ZyXel ISDN router - $575

1 - Bay Network router - $823

1 - Zoom ISDN modem - $300

Total: $4,563

Discount: 10% = $4,107

Delivery within 24 hours, 30 days full-return, no-questions-asked policy, 1 year manufacturer's warranty on all parts. Service and repair available at our site or through the manufacturer.

You call the three references for Supplier 1 and find that they all endorse the supplier's products and services. You ask about the substitution of the ZyXel router and the supplier indicates that this should give better compatibility with the ISDN modem and the proposed firewall schemes.

Supplier 2:

1 - 166 MHz Pentium machine with 64 megs RAM, 2.5 gig hard drive, video card and 15" monitor, CD-ROM drive - $2,195

3 - Fast EtherLink cards - $270

2 - Bay Network routers - $1600

1 - ISDN modem - $300

Total: $4,365

Discount: 15% = $3,710

Delivery in two to three days, defective material can be exchanged, one-year manufacturer warranties on all products.

You call the references and they all say that the company provides "O.K." service. You call and ask the supplier about the 166 MHz chip instead of 233 MHz. They indicate that 166 is adequate for the application proposed and will shave $400 off the price of the computer.

Supplier 3:

1 - 233 MHz Pentium machine with 64 megs RAM, 2.5 gig hard drive, video card and 15" monitor, CD-ROM drive - $2,695

3 - Fast EtherLink cards - $270

2 - Bay Network routers - $1,650

1 - ISDN modem - $495

Total: $5,110

Discount: none

Immediate delivery, no-questions-asked exchange policy, 1 year manufacturer's warranty and three year replacement of defective parts by supplier. They also suggest the use of a separate firewall and screening device between the router and the web server to replace the gateway machine at a cost of $2,000.

You call the three references for Supplier 3 and they all report "outstanding" service. You call to ask about the security device and they make a somewhat convincing argument that the gateway machine is "overkill" for the level of security desired.

Now you have to make some decisions. One supplier responded with their idea of which components you should buy. Another responded with exactly what you requested. The third also responded to your request and then proposed an alternative. Two offered a discount and different levels of service. References varied between suppliers. Which offers the best combination of price, service, and delivery?

There is no correct answer. You need to evaluate the existing information against your particular needs. In this case you need to trade off one advantage for another, since no one supplier is outstanding in your three criteria.

However, you are not helpless in this situation. You now are armed with written quotes from three companies. The best warranty, replacement, components, and service potential is supplier number three. Call this supplier and try to negotiate a discount. The gap to close is about $500, to match the quote of the first supplier.

At the same time, if you haven't given up on supplier number two, call them and see what their price is to give you exactly what you asked for in the request. If they cannot do this or seem unwilling, then you can quickly eliminate this supplier.

Finally, you can look at the suggestion of the third supplier on using a dedicated firewall device instead of a gateway computer. If you prefer the ability to have flexibility and upgradability with the gateway machine you might not want to pursue this alternative. However, if you agree with the supplier that this meets your current and future needs, then you can potentially shave $700 from the bid. Still, you will want to ask for a discount.

Summary

This chapter has shown you how to select hardware for your internet project and how to prepare requests for quotes. In Appendix B, an actual request is reproduced in its entirety. You can use this to study the techniques we have discussed in this chapter.

Internet search strings

"computer hardware" + "method of evaluation"

"Software selection methods"

"computer product evaluation"

Also target specific brands and models of equipment in the World Wide Web, newsgroups, and mailing lists.

Internet addresses

The usual companies should be consulted on their network, server, and workstation hardware.

www.pc.ibm.com

www.ibm.com

www.intel.com

www.wyse.com

www.compaq.com

www.apple.com

www.novell.com

Chapter 8
Selecting Software

In many situations, the type of software you wish to run determines your hardware needs. Internet technology is no exception. As discussed in Chapter 7, you can purchase the fastest and most capable hardware available for internet applications; the cost of hardware is now so low there is not much point in trying to economize.

The purchasing of software should occur at the same time as purchasing hardware. The two are strongly interrelated. Therefore, you'll be carrying out steps in this chapter while at the same time you are making decisions about which hardware to buy. In addition, you'll also be investigating your internet connection. These three items constitute the physical components of your internet technology system. As we shall see in later chapters, the cost of hardware, software, and the actual internet connection are going to be a fraction of the money you spend on your internet project.

Selecting the Best Internet Technology Software

Depending on the type of internet connection project you are heading, there can be a wide array of software involved. The minimal amount of software needed is an operating system and packages to create internet content. This would be the case with the Dickerson County school district. Since they are leasing space from the ISP, their only software need is web page creation applications.

Avix Manufacturing will be installing a web server and extending their E-mail system. This will require them to upgrade the operating system they currently use, purchase web page creation software, purchase E-mail software, and invest in a few different security programs.

The Law Firm will be beginning with the internet. They need a new operating system that includes software to serve up web pages, web page creation software, training packages, security programs, and a few other applications. Some of their existing software will have to be upgraded so that its work can be imported directly into the web server.

Megalith will be making a substantial investment in software. Because of the large and wide ranging nature of their project, they will be buying all of the software listed above plus specially designed software just for Megalith and vertical application packages. Therefore, Megalith will be spending the most time evaluating and testing software before it is migrated into the system. Software purchase for Megalith will occur over time, during the implementation phase of the project. Our other three example companies are capable of purchasing all the software at the same time and installing it over a very short amount of time.

The most important point to remember when selecting software is to buy what you need. Because of the advanced planning that involved both goals and objectives, it will be easy for you to determine exactly what you need to make your internet project a success.

Unix versus Windows NT

Most companies have to make a key decision early in the software purchasing process. This involves whether they will be basing their internet technology on an existing operating system, on Unix, or on Windows NT. A company like Avix Manufacturing might already be running NetWare on their local area network. Through careful evaluation they may find that all they need to do is get the web serving software available from Novell. Other companies running proprietary operating systems, such as AS/400, can also purchase internet software designed for that particular platform.

In the majority of situations the decision will come down to whether to use Unix or Windows NT. Both of these are powerful operating systems with a wide variety of internet software available. Both are about equally painful to maintain and support. Unix tends to be the favorite of companies where the IS department has people familiar with Unix and are not afraid to do some serious programming. In this situation, the IS department usually centralizes the internet technology with its own personnel.

In contrast, Windows NT typically requires very little programming and it is fairly easy to teach to people already familiar with the Windows environment. This allows the internet technology to be decentralized across the company. It is also a favorite of companies already running Windows as the chief operating system of the personal computers within their organization. Windows NT has the unique ability to migrate software to these workstations.

Either operating system is more than powerful enough to allow you to load on software such as E-mail servers, web page servers, database applications, and other high-end applications. Both operating systems require a good deal of maintenance. We are still a long way from a "fire-up-and-forget" software environment.

The selection of the basic operating system to run the internet software depends on both the personal and technical preference of your company. If the IS department is already heavily involved with Unix, it would make sense to stay with this operating system. If the company is heavily dependent on Windows as an operating system, then Windows NT may be the logical choice. Another consideration is whether the other internet software you will be selecting can run under one or both of these operating systems.

Analyzing Server Support Software

The next level of decision-making will revolve around the types of servers your company will be purchasing. File serving hardware requires software to complete its mission. With internet technology there are several forms of servers you could load onto a file server. These include:

- Web servers
- E-mail servers
- Database servers
- Audio servers
- Video servers
- Secure transaction servers
- Encryption key server

This is only a partial list. Your company has to look at its internet technology plan and decide which of these types of servers it will be purchasing. Then you have to track down a list of available software.

Let's take a single example, web serving software. This is the software that serves up web pages onto the internet. Let's assume that your company has decided to use Unix as the basic operating system for your web servers. A partial list of software available for web serving applications would be:

- Apache
- Netscape enterprise server
- Netscape fast-track server
- O'Rielly's professional web server
- Other third party web serving software

With a fairly wide selection of possible software you can use, you have to decide the correct package for your mission. At the same time, prices vary widely. Apache software is essentially free. Some of the high-end web serving software can cost thousands of dollars. You need to strike a proper balance between cost and capabilities. In this book, the prejudice leans toward capability. We feel that the most important part of software selection is to fulfill all of your needs and anticipated future needs before considering price.

Checklist of Server Software Needs

In Chapter 6 we discussed how to select the proper software vendor. Now we have to talk about how to select and evaluate software packages. The plan for your internet technology created in the early chapters of this book are now used to help you decide the proper software to use. For server software, this will involve the evaluation of the capabilities of the software versus the anticipated demand that will be placed on your web sites.

The following checklist can be used or modified to assist you in your evaluation method. This is the basic software checklist used for virtually any software package you will evaluate. The first portions of the checklist are used with all software. With each type of software we will be discussing, a module of additional questions can be applied. These will be noted throughout this chapter.

Checklist for Evaluation of Software Before Physical Testing

Name of your project:

Software Package to Evaluate:

Manufacturer of package:

Support Source for package:

Names of evaluation team members:

General Questions:
- Is there an "industry standard" for this type of software?
- Are there any standards this product complies with as required by the project?

Accuracy of Advertising Material:
- Is the advertising provided based on the product and version you are evaluating?
- Are the capabilities stated in the advertising accurate?
- Is the minimum hardware configuration suggested by the software maker realistic?

Their suggested configuration:

Your suggested configuration:
- Does the operating system suggested match your existing system?
- What are the warranty terms?
- Are you buying, leasing, or renting the software? (Check software agreement carefully.)
- Number of users able to run the software:
- What is involved in registration of your copy of the software?
- Other benefits of purchasing the software?

Support within the Software:
- How do you rate the usability of the documentation?
- How well organized is the index, both in the software and in the manuals?
- Is installation fairly straightforward?
- Do you need to make many decisions on configuration?
- Can help files be uninstalled?
- How well organized are the help files?

Perform the following tests of the help files:
1. See how quickly you can find information on connecting to the internet. Is it complete and helpful advice?
2. Look up how to uninstall the program. Does it give complete instructions?
3. Look up the use of encryption technologies.
    - Is the help file clear, concise, and accurate?
    - How often will the product have to be updated or upgraded? What is involved? At what cost?

Technical Support Outside of Software:

- Is a help line provided? What charges?
- Test the help line and measure response time to a question.
- Does the technical support staff seem knowledgeable?
- Will this software require the formation or expansion of your internal help desk?
- Are there software support products available so that users can perform their own diagnostics and troubleshooting?
- Does the technical support organization use good telephone manners?
- How many web sites support this product? Conduct a search.
- How many discussion groups support this product? Conduct a search.
- Does technical support include E-mail, phone, fax, and other support channels? Costs?

References:

- Ask for and check at least three sites already using the software. Ask what jobs the software is performing.
- What do the web sites and discussion groups say about the software?
- Can you work with the local sales representative?

List the key features you want in the software package:

- Ease-of-use:
- Accessibility:
- Security features:
- Performance characteristics:
- Cost of purchase:
- Cost of implementation:
- Cost of support:
- Supportability:

List the mission you have assigned to this software:

- Goals:
- Objectives:

What you are trying to accomplish with this form is to eliminate competing products to reduce your list to two or three products. Then you can begin the physical testing of the software on your platforms to ensure that they will really work. The checklist below is a starting point for designing a procedure for the physical test of software.

A quick word of advice at this point involves initial research described in this checklist. When looking for information on software packages, you will be tempted to study the reviews of software conducted in the popular computer magazines. A major problem with such reviews is that you cannot be sure of the version being tested or whether the tester was being thorough. Many times, these reviews contain facts about capabilities in software that simply didn't work or even exist in the actual product. The lesson here is to use these sources of information sparingly and do your own testing on your own equipment.

Checklist for the Physical Testing of Software

You should set up a prototype platform that matches as closely as possible the hardware configurations to be used in your internet system. The machine should be cleared of viruses and configured to match the machines that will actually be used. All activities on this prototype should be closely monitored and logged. Wherever possible, objective measurement criteria should be used to judge the suitability of software.

Installation:
- Measure the current system resources being used before installation.
- Install the program under the recommended operating system.
    - ✓ Is installation straightforward?
    - ✓ Was the package successfully installed on the first try?
    - ✓ Was technical support required?
    - ✓ What impact on system resources occurred? (RAM memory, processor resources, hard drive space, etc.)
    - ✓ Did instructions match actual installation sequence? Note differences.
    - ✓ Were other software packages on the machine affected?

Running:
- Configure the package for the mission. Develop a simulation of the type of data to be processed by this software.
    - ✓ Does the package handle the type of assignments it is likely to receive?

✓ Does it show signs of needless delays, hangs, lock-ups, interruptions, error messages, or other problems?

✓ What impact on system resources occurred?

✓ Backup the system, erase all directories and restore the backup. Does the software still function correctly?

• Use a specific checklist of tests and results for each package tested.

Stress Tests:

• Load into the package unusual data or large data files to test its ability to be stressed.

— Example: Enter a negative number where only positive values are expected. Any error message? Does it self-correct?

— Example: Load a web page filled with illustrations on a web server and test responsiveness.

— Example: Attach a web page to a huge database and request a complex search.

— Example: Enter strings of data into a form field that are longer than the field. How does it handle this?

— Example: Simulate hundreds of users making a file access at the same time.

Uninstall:

• Upon completion of all tests attempt to uninstall the package.

✓ Does it uninstall completely?

✓ How easy was the process?

✓ What resources were left behind?

• Compare the new system resources report to the one generated before the software was loaded. Are they the same?

Support:

• Open the help files and test the index and searching capabilities. If direct connections from the program to the internet-based technical support is offered, test it.

• Can you connect? Is the information useful?

• Test any support programs provided for this package.

Year 2000 Compliant:

• Will current dates, year 2000 dates, or year 2001 dates cause interruptions in the program?

- Are all date-based functions set for four-digit years?
- Enter 1999, 2000, and 2001 dates and then conduct searches to see if retrieval and operations are consistent.
- Do interface and data storage routines support the year 2000 compliance rules?
- Does the software understand that year 2000 is a leap year?

As you can see, these two checklists are extensive. However, you must be thorough with your software. One of the worst things that can happen to your project is to be several months into implementing a web server to discover it can't perform one of your critical missions.

Example of how the checklists are used for web servers

In this particular example, let's evaluate possible web servers. You can use the basic checklist for software evaluation, but supplement it in a couple of spots for the specific needs of web servers.

For example, first take the mission portion of the checklist and spell out exactly what you expect the web server to do in the internet technology system. Taking the case of the Law Firm, they might create the following list:

Mission—Provide intranet services within the corporation
- Goal—support up to five concurrent intranets
- Goal—support audio and video streaming
- Goal—run under Windows NT
- Goal—cost less than five thousand dollars a year to support

From the statement, they were able to draw several criteria characteristics to use in evaluating the software. One of the areas where the criteria would be most prominent would be in the physical testing of the software. Here the IS manager develops a list of specific performance goals for the software.

For the Law Firm, the checklist might look like this:

1. Load the web serving software. Does it seem to be compatible with the operating system?
2. Load in a standard training package. Are several people able to access the package at the same time?

3. How many simultaneous intranets can be supported on this package?

4. Are there special configurations needed to run in intranets? For example, must the local web be called "localhost" to form an intranet?

5. Is the package compatible with our existing word processing software?

6. Can the new software work with existing database engines?

7. What is the extent of systems resources used by the software package?

8. How are encryption keys managed using this software?

9. Can multiple public keys be presented using this web software?

10. Which web page programming will this package support? HTML? CGI? Java? Perl?

For your specific company, you'll need to look over your goals and missions for the project to develop your own list of criteria. Add these to the checklist already provided. Feel free to remove items that you feel do not apply to your particular situation. What should result is a document you can use to make an objective decision on software for your company.

For web browsing software, it is necessary to find a package that will support both your current needs and future growth plans. It may be enough to have a web server that can support single intranets and several dozen web pages now, but you may find that someday you need one with multiple web capability.

The compatibility of the software packages that will provide content to the web server is also a critical issue. If you planned to centralize the creation of your web content, you need to carefully check that every package you will be providing content for is compatible with the web server. It is not enough to have a package that says it can create HTML compatible files. Each department that is expected to contribute content should prepare a simulated document, page, database, or whatever. These are then fed to the web server and your expected web page creation software. Transfers should be flawless and hassle-free. Otherwise, you will need to budget for better software or more personnel time for conversion.

Selecting the Browser

Once serving software has been selected, you then reach another critical decision. Specifically, you must decide on the internet browser to use throughout your organization. By selecting a single standard browser for all users you can better plan the look and feel of your web site. The type of browser being used will determine what features a web site can successfully present to the user.

The current battle is between Netscape Navigator and Microsoft's Internet Explorer. It is more than just a battle between these two browsers. The version level of the browser is also important. For example, some companies insist on only using version 3. Others are delighted with the additional features of version 4. Earlier versions of both programs are not capable of displaying some of the newer features available to web pages. All have limited capabilities of using add-on programming modules.

Just to complicate the picture, some of the used browsers were bundled with other software that came with your personal computers. Therefore, in most situations you'll discover that your corporation has both types of browsers in several different versions. Eventually, you'll have to decide which will become the official browser of your company.

For the Dickerson County school district they have no choice. The number of parents, staff, and students logging on to the system is so large that they can be assured that several types of browsers are being used. When they reach the page design phase of their project, they will take this into account.

Avix Manufacturing, the Law Firm, and Megalith will all attempt to adopt a standard browser for use within the corporation. This will allow them to carefully design intranets for uniformity of presentation. However, they'll also be sending web pages out onto the internet. On the internet an even wider range of browsers is being used. In some parts of the world text-only browsers for the World Wide Web are still in use.

The best way to evaluate which browser to use is to download from the manufacturer's web site its list of the features offered by the newest version of the browser. This should be compared to your internal needs. Pay particular attention to the amount of resources used by the browser. If it is particularly high, and you have a large number of computers with limited resources, you may want to go down one version level. On the other hand, if you plan to use any of the following applications in your internet technology system, the newest version of either browser is highly recommended.

- Audio
- Video
- Multimedia
- Software migration
- Custom applications
- Java, CGI, Perl, or other programming-intensive content pages

- Any applications which will require the browser to run complex add-ons

The future is interesting for browser software. Already when you load Windows NT, it is the browser that guides you through the process and loads the software for you. The next generation of Windows software promises to be intensively browser based. The current thinking is that software in general is pushing toward the browser model. This will have many implications for your own internet technology plan.

Whatever the future of browser software it will most likely involve needing more RAM and faster processors on each personal computer. Just as the need for CD-ROMs, sound, and high-end video is becoming apparent in business, so will be the need to support the even more powerful browser software.

Selecting Software to Create Content

Now that you have evaluated and selected software to establish your internet presence or corporate intranets, you have to begin selecting programs that can create content to fill your new system. Now you are into an area where there is a very wide range of available programs. Web page creation programs such as FrontPage, Net Objects Fusion, Home Page, Hot Metal, Hot Dog, and HTML Assistant are prominent software packages. However, many existing packages can also translate their contents into Web pages. This includes programs such an Adobe PhotoShop, PageMaker, Office 97, and so on.

In later chapters we're going to point out that existing software can be used as part of the content creation process. For the sake of clarity we'll restrict the discussion right now to software deliberately designed to create internet content; specifically, the web page creation software packages. Later we'll worry about the packages that can support the web design software. This will include the database engines, art design software, video content creators, and so on.

Checklist for Web Page Creation Software

The following checklist can be used as a helpful guide for narrowing down the type of software you wish to select for web page creation.

Checklist for Web Page Creation Software

This checklist should be used to modify the general software checklist presented earlier in this chapter.

Install the demonstration version of web page creation software. Have ready several word processing files representing the different types of software you use within your company. If database applications are desired, have a couple of typical databases created and copied into a separate file that can be used for testing. Also make ready several graphics. This should include graphics that have been converted using other software available to your office into the following formats—.gif, .jpg, .tiff.

- Does software create individual web pages or is it capable of creating webs of pages?
- Open a new web page or web. Create a home page using the word processing files, a spreadsheet, and some of your graphic files.
  - ✓ Is the creation of a new page intuitive?
  - ✓ Do all conversions from data files into your new web page proceed successfully?
  - ✓ Are you able to place elements where you want them on the page?
  - ✓ What size file does your page create? How much of this file size is the sum total of the example data fed into the page?
  - ✓ Does the software offer wizards or other types of systems to help you create pages?
- If so, open the assistance portion of the program and attempt to create another home page.
  - ✓ Is the creation of the new page using the assistant intuitive?
  - ✓ Are there enough choices for formats, graphics, and placement of elements?
  - ✓ Are files converted successfully by the assistant?
  - ✓ Was the creation of the page completed successfully, or would you have to take additional steps?
  - ✓ Are the web pages for a single site easy to organize within the package?
  - ✓ Can you keep pages from different sites separated without trading separate subdirectories?
  - ✓ Is it possible to back up several group web pages? Can webs be backed up to movable media?

✓ Is checking available within the package?

✓ Are your web pages published to your web site? Is a separate FTP program required?

✓ Are templates available to help guide you in the creation of page layout?

✓ Can elements be assigned to multiple pages? For example, can your company logo automatically appear on all pages?

Naturally you would supplement this checklist with additional tests and questions related to the specific mission you wish to accomplish. You would also take time to see if existing software packages can be used for the bulk of content creation. A separate web page creation program is a powerful tool for creating a dynamic web presence. However, it is not always necessary for all applications. This will open the door for something we will discuss in later chapters—the decentralization of the production process.

During the testing of page creation software it is important to have people who will actually be using the software performing the test. This type of software tends to be fairly quirky. It seems to have a personality of its own. Some packages follow well-known models of page creation such as the PageMaker format. Others are very broad HTML editors in which the operator has to visualize the effect of the code being placed on the page.

It is important that the people using the software feel very comfortable with the way the software performs. Part of your checklist should be a subjective measure of how well they like to use the software being tested. Page creation software is also widely discussed on the internet, where you can gather a great deal of information about what people are doing with their software. If you check carefully the web pages you have found in the past that were excellent presentations of information, you could determine what type of software was used to create the page.

Feel free to search the internet for other corporate or business sites that have interesting ways of presenting themselves without fancy multimedia presentations. Send E-mail to the web master of these pages asking which type of software they used. Also ask them how well they like working with the software.

Integrating databases into the web site

Once you have selected your web page content creation software, you can now select the programs that will also support web pages. One of the most popular of the support programs are the database engines that can be integrated into your web page. As mentioned in Chapter 1, it is possible to create web pages that allow browsers to make requests to one or more databases at the same time.

For example, Avix Manufacturing is going to put their price lists on their web page. Putting the price lists into database software allows the company to update the price lists in real-time and have the results immediately available to web pages. Therefore, a price change at 4:00 in the afternoon is seen by web browsers at 4:01.

There are several database engines that can be tied to a web page. The most popular of these are created by Oracle. Oracle software is the most used when an intensive database application is being tied to the web page. For smaller database applications, such as the one at Avix Manufacturing, there are several database engines available, including Access, Approach, FileMaker, and the like.

When you evaluate a database engine for use with a web page there are a few key concepts that are critical to your decision.

1. Does it have a capability of smoothly integrating with your web pages? In other words, can requests be passed from the web page to the database engine through a robust utility? Can data then be passed back to the web page for presentation?
2. Is the speed of response of the database engine fast enough to serve the traffic you expect at your web site?
3. Is the database engine capable of handling the complexity of your database application?
4. Is it fairly straightforward and intuitive for database design and maintenance?

In some high-end applications you'll be required to custom-design the database integration. This can incur a large use of your existing resources. Therefore, you need to balance the power of the database against its ability to work with web pages versus its ease of programming. In the end, prototyping your system will be the only way to be assured you have selected the proper package.

Selecting Security Software

Along with the internet technology software you have been selecting so far, you need to also select the security software that will protect your system. By selecting your operating system and server software first, you will have a better idea of what type of security software will be required.

Both Unix and Windows NT offer existing security levels within the software. For example, in the case of the Internet Information Server (IIS) you can establish user accounts and various levels of file access. Windows NT's NTFS file structure limits the number and types of software that can be used to complement the existing security features.

Next, pull out the list of security threats that you originally brainstormed during the planning phase of your project and pick several of the most critical threats from the list. Design simulations of these types of threats. For example, one threat is that someone will use a password-cracking program to try to get into your system. If you can, download or purchase a program that is used to test the password protection that your security programs present. Otherwise, you can place a person at a terminal to try several thousand possible passwords to see if it is fairly easy to get into your system.

One threat to security you have to simulate very carefully is infection by a virus. Deliberately introducing a virus into your system, even a prototype, is extremely dangerous. Therefore you need to find a virus simulation. This is a small algorithm that will perform some of the characteristics of well-known viruses without actually doing damage or replicating more than once. In other words, it's a great deal like a vaccine virus that is already dead. However, it will leave behind the same traces as a real virus would. Therefore, you can see how effectively anti-virus software finds the source of the problem and eliminates the sites of contamination.

The additional questions you added to the general software checklist would involve the efficiency of the software to be operated, modified, and eventually uninstalled or upgraded. Not only does security software have to be fairly easy to operate, it also should have the additional requirements of protecting itself. You should run some tests to see how difficult it is for a nonauthorized person to reach the security software. When that occurs, the "authorized" person is inside your security system and can alter it to his or her own advantage. For example, entry points into your system can be created for later intrusion. You can quickly see the need to thoroughly test and prototype all security software.

Selecting Utilities
and Programming Languages

Wise general advice on programming languages and utilities that support your web sites is to use it as little as possible. Try to avoid the need for a separate programming language. Once you start writing custom programming modules for your web site, you are greatly increasing the use of your resources and limiting the number of people who can participate in the creation of content. You are also introducing the difficulty of monitoring, inspecting, testing, and troubleshooting software code.

Some of the newer web page creation software packages come with preprogrammed features for common web site applications. For example,

- Discussion groups
- Feedback forms
- Questionnaires
- Online commerce
- Subscription services
- Online training
- File downloading

This eliminates the need to program these applications into your web pages. If you are planning to use any of these types of features with your web site, be sure you test them thoroughly before purchasing the package. Even though the advertisement might say it can perform these functions you may find that some of them in reality will not work with most web servers.

Now let's talk about common utilities that can supplement your web page creation and web server activities. The most popular ones to use are the FTP programs. These allow you to send web pages, databases, and other information files to a web server using the FTP protocol. Thus, a person anywhere in the world with an internet connection can send files to your web sites to have them posted.

The good news here is that most of the FTP utilities are available at no charge. You can go to the internet or your ISP and usually download the files you need.

Another famous utility that has grown into a program of its own is the separate E-mail reader. Most browsers come with their own E-mail reading package. However, you can buy more powerful versions of this utility such as Eudora Pro. These programs allow you to download the E-mail for multiple sites. They have advanced reply and forwarding features. They can also actively filter messages into separate mailbox areas. They can be set up to automatically check your mail at regular intervals and send the unread messages to the E-mail processing software at your workstation.

Training packages, audio file recorders, and video recorders are also available to supplement both the creation of web pages and the browsing of web pages. Plug-ins for the browsers can expand their capabilities to view and interact with web pages. Although useful, it is a good policy to limit the number of plug-ins actually installed in corporate machines to a minimum. The web server or FTP server will have to be configured to make such plug-ins available for dissemination to all workstations. Required plug-ins should be made part of the browser package before the browsers are disseminated.

One of the "must have" utilities for web pages is Adobe's Acrobat. The full-feature program runs on your server or production machine to convert text and illustration files into the standard PDF format. A no-cost reader plug-in program can be downloaded by the users within your company or by people at home from the internet. This allows you to "publish" reports, brochures, and other printed matter in a standard format any internet browser can retrieve.

For example, Turner Classic Movies publishes their monthly schedule with movie listings, photographs, and illustrations in Acrobat. By downloading the file from their web site you can print out a faithful reproduction of the monthly listings magazine on your own printer. This saves time, money, and postal delays. Customers get instant response and publication quality.

The same tactic can be used within a company. However, this means that you will have to expand your checklist for production software to check for the ability to work with Acrobat.

A reality check at this point will show the wisdom of our minimalistic approach to software. The Law Firm discovers that they will need to test MicroSoft Word 7.0 to see if the copy it creates can also incorporate drawings from Corel Draw. At the same time, the resulting documents should be directly transferable into Net Objects Fusion for web pages and Acrobat for .pdf files. Word also has to interface with the other office software so that spreadsheets from Excel and the reports generated by the docket software are all compatible. As you can imagine, this will be quite a test for the software.

Once you decide that you need features beyond what the page creation software offers and the utilities can accomplish, then you are thinking about internet compatible programming languages. These allow you to create special effects, extended features, and other niceties for your web pages, database applications, and so on. The major contenders in this field are:

CGI This stands for Common Gateway Interface and is a set of standardized variables and conventions for moving data between your HTTP service and other applications. This allows data to be transferred between the server and the browsers. This allows you to write programs to perform such tasks as separating data filled out on a form within a web page and sending each piece to the appropriate location on a database.

Java This is an object-oriented programming language created by Sun Microsystems. Java allows you to implant an executable programming code into your web page. Because it is similar to C as a programming language, many people have easily learned its capabilities. It is a very forgiving language that creates fairly robust applets (small applications). Thus, you can program a capability such as a scrolling banner and share the applet with other web page designers.

ActiveX This allows browsers to access MicroSoft system-level resources. This allows OLE, active scripts, other applications, and software components to be accessed and used by the browser. This opens up many ways to liven up the capabilities of web pages.

Perl CGI variables and conventions need a programming language to make creation of applications easier. Perl is one such language. It stands for Practical Extension and Reporting Language. It is a very popular language for CGI programming, especially for Unix systems.

C The C programming language can be used for creating system-level applications. This is a language commonly used for many software applications today. However, you are entering a realm of serious programming work and the consumption of valuable resources.

Scripts and macros Many software packages and some operating systems allow you to write short scripts or macro units of code to control existing applications or to create a new application. Logon scripts are the most common ones encountered for internet applications. Windows NT provides standard scripts you can modify to make log-ons to your ISP automatic and to have interrupted communication lines restored.

As you can see from the discussion of these types of programming languages, their capabilities overlap. You must carefully evaluate the power, ease-of-use, and compatibility of any program language you plan to add to your system. As soon as you add such a capability you now have to think about programmers, debuggers, support, and a variety of other issues. As we shall see shortly, the existing capabilities of web creation software, the need to keep internet presence simple, and the limited availability of resources will justify the position of avoiding programming wherever possible.

HTML is another programming language and a separate subject we will deal with in Chapter 10.

Selecting Vertical Applications and Custom-Designed Software

Commercial software is assumed to be fairly robust, but you will want to perform tests to ensure this assumption. Being robust means that it can survive extended use under normal operating conditions and also survive stressful conditions. Vertical applications software, in contrast, is not always as robust as you would like. Therefore you need to test vertical applications fairly well to make sure they will survive the day-to-day demands of your internet system.

A good example of a vertical application is a special security program designed for a particular type of web server. The market for such a product is typically small. The application is very specific on the jobs it can perform. The checklist we used above for any software would still be in place. You want to be especially sensitive to the accuracy of the documentation and the technical support ability being offered by the supplier.

You may run the same test that we recommended to make sure that the application can withstand the normal use that is expected of the program. However, you would repeat this test under several simulations to ensure that the product is very robust and doesn't crash frequently.

Software being custom designed for your system presents a different problem. In most cases this will be designed module by module by an outside contractor or internal department. Therefore, software will be arriving in stages and needs to be tested at each stage to ensure the success of the overall package. This requires you to develop a series of tests each module must go through before acceptance.

Let's take a specific example. Imagine that your company has hired an outside software contractor to develop a database warehouse application. Three different databases will be accessible through a single web page that allows users to generate any one of a dozen different reports.

The first test will be on the existing databases. Here you will ensure that variables and conventions specified for the database are still in effect and can be reliably used in a new application. You will have to develop subroutines that call for specific variables, fields, and search options. All of these tests should be completed successfully. Any failure should be noted in the system designed around the known failures, and then reduced and corrected.

The second set of tests would look at the integrity of the web page used to create the reports. Here you would ensure that different browsers can use the web page successfully to call up a variety of reports. A third set of tests would be performed on the actual calls for various reports. In this case you would give both valid and invalid requests to the report generator. The request for reports should accurately retrieve the needed information while, at the same time, warning the user of invalid requests.

The final set of tests will be the fully integrated systems. Using the prototype models (see Chapter 9), you can attest to the combined database warehouse under actual users' conditions. This is known as validating the entire application. As you can see, the process of checking and installing custom-designed software can become complex and difficult.

Other Software Options and Actions

This is only a limited look at the types of software involved with an internet technology system, and some of the most common application programs used. In the real world you would be presented with hundreds of choices of programs that you could create to support internet technology.

The trick in being a successful IS manager is using internet technology with the minimal number of software packages for maximum impact. In addition, you must always be forward-looking. New versions of software are released frequently. Each time a revision is released, you must make the decision about whether to upgrade or hang on to the existing version of the software. By having an evaluation procedure already in place, you can make this process much easier.

Upgrading existing software

With every software package you purchase you'll be given repeated options to upgrade to newer versions. These upgrades come in two basic stages. With minor upgrades the version number does not change when the sub version number is increased; for example, an upgrade from version 5.1 to 5.2.

In this situation you must look at the features, fixes, patches, and other characteristics that have changed with the minor upgrade. Then you can evaluate the value of these changes against the cost of the upgrade. You should calculate the cost of the upgrade as well as the expense of buying the software plus the cost of disseminating the new versions to all affected computers. Typically, upgrading a single computer, such as a web server, is fairly inexpensive. In contrast, to upgrade all browsers throughout the corporation can be a time-consuming and expensive proposition. Therefore, you may want to wait for a more serious upgrade.

A significant upgrade is usually indicated when the version number of the software increases; for example, an upgrade from version 4.2 to 5.0. This is supposed to be a major change in the software. That makes your first job an evaluation of whether the upgrade was indeed significant. You should see the following characteristics change in a significant upgrade:

- Look and feel of the user interface
- Major capabilities of the software
- Significant expansion of file formats that can be handled
- Number of other programs with which the program can co-function
- Levels of security

- Speed and accuracy
- System resources used

A significant change in any or all of these characteristics represents a true major upgrade. Once you have established that the upgrade is truly significant, then you need to weigh again the value of the changes against the needs of your system. For example, our office is still using WordPerfect 5.2. Despite several major upgrades of this product, the version we're using still fulfills all the needs we have for word processing. You must always ask yourself whether it's worth the expense and time to upgrade.

Maintaining software

Outside of upgrades, some software requires frequent downloading of patches and fixes to minor problems that are encountered by users. Windows NT is a notorious example of this. When you load Windows NT you also need to load what is called the service pack. Each service pack is the newest set of upgrades, fixes, and patches for the software. From time to time, Microsoft releases new service packs.

FrontPage is another example of software that has had a steady stream of patches released. Recently, the discussion group Wizard had problems that required a patch. The patch can be entered manually by the user. However, the web servers needed a software patch to upgrade their entire level of functionality.

Both of these examples show you why you need to have regular monitoring of software needs. Specifically, for each major software application you purchase, someone should be assigned the task of regularly checking with the manufacturer on upgrades, patches, and other related issues. The internet is an excellent way to stay in touch with any changes being made to software. By bookmarking the location of the software manufacturer you can regularly review any upgrades that are being proposed or offered for immediate download.

This, of course, requires that you have a written procedure on how this will be done. The procedure needs to state who will be in charge of these activities, when they will be conducted, and to whom the information will be submitted for approval. You must resist the urge to automatically upgrade software when changes are made available. Instead, each opportunity for upgrading must be evaluated. Patches and fixes should be tested on the corporate prototype machine to make sure they will not have disastrous effects on existing configurations.

Finally, you need to investigate the field of configuration management. Somewhere you need the database of the current versions and characteristics of the software you have in use. The internet technology system should be a complete database in and of itself.

Evaluating the readiness of existing software to join the internet system

You will come across situations where existing software can be integrated into your internet system. For example, a new page layout program purchased by the production department has the capability of generating web pages and web content. The production people use the package to create user instructions for their products. They would like to have copies of these instructions posted to the technical support web page of your corporation.

This now presents you with the issue of accepting an already purchased software package into the internet technology system. The checklists we listed above would not be used in their entirety. Hopefully, the production people performed many of these tests when they purchased the package. This is the issue you need to discuss with them directly. What you need to do is to use the portions of the checklists that apply to the software's compatibility with your current internet system. A series of tests should be designed to verify the adequacy of the software to participate in your system.

You'll also want to discuss the issue of security, access, and accepted usage of the software. These should be spelled out in a short memo to the production people. For example, you may want to agree on the system the production department creates. The work instructions and templates are created and then copied to file servers in the IS department. Here your web page creation specialist will use the files to create the necessary technical support pages. At the same time, the template used for formatting technical support web pages is shared with the production department.

In this way you are mutually confirming the level of quality the corporation expects within its internet presence.

Exercise: Form a list of your additional software needs

When it comes to the maintenance and upgrading of software, you need to form an action plan to combat obsolescence as well as unnecessary expansion. This action plan can be formed by creating a list of all your anticipated future needs in software. For each major software package you use, note the anticipated need for upgrades, maintenance, and other changes.

Checklist for additional software needs

Operating System:
- Upgrades anticipated by date:
- Necessary maintenance:
- Fixes and patches:
- Reconfigurations:
- Other changes:

Web Serving Software:
- Upgrades anticipated by date:
- Necessary maintenance:
- Fixes and patches:
- Reconfigurations:
- Other changes:

Other Server Programs (please list):
- Upgrades anticipated by date:
- Necessary maintenance:
- Fixes and patches:
- Reconfigurations:
- Other changes:

WebPage Creation Software:
- Upgrades anticipated by date:
- Necessary maintenance:
- Fixes and patches:
- Reconfigurations:
- Other changes:

Utilities:
- Upgrades anticipated by date:
- Necessary maintenance:
- Fixes and patches:
- Reconfigurations:
- Other changes:

Programming Languages:

- Upgrades anticipated by date:
- Necessary maintenance:
- Fixes and patches:
- Reconfigurations:
- Other changes:

Security Software:

- Upgrades anticipated by date:
- Necessary maintenance:
- Fixes and patches:
- Reconfigurations:
- Other changes:

For each of the listed programs you would describe as nearly as possible the anticipated needs. Let's look at a brief example of this list for MicroSoft's Internet Information Server (IIS).

Web Server IIS:

- Upgrades anticipated by date: Version 3.0 in 4th quarter 1998, 4.0 in 1999;
- Necessary maintenance: Service pack roughly every six months
- Fixes and patches: Weekly monitoring, only about three approved patches per year
- Reconfigurations: Change to intranet applications 1st quarter 1999, Change network role to primary domain server in 2nd quarter 1999
- Other changes: none

This information is then used to form a project management timeline for upgrades, maintenance, and other fixes for the entire internet technology system. You now know that you will need a couple of technicians familiar with Windows NT around December of 1998 and January 1999. The first project will be the upgrading to version 3.0. The second project will be a reconfiguration to add an intranet a month later. By adding time involvements and other resource information you can also budget for the regular servicing of the software resources of your internet services.

Further References

It is highly recommended that you obtain the popular computer guidance books on target software you're considering to gain a greater insight into the product's performance and features. For example, *Windows 95 for Dummies* up to the *Complete Guide to Windows 95* and the *MSCE Certification Course* for Windows 95 can provide you with valuable data. These books are typically written for audiences such as the novice user, expert, administrator, or technician. Choose the ones that match your audience and scope of application. Go to www.amazon.com to get a current listing of books for particular software packages.

Internet Search Strings

"Software Evaluation" + Windows 95

"Software Evaluation" + Unix or Linux

"Software Evaluation" + Web Servers

"Unix support group"

"Internet related software" + "user group" or "support group"

"Security software"

Internet Sites

www.microsoft.com

www.netscape.com

Chapter 9
Establishing
an Internet Connection

At last we reach the core of your project, to make the actual connection to the internet. This is the whole point of this book and your internet technology system. It is no accident that the actual intention of your project occurs nine chapters into the book. Without the thinking, planning, testing, and documentation we have already done, the connection would be problematic at best.

The connection to the internet is likely to be the biggest bottleneck in your entire system. While your network is communicating at 100M bps, a bad internet connection can drop that to speeds of 56K bps or less. Magnitudes of lower speeds can quickly cripple your system. The intention of this chapter is to help you find the connection that is fast and reliable enough to cause no pain to your users.

Normally, the discussion of internet connectivity is a discussion of dedicated data lines. Before we talk about dedicated lines we need to discuss their alternatives. Many people are not aware that there are other alternatives for finding a connection to the internet for your company. These alternatives must be studied and rejected before you proceed to the dedicated data line selections.

The reason that you studied these alternatives first is for the occasional situation your company finds that one of the alternatives makes more sense than paying a high monthly fee for a dedicated data line to the internet. The two basic alternatives are using ISP equipment and forward-locating a server for your network.

Evaluating the ISP

In the case of the Dickerson County school district, the IS manager realized early on there are several advantages to renting space at an ISP. Most of the school district is going to be represented by a single web site. The need for communications between schools was minimal. The same was true of the amount of E-mail that was expected to come from parents and students. The cost of a single web site with all the features necessary to support their mission was only $15 a month.

Obviously, the cost of having their own web server, data connection, and backup system was a far greater expense than merely renting space from a web hosting service. For most small businesses performing low-level commerce on the internet, this option makes sense. The cost of a web site that supports money transactions with a security agreement is usually less than $50 a month.

When you compile your list of goals and objectives for your internet technology system, you should calculate the annual cost of running the system and the total capital investment in the system. Then you should compare this to the cost of creating the same system on rented space at an ISP. You may be surprised to discover that it is more economical to rent the space. This also means that backup, upgrading, and technical support will be problems handled by the ISP.

At the same time, you must also make considerations for how much control you want over your system and how big an issue security will be. Let's look at an example of a company that would probably benefit by just renting space at an ISP. The Brown Sharp Knife Company produces 50 different products which it sells to the public through catalogs. The business does less than a million dollars in sales per year. All of their sales are done through catalog shopping.

This small company decides that they need an internet presence. They decide to set up a web site which will advertise the different products they offer. An order form will be provided so that people can use a charge card to order any of their items. Orders are E-mailed to their sales department, which then fulfills the order and ships the product. The knife company anticipates that an average day will see about a hundred or fewer orders coming in from the internet.

Such a web site would need less than five megs of memory storage and a few E-mail addresses. This could be rented from an ISP for about $30 a month. The site would rarely change since new products are only introduced about once every three months. Clearly it would make economic sense to rent the space rather than to invest in the hardware, software, and internal technical expertise required to run a single web site.

The following would be reasons to reject the alternative of renting space at an ISP:

- Multiple web sites
- Need for high security
- Need for direct control of hardware
- Use of large areas of disk space as part of web site
- Incorporation of corporate E-mail system
- Need for multiple web servers
- High volumes of traffic expected
- Requirement for high levels of reliability
- Use of intranet

There are other reasons you may find to reject this option. However, rented space on an ISP could be part of your redundancy plan to insure continuous internet presence. The web sites that are presented to the public could be copied and stored at an ISP. Traffic could be routed to these backup sites in the event of a massive failure within your own system.

Most companies will find that they can easily reject this option for their internet technology system. Therefore, you examine the next option.

Located-forward web server

A good ISP will have a combined communication line system that provides 10 megs a second and greater speeds to the internet. A really good ISP will let you link your web server directly into their network so that you can access these speeds. We recently were quoted a price of $175 per month for this service. Our server would be physically located at the ISP (hence the name "located forward"). The connection would be directly to the ISP's network via the network interface card.

The primary advantage here is that you are able to achieve connection speeds much greater than the one that is normally available for your company. As you'll see below, the cost per month is much smaller than a dedicated data line running at much slower speeds. Therefore you get a more efficient and wider bandwidth access.

Unfortunately, this massive bandwidth comes at a price. Because your server is located at the ISP, access, control, and security become serious issues. You'll never be quite sure who has access to your machine. The possibility of theft, fire, and other hazards are also hard to predict. However, you can run an inexpensive dedicated data line directly to your web server so that you can post web materials directly from your corporate site.

This results in an option that can give your company tremendous bandwidth at a low price. This would be desirable in the situation where a company wishes to present web pages to a very wide audience and security is not an issue. An example of this would be a public service organization that would provide valuable information to the public. At the same time, they would have a very limited budget.

The recent example of an organization that required a large bandwith for a short period is the Jet Propulsion Laboratory. When photographs from the Mars surface and from the Mars orbiter were returned, literally millions of people a day attempted to download these images. The need for bandwidth was so large that the Jet Propulsion Laboratory has voluntary sites that duplicate the information. This gives the average internet user several locations from which to get the same photograph. As bandwidth on one site becomes clogged, other sites are still open for business.

Locating a server forward also gives your company the ability to test its web presence before making major commitments to the internal hardware and human resources. In other words, when you are not certain how much bandwidth you need for your connection, you can always test from the ISP site using a less expensive option to determine the actual number and sizes of dedicated data lines to put in place.

It also gives you the option of breaking off some of your more popular public services and placing them on a located forward server to free up your internal bandwidth at the company, especially your existing internet connection lines. For example, if your company created a search engine that helps customers locate competitive information from hundreds of internet sources, you may find that a flood of traffic to this one feature is tying up your connectivity. By moving it to a separate server located at the ISP, you can accommodate the large traffic volume while freeing up bandwidth for company employees.

Forming a Direct Internet Connection

To understand how to connect your company to the internet, you must first understand how the telephone system works. The internet is actually a series of high-speed backbone data lines stretched all over the world. In a country such as the United States, access to these backbones is controlled by a handful of companies. Typically, the long distance telephone companies have access to the internet. These are companies such as AT&T, Sprint, MCI, and so on. They make the connection between the internet backbones and your local telephone provider. The point where the hand-off occurs between the long distance network and your local provider is called the point of presence or POP.

When you make your connection to the internet what you are actually doing is finding an internet service provider that will lease to you dedicated data lines connected to their POP source. This allows your company to have a dedicated connection to the POP source and to the long distance network and eventually to the internet backbone.

Also available are companies such as UUNet that will lease you a data line directly to the backbone. However, you must use caution in selecting your method of connection. First of all, you want to find a lease data line that stays within your local telephone system. Otherwise you'll be paying long distance charges on top of the lease rates for the line. Second, the phone companies that sell you the leased lines tend to forget to tell you about their lower-cost options available. Therefore, arm yourself with as much information about the services available as possible. This will help you to hold down costs and can help you deliver the highest quality line to your company.

When you're shopping for an ISP, one of the key issues will be the amount of service they provide with a leased line. You'll need an ISP that already has a large bandwidth connection to the internet. Then you want to find an ISP that can also configure and install your leased data lines. Better still, find one that also provides technical support for keeping the data line running trouble free.

Finally, a critical decision is to select the correct data line for your application. Although the cost of dedicated data lines continues to fall, most of them are not inexpensive. At the same time, the dedicated data line is one of the great sources of bottlenecks in network communications. Therefore you must select wisely when choosing a dedicated data service.

Selecting the Right Connection

To make the right selection you need to first understand the choices. There are three basic types of data communication lines available. They are:

- Analog services
- Switched digital service
- High-speed dedicated service

We need to take a moment to discuss the features and limitations of each of these potential services.

Analog services

In almost all cases analog services will be greatly avoided in commercial applications. Analog services are the use of voice telephone lines and telephone modems. This is in the realm of the 28.8, 33.6, and 56K bps modems. These types of connections are best used for linking a single user to a single remote computer. They can also be used for individual access to their own private internet account.

Digital information from the computer is translated into analog form and then sent down standard telephone lines to the waiting computer. Although it is possible to connect the web server to the internet over a 56K bps modem, you'll find service frequently losing contact with the data line. On a good day it can support up to 20,000 requests for web pages.

Therefore analog services are best used by individuals or by a company that wants a low-cost option for testing a web service prototype. A 56K bps ISP account, which can be left on at all times for 24-hour testing will cost about $50 a month. This gives you an inexpensive option for testing select hardware. However, experience shows this is not the best way to test prototypes and should probably never be used for your web server to present web pages to the public. In practice, transmission rates are usually 40K bps or lower.

Installation of analog service is fairly easy. You install the dedicated telephone line in your office the same way you would any telephone extension. With your modem you dial into the ISP to a number that allows a dedicated link. If your ISP is in your local phone area you will pay only a few cents for each call you make. If you write a script to run online each time the connection is dropped, you can keep a pretty consistent connection.

Analog services use one of two types of protocols: either the serial line internet protocol (SLIP) or the point-to-point protocol (PPP). SLIP is known as a packet framing protocol. It takes data packets from one network and transforms them into a stream of IP data grams to be sent to another network. It allows data to move smoothly from one network to another over analog phone lines. This is done one piece of data at a time and thus, the name serial.

The PPP is much more sophisticated than SLIP. It realizes that error checking is already being done by TCP internet. Therefore it takes away the need for error correction sequencing or flow controls. This gives the protocol simplicity, transparency, and great efficiency. PPP is noted for its ability to squeeze the most out of a given bandwidth. It is frequently the first choice of a company using an analog phone connection to the internet.

Switched digital service

Telephone companies today are not made up of just analog telephone lines. In the last two decades there has been a considerable effort to install widespread digital service. Digital telephone systems such as the PBXs are what run most corporate phone systems. Digital phone service was originally installed to improve voice quality and add features to the existing phone system. Unfortunately, the phone systems did not anticipate the explosive growth of the internet. The hardware was focused on voice use and not data.

However, the phone companies are moving rapidly to correct this problem. High-speed dedicated digital data service is available with many new services now being designed and delivered. This includes services such as the dedicated 56 KB data line, 64 KB dedicated data line, and ISDN services.

Let's begin with the dedicated 56 KB digital data line. Digital communications for data transfer are greatly preferred over analog. First of all, very little translation of the data is required. Second of all, digital lines are very robust against noise. This makes digital lines extremely reliable. Digital processing also allows a lot more information to be fed to them with the same size copper wire, increasing bandwidth.

One version of a dedicated data service is the switched connection. This is where the telephone company creates a dedicated circuit between your company and the ISP. The circuit is only opened upon request. Thus, you only pay for the amount of time actually used. For companies making outside connections to the internet for occasional research and other internet requests, this is a viable option.

For companies wishing to hook their web server to the internet, they need around the clock continuous service. They need to get a dedicated data line. This is simply a telephone line which always remains open between your company and the ISP. The telephone company then charges you the price of using one circuit full-time. You'll find such dedicated data lines can cost anywhere from around $100 to $200 per month.

At the same time, you'll need to use a router at each end of the dedicated data line. The router will also require a Channel Service Unit (CSU) and a Data Service Unit (DSU). The Channel Service Unit provides the interface between your network and the telephone company's network. The Data Service Unit provides filters for the digital signal, synchronizes the signal, and provides all needed network control. A good ISP will provide you with the equipment you need, already configured so that you can set up your dedicated data line as quickly as possible.

You should also be aware that dedicated data lines take time to install. The typical wait for dedicated data line is at least three weeks. When planning your internet technology system, allow plenty of lead time for the dedicated lines to be selected and installed. Plus, you also have to account for testing. Make sure that all of the equipment and configurations are correct to support the dedicated data line.

ISDN

Integrated Services Digital Network (ISDN) is one of the fastest-growing, most popular, and most controversial of the dedicated data lines. ISDN is basically a bundling of dedicated 64 KB data lines in the various forms of telephone service. Not only can you make connections to the internet using the service, you can also provide voice transmission, fax service, and other forms of digital communications over the same twisted pair of wires.

Unfortunately, there is no universally accepted format for presentation of ISDN services around the world. You have a wide range of formats, configurations, and services to select from under the name ISDN. Let's look at the basics of ISDN to understand how you make a wise decision in selecting this service.

The most common format of the ISDN service is called the basic rate ISDN (BRI). This is actually three communication channels delivered over a single twisted-pair wire. There are two 64K bps channels referred to as the B channels. A third channel is called the Delta channel or D channel. This channel is used for the coordination of the two B channel operations.

When you select a dedicated 64K bps data line you are really getting just one of the two B channels activated. In most situations you'll be selecting the full BRI service. This is where both B channels are used to transmit data from your site to your internet service provider. Other formats of ISDN will allow the B channels to transmit voice, video, fax transmissions, and other services at the same time.

For the point of this discussion, you'll be looking for the ISDN service that provides dedicated data lines. You'll need to have ISDN modems with network terminators placed at the end of the connection. A similar set of hardware will be placed at the ISP. At your end of the connections, the router is connected to the ISDN modem. This allows digital signals to be routed to the ISDN line and then upstream to the ISP. Here their routers send the data packets on to the internet.

With the two B channels bonded together as a dedicated data line you achieve an effective 128K bps of transmission speed. All in all this sounds like an excellent and inexpensive way to have a dedicated data line. Currently Ameritech is offering ISDN service for $42 per month. If the ISP is in your local telephone area, there are minimal phone charges. However, the ISP will typically charge about $200 a month for the dedicated access account.

There are also several problems associated with the use of ISDN service. The largest of these is the fact that is not available in all areas. Your company has to be located within 18,000 feet of a telephone switching site to receive ISDN service. Therefore, you run into situations like we have at our office. We live in a small rural village just outside a medium-sized city. The medium-sized city has ISDN services available throughout the metropolitan area. We have access in the small village because the fiber-optic telephone cable runs through the village and has a switching station. However, the next village just seven miles down the road does not have ISDN service. They do not have a telephone switching office with ISDN capability.

Another problem is that the telephone companies will attempt to sell you more ISDN service than you really need. A short conversation with our ISP revealed that we wanted to order the following from the phone company.

- BRI service
- Two channels only, no D channel
- Data only usage
- Two-wire connection to our building's demarcation point
- No inter-LATA
- No intra-LATA
- No long-distance

The elimination of the D channel saved some money because we don't need to coordinate a dedicated line. Specifying data only prevents the telephone company from charging you for voice availability and other services you will not be using. Connecting a two-wire line to the demarcation point limited labor and parts to $60. We connected a twisted pair from the demarcation point into our office using the existing telephone wiring. Knocking out LATA and long-distance phone services eliminates their ability to charge you a monthly fee for these services. You don't need these on a dedicated line to a local ISP.

You should also be aware that when you make an ISDN connection you are really making two phone calls. Each line is treated separately. You get a separate phone number for each line. In turn, when you dial you connect to two phone lines at the ISP. Once connected you usually stay that way on an ISDN line. Failure rates are a tiny fraction of a percent.

Finally, you should establish ISDN service for data only. Although you can send voice and other transmissions across an ISDN line at the same time data is being transmitted, this is not recommended. Inevitably, someone places a phone call at the moment of peak data transmission. The result is a serious delay in data response for internet requests.

T1 and T3—The most popular high-speed dedicated lines

The T-carrier services are able to deliver very high data rates over local and wide area telephone services. Much like the ISDN lines they can carry both voice and data transmissions. With T1 there is the D channel to control transmission. It is controlling 24 B channels bundled together. Each B channel is a 64 KB digital line. This gives you the total throughput of 1.544 megabits per second.

The T3 service is the equivalent of 28 T1 lines. This produces a total throughput of 44.736 MB per second. If you are running a local area network at 10 MB per second you can see that this type of dedicated data line produces a bandwidth larger than the communications speed of your network.

ISPs tend to use either T1 or T3 lines to make their connections to the internet. When you lease space at an ISP you're actually leasing a piece of the bandwidth that they control. The ISP that we use for testing has three T3 lines, each leased from a different long distance carrier. There is redundancy so that if one long distance carrier loses service the other can take over. It would take a failure of three separate phone companies to bring down their internet connection.

It is also possible to lease a fraction of one of these dedicated data lines. What our ISP does is let you actually share some of the B channels in their bundle. This gives you the flexibility to choose the exact amount of bandwidth you need for your particular application. It also gives you an upgrade path. You can start with, say, a fractional T1 and later move up to a full version of the T1 circuit.

However, once you start talking about T1 and higher speed dedicated data lines, you've entered a new universe of internet connectivity. Installations, support, and usage of these lines require exponentially higher amounts of your resources. For example, a T1 dedicated data line costs about $1,200 a month. This is not including the $2,300 fee to put the line in your company. Then there's a host of equipment that must be connected by both the ISP and the telephone company to make the circuit work. When we installed our T1 we learned how many different labor agreements are involved with the connection of the circuit. One person was responsible for bringing the cable into the building. Another was responsible for actually connecting to the hardware. A third person had come to do the physical separation and splicing of the line. A fourth person had to come to configure the equipment to accept the T1. A fifth person had to actually string the final data line to our computers. You get the picture.

Therefore, you do want to investigate turnkey solutions to T1 connections. The same is true of T3 connections. There's a lot of equipment involved at the telephone company and the installation. In our case the telephone company installed a second, redundant line. That means that all of the physical equipment supporting the telephone communications portion of the line had backup units that would take over any component that failed.

Today it is possible to buy some of the equipment you need to make the T1 connection. Routers are being equipped with CSU/DSU units that allow you to plug directly into a T1 lead-in. However, you'll want to talk with your ISP about the configuration that is required for this type of high-speed dedicated digital line.

In short, plan to have the telephone company and the ISP contracted to install these types of connections.

Other connection options

Beyond T3 is there is a whole class of dedicated digital lines that are based on fiber-optics. These are based on the Synchronous Optical Network standard, or SONET. These carry names like OC-3 and OC-48. These optical cables are capable of carrying massive amounts of data. For an example, an OC-3 circuit can carry 155.52 megabits of data per second. One of the web posting sites that we work with uses three OC-3 circuits. Data speed goes as high as 488.32 megabits per second.

This allows you to transmit both voice and video along with your data across your internet connection. These types of connections are for extremely serious internet usage. These and the TE carrier lines can also be used as a physically linked local area network. We will look at how that is done a little later in this chapter.

Another option is the frame relay. The frame relay is based on two principles. The first is the way you are sending data. It is assembled into frames. These frames are sent through what is called a virtual circuit. The virtual circuit is the second important concept of frame relay.

A virtual circuit allows several connections to be made across a single physical circuit. You can develop any one of a variety of wide area network connections. Basically you send information from your company through a leased data line to a frame relay site. This site will then re-transmit your data frames to several other connected sites at the same time. This replaces your need to have dedicated data lines between all of your remote locations.

Instead, each location is connected to a central frame relay site. Flow control at the frame relay steers messages around areas of congestion and delivers data frames to the correct locations.

In short, frame relay is something to investigate if you have wide area network needs. You can also use it for internet time, although its usefulness for this is somewhat limited.

Beyond these options there are also microwave transmission possibilities and satellite communications. These are extremely complex and very expensive modes of achieving dedicated data lines. Most companies will not have to worry about these.

Exercise: Calculate Connection Needs (A Progressive Checklist)

To install a dedicated link to the internet requires you to select the correct amount of bandwidth. Then you work closely with your ISP for the actual configuration and installation of the selected line.

Let's begin with an exercise to help you select the correct bandwidth for your application. This will require a bit of estimating on your part and should give you a rough idea of which dedicated connection to begin with. Following is a basic formula to use to calculate the amount of bandwidth you might need.

Web demand + E-mail demand + other internet services demand
+ overhead = bandwidth required

Web demand is the number of hits you expect on your web sites multiplied by the average size of your web pages. What you are trying to do is estimate how many megabytes of data need to flow each hour. To make the calculations realistic you need to make an estimate for your peak hour of the day. Let's assume that you are running a single web site and estimate that you will have 500 hits during the peak hour of the day. The average size of your web pages are 12 KB. Thus,

Web demand = 12,000 x 500 = 6,000,000 or 6 MB/hour

The number and average size of E-mail messages flowing into and out of your system also has to be calculated. You will need to estimate the number of E-mails sent and received during the peak hour times along with the number of people using E-mail. For illustration purposes, we will assume that 25 staff people will send and receive an average of 10 E-mails during peak hours. The average size of these is 3 KB. Thus,

E-mail demand = 25 x 10 x 3,000 = 750,000 or 0.75 MB/hour

Next is an estimate of your other internet services. This would include activities such as Telnet, FTP, Usenet, and so on. Let's assume that your site offers a Usenet service and FTP service for customers to download demonstration software. At peak hours you expect 2 megabytes of FTP activity. Your Usenet feed is described by the provider as needing 80 megabytes per hour to download the hourly updates. Therefore your other internet services demands are,

Other internet services = 2 + 80 = 82 MB/hour

Finally, there are overhead activities on your web site. These include security activities, DNS, routing, and the like. The volume of this can be estimated by monitoring resource usage during prototype testing. For the purposes of our illustration we will assume that you need another 2.5 megabytes per hour to support ongoing activities. This gives the following total peak requirement:

6 + 0.75 + 82 + 2.5 = 91.25 MB/hour

You can subtract from this total if you are using gateway servers with caching or other internet caching services. These can reduce the total throughput placed on your connection. In this case, none is assumed to be in place as a safety factor in the estimation.

What remains is to calculate the number of bits per second this represents and then select the data line that best fits the peak rate. To do this we have to convert our final figure into bits, then divide by minutes and seconds. (There are 1,048,576 bytes in 1 MB and 8 bits per byte.) The formula is,

Peak requirement in MB/hr x 1,048,576 bytes x 8 bits ÷ 60 minutes ÷ 60 seconds = data bits per second

In our example,

Peak requirement = 91.25 MB x 1,048,576 x 8 = 765,460,480 bits an hour ÷ 60 minutes = 12,757,674 bits a minute ÷ 60 seconds = 212,627.9 bits a second

A 56K modem could not handle this load. (A modem is an analog line and cannot handle the digital routing of an internet connection anyway.) Therefore, the chart you use to find the best connection line begins with digital services.

56K bps dedicated digital line = 56,000 bits per second
64K bps dedicated digital line = 64,000 bits per second
ISDN service = 128,000 bits per second
Fractional T1 = 128,000 bits per second with 64,000 increments available
Full T1 service = 1,544,000 bits per second
Fractional T3 service = between 1,544,000 and 44,000,000 bits per second
Full T3 service = 44,736,000 bits per second
OC-1 service = 51,840,000 bits per second
OC-3 service = 155,520,000 bits per second
OC-12 service = 622,080,000 bits per second
OC-24 service = 1,244,160,000 bits per second
OC-48 service = 2,488,320,000 bits per second

As you can see there is a wide range of selection for services. It takes a considerable amount of traffic to demand a service above T1 speed. In our illustration, the T1 speed is more than adequate.

Example: Avix Manufacturing's needs

Let's take a moment and look at a couple of examples of how these calculations would fare with two of our example companies. As you look through these examples, note particularly the small sizes of the web pages and the E-mail being sent. The actual sizes of web pages and E-mail in your company will vary from these numbers. The figures we are using are small because the procedures described later in this book will encourage the use of minimal web resources.

You can discover the average size of web pages that you will create through prototyping, inquiry to the software producer, or the educated opinions of people experienced in this field. Overhead can be estimated by using prototype exercises and by observing how much hard disk space is being consumed by management operations. You can also monitor the amount of data flowing over your communication lines during the processing of internet services. By subtracting the amount of data that you intended to send you get a rough estimate of the overhead being used.

In the first example, the IS manager at Avix Manufacturing needs to estimate bandwidth that will be required to support the internet services. As you may recall, Avix will be setting up a single web server which will be presented to the public. Therefore, the communication line will run from this web server to the ISP. E-mail sent by staff to the internet and received from the internet will also run up and down the line. FTP service is being established so that customers can download copies of the catalog or specifications as data files. In other words, this is a fairly light use of the data line connected to the internet. Because it has to be available 24 hours a day and be very reliable, a dedicated digital line is necessary.

The IS manager looks at peak usage for the data line. Some of the new services coming online are rated according to actual usage of the line. It may be better to estimate an average use of the line and leave enough room for peak performance. In this case we will assume that peak performance is the major concern for the dedicated line.

The IS manager begins by estimating that peak hours on the web site will receive 2000 hits. The average size of their text-based web pages is 7 KB. (Remember a KB = 1024 bytes.) Thus,

2,000 hits x 7,168 bytes per page = 14,336,000 bytes an hour or over 14 MB per hour

There are 180 employees within Avix that will have access to E-mail. Assume that in a peak period the average employee would send and receive about five E-mail messages each with an average of 8 KB. The resulting data demand would be,

180 employees x 5 E-mails x 8,192 bytes = 7,372,800 bytes per hour or over 7 MB per hour

Taking the size of the catalog file and the likely number of people to download it within one hour, the IS manager estimates that the FTP service will consume about 25 MB per hour. At the same time, three of the staff people are going to be conducting regular research on the internet. It is estimated that they will consume almost 6 MB per hour. Supporting all this would be close to another 1 MB of data for overhead. The addition of all of these demands would result in the total demand of,

14 MB + 7 MB + 25 MB + 6 MB + 1 MB = 53 MB per hour

Because a megabyte of data represents 1,048,576 bytes of data you need to multiply that number by 53 megabytes and then by 8 bits per byte to get the number of bits per hour. This, in turn, is divided by 60 twice to calculate the number of bits per second. That is,

$$\frac{53 \times 1,048,576 \times 8}{60} \div 60 = 123,498.95 \text{ bits per second}$$

Now using the chart on page 214 you can see that the ISDN line is more than adequate to handle this load. For about $200 a month, Avix Manufacturing can establish their internet link and expect to endure peak demands.

As you do your own calculation you'll no doubt come up with a figure higher than these. Yet, most IS managers are surprised to learn how small a dedicated line you need to handle some fairly large loads of data. For example, we have tied together the local area networks of major firms using nothing more than dial-up ISDN service. To this day we have yet to maximize the capability of these data lines despite the heavy traffic being sent across them.

Example: Megalith's needs

Stepping up to the much more demanding and larger scale, Megalith Corp. would expect the need for either multiple dedicated data lines or a very large pipeline to the internet. This example will demonstrate that they could be wrong on both accounts.

Megalith plans to have at least six web servers and two E-mail servers connected to the internet. Then they will have to make a key choice on whether each server should have its own dedicated line or whether to set up a gateway machine with a proxy server and hook all internet serving devices to this one gateway. Before making that decision, they will want to see what the total data demand is for the corporation's world headquarters.

The IS manager estimates that each web server will receive up to 2,500 hits per day. The average web page will be 9 KB in size. This creates a web demand of almost 129 MB per hour at peak periods.

6 servers x 2,500 hits per hour x 9,216 bytes per page = 138,240,000 bytes per hour
138,240,000 ÷ 1,048,576 = approx. 132 MB per hour

With 5,000 staff members each sending an average of 10 E-mails an hour and each E-mail message averaging about 8 KB, the E-mail demand is expected to be close to 391 MB per hour. In addition, the corporation will be piping both audio and video data to internet customers. This is expected to require 1200 MB per hour. The FTP service will add another 80 MB per hour. The Usenet connection will require 100 MB per hour and the telnet activity an additional 40 MB per hour. Overhead for operations will be at least five MB per hour.

Expected Peak Demand = 132 + 391 + 1200 + 80 + 100 + 40 + 5 = 1948 MB per hour

Performing the equation that translates this figure into bps results in the following:

$$\frac{1948 \times 1{,}048{,}576 \times 8}{60} \div 60 = 4{,}539{,}169 \text{ bits per second}$$

In other words, fractional T3 service would easily handle these peak loads. A multiple full T1 service could be an option, but the company would have to see the price for the fractional line versus full service. At the same time, they would want to have the margin built in so they could accommodate any sudden growth in their internet system.

As you may have been able to observe in these calculations, there are a couple of key points that determine the amount of data flow you need for your internet connection. The first is the average size of the data files that are being sent up and down the internet line. A web site that has very small text-based files requires very little bandwidth. The same web site with the same number of hourly hits using audio files, video files, multiple graphics, or any other source of larger data files will quickly consume your bandwidth.

Another big consumer of bandwidth is the number of hits the web site receives. A small company on a good day will only get about 2,000 hits on its site. A popular financial advice area on the internet can receive over 21 million hits on a single day when the stock market is in crisis. Web sites supporting breaking news stories have been known to receive over 10 million hits in a single day. Individuals, such as the JenniCam, have had to lay in multiple T3 lines to support the number of hits their site receives.

The lesson to be learned here is that these calculations need to be realistic in your estimates and to always slightly over-estimate how much bandwidth you'll need. You can always lay in redundant data lines for upgrading, and scalability is usually not difficult.

Offering Internet Access to Existing LANs

In some situations you'll run a dedicated data line right to the web server you will use to present your internet presence. Avix Manufacturing is doing just that. However, in many more situations your company will have an existing LAN and all users on the LAN will want internet access. This is done by introducing an "internet gateway" to your LAN. There are several ways this can be done: a separate gateway machine, a separate router, software in your web server, and other similar tactics.

Example: Using Windows NT to create a two-way internet gateway

In Windows NT 4.0 the procedure for establishing the physical link to the internet is fairly simple. As we mentioned in Chapter 1, IP addressing is critical to the understanding of internet technology. The physical connection to the internet will also depend on IP addressing.

To begin with, you need to set up Windows NT and tell it to configure your network interface card and set up specific IP addresses. The card has its own IP address. For the purposes of this discussion we will assume that it was given the address of 145.44.124.2. If you were using an ISDN card for your connection, the card would be given a unique address as well. At this point you can also assign a default gateway address of say, 144.75.224.1.

At the same time, you have applied for a domain name with Network Solutions, Incorporated (InterNIC). You have secured the name "avix.com" with an IP address for that name of 207.75.224.3. When someone on the internet enters www.avix.com the packets are labeled to be delivered at IP 207.75.224.3. The actual point of delivery is the server at the internet provider's location. Their router sends the packets on to the connection to your company.

Under Windows NT, you activate the TCP/IP services of your web server, enter the proper IP codes, and then make the connection. For modems, you use the Remote Access Service (RAS) to dial up the appropriate line to the ISP. For other connections, you go through the NIC to a router and then on to the connection. Your ISP provides you with the equipment and configuration you need. Your only responsibility is to direct outgoing internet traffic to the right IP address and configure the reception of incoming traffic.

At your server you can establish virtual directories with their own IP addresses. This allows you to create several domain names under your registered name. Using the 207.75.224.3 IP address you can have the ISP submask more IP addresses, such as:

207.75.226.12
207.75.226.38
207.75.226.45

These are IP addresses that will be routed to your web server by the ISP. This allows you to act like a web hosting service to create new domain names such as "www.sales.avix.com," "www.support.avix.com," and "www.suppliers.avix.com." The important point here is that a wide variety of connection options are available. You need only know how to tell the appropriate software and hardware where packets should flow.

Outside Access to Your Intranet

An issue often overlooked by IS managers is whether employees will need to gain access to the internet from within your company. To physically form this link you can establish your web server as a gateway to the internet. The web server is set up as a master domain controller on your LAN. This gives it the ability to route traffic on the net effectively using existing account properties. A gateway can be formed so that a new IP address is created. A user only needs to enter this IP address to gain access to the internet connection from within your company's LAN.

At the gateway machine, IP packets addressed for the gateway IP address are examined and sent on to the IP address of your ISP account. The examination phase of the handoff is vitally important. You should carefully examine the options available at this point in the operating system and server software you select. The examination of IP packets allows services such as security checks, organizing packets by priority, bandwidth management, and rejections of selected accounts.

Connecting the Intranet to the Internet

Another interesting situation is when you have an intranet and you want external people to be able to access your system remotely through the internet. As we have discussed before, you can set up direct lines into your local area network with high security to permit a few employees access to your intranet.

However, we are now talking about the case where many approved people, such as vendors and customers, need to have limited access to your system.

At the same time, users in your intranet want access to internet resources. Making such gateways available is relatively simple on the hardware side of the equation. The difficulties lie with establishing network policies for access and usage at these connection points. Another problem is careful control of network traffic loads. An example can illustrate both challenges.

The Law Firm will establish a simple intranet with the use of three or four file servers handling E-mail, web pages, training packages, and the like. The physical connection to the internet will be over a dedicated 128K bps ISDN service hooked to a gateway computer. This gateway machine will have a gateway IP address so that people inside The Law Firm that want to gain access to the internet can route their requests through this machine. A second ISDN line will be hooked to the primary web server to support clients accessing resources at The Law Firm.

The first problem is that you now have a handful of routers (both physical and in software form in the servers) trying to direct heavy network traffic. A user in the research department can send a request to a World Wide Web page on a distant internet site. This is routed from his desktop computer through the network hub in his department, through the router on that floor to the gateway machine, through a firewall, and finally out to the internet. This one request takes up the resources of several machines. Multiply this by dozens of active workers and you can see where congestion becomes a problem.

Next, there is the problem of making sure that only authorized people are allowed to go through a gateway connection. The researcher may have permission to access the internet, but he is working at a computer in the library instead of his desktop machine. Unless he logs in as an authorized internet user, he won't get out of the LAN. Your internal checking mechanisms may approve his account but filter out his current IP address as invalid and stop the transfer. In other words, once you start setting up permissions with employees that use multiple machines, the job of keeping all of this straight becomes difficult.

For a company like Megalith, the problems are even larger. Even though the web page serving is divided among several servers for better efficiency, they placed all outgoing internet traffic through a single gateway. This results in a traffic jam at that point.

Strategies for solving these types of problems consist of using network management tools where primary domain controllers can form trust relationships. This allows users from one area to smoothly access resources (such as a gateway) located in another area.

Connecting Two or More Distant Intranets

Another common situation is when two intranets are being operated in two different corporate locations. You need to link the two systems over long-distance lines to facilitate the exchange of files, E-mail, web site browsing, and the like. The type of connection to make depends on the needs of the intranets to talk to each other and the number of remote sites involved.

Your first step is to determine how many sites will be involved and how much traffic will flow between particular sites. If, for example, you have three sites, then they can be joined by direct lines. That way any one site can connect directly with another site. In contrast, if several sites are involved and the traffic is fairly heavy, then frame relay may be your best solution.

Let's look at two specific examples. The Law Firm needs to connect its intranet with the LANs at three distant offices. To do this, they set up dial-up ISDN lines to each location. When a request comes from a user to contact a distant site, the appropriate gateway directs the packets to the ISDN line between the two sites. The dial-up occurs to make the contact and shuts off when all packets are sent. In this way, you only pay for the time used.

For Megalith, they have several internal LANs that need to be in contact with twenty of their worldwide locations. The solution is a frame relay where each affected LAN calls into the frame relay service. Packets are then routed to one or more sites at the same time. The heavy use of communications between sites and simultaneous broadcasts to many sites make this type of arrangement necessary.

Accessing and Running a Web Site Remotely

You may encounter a situation where you, as a systems administrator, need to access your internet technology remotely to perform fixes while you are on vacation, at a conference, or at home. Under Windows NT the Remote Access Service provides you with pathways into your system. You can attach a 56K bps modem or ISDN modem to a server and create a backdoor to your system. As such, you will want to set up the remote access path for call-back and other tight security measures.

Another approach is to load a program such as PC Anywhere or Carbon Copy so that users can dial into the system from remote locations and run their workstations as if they were sitting at the office. This allows employees to continue work assignments from home, during travel, or from other sites in the company. For example, an employee could be at a different building on the corporate campus in a meeting when she discovers a file is needed from her workgroup's server. Using a laptop and phone line, the file can be quickly retrieved. This avoids the need for chasing down an open terminal and hoping her account has a trust relationship with the LAN in the other building.

Prototyping the Components of the System

Finally, we have reached the point where you have found your appropriate hardware, software, and data line connection. The assumption being made is that all of these components will work together. You may even have assurances from each of the different manufacturers. This is all well and fine but it needs to be proven before you implement your system. To do that, you need to make a prototype.

Prototyping a system means that you take a representative portion of the system and test it in isolation. You'll try to subject this experimental version of your full system to a wide variety of stresses and simulation of normal traffic. The objective is to see if all components work together smoothly and can achieve their mission goals.

Let's take a simple example of how this is done. Avix Manufacturing will be using a web server connected to an ISDN line. The server will also be routing E-mail to and from the internet for the company. Avix begins by purchasing the computer that will work as the file server. Into this they load the various software packages they plan to use. Then they hook up the ISDN line and create the connection to their ISP.

The system is not yet connected to the local area network. Instead, it serves as a prototype to test the assumptions of the functionality of the complete system. The first test is to access the internet over the ISDN line. The browser that will be passed out to all employees is thoroughly tested. Then web pages are created and placed on the server. Using a computer with a modem hooked up to different ISPs, they access their web sites and begin testing the retrieval of web pages. They'll also begin the process of testing E-mail traveling to and from different locations.

For each of these tests, they keep close track of the response time, resources used, and any problems that are encountered. This is a shake down. Avix's staff tries to find where the weaknesses are in the system they have designed.

Once Avix is satisfied with the performance of the server, they then hook in through the network interface card to another computer. A technician at the new computer sends E-mail requests through the server out to the internet. This person also requests web pages and other simple transfers. The idea is to simulate what the whole community of users will be doing with the system. Again, response times are noted and problems are addressed. The objective is to get the bugs out of the system before it is introduced formally into the company.

Once prototyping is completed, it is time to actually implement your system. In a company the size of The Law Firm or Megalith, small parts of the system would be prototyped one at a time. For example, the web servers would be tested as prototypes. One web server would be thoroughly tested and the successful configuration would be used to set up all other web servers. The same would be true for servers used for E-mail, dedicated digital communication lines, router configurations, and so on. By testing a representative component, you can assure better success for all components.

Summary

You may have noticed in this chapter we did not give specific instructions for creating the internet communications links. The number of variables involved and the rapidly expanding number of services being offered makes this impossible. Instead, we have given you the information you need and the questions you need to ask to determine the best type of connection and the best service for your company.

Once you have selected the proper communication links for your company, you should contact telephone companies and the ISPs to get the specific information you need on equipment, configurations, and other issues. Then, through proper prototyping you can test both hardware and communications links to ensure that your system was properly designed.

From this point on, we will be discussing the implementation of internet technology. From this moment on, people are going to begin using your system. Therefore, our emphasis now changes from planning to continuous improvement.

Further References

Leon Salvail's "Guide to Internet Server Connectivity," New Riders Publishing, 1996.

Internet Search Strings

- "ISP Evaluation"
- "Web Hosting"
- "Internet Equipment"
- "ISDN"
- "T1 Service" and "T3 Service"

Internet Sites

The site of any internet hardware producer such as Bay Networks, Cisco Systems, Hayes, Zoom Telephonics, and the like.

Chapter 10
Understanding HTML

One of the first implementation projects for your internet technology will be the creation of web pages. It might be web pages for presentation to the public, pages for internal use, pages to link databases, or any of a dozen other applications. Whatever the reason, the employees involved with page creation need to be aware of several important aspects of web pages, the HTML language, and how browsers work. This knowledge will assist them in several ways: creating pages that people will want to read and use, using resources effectively, and avoiding major internet problems.

Contents of a Web Page

To understand a web page, you must first understand a web browser. Your web browser is the client in the server/client architecture of the internet. In other words, the browser receives from the user a pointer to a specific location of information, the URL. Using the http protocol, the browser is able to read the hypertext at that location. The hypertext at the given location is assembled on what is called a web page.

A web page can contain information, links to other sites, and links to other services that can be offered over the internet. These other services include E-mail, FTP, Usenet, audio, video, graphics, and other such services. Therefore, the web page is the basic building block of internet technology. It is the one place that can have a common interface with all users. Thus, it is the most important component of your implemented system.

Your job as IS manager is twofold. First, you must teach people each level of creating web pages, and how they are to be assembled, tested, and

225

placed on your servers. Second, you must establish the policies and procedures to keep the content sensible, usable, and competitive. Part of your objective will be to assure the maximum use of resources in the most efficient way
possible. In other words, you want your web pages to be as effective as possible for the missions they are assigned.

What is HTML?

HTML stands for hypertext markup language. The most basic web page is
blank. What HTML does is instruct the browser where to place information on
that blank page. HTML is a language that describes the structure of a page. It
is different from a page layout program such as PageMaker. However, web
page creation software has joined together the concept of page layout with
HTML. In this way you could have style sheets, templates, and content wizards that will create the HTML code to imitate page layout functions. Thus, you
get the ease of the page layout program.

HTML relies on a series of tags to tell a browser how to order and present the contents on the web page. These tags are attached to the text and
images on your web page. An example can best illustrate a few of the tags that
are available and how they are used.

Let's take the case of the Dickerson County School System. They wish to
create an opening web page for their web site. The beginning of the document will name the school system and indicate their mission on the web site.
The text they wish to place on the page is as follows:

"Home page

Dickerson County School System

Welcome to the home page of the Dickerson County School System.
This web site is provided to students, faculty, parents, and other stakeholders for the exchange of information and the promotion of education."

If this text were placed on a web page without HTML tags, there would
be no spacing between paragraphs or sentences. All of the letters would be
slammed up against each other. What the tags do is establish the title of the
page, its format and the presentation of text. Therefore, a properly formatted
web page would have the following tags attached in the example below.

```
<HTML>

<Head>

<Title> Dickerson County School System </Title>

</Head>

<H2> Home page </H2>

<HR>

<H1>Dickerson County School System</H1>

<P>

Welcome to the home page of the Dickerson County School System. This web
site Is provided to students, faculty, parents, and other stakeholders for the
exchange of information and the promotion of education.

<P>

</HTML>
```

As you can see, the tags are enclosed in angle brackets. Each has a particular function. Each tag has a countertag. For example, <H1> indicates that this text is to be presented as a level 1 heading. The browser is preset for how a level 1 heading is presented. Typically this would be large point size font in bold. The countertag of </H1> marks the end of the text to be presented. Thus, most tags appear in pairs.

```
<HTML> </HTML> marks an area of HTML coding

<Head> </Head> marks the heading of a page

<Title> </Title> marks the title of the page which is repeated at the top of your
browser

<H2> </H2> second level header

<HR> inserts a horizontal line
```

One tag in our example without a countertag is <P>, which marks a paragraph of "normal text," or the type of text you would find in the body of any publication. When this portion of HTML code is read by Internet Explorer, it appears as in Figure 10–1.

Graphic elements, audio files, video clips, links to other URLs, and the like can also be included in a web page. We will discuss how these features are added later in the book. For right now, our concern is with the basic structure of a web page and how to establish corporate "look and feel" properties that minimize the use of your internet resources.

An important point to remember is that there are several types of browsers available in the world. Each acts a little differently with HTML commands. The more exotic the web page, the more difficult it is to have a similar look and feel for your page across browsers. As we shall see, getting a web page to work with all browsers is more difficult as your pages become more complex.

Figure 10-1. Internet Explorer Normal Text

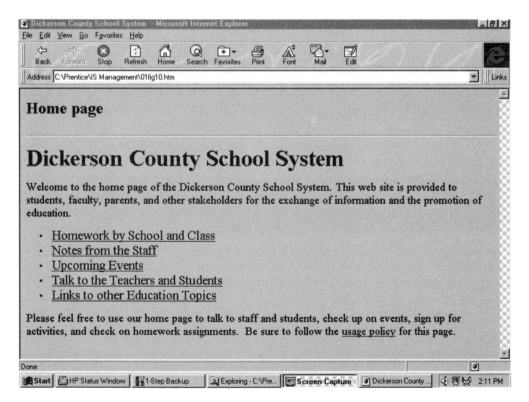

Understanding Critical HTML Tags

Some of the HTML tags are critically important to the success of your web site. This is especially true when the site is being presented on the internet. For example, the tag for the title of your page is critical even though its text does not appear on the actual web page. Instead, it appears in the blue bar at the top of your browser software. Thus, the user can glance up and see what location they are currently monitoring.

Probably the most critical tag to include on web pages is the meta information tag <META>. This is used to contain information that can be read by internet search engines. You can enclose additional descriptions of your web page, expiration dates, and other valuable information in your meta tag. By carefully designing the contents in this area you can ensure that your site is quickly located by any search device on the internet.

The pair of tags <A> and </A> indicate the link to another web page or URL. This allows a web page to be linked to the other web pages at your web site. It also allows you to link to other web sites anywhere on the internet. You can also place bookmarks within a page at your web site or another web site and hyperlink to that point. For example, you could have a large glossary of technical definitions used within your company's web page. By carefully bookmarking each definition, you can create dynamic links from all your documents to the appropriate definition. This would allow people reading your procedures and specifications to quickly jump to the appropriate definition and then back to the document.

Advanced HTML options give you the ability to put data tables on your web page, use captions, send E-mail, and other interesting capabilities. This gives you a wide variety of possibilities in the design of your web pages. In addition, there are programming languages that can work with HTML to expand your capabilities even further. We'll talk about those later.

Using an HTML Editor

HTML code can be created on any text editing program. However, that would require you to manually enter each tag along with the text. To speed up this process, several companies have developed HTML editors. These allow you to enter the raw text and then click for the appropriate HTML tag to include.

For example, in the Dickerson County school district's web page, you can type out the mission statement, highlight it with your cursor, and indicate this is normal text. The heading of the page could be highlighted and given

"Heading 1" to indicate how this text is to be presented. The tags would then automatically be inserted. Tags such as <META> would still have to be inserted manually.

There are also software packages that work like page layout programs with embedded HTML editors. These allow you to lay out the page as you want it to appear on the web. Text is entered, highlighted, and then changed to the format and size for presentation. The HTML tags are not shown. However, they are being embedded in the code being created to reproduce the page the way you wish to see it.

Some of the most advanced of these programs allow you to switch between various modes when using the software. The first mode may let you see the page in page layout format. A second mode shows you the raw HTML code so that you can add or subtract codes or text as needed. A third mode may be available which previews the final appearance of the page through a selected type of browser.

For the IS manager there will be a wide selection of possible software to use to create web page content. The problem does not lie so much with software as with the people that will be expected to create the content. If the content producers are a group of Unix programmers on your staff, you may find that they prefer doing raw HTML code entry. In contrast, if the production will be carried out by staff members of the public relations department, they may prefer the page layout type of editor.

Therefore, when you are selecting software for web page creation, you should involve all of the parties that are expected to create the content. When it comes time to test the software you'll need to have at least two or three of the most popular browsers available. Once typical pages are created, as part of the software test you'll view them through at least two or three different browsers. You are looking for the type of software that allows the greatest number of browsers to successfully view your page.

Once the software is selected and put into place at your company, you need to supplement that with a set of policies and procedures. A single policy is created that will spell out the intention of web pages, restrictions on content, corporate "look-and-feel" issues, and other such topics. Basically, you need to establish a corporate format for web pages.

Procedures are then written to help guide the people creating the content on how this format is to be achieved. To support the procedures, you need to create templates and outlines the people must follow when creating web pages.

For example, if your technical staff has elected to use a raw HTML editor, then you must specify the minimal amount of code to be included on any page. This would include the following requirements:

1. All web pages must have a title.
2. All web pages must include a meta tag with basic information about the page, including expiration dates where they apply.
3. The heading of the page will be tagged.
4. The body of the page will be clearly marked and tagged.
5. Any programming code included on the page will be documented.
6. All new pages shall be tested and approved by the internet administrator.

To assist in implementing these guidelines you can create a starting web page that has the minimum number of tags placed on a page. Since these tags are used by many page programmers, you can save time and effort by having these basic elements all ready for the employees when they start. They may look like the following:

```
<HTML>

<Head>

<Meta> </Meta>

<Title> </Title>

</Head>

<HR>

<Body>

<P>

</Body>

</HTML>
```

The web page creators start any project by filling in the title, meta information, and the basic text of the document. Programming links, format tags, graphic elements, and the like can also be added. The point here is that the first five or so minutes are not spent putting in the basic required elements. Time and effort are saved.

Example of a procedure for page creation

Let's begin with a brief review of what a procedure does for your company. Policies establish why something is being done. Procedures describe the stages of a single process, or in other words, the what, who, when, where, and with which tools, for a process. The series of tasks to be completed are listed for the process. Work instructions would be a further elaboration of each task.

The creation of a web page is either a task or a process. If one person creates the pages for your company and the pages are simple, then this is seen as a single task. However, if several people can create pages, or if teams create pages, a review and approval process is used. If the pages are more complex, then a process of creation is involved and a procedure is required. In our example we will assume that the Law Firm wishes to create a web page with links to all internal documents stored on the intranet. Essentially, a table of contents for all documentation on the intranet is needed.

This will be a dynamic document that will have to keep up with the introduction of new documents into the system. The page is easy to envision but challenging to create and maintain. Therefore, the creation of such a page can be made easier by the existence of procedures and policies to guide the efforts of the people tasked with this project. First there would be the project management guidelines used at the Law Firm to help shape how the team works together, tests their progress, and reports to management. Next would be the general web page policy.

4.4.1 Policy on Web Content and Appearance

The Law Firm is a professional organization serving a select set of customers. As such, their web pages should reflect that level of professionalism while avoiding excessive use of intranet resources.

The IS manager is the ultimate authority granting permission to create a web page and approving of its content and format. The header information, footer information, background color, and navigation bar are established by the standard templates noted in the web page creation procedure (SOP 4.4.12).

Content of web pages are to be text based where possible. Grammar and spelling should be correct. All links should be tested and found valid. Web pages with links will be tested by the key programmer at least once a month.

Notice that the policy is a general statement about web pages and leaves the details to the procedures. The IS manager is assigned the role of making sure that this policy and its related procedures are followed. Also, the basic content of the web pages is outlined. Enough flexibility is given for imaginative pages while enough formatting is fixed to give a universal "look and feel" to the pages at the Law Firm.

Now let's look at the web page creation procedure. Here we can see the details of how the page will be created.

Standard Operating Procedures 4.4.12—Web Page Creation

12.1—Purpose

To promote professionally formatted web pages that are reviewed and approved for use.

12.2—Scope

This procedure is for any web page used with the company, whether for intranet or internet presentation.

12.3—Responsibilities

The IS manager will approve the final appearance and functionality of all web pages.

12.4—Procedure

12.4.1 All non-database related web pages will use G:/FrontPage/Webs/Corporate.htm as the template for web page work. Content is added to the page after it is saved under the name of the proposed web page. A multi-page web site requires the creation of a web and related directory. Web pages in draft form are placed in the "Temp" subdirectory.

12.4.2 Database related web pages use the G:/Data/Pages subdirectory area and one of the three basic templates for creating new pages. Database pages need to have available a test set of the database that will be eventually connected to the web page. This test set is stored with the web page and used for testing the functionality of the page. A full-scale test with the actual database is conducted according to plans developed between the page designer and the IS staff.

12.4.3 All web pages must include a title, a contact point for questions about the use of the page, and a date of creation. The most recent update of the page should also be noted. Any page can have up to three graphics and four graphical elements (lines, boxes, etc.) per page as long as the total size of the page does not exceed 150KB. Graphics will be in .gif format.

12.4.4 To create the web page the designer should have a list of objectives the page is designed to meet. A rough draft of the page should be created and posted in the Temp area of the intranet. E-mail should be sent to interested parties with links to this draft and comments encouraged. The feedback should be used for the final appearance of the web page.

12.4.5 Once in final form the IS manager and the production leader should be notified by E-mail. Within 5 business days a decision should be reached on the acceptability of the new page. If accepted it will be moved by an IS technician to its permanent location. The production person should retain a backup copy. If not found acceptable, the needed corrections will be noted and the designer will have 5 business days to make changes and resubmit for approval.

12.5—Reference forms

12.5.1—Use Reference Document 21.12—Definitions for any terminology questions

12.5.2—G:/FrontPage/Webs/Corporate.htm is the standard format template for general web pages

12.5.3—G:/FrontPage/Images/ is the location of acceptable clip art for web pages

This is a scaled-down version of the procedure, but it gives you a rough idea of how the Law Firm wants their pages created and reviewed. Now let's look at the actual process.

To complete their job, the web page team first creates a list of objectives the page must accomplish. These are simply:

1. Provide a central location for a list of existing web documents in the Law Firm.
2. Dynamically link to each document or to the table of contents for a set of documents.

They envision that the page will look something like this:

General Table of Contents for Law Firm Intranet

Use this page to find your way to any of the documents currently stored on the office intranet. Just click on the document you wish to view. Use the "Back" button on your browser to return to this page. If you cannot link to a page or have other problems, call Tom at extension 2745.

I. Research

1. New cases received
2. Breaking news
3. Supreme court rulings

II. Human Resources

1. Vacation policies
2. Sick leave
3. Maternity leave
4. 401k results
5. Temporary workers
6. Medical benefits

III. Calendars

1. Corporate law team
2. Civil law team
3. Patent law team

IV. Training

1. Procedure writing
2. Phone procedures
3. How to file a brief
4. Confidentiality

On the surface this appears to be a fairly simple document. The designer has only to come up with an interesting format for what is basically a text only document. The difficulty will come with the links to other sites. For all of the items listed on this draft page, the designer must know where the related documents are located in the intranet. Let's take a couple of items such as recent Supreme Court rulings that are on the internet. The link will have to be designed to jump successfully from the intranet to the internet and back again.

This is made possible through the linking tag in HTML. To make a link you must first know the URL of the page you are seeking. In the case of our example there will be two basic types of URLs. The first type is a location under the intranet. For example, G://Temp/index.html is a file which serves as the home page for one of the items listed on our example. The link we will create will tell the web browser to go to the web server and retrieve from the temp directory the file "Index.html."

The second location will be on the internet. To make this link we must invoke the http protocol. For example,

http://www.9000.net/index.htm

This instructs the browser to link to the internet and then to the domain 9000.net to retrieve its home page.

The actual link tag pair is <A> and </A>. Within this tag are the commands which html passes down to http to execute. The resulting line of code might look like this:

<A HREF="http://www.9000.net/index.htm">Training Courses</A>

The HREF command tells the browser where to make the link. In this example it is going to the home page at 9000.net. The link itself is not shown on the page. Instead the phrase "Training Courses" appears on the page. Typically it will appear in a different color and underlined to indicate that it is a link. This ability to create a link with a short name, instead of having to list the actual address of the page that is being linked, gives the designer the ability to make a clean looking web page.

Figure 10–2 shows what the final web page looks like within a browser. The user only needs to point at one of the links to be taken to a location to get a specific piece of information.

Some of the links will take the browser to a table of contents page at a different location. This cascading of tables of contents is one way to design the web sites to keep selection sequences short for users. For example, instead of listing all the current court cases pending for this law firm, a single line can be inserted in this table of contents that says "Pending Cases."

This link would take the user to a list of different types of cases. There the user would have additional selections for, say, civil, criminal, real estate, and so on. By clicking on the civil law case section, a list of the current civil cases would be presented by title. Thus with only a few clicks, users can locate the cases they are interested in. The alternative of listing all pending cases on a single page would make for a long and difficult to use web page.

Figure 10-2. Final Web Page Design

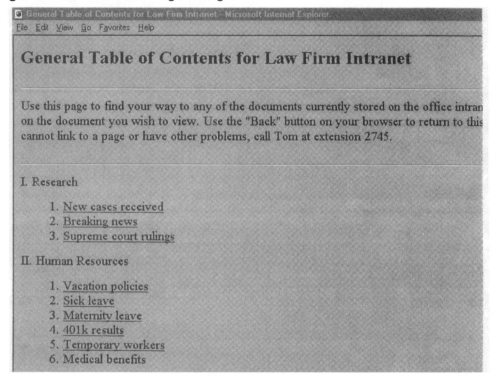

Minimizing Programming
for Maximum Efficiency

The next issue to discuss is whether you should include additional programming on top of the HTML. There are additional programming languages which take advantage of the HTML code and other aspects of http to expand your capability with web pages. Examples include CGI, Java, Perl, and the like.

Our emphasis continues to be to use these extensions as little as possible. They should be used only when absolutely needed. It is very easy to import a job applet that will allow you to have a scrolling banner on your web page. However, this assumes that the users will have browsers capable of using the applet and that it does not consume too much of your web page resources. Therefore, there should be a moment when the designer pauses to decide if the special effect being added to the page is worth the cost of incompatibility and wasted resources.

The procedure presented earlier in this chapter briefly noted that no web page should be more than 150 KB if possible. This size limit forces the designers to think carefully about what goes on a web page. This is also an issue to anyone creating content. The general guidelines to follow are to keep pages:

- Short
- Easy to read
- Easy to use
- Efficient

Maximum efficiency is achieved in two ways. The first is to take advantage of any programming applets your page design software provides for you. For example, programs like Net Objects Fusion and FrontPage can create discussion groups on your web page automatically. This saves you from hard coding the extensive number of instructions needed to create such discussion groups. Also you will be avoiding the need for troubleshooting and debugging your own programming.

The second approach is to restrict any programming to short easily run applications. There should also be a restriction on programming languages to those that all browsers within your company can pick up and use. That would tend to limit use to CGI.

As we have discussed before, CGI (Common Gateway Interface) is a programming language that works with the browser. CGI programming involves the creation of scripts that are stored on your server along with the associated web page. When a user is browsing the page and requests some information or otherwise interacts with the web page, the page generates a URL that points to your script. The script is called up just like any other URL (i.e., http://www.9000.net/cgi-bin/form). The difference is that the user's browser only sees the results of the script, not its actual operation.

CGI allows you to create a wide variety of interactive components that can be used by most browsers. These include:

- Forms
- Discussion groups
- Input fields
- Database queries
- Calculations
- Customized responses

and so on. Most web page layout programs today offer some level of self-scripting in the form of templates or wizards.

As the IS manager, you have a difficult series of decisions to make about programming languages for web pages. The first is the actual programming language you will select for use within your company. Not only do you need to select the type, level, and nature of programming language to be used, you also need to know how intense your programming requirements will be for several years.

With companies like Avix and the Dickerson County School System their web demands will be slight. They may need to generate discussion groups or database links, but the scope of these will be limited. Either group could subcontract this work and avoid the need for any programming. The Law Firm and Megalith both will use extensive database linking and other programming intensive activities as part of their systems over the next few years.

Let's assume that Megalith decides to endorse Java as their main programming language. The IS manager must then decide which version of Java to usc, where it will be purchased from, who will support the programming language, method of updating, training of programmers, and a host of other issues. Will beta versions of updates be allowed? Who will test and debug applets created by programmers? Who will approve the code before it is incorporated into web pages?

These are all questions that you answer in your procedures. If you already have a programming procedure, then this new language will follow the same rules. The description of coding, testing, verifying, and approving web pages will include a discussion of programming issues. You will also need a procedure for the acquisition and updating of software that includes instructions for the web page language you choose.

Dynamic Yet Secure Linking Through http: and https:

Within your web page we have seen that you can make links through the HTTP protocol. The internet works well because you can freely make the links between sites and within a server. Unfortunately, these links include links to scripting and other programming forms. This opens up a huge security problem. Unless it's protected, other people can enter your system and execute a wide variety of commands.

This is why access control is so important to your system. The first level of defense is authorization accounts that only allow your programmers access to critical parts of your web server. Firewalls can also prevent other people from freely monitoring the activities of your server or porting themselves to locations outside of your web pages.

When making links to other locations within your server and your intranet, you need to install encryption and other security schemes to keep your links open and easy to use for browsers, but secure from tampering. You will want to investigate the HTTPS services which stands for HTTP Secure. This allows the use of challenges for people trying to access a site located under this service. It also facilitates the secure exchange of financial information for online transactions.

Maintaining Secure File Transfers Through FTP

The FTP file system can also be used like a link on your web page. This allows you the ability to transmit files openly on the internet. However, this also opens up another security problem because the browsers will tend to default to listing your file directory when problems occur. Thus, a user suddenly is able to examine a complete list of the files in your FTP area. In most cases, any of these can be downloaded or the user can change directories and examine other files. Therefore, you need an FTP service that prevents this, or you need to design your FTP links to be secure. The following steps are highly recommended:

1. Create an FTP directory that is highly protected and contains only the files you want to transmit to the public.
2. Make the files read-only.
3. Set up anonymous log-ins with their own access privileges which restrict them to the web pages and the FTP site only.
4. Perform IP address filtering to keep internal access restricted to internal people.
5. Use a virtual directory for the FTP files and isolate this area from the rest of your server.
6. Keep complete log-in and audit logs on everyone that accesses the FTP area.

There are additional measures you can take depending on the critical level of the FTP mission.

Increasing Site Appeal

Your main strategy for web pages is to keep them simple, usable, and appealing. You want people to readily use and enjoy your web pages. The more helpful people find your web pages the more often they will return to your site. This is equally important with getting and keeping new customers as it is with encouraging employees to use your intranet.

There are several strategies you should use when designing a web page. They include the following:

- *Keep it short, simple, and logical.* Use the same effective business writing rules used for letters, reports, and the like, for your web page.

- *Content, content, content.* The main goal of an internet site is to capture new users and hold their attention. This requires your site to have compelling information that is of value to your existing and new customers. For an intranet site, the goal is ease-of-use combined with a well organized site. You want people to quickly locate the information they need and not linger on a particular page.

- *Simplicity, simplicity, simplicity.* The best design for a site is one that has the most information in the fewest words. Ideally people should not have to scroll down more than one browser field on any one page. Complex information should be broken up into several logical pages.

- *Effective navigation.* A user should be able to reach a desired point on your web site within one or two clicks. As in our previous example for an intranet, the first click takes them to the desired subject, the second click to the topic of interest. Also, every page should have an obvious navigation button to the home page, the first in a series of pages, and other common points. Such a navigation bar should be on the top and bottom of each page so that it is always within the user's sight.

- *Always exercise strict control over web design.* Designers like to think that they should have freedom to pursue their own "vision." Unfortunately, this leads to a hodgepodge of designs that ruin corporate identity. Radical and new design concepts should be reserved for radically new products.

- *Know your user.* Web pages must be designed to meet the needs and expectations of your users. For an intranet this is fairly easy to calculate based on the amount of computer savvy your staff exhibits. For the internet, this is so hard to estimate that the best approach is minimalism. Just present the information.

- *Always include a help link.* For people that find your page but don't know what to do, this help link should explain how to find related material, how to make selections, what specific commands are available, and so on.

- *Include your E-mail address.* An E-mail path for feedback should be included on most pages. If a person finds your web page and wants to ask a direct question or wants clarification, the E-mail link will get the message to you fast.

- *Test your links* and keep them up to date.

- *Avoid dead-ends in the stream of web pages.* For example, if you have a series of pages explaining the corporate phone procedures, the last document should give the reader choices such as going back to the home page, to the beginning of the series, to the next related series, or to a specific page in the series. Each page in the series should have routes back to the table of contents for the series, the home page, the next page, or the previous page.

- *Simple font, simple colors, no backgrounds.* Even though a fancy background pattern looks good on your 21-inch monitor, running the latest version of Internet Explorer, it will look like mud on a 14-inch, 16-color, VGA monitor running Netscape Navigator version 1.0. Use fairly large simple fonts on a blank white background with only a few colors at most. Your page is designed for reading, not a massive illustration.

- *Keep graphics simple.* Unless you are in business to sell items requiring elaborate drawings, pictures, or other illustrations, avoid these to conserve resources and prevent distractions from your main message.

- *When possible, be interactive.* When you show a catalog, include ordering boxes so the reader can place an order while scanning your selection. When you design training, interrupt after each key concept with a short exercise or quiz.

- *Show information about the page.* Include the date of creation, date of revision, name of page creator, and alternative contact information on each page. This allows users to know the freshness of the data, who to contact for questions about the page, and how to reach you outside of the internet. This is usually done as a footer for each page. Copyright and trademark information, when applicable, should also be included here.

- *Test the speed of your page.* How quickly will your page load into various browsers using slow modems? The 14.4K bps modems make a good benchmark of slower modems or faulty internet connections. Most studies indicate that a user will wait up to 20 seconds for a page to load before they consider going somewhere else. Most studies are optimistic. A page should start to appear as soon as possible and be completely loaded in under 20 seconds. Give people a feeling that they are getting immediate feedback to their URL request.

- *Be conscious of image size.* If you are going to use large images, create a table of contents or page of thumbnail images that can load quickly because of their small size and limited resolution. The user can then click on a desired image to get the larger, full-resolution image. Be sure to warn the user of the size of the image file involved and how long it takes to load on a 14.4K bps or 28.8K bps connection.

- *Support text with easy-to-read headings.* Lists, clusters of links, menus, and the like are good ways to have both a summary of what is within a site and how to reach it quickly.

- *Highlight key words.* If you are a law firm running an internet site, you may want to highlight the key words in the paragraphs containing valuable, related information such as "divorce," "civil rights," and "living trust."

- *Include a corporate logo.* The logo of your company should be tastefully placed on every page you create. Many intranet and internet users like to print off a single page from a site to use for reports or presentations. This way you know the source of the document is clearly presented.

- *Spelling and grammar MUST be perfect.* We once created a web site with over 100 web pages with one major spelling mistake on a famous person's name. Half of all our E-mail was about that mistake until the problem was corrected.

- *Stick to successful designs.* Browse the World Wide Web and select pages that you find particularly clear, easy to use, and useful. Copy the design elements that made your positive impression possible.

- *Be aware of differences in browsers.* When you do not know which browser your users have, do not use browser-specific commands such as "back button," "bookmark," or "plug-in." Instead, give specific instructions or use navigation buttons that say "I need a quote," "How can I order?," and "Take me back to the table on prices."

- *Never use the phrase "click-here."* See previous rule.

In addition, you will need to translate the strategies you endorse into a general guideline for web page creation. Earlier in this chapter we looked at a procedure for creating a web page. One of the supporting documents should be a style guideline. Starting with the basic template for corporate web pages, the designer is free to create the remaining web page. To keep this design work focused on a specific target, include the list of objectives for the page with the style guideline. The guideline can also be used in the training of people who will provide content for your web site.

The way to test new web pages is to have someone outside the development team call up and use the pages. Specifically, find someone unfamiliar with the topic being covered. Instruct them to scan through a small set of pages on their browser. They should be able to navigate their way through your site with no difficulty, read and understand the material, and easily respond with feedback or ordering information.

In fact, if you want a really effective site, you repeat this test several times. Each time, you reduce the number of words used and then keep simplifying the documents. Your goal is to find the smallest amount of information and links that have the highest effectiveness. The faster and easier a user can reach desired information or carry out needed actions, the better the design of your web pages.

Style Sheets and Design Guidelines

A design guideline is a set of written instructions on how a web page is to be laid out. Each corporation can develop these for their web sites. A style sheet is the organizing of common required design elements into a central location within your page design software. That way, a designer can quickly call up the layout for any page and immediately start to create web content. The style sheet option or document template is an important option to seek out in selecting your web design software.

Let's take a look at the design guideline for Avix Manufacturing. Note how much of it is based on the rules given above.

Guideline for Web Page Creation—Avix Manufacturing

Web pages should use the following guidelines for layout and general ease of use.

- The "corporate.html" file in G://AvixPage can be used as a starting point for all web pages.
- Use white backgrounds.
- The company logo should be on each page between 40x40 to 80x80 pixels in the upper left corner of the page.
- Avoid pages that consume more than two screens of a browser.
- Headings should be Arial font, 18 points, no bolding.
- Body text should be Arial font, 12 points.
- Use bold and italic only where necessary.
- No more than two horizontal lines per page.
- Spelling and grammar MUST be perfect.
- Test your links.

This simple guideline would have at least three example pages attached that used the design philosophy of the company. Between these examples and the guidelines, the page designers can create a consistent look and feel to their pages while keeping them very useful.

Demonstration: A Walk Through Page Layout using FrontPage Editor

With our policies, procedures, and guidelines for web page creation in place, we can now look at how they affect a simple project done on a specific software package. Avix Manufacturing needs to create the initial page for their web site. They have laid out the following objectives:

1. Fits on one browser screen.
2. Invites the user to scan their catalog.
3. Is simple and straightforward.
4. Provides basic contact information.

Looking at the guidelines above, it would seem that a lot of rules have to be applied to the page, thus trading off a lot of content. This is not true. The idea is to create the minimal amount of content that will accomplish the stated objectives.

For example, they need to have the company logo, contact information, obvious instructions to direct the user to the catalog, and other helpful information all fitted onto one screen. The program FrontPage from Microsoft includes a web page editor for creating a single web page. Elements can be placed on this page almost at will.

Let us create the Avix page in only a few steps using FrontPage. Figure 10–3 shows what FrontPage editor looks like with a blank page ready to be filled in. The designer would begin by calling up the corporate template sheet. Using the file pull-down menu, the option "open" would be selected. The corporate template sheet, "corporate.html," would be selected and the results would look like Figure 10–4.

The template would be renamed and saved. The designer would add the corporate logo, the text inviting the user to look through the Avix catalog, and other basic information. Using the guide sheet for formatting and use of color with a white background, the results would look like Figure 10–5.

Figure 10-3. Front page Editor with Blank Page

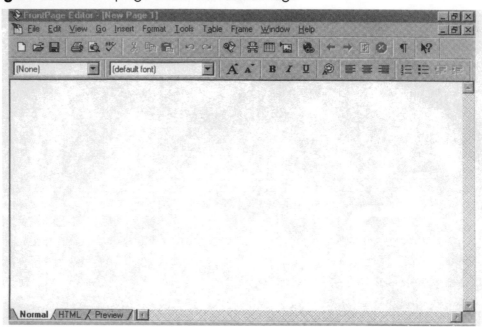

Figure 10-4. Corporate Template Sheet

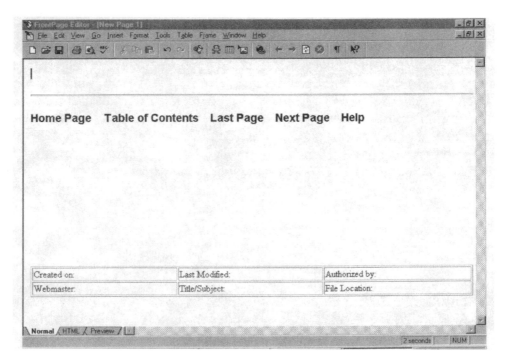

Figure 10-5. Finished Template of Home Page

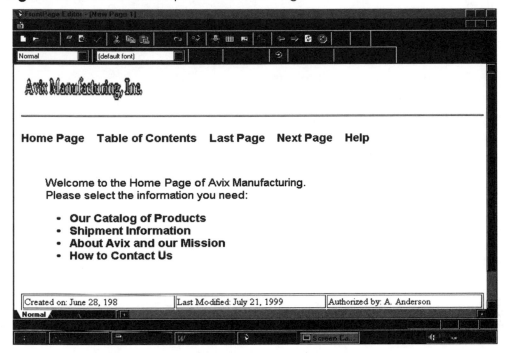

This final form of the opening page of their web site is simple, effective, informative, and fits on one browser screen. The objectives set out by Avix Manufacturing have been met.

Despite the temptation to use as much clip art and glamour as you can fit on a web page, you'll quickly learn that simple and informative pages are widely used on the internet. In business environments people want information and they want it now. Web pages that are easy to read, easy to navigate, and have very valuable content will be widely used if effectively promoted.

Examples: The web pages of our four example companies

As Figure 10–5 has shown us, the Avix Manufacturing home page is very simple. The thinking here is that if a person hits the site by mistake they quickly realize it and will leave. At the same time, a person looking for the Avix site will have this page load very quickly into their browser, confirming they have made the correct selection for a URL.

This ability to quickly bring up a page confirming that a user has reached the proper site and inviting them to explore the information there can conserve resources for your internet connection. Because the opening page is usually the one that receives the most traffic, it should load quickly.

The Dickerson County School System created its web page using a different set of objectives. They are:

1. Provide the menu of all resources.
2. Be easy to read, especially for younger students.
3. Be visually appealing.
4. Encourage participation.

What The Dickerson County School System created can be seen in Figure 10–6.

The Law Firm has a different set of objectives because they are using an intranet. The pages have to be very consistent and professional. Internal personnel are using the intranet the same way they would use a procedures manual or reference text. Their objectives are:

Figure 10-6. Dickerson County School Sytem Web Page

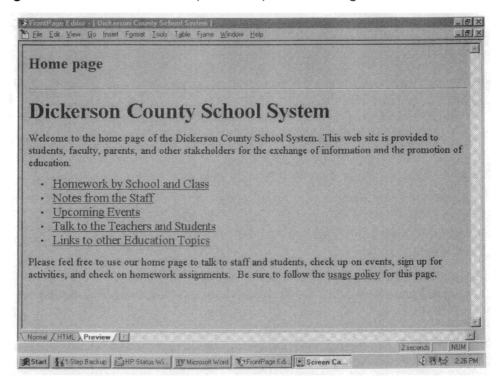

1. No more than three links to reach the needed information.

2. Professional appearance.

3. Law Firm name on each page with standard document control information.

4. Limited access for selected parts of the intranet, and Strict access control.

Figure 10–7 shows the home page of the Law Firm.

Megalith Corporation has several web sites, each performing different tasks. For example, the sales department has the "corporate image" site. This is the site that projects the official corporate positions and public relations. Links are made from here to the actual order entry site, technical support, and the other Megalith web servers. This site explains the power and majesty of the Megalith Corporation.

As such, it needs to have large flashy photos of the products and of employees providing important services. It also features a site map where the

Figure 10-7. The Law Firm Home Page

user can click on images to get to the information they need. The objectives for this site's home page are:

1. Quickly confirm that a user has reached the Megalith site (readable by all browsers).
2. Trendy style, simple background.
3. Alternative site for Spanish or French language version of this site.
4. Easy to navigate to other Megalith sites.

Figure 10–8 shows how this type of home page looks very different from the other three. This is due to the mission of this page. The intention is to look like the newest and trendiest page on the internet. Part of the corporate image is to use cutting edge styles. Megalith doesn't want their site to look like others or to be overly simple. Therefore, the exceptional mission and objectives result in a different looking page that deviates from the "minimalism" we have encouraged in this chapter. This is also perfectly acceptable. Always design in the direction of your objectives.

Figure 10–8. Megalith Home Page

Summary

Implementation of your internet technology takes place on two fronts. The first is the implementation of the technology internally so that people within your company know what to do, when to do it, and how to use the technology. We will discuss this in the final chapters of this book.

The second front is the presentation of your internet technology to the public. The public can be the general public, your customers, your suppliers, your partners, or even your internal personnel. By simplifying your web pages until the minimal page still has the critical information, you create web resources that people will use and enjoy.

Chapter 11
Implementing Different Types of Intranet

In the last few chapters we have been discussing the methods used to implement internet technology. This chapter is a brief diversion to discuss the implementation of intranets. These internal versions of the World Wide Web have some unique concerns and applications that are different from the internet. They are:

- The information tends to be proprietary and not for public consumption.
- The sites tend to be very mission-oriented.
- You compete for bandwidth on your internal network.
- Open access is encouraged.

In this chapter we discuss how the intranets are actually established. The planning and preparation is similar to that for any internet site. Therefore, you would use the same checklists and other planning aids already presented in this book.

The Intranet

Once you have an established local area network, you can create an intranet. You can do this fairly easily using your existing network software's web serving program or with an operating system such as Windows NT. By giving each workgroup a name and each computer in your network a name, you establish the intranet structure. Each computer should have a unique IP address. At the same time, you can also set the level of sharing that is allowed within specific directories.

Once you have finished identifying your network, you need to establish a directory that will be shared across the network. In this case you will make a primary subdirectory called "Procedures." Under this subdirectory we will make additional subdirectories for each department. For right now the first one will be called QA. This will be the subdirectory for your quality assurance procedures.

The file structure will look like this:

```
C:\Procedures
C:\Procedures\QA
```

Inside the quality assurance subdirectory you'll place the web pages containing your standard operating procedures for quality assurance.

Assuming that your network shared drive has the name "D:" any computer on the network can access web pages by using the open file command in the internet browser. By selecting the following, your other computer users have entered your intranet.

```
Open ... File... D:\\Procedures\QA\Index.html
```

This series of commands will open the home page of your intranets. What your users will find are the standard operating procedures for the quality assurance department. The intranet would also have the procedures for other departments in other subdirectories. Because web pages can be linked, the user will find it easy to jump between the procedures and references. At the same time, you now have full control of the distribution and use of the documentation. The users can only look at the standard operating procedures. It takes special permission to actually print, save, or edit these documents.

Setting up the Intranet Using Windows NT

Windows NT is what is called a client/server based operating system. That means it is sold in two parts. One version of the software is called Windows NT server. The other is called Windows NT workstation. You'll need one copy of the NT server software for the central computer of your network. Each computer connected to your network will need a copy of Windows NT workstation. Microsoft sells Windows NT in logical bundles for setting up networks. In other words, for a single price you can buy all the software needed to set up, say, five machines in a local area network.

Another option is to use Windows 95 machines to connect to your file server. That way you will only need the Windows NT server on one machine and you can use the existing Windows 95 software on all of the other machines.

The use of Windows NT is a subject in and of itself. There are many capabilities that are hidden inside this software. The one that you have to worry about is a program called NT Executive. This is the program that handles all requests from the other computers to use your resources. It can also assign different resources to different microchips. This opens up the possibility of using more than one microprocessor in a single computer to function as the server.

To set up your intranet, you need to first install Windows NT for your file server. Place the Windows NT CD-ROM into your CD-ROM player. The software comes with an automatic installation procedure. If it does not automatically install, then follow the instructions that come with the software.

If you are familiar with Windows 95, then using Windows NT is really easy. Let's begin by setting permissions on our files and directories. Permissions define who can see which files and what they can do with them. For example, you can allow all users to read the standard operating procedures of your company. But, the same users cannot alter or move these files.

To set the directory and file permissions, open up the Windows NT Explorer. This is the same file exploring program that you have on Windows 95 called Windows Explorer. To set permissions, you select the files or directories you wish to protect. You then click on the security tab to display the permission settings. Click on the "permissions" button and the permissions dialog box will appear. From this point you can choose the type of access you want the different users to have to your files and directories. Once you click the "OK" button, the new file settings are established for the network.

To install the TCP/IP addresses for your local area network open the control panel in Windows NT. Now double-click on the network icon that appears on the desktop. In the network dialog box click on the protocols. Next, click on the "add" button. What will appear is the select network protocol dialog box. Select the TCP/IP protocol from the list of available protocols. You will be asked where your network files are located. Typically this will be your CD-ROM drive with the Windows NT software loaded.

At this point you're into the TCP/IP properties dialog box. Here you can specify the make and model of adapter card you are using for each computer. You can also specify your own IP address. In most cases however, you should use the automatic system for establishing that address. The same will have to be done on each of the computers that are connected to your local area network. There is also the mask and default gateway used to form connections between your machine and the internet, if this is in your plans.

There you have it. Once you have installed your software and told Windows NT where the adapter cards are by IP address, and set your file permissions, you have an intranet.

Establishing Intranet-based Training

There are hundreds of mission-specific intranets that can be established at a company. We will examine a few examples to see how you would implement different systems. For example, the Law Firm wants a training intranet.

Training is one of the most popular applications for an intranet. It allows a company to place standardized training material into a format that the employees can access anytime, day or night. Just like a book, audio tape, videotape, or computer-based training on a CD-ROM, training material can be placed on the intranet for ready access. The advantage of the intranet is that the training material can be modified and updated at will.

Take the case of a videotape training package. Let's say that you have a training package containing a health benefit form. Each time the form changes the videotape becomes obsolete. However, the same material presented on the intranet can be updated to reflect changes in the forms. Thus the training stays fresh and updating becomes inexpensive.

To set up a training intranet you first need a list of the training packages the company expects each employee to take. This can be in the form of a training matrix where each job category is matched to the type of training required for that position. This list is reviewed to see which training modules are suitable for delivery through an internet browser.

Those that do fit the internet model are slated for implementation on your intranet. Those that require hands-on activities, extreme interaction, or other characteristics that do not make them suitable for training over the intranet will be delivered by traditional methods.

The candidates for intranet training delivery are then examined when the schedule is created. The schedule is the list of learning objectives and the order in which the training modules will be transformed into an intranet format. This is done for your browser using the following steps:

1. The entire training package is broken down into its most basic components. Each component teaches the participant one particular concept or skill.
2. Each component should be summarized by a single web page.
3. Each web page should have an illustration reinforcing the concept or skill being taught.

4. Definitions and references to other concepts are hyperlinked so that the student can jump to another web page to completely understand the term before completing the original page.

5. Each page should end with an interactive segment. Such interaction can be very simple, such as asking the participants to correctly identify the concept being taught, or more complex.

Let's look at a particular example to see how this is done. Below is a page from an internet course teaching someone how to write the standard operating procedure. It is taken from a course normally given in person on the same topic.

What is a Procedure?

A procedure is a written record of how a particular process should occur within an organization. The procedure tells you who should do what, where it should happen, what equipment should be used, when it should happen, and the sequence of tasks to be performed. In short, a procedure is a description of the tasks that go into the operating process. In contrast, a work instruction would be written to tell one person how to perform one task within the procedure.

<u>An example of a Procedure Used at the Law Firm</u>

Pop Quiz: The document that tells you who does what, when, and where is called:

_____a. a <u>work instruction</u>

_____b. a <u>procedure</u>

_____c. a <u>policy</u>

This is a very short and simple example. The concept being taught is the definition and description of a procedure. This is done in a short paragraph. You could follow this with a small reproduction of an actual procedure. Instead, this intranet training package has placed hyperlinks to one of the procedures used at the Law Firm. If the participant is interested in the actual procedure, a click on the hyperlink would bring up a web page representation of the procedure. This is an example of how participants can choose how deeply they need to study each topic.

The training web page ends with a pop quiz. Here the person is asked a question that reinforces the definition of a procedure. Notice that each of the answers is also a hyperlink. If they read the question and choose the answer "policy" they will be taken to a web page that will explain that this is an incorrect response and will again reinforce the correct definition. If they choose the correct answer, "procedure," this will take them into a different web page that will explain that the answer is correct and will still reinforce the definition of procedure.

There are dozens of techniques available to simulate the normal interaction that goes on in a classroom. By incorporating these into your intranet-based training you can develop an effective training package. However, it is highly recommended when you make training available on your intranet that you regularly test the participants of that training to ensure that the skills they should have acquired have been successfully transferred.

The final phase of implementation of a training intranet is to create a table of contents that not only lists the types of courses available, but makes it possible for a person to search, by job title, for the type of training he or she should be taking. This allows any employee to enter the training area and select the type of training they need to receive. By breaking up the training packages into many web pages, you can also have the participants bookmark how far they got in the course before they went to take a break. That way a person can return to where they left off in the course at any time. This allows participants to spread out their training efforts over several days, if necessary.

As you can imagine, requiring people to take the training and tracking how quickly they are taking the training and picking up on the concepts is a difficult task with an internet-based system. You'll need to work with human resources to develop a method for performing these tests. Still, a successful intranet training system greatly reduces the training cost, increases the availability of training, and frees up the human trainers for more involved courses.

Establishing Customer Service/Technical Support on an Intranet

One of the most popular intranet applications is the consolidation of customer support and technical support information. Take the case of the corporation Megalith. Because of the wide range of products and services they deliver, they have several customer support and technical support teams. Each one has its own philosophy and database for addressing customer needs.

One way to efficiently share the information each group has with all other groups is to create a corporatewide philosophy for dealing with customers. Megalith could use an intranet. They could begin with top management and could work with the existing customer support departments to create a common customer philosophy. This can be transferred to the intranet along with a brief training segment to demonstrate to all customer support representatives how to handle different customer situations.

Next, Megalith could develop a logbook which is shared across the intranet for all customer contacts. Whenever anyone at Megalith is contacted by a customer, the date, time, nature of the call, and the response is all loaded in the log. Because anyone on the intranet can call up the log and make the data search, this allows a powerful new tool to be used at Megalith: personalization. Let me illustrate how this happens.

One of the small customers of Megalith products makes regular calls to the warranty department to report problems. Each of these are logged on the intranet. One day, the same customer calls technical support with a software question related to one of their products. This caller and the technical support person have never talked to each other before. The support person uses their internet browser to hyperlink to the intranet's customer logbook. Here she quickly enters the name of the customer. A summary of all logged contacts with this customer now appears.

After taking some basic information from the customer about the problem, she begins responding by reviewing related questions the customer has asked before. She also reviews with the customer that they are well within their one-year warranty on the product involved. She notes that this customer receives a 10 percent discount on the price of any additional services related to this product. In other words, the technical support representative is immediately up to speed on how Megalith deals with this customer. In addition, the customer does not need to relate any history of experiences with the product to bring the technical support representative up to speed. Both parties benefit.

Finally, a good customer service intranet involves a database of documented patches, fixes, and other solutions to any problem reported by customers. There are software packages available today that perform this function over local area networks. Your intranet can always be hyperlinked to that type of package. You can create your own database on the intranet by creating a web page form that each customer contact person fills out to fully report problems and how they were solved.

In this way, any technical support person can quickly search through common solutions used to attack similar problems. In the case of some of your more important customers, you would give them limited access to your intranet to obtain the same information. This is already being done by corporations such as Microsoft and Hewlett-Packard. Their internet sites allow you to search through lists of common problems with their products. By clicking on the problem, you can read about similar problems and the common solutions that are used. An FTP site also allows you to download software patches where necessary.

Maintaining Supplier Relations on an Internet/Intranet Site

The big trends in industry today are integrated supplier networks and just-in-time (JIT) delivery systems. An intranet can be a great assistant in achieving goals as large as these.

Take the example of just-in-time delivery. The intranet you establish will have linked together the key people within your company that schedule delivery of goods from suppliers. Typically this would be the purchasing personnel, production planners, the dispatcher, engineering, quality assurance manager, and possibly several other people. Take the case of Avix Manufacturing. They need to produce a simple valve.

To build the valve, they need seven components that come from different suppliers. Engineering has information on the types of components needed, on how they are assembled, and standards to be met. The production planning department has determined the number in the run, when they will be produced, and the disposition of the valves to customers. For example, we will assume that 500 units need to be created.

The intranet for the production area already tracks common problems by product. This log shows that the valves require extra ball mechanisms for successful assembly. Because the ball chamber does not always accept the ball mechanism, they need to order 10 percent more of them. This information is then passed on by E-mail to purchasing. The production planning people also have information from the intranet on the lead time each supplier needs to build and deliver the needed parts.

Using their gateway to the internet, E-mail is sent to each supplier requesting the specific number of parts to be delivered within a one-hour window at Avix. Each supplier, in turn, sends back confirming messages. The use of two digital signatures insures that the documentation is authentic.

Next, the quality assurance manager prepares inspection routines for the incoming material. These are posted on the intranet for the manufacturing people to use. An alert about the manufacturing of the valves is posted on the production schedule, which is also part of your intranet. Confirmation that all suppliers are still on target for delivery is achieved by E-mail a few days before production.

At the magic hour, all of the different parts arrive within a few minutes of each other at Avix. This is noted on the intranet so that all personnel are notified of the successful delivery of the parts. The parts are then immediately wheeled over to the assembly area where within a few hours, 500 valves have been put together. Problems encountered while putting the valves together are addressed by assembly personnel who will consult the intranet problem log. This gives them tips on initial corrective action for common problems. Because this information is at their fingertips, they are able to correct problems as they occur without the need of stopping production or calling on other personnel.

As you can see, technologies such as just-in-time delivery are achieved through a ballet of coordination and communication. Intranets are famous for being able to make such coordination and communication possible. This is especially true when the intranet has a gateway to the internet. This can also be achieved when key suppliers have limited access to your intranet. In this way they can monitor upcoming projects and start to anticipate your needs. They can also download specifications and standards to be used in the assembly of needed components.

This type of application of an intranet is extremely effective in increasing your company's competitive position. To implement an intranet for such a difficult mission requires the use of an implementation team with representatives from each key department. You would bring in production people, key suppliers, engineers, purchasing, and other representatives. This team would need to agree on which way they will communicate and what forms of communication are to be used. Your job as IS manager is to educate the representatives of the capabilities of the intranet. You should point out the different options that are available to facilitate the meeting of their particular needs. You should also coordinate who is going to develop which services on your intranets to meet the mission requirements.

Using Discussion Areas and Workgroup Intranets

One of the most popular applications for your intranet is to facilitate workgroups. This can be accomplished using products such as Lotus Notes over your local area network or with an intranet. Either way, technologies such as an intranet have the one powerful feature often overlooked by workgroups: anonymity. Let me illustrate.

You have formed a workgroup to brainstorm a new service for your company. Members of this group are taken from key departments such as sales, finance, and technical support. One member of your group is the executive vice president of the entire division. No one in this workgroup is going to contradict this top executive's opinion.

In contrast, the same group of people placed on an intranet can communicate by using technologies from the internet such as mail lists. As the internet web master you can arrange for the identity of each participant to be masked in a discussion area. Each participant would enter the discussion area under an assumed name. That way when the executive vice president suggests an idea that will not work, no one will realize who made the suggestion. Thus, you may find a technician pointing out the flaw in the argument. Anonymity ensures an open discussion, and this helps prevent political problems.

The discussion group is just one of many tools you can use to facilitate workgroup activity. To implement a discussion group in an intranet, you need to set up a separate directory. In this directory you create a web site based around a discussion group. The selection of the software used to create the discussion group is very important. Some packages allow the group to operate like a chat room on the internet. Participants can sit at their own desks anywhere on the internet and participate. Comments are typed on the screen and shared with everyone in the discussion area.

Another form of the discussion group has people entering comments via E-mail. These are posted in "threads." Threads are messages related to a common theme. A participant can look up one of the issues involved in any ongoing project. Reading through the comments made so far, the person can then add comments which are attached on the end of the string of messages. In this way people can participate in the workgroup on their own schedule.

We developed such a discussion group for a client recently. They were a start-up company and wanted to tie together their marketing personnel with the field sales representatives. An intranet was set up with a limited access dial-in modem available for field personnel. The discussion group was created. Each thread was based on the name of a client. In that way, sales personnel could enter messages based on which customer they were talking to.

Whenever a new customer would call the marketing department at the company, the marketing representative was able to call up all conversations the salesperson had had with that customer. The marketing person would then enter his or her own conversation notes and post it back to the discussion group. In this way the sales personnel also knew what the marketing people were telling these customers. At the same time, both sales and technical people would post comments to each other in the discussion group on how this customer should be handled. For example,

"Jim, I talked to Zyxlex and Ed says he wants to see the discount clearly noted in the contract."

"Fred, I have edited the contract and highlighted the discount. I faxed one copy to Ed on March 3 and also mailed a copy. I will fax you a copy as well. Is this emphasis on the discount something we should think about with all customers?"

At this point other sales representatives would read this message and respond to the question. In fact, the marketing people could post a general message asking all sales representatives to comment on the need to emphasize discounts in future contracts. In this way the marketing and the sales force work together as a team, but, they never see each other face-to-face.

Gaining Wide Area Control of the Organization

In this book, one of your objectives is to use internet technology to improve the competitive position of your company. One way to do this is to use the internet technology to improve internal performance. One option which also increases your company's reputation, is to become ISO 9000 compliant. ISO 9000 is a voluntary, international standard on how to structure a management system for quality assurance. The standard spells out 20 different areas where control is necessary within your company. All of these requirements depend on your ability to document what systems your company has, to show how the processes within these systems work, and to have ready evidence of their consistent application. An intranet is an ideal tool for creating and publishing such documentation. This allows your internet technology to solve a major management goal.

Example: Establishing an ISO 9000-based system

All you need to do is to establish standard policies and procedures and put them in a format that intranet browsers can read. Let's examine how Internet Explorer or Netscape Navigator can be used to look at your corporate documentation. The best place to start is with Section 4.5 of the ISO 9000 system—document control. This is the first procedure you always put in place when establishing an ISO 9000 system.

Section 4.5 Document Control Let's begin by looking at what we need to do to establish document control. ISO 9001 spells out some specific requirements for the control of documents for all company departments. To interpret the requirement and get specific information, you need a copy of ISO 9001 and a copy of ISO 9004-1 to glean hints as to the application of the requirement.

In 9001, several points are made on this particular topic. All documents related to ISO 9000 have to be strictly controlled, there has to be a document approval authority, documents have to be stored at the right locations, only current versions of a document should be available, changes have to be made using a standard procedure, a master list of documents should exist, and reissue of a document is recommended after several changes.

The following are examples cited by ISO 9004-1 of the types of documents requiring control:

- Drawings
- Specifications
- Blueprints
- Inspections instructions
- Test procedures
- Work instructions
- Operation sheets
- Quality manuals
- Operational procedures
- Quality assurance procedures

In addition, this section of ISO 9004-1 specifically allows the use of computer-stored forms and documents. It also calls for identification on each document, with dates and revision information. It hints at the need to demonstrate that achievements of desired quality results have been documented. And, it calls for the removal of time sensitive documents from the manufacturing process.

Determining the Structure of Your Intranet

As you can see, there is a certain structure that will have to be achieved in an ISO 9000 documentation intranet. To begin with, you need a standard form for each of the documents. For our example, we will be using Microsoft's FrontPage 98.

FrontPage 98 allows you to create web pages easily without knowing HTML code. It also allows you set up standard page elements that show up on all pages. Because of this you can create standard and draft documents called templates. The templates will conform to the suggestions of ISO 9004-1.

The company name, identification of the document, revision information, date of creation, date of revision, and a signature of authorization should appear on each page. Unlike a written system, you do not need a page numbering system. Each procedure or policy will occupy a single page. Remember, the web pages can be as long as you like. What you need to establish on the longer documents is a table of contents with anchors, so that people can jump immediately to the section they wish to see. Hyperlinks can connect definitions, procedures, and related policies with work instructions to make a very dynamic documentation system. (More on this later.)

Let's start by looking at the difference between a written policy and the same policy on an intranet. We will begin with the policy statement for document control.

The checklist

Your first step is to pull together all of the above information so you can create your final checklist of items to cover in your policies and procedures.

- Central document approval authority
- Identify central authority by job title
- Master list of documents
- Right documents in the right place
- No obsolete documents in circulation
- Nature of any change shall be explained
- Reissue documents after a specified number of revisions
- Sub-contractor documents are included
- Documents should be signed, dated, and numbered
- Time-sensitive documents are removed when out-of-date
- Internal audits will check on this document control procedure
- Approval is needed to revise, remove, or copy a controlled document
- List which documents are under control of procedure
- Describe procedure for each unique set of documents (if applicable)

- All corrections should be signed and dated
- A separate procedure is used to initiate corrections

Writing the policy document

The Level I document is a policy statement. Keep it simple and to the point. Begin by identifying who is responsible for meeting the requirements, then briefly describe what objectives are being achieved.

For the written version of the policy statement, use a single page with the identification information required by ISO 9004-1. Onto this piece of paper you would write a standard document control policy such as the one following.

Section 4.5—Document Control

4.5.1   All new or revised documents shall be approved by a central authority. This central authority will then track the status, revision number, and location of all documentation.

4.5.2   The central authority for each type of document is as follows:
- QA Manual and documents related to testing and inspection—QA Manager
- Engineering drawings, customer specifications, and similar documents— Engineering Manager.
- Purchase orders, customer contact forms, and similar documents— Purchasing Manager.
- Sales-related documents—Sales Manager
- Other documents—Office Manager

4.5.3   Each authority will assure that the documents under his or her responsibility are up to date, available where needed, signed and dated with revision numbers, and reissued when appropriate.

4.5.4   A master list of document locations and revisions will be created, maintained, and audited at least once a year for effectiveness.

This policy meets the requirements of Section 4.5 of ISO 9001. This is a short and simple Level I document. Essentially, it is a statement of the policy on how to assure quality and control of documents within your organization. Documents are approved, distributed, monitored, and removed by a central authority. Control of revisions and distribution is clearly delegated to decentralized authorities. A master list of document status is maintained and regularly audited. This policy would be placed in your quality assurance manual. It would be the job of management to make sure everyone was aware of the policy. Now let's look at the same policy statement but this time in web page format.

Section 4.5—Document Control

4.5.1   All new or revised documents shall be approved by a central authority. This central authority will then track the status, revision number, and location of all documentation on the intranet.

4.5.2   The central authority for each type of document is as follows:

- QA Manual and documents related to testing and inspection—<u>QA Manager</u>
- Engineering drawings, customer specifications, and similar documents—<u>Engineering Manager</u>
- Purchase orders, customer contact forms, and similar documents—<u>Purchasing Manager</u>
- Sales related documents—<u>Sales Manager</u>
- Other documents—<u>Office Manager</u>

4.5.3   Each authority will assure that the documents under his or her responsibility are up to date, available where needed, signed and dated with revision numbers, and reissued when appropriate.

4.5.4   A <u>master list</u> of document locations on the file server and revisions will be created, maintained, and audited at least once a year for effectiveness.

The first thing to notice is that it now mentions the intranet and the web server. However, the more important things to notice are the words that are underlined. These are hyperlinks to other web documents.

Let me give you an example of the power of these links. In element 4.5.4 of the policy statements, the words "master list" are underlined. If you want to see the master list of documents in the system, you click on the words "master list." This will whisk you away to the actual master list which will appear on your browser screen. With a click of the "Back" button on the browser, you go back to the policy statement.

These links allow you to do clever things such as have a single glossary for the entire documentation system and link all definitions to that one glossary. Therefore, you do not have to end each policy or procedure with a list of definitions. Instead, people can just click to read the definitions.

Another example is the links to the various managers. If you are wondering what it is the purchasing manager does under the responsibilities of your management system, just click on the link "purchasing manager." This will take you into the web pages for the purchasing area. Here you can explore some of the policies and procedures they follow. If you wish to jump back several pages to the policy statement again, use the "Go" command on the menu bar in your browser and select the policy statement.

In other words, the powerful advantage of an intranet is that all documentation in your company can be just a few clicks away for any one person. Instead of trying to track mountains of books and binders all over your company, all documentation is stored on a single file server. With one location and one format for publication, the job of document control becomes infinitely easier.

Another example

To reinforce the point made above, let's look at a second example—the creation of the procedure for document control. If you go to the web site (www.isogroup.iserv.net) you can read the description of the procedure for a written document system. What we'll look at here is the same procedure rewritten for an intranet. Note that the use of a single file server and a standard browser are emphasized. Also note that this procedure would be the first one you would put into an ISO 9000 intranet. It would also be the one you would use to train people not only to use their browsers but to understand how documents are now controlled in your company.

Example of a Level II document

The following is the quality procedure you'll find for document control in the Quality Assurance department.

15.6 Quality Assurance Document Control

15.6.1 Authority and Responsibilities

The Quality Assurance Manager will be defined as the central authority for the control of quality assurance documents. This will include:

- Use of FrontPage as a standard document publishing tool
- The twice yearly audit of the effectiveness of the control system
- The maintenance of a master list of documents for the subdirectory on the file server E:\Procedures\QA and E:\Procedures\ISO
- The approval of new or revised documents

15.6.2 Document Tracking

All documents created or revised by the Quality Assurance personnel shall have as minimum identification a title, date of creation, date of revision, signature of the Quality Assurance Manager, page number, and file name. The template file to be used for all procedures, policies, and work instructions will be E:\FrontPageWebs\Doc.htm.

Documents will be produced using the Microsoft Word word processing system. Draft documents should be stored in local workgroup hard drives. The submission of a finished draft should be sent to E:\Documents\Draft\QA. An E-mail should notify the quality manager of the submission.

15.6.3 Initiating a Document

To initiate a document, an individual needs to submit a <u>document approval form</u> (DAF) to the QA Manager. Attached to this form should be the proposed document. The QA Manager will then check the proposed document to assure that it is in the proper format, does not duplicate existing documents, and that a list of people who should receive copies is completed. Approval shall be indicated by the QA Manager's signature and appropriate distribution of the document. Once approved, the document is stored in the database of the QA Local Area Network (LAN). The distribution list is noted in the document description section of the software. The QA Manager's Administrative Assistant is then charged with printing enough copies of the document for all destinations listed on the circulation sheet.

15.6.4 Changing an Existing Document

To change an existing document, a <u>Change Request Form</u> (CRF) is submitted with a link made to the appropriate document. The CRF should specify what is being changed and why. This is then processed by the QA Manager for approval. When distributed, an E-mail shall be attached explaining why the change was necessary. Now obsolete versions of the documents will be removed from the system by moving it from the active procedure subdirectory to the archive area <u>(E:\Documents\Archive)</u>.

15.6.5 Removal of Obsolete Documents

After no more than six revisions of a document, a new document should be issued under a new version number. If a document becomes obsolete, or if time-sensitive documents expire, then the QA Manager should be notified. Again, the document is removed to the archive area.

15.6.6 Audit of the Document Control system

Twice a year, the QA Manager will initiate an internal audit of this document control procedure. An internal auditor will be selected from outside of the QA function. This auditor will receive a mandate and a set of instructions from the QA Manager. The auditor will follow the <u>internal audit procedure</u> listed in the Quality Assurance Manual.

One of the big differences between the written version of this procedure and the intranet version is the removal of the discussion of how to chase down documents. In the written version we talk about the need to go out and look for copies of the affected documents and either update or remove them. All of that is now unnecessary on an intranet. Because only one copy of the document exists in electronic form on a file server, it is very easy to find, retrieve, or update.

The intranet procedure also has the underlined hyperlinks. I would like to point out a couple of them and how they are used effectively. In section 15.6.3 it talks about a document approval form. By clicking on this link you are taken immediately to an electronic version of the form. This form can be filled out right on the computer and with a single click sent to the QA Manager. By listing on the form the location of the document involved, the QA Manager can call the document up instantly on his computer screen. This eliminates a lot of paperwork and confusion.

In section 15.6.6 the internal audit procedure is underlined. This link will take you straight to the internal audit procedure. Therefore an internal auditor working on a checklist for the audit would read this section and click on the link. Now presented with the actual internal audit procedure the same auditor would press the "Print" button to print out a copy of the procedure to follow. There is no need to sort through several different manuals to look for the proper procedures to supplement the internal audit because the internal audit procedure also has links to all of the work instructions, checklists, and history of previous audits.

Finally, the QA manager's name is underlined in the procedure. If a person is looking through the procedure to see what to do to solve a certain problem and sees that they need to notify the QA manager, a mere click on the manager's name sends an E-mail message. After filling out an E-mail describing the nature of the problem and what assistance is needed, within seconds, the message appears on the QA manager's screen, whether he's a few feet away or several miles away. At the same time, the communications between the employees and management are now being documented. When it comes time for your certification audit, the documentation you need now exists on the computer. From any screen in your company you should be able to bring up the documentation your auditors need to see.

Summary

Needless to say this is an effective way to implement your ISO 9000 documentation system. At the same time, you are improving communications and your management system for the company. However, you must carefully plan the system and train people for it to work successfully. This is what we will be discussing in future chapters.

Further References

You can learn more about ISO 9000 at the following web sites—

> **www.isogroup.simplenet.com**—The home page of the ISO 9000/QS-9000 Support Group
>
> **www.iso.ch/welcome.html**—The home page of ISO in Geneva
>
> **www.asq.org**—The home page of the American Society for Quality
>
> **www.euroqual.org**—The home page of the European Organization for Quality

Recommended Reading

> *Intranet Web Development* by John Desborough, New Riders, 1996.
>
> *Running a Perfect Intranet,* by Rick Casselberry, Que, 1996.
>
> *Building and Managing the Corporate Intranet,* by Ronald L. Wagner and Eric Engelmann, McGraw-Hill, 1997.

Chapter 12
Training Employees to Use Internet Technology

When you introduce internet technology to your company, you need to accomplish the following:

- Explain the services being introduced.
- Make clear to each person his or her role in using the new technology.
- Portray the technology as vital to future job performance.
- Remove any hesitation to use the technology.
- Teach each person how to use the new services.
- Convert many people to supporters of the new system.

This can all be accomplished through properly designed and executed training; specifically, through the use of a technique called instructional design.

Instructional design is a process of creating training material that meets the needs of your employees. However, it is more than just a systematic way of creating training material. The objectives of the process include the change of individual behavior and the organization as a whole through learning. You want the participants to react to the training. People who experience the training should show not only competency in using internet technology, but they should change their behavior to accept and effectively use the new services.

Understanding the Importance of Training

Commonly underestimated in importance is the role of training in the process of implementation. With internet technologies this is doubly true. Not only are you introducing a new technology to your company, but this technology

273

comes with baggage. Most people have already formed an opinion about the "internet" long before they actually see or use the technology.

Within a company you usually get only one chance to convince everyone that internet technologies are a good idea. Training is the one opportunity where everyone in the company can be addressed face-to-face on the intentions and benefits of your new services. Therefore, training is where you want to spend a considerable amount of your time and effort making sure that the right message is delivered and that everyone experiencing training picks up the skills they will need to smoothly integrate internet technologies into their daily lives.

You need to begin with a list of the information that will be transmitted to training participants concerning the role and function of the new internet services. This general information is in addition to the specific skills you expect each participant to acquire. To create this first list, you turn to the goals and objectives you drafted as part of your overall internet implementation plan. You should pay particular attention to the points of resistance you anticipate during implementation.

Let's look at a couple of examples of how your planning is used to design parts of a training package to counter expected points of resistance and to fulfill some of your goals and objectives. Let's assume that your plan includes a goal of getting all employees to embrace the new internet connection. To achieve this goal, part of your effort will be to make it clear to all employees that they are expected to endorse, and use, this link to the internet.

Therefore, you add to the beginning of any training seminar a five-minute talk given by one of the senior managers from your company. This person outlines the importance of the new technology and how it fits into the strategic plan for the company. For example,

> "As VP of operations, I can assure you that we are counting on each of you to use the internet effectively to help promote our company, communicate faster with suppliers, and serve the needs of our customers."

Such a clear message from a top official sends a strong signal to the rank and file that this new technology *will be used*. Follow-up messages within the training material can reinforce this signal. One way to do this is to add a page in a training manual specifically written for the participants in the class telling them their role in the new system. Take the case of a seminar on using internet E-mail given to the production personnel:

> "In the case of production, internet E-mail will be used for daily communications with suppliers and distribution points. In addition, E-mail will be

used to coordinate schedules between the home plant and our Wixom facility. Below are several examples where this is already being done."

Then you would show several examples of where a specific person sent communications to other parts of the world. Each example should show where this reduced time, saved money, increased understanding, or caused some other valuable benefit for the people involved. The idea is to make the training personal, and immediate, to the participant while also reinforcing the positive points of the new technology.

As we will see, later parts of the training will take these same participants through simulations of the actual E-mail communications they are expected to use. One central message of usefulness is repeated several times in several ways during the training.

A second example is the famous need to quiet the fears people have of using the internet. We talked about one at the beginning of this book where some people equate the internet with pornography. Indeed, it is out there and in large quantities. However, you must demonstrate that there is vastly more information of use to a company employee also on the internet.

This can be done using a two-stage approach. The first would be to conduct a "key word" search as described earlier, where you have participants compare the number of hits for a word like "sex" with other key words like "love," "Christian," and such. Another approach is to find an "adult only" site that doesn't show anything but asks for your credit card before you can get into the site. This demonstrates that access to such material is not as easy as the news media suggests.

However, spend as little time as possible on this part of the demonstration. Instead, the bulk of your time is spent showing several productive sites to the participants. Here are some possible examples:

- The company is pursuing ISO 9000 registration, so show them one of the support sites that can explain the process.
- You do business in Hong Kong, so go to one of the Hong Kong business support sites to read about local events.
- Your financial people can be shown the IRS site that makes all tax forms downloadable.
- Tour the library of Congress to do some basic research.
- Find the owner of a famous web site using the Internic site.
- Watch investment and business news stream into your browser from CNN financial network.

The idea is to give several examples so that each person will find at least one of the sites interesting. In that way, they will want to learn more about how to access this type of information.

Designing Easy-to-Understand Training Materials

All of your training material must be easy to read and understood by your audience. Good training draws in its audience and encourages them to continue participating because the information and skills they are obtaining are fun to learn and beneficial to their lives. Achieving this takes time, testing, and practice.

The time is spent understanding the needs of your training audience. Testing is used to further refine your material. Practice is used to make the presentation of the material smooth.

What follows are some basic guidelines used to create proper training programs. Some companies like to use as much third-party material as possible. In such cases you would use our suggestions to evaluate the materials to select the ones that best reinforce your message and meet your goals. In many cases you will find that you still need a live instructor introducing the course to complement the material and to be available to answer questions. In some cases you can place material onto an intranet for delivery or have it on CD-ROM for review at the leisure of the participants.

One key planning tool will be a training matrix. This is created by listing the basic job functions in your company down one side of a piece of paper. Across the top of the page you list the titles of the training packages to be used in introducing your employees to the new internet technologies. The resulting matrix is marked to indicate which groups receive which training.

This matrix can also be used to create the final schedule for training, or as a discussion enhancer to help the internet technology team work with department managers in determining the skills each group needs to have as part of the new system. For example, you may offer the following courses:

- Introduction to the internet
- How to use E-mail
- Effective web searching
- Using the new intranet database
- HTML programming

- Using Net Objects Fusion
- Windows NT basics

Not all employees need to take all of these courses. For example, suppose the quality assurance department is expected to communicate with suppliers and internal personnel using E-mail. They are also expected to use the web to support their research and engineering efforts. Therefore, it may be decided that each person in that department would receive the introduction to the internet, how to use E-mail, and effective web searching classes.

In contrast, the IS staff already knows how to use the internet E-mail and web searching functions. They will want to take the HTML and Net Objects Fusion classes. They are already familiar with basic Windows NT functions. A special class on advanced techniques for a selected small group might be added as a one-time training event. Or, you could be already conducting certification training for MicroSoft software and note this in your internet implementation plan. Such existing training plans that overlap your implementation training have to be integrated into the whole package.

Understanding Instructional Design

Instructional design is a systematic process that creates teaching material, changes behaviors, and used properly, can promote the effective use of your internet technologies. The actual delivery of training is just a small part of the process. The following is a simple overview of how the method works. You should research this topic in detail for a better understanding and for obtaining the full benefits of implementation.

1. *Front-end Analysis.* Here you look at the needs of your target audience. You need to find out which skills they need to master for a particular mission. To this list you add the goals and directions you want the participants to pursue when training is completed. Finally, you determine how to achieve this list of objectives.

2. *Task Analysis.* This is used to determine how much effort you want to put into creating or modifying a training package versus the type of result you want to get out of the training.

3. *Product Survey.* Now you look at in-house and third-party training packages that may fit your needs. These can be modified to make an exact fit.

However, the economy of doing this is compared to the results expected. When no existing training package is found, you create your own.

4. *Design of Instructional Material.* If you have to create your own training package, then you need to have a comprehensive design for the course. The instructor should have instructions on how to deliver the course, material should be interactive and relevant, and some form of evaluation must be used to ensure that the message of the course is correctly received by the participants. The standards used for the design of course materials can also be applied to evaluating an existing package.

5. *Development of Materials.* The actual course materials are developed. There is a wide variety of ways to deliver training effectively. You need to decide early on which approaches work best for your employees.

6. *Evaluation.* The finished materials are tested with a pilot group of participants. The idea is to adjust the material until you have a package that is effective and well-targeted for your audience.

7. *Delivery.* It takes careful planning and management support for the successful delivery of training. People need to be in a conducive environment, informed of what to expect, and encouraged to participate.

8. *Application and Further Evaluation.* People should leave a training course on internet technology and be able to put it to work immediately. For example, a class on E-mail should end with the participants having their new E-mail addresses and being able to send messages as their final exam. The effectiveness of the training should be evaluated again to see if, weeks after the training, participants are still effectively using the new techniques.

As you can see, this is an involved process. However, using it will help to prevent many of the training problems you may have experienced in the past.

Evaluating Student/User Capabilities

To get an idea of how this works, let's look at a specific example. Megalith is planning to have all corporate headquarters office personnel go through a course on how to use an internet browser. To ensure the success of this training they will borrow many of the steps described above.

The first step is to conduct front-end analysis. A training design team is formed using representatives from the human resources department, management, information systems, and potential participants of the course. This group reviews the skills each participant should gain from the training, including:

- Ability to open and use Internet Explorer
- Enter a URL successfully
- Work with interactive forms on web sites
- Understand the use of the Back, Forward, and Go functions for navigation
- Understand how hyperlinks work
- Use the mail function to read and answer mail
- Is able to attach a file to an E-mail message
- Print out a web page

To this list is added the behavioral and organizational changes that are expected from the training, including:

- Overcome resistance to use the internet
- Calm fears about "accidently" finding a discouraged site
- Encourage proper use of the internet
- Promote professional presentation on the internet

It is decided that the best approach for an audience of over 2,000 office professionals is to use a hands-on training course. That is, an instructor will lead about 20 people at a time through the basics of using an internet browser. Each participant will have a personal computer and instruction booklet. The class will make heavy use of having the participant actually carry out the steps described in the booklet. This will include browsing, printing, and responding to real web sites.

For successful training you need to know your audience. This is especially true during the front end analysis phase of the project. You need to know the skills and knowledge the audience brings to this course. Megalith may find that about one-quarter of the potential participants already have an internet browser on their home computers and are quite familiar with its operation. This group will be given a shorter course designed to focus on proper use of the corporate browser.

Half of the potential participants at Megalith are not regularly using computers in their current jobs and they indicate that they have very little knowledge about the internet. This group will need additional instruction on basic computer skills and the structure of the internet.

By looking closely at your audience, you can anticipate how the training must be delivered to prevent training-related problems. Clearly, giving one course with no modifications or adjustments to all 2,000 Megalith employees would be a mistake. The people already familiar with browser operations would be bored. Changing their attitudes as part of training would be difficult.

How Much Effort is Required to Create or Modify Materials?

The second phase of instructional design is to evaluate how much effort and resources you want to put into the proposed training class. In our example, the large audience of 2,000 people makes it justifiable to spend considerable resources. However, if a third party already has an effective and adjustable training package, then further development work and expense would be unnecessary.

A good way to judge the effort required for a project is to compare the size of the audience and the cost of development versus the goals to be achieved. A couple of examples can show how this is done.

Case #1   Avix wants to teach five office workers how to effectively use an intranet. The main goal is to get these people to actively endorse using the intranet. Without their "buy-in" the office intranet will probably never get implemented. The intended course would be an overview of intranet possibilities using Windows NT, Net Objects Fusion, and Office 97. An existing course is available for a cost of $5,000, but requires considerable of modification. Thus, the audience is small, the goal is very important, and the cost of developing or leasing the training material fairly expensive.

In this particular situation, money would be spent to develop the special course just for these five people. This would make the training expense but the objective is even more important.

Case #2   The Law Firm wishes to train almost a hundred clerks on how use a World Wide Web browser and the internet connection to conduct legal research. This class is a combination of an existing course on the use of a browser and special material on sites available on the internet that are good for legal research.

In this situation the objective is modest, but so is the cost. Much of the material already exists and is available at a fairly low cost. The training objective is to give one more research skill capability to the law clerks. Therefore, training would focus on testing whether the clerks can successfully use internet sites to conduct research.

Checklist for Successful Training

When you are evaluating, conducting, or developing training material, it is helpful to have a checklist of what makes training successful. The following checklist can be used for this purpose.

1. Were the needs of your target audience evaluated and listed?
2. Were the needs of the target audience broken down into skills and knowledge points?
3. Did a team of potential participants, their supervisors, and training specialists review the skills and knowledge points to confirm their relevance?

Using the Intranet to Deliver Training

Often overlooked by the administrator, a local area network has the potential of using an intranet to deliver training. An intranet allows you to deliver web pages, audio, video, and other interactive forms of training directly to the desk of the participant. It is best used for a wide range of training material for people who cannot free up large blocks of time to sit in a training seminar. It also works well with specialized training for very specific topics where people who need the information may have to obtain it immediately.

A couple of examples can illustrate situations where intranet-based training works well.

- *A company wants all employees to be familiar with its method of document control.* However, the explanation of how it works and a demonstration will only take up about half an hour of training time. Also, the employees are already working on tight schedules. Therefore, instead of putting up with the headache of trying to schedule groups of people for half-hour seminars, the training is placed on the intranet.

- *Another company keeps a database of employee backgrounds and capabilities.* From time to time, someone within the corporation may need to look at this information to learn more about team members they are being assigned. However, it is almost impossible to predict who might need to know their way around the employee database. Therefore, the instructions for searching and using the database are placed in web page format on the intranet. That way, when an employee needs to learn how to run the database they just click the "learn here" hyperlinks to take the training.

- *A third company wishes to have people take training in basic blueprint reading.* They also want people to have confidentiality maintained on their ability to work with blueprints. Therefore, a self-paced training class is translated to intranet format. It is supplemented with a feedback mechanism that detects people having trouble understanding the material. Additional web pages are then presented to help these people through the material. Thus, individuals taking the course have it custom designed to their particular needs; they can take it anytime they wish, at the pace they wish.

All of this is made possible by the great flexibility and power of a web page. Just about any form of interaction that takes place in a classroom can be simulated on the web page. Only a few exceptions are known to exist. For example, you cannot have hands-on exercises for a laboratory-type of environment on the web page.

However, you can simulate team exercises, group discussions, communications with the instructor, and other forms of interaction. In addition, when a quiz is a given, there can be immediate feedback to the user.

Testing the Effectiveness of Training

It is still surprising the number of companies that do not bother to test to see if training is effective. The thinking goes that if someone attended a course, they must have learned something. Next to this opinion is the one that if you give out an evaluation form at the end of a course, you can determine whether people enjoyed the training. Neither approach is effective or useful.

Instead, you continue the meticulous planning and preparation you did for the training with follow-up activities designed to assure that skills were transferred and retained. This process begins with the pilot testing of a course with a small sample of potential participants. Then, carefully interview the participants and test them for how well they retained the material being presented. A lot of feedback is collected to learn how the course can be made quicker and simpler yet still transfer the necessary skills. The goal is to design a course that can appeal to a wide audience and have a high rate of success.

Participants in the training can receive evaluation forms as the final exercise in the course. Such a form should be designed to determine how well people absorbed the material, what changes they would make, and the strong points of the training. Better still is to conduct competency tests during and at the end of the course. In the following example, people will be learning how to use an intranet browser. As part of the course they should demonstrate that they can enter a URL successfully, reach the page they are seeking and use the hyperlinks to maneuver to other pages. Hesitancy or mistakes should be noted and studied for patterns.

The supervisors of the participants should also be present during the training. Within a week or two of the completion of training, the participants should be required to use their new skills on the job. Working with a supervisor you would then go back to see how well the people are using the skills they learned. Further discussion with these participants will reveal any weaknesses they've had in retaining the material. The supervisor should then be encouraged to report any problems with people using the newly acquired skills.

The idea here is to take a proactive stance on the evaluation of the effectiveness of your training. There are a whole range of methods that can be used to make such evaluations. We looked at only a few. You can work closely with your human resources or training department to design and develop even better ways to evaluate. This information should form a feedback loop which is used to change or modify the course appropriately.

Continuous Improvement of Training

This type of feedback mechanism is a major part of the continuous improvement of training. Training is not a static item. The skill level of people and the demands of the company are constantly changing, so training must change with it.

Management should review on a regular basis the training matrix for the company. The needs of various job functions have to be constantly re-evaluated for the skills they wish these workers to possess. This information is combined with feedback on the effectiveness of current training, and then supplemented with a list of new skills that supervisors feel the employees should learn. Both the IS manager and the human relations director should work together to see where training can be combined or reduced.

It is very common to find that one type of training complements another. For example, people who are unfamiliar with the use of a personal computer could incorporate network browsing as one of the exercises they work through. This would lead naturally into the second course on how browsers work. That, in turn, would be followed by a course on how they perform their specific job. This final course would be built on the idea that much of the information they gather will be done through an internet browser.

Each day the IS manager must think of a new way to slightly improve training within the company, and specifically, the training related to the internet system. This is how continuous improvement works. You do not do this in a vacuum. Instead, you must actively seek out feedback from the people using and maintaining the system.

Example of a Training Package You Can Use to Introduce the Internet

The best way to introduce people to the internet is to first make them familiar with the functions of a network browser. Let's walk through a short course on using an internet browser. This will also illustrate how to correctly deliver training.

We will assume that one of our example companies wants to deliver a two-hour course on Internet Explorer. The objectives of the class are to have employees:

- Understand how a browser works
- Discover their role in using a browser
- Learn how to launch the browser
- Be able to understand and enter URL's
- Be able to use links within a web page
- Learn how to use the Home, Back, Forward, and Favorite buttons
- Be able to read their E-mail through the browser
- Learn how to print a web page

These objectives will form the introduction of the class. Let's walk through the actual class to see how the planning process for training helps send a clear message.

Before the class even begins a coordinator sends out a memorandum to the potential participants. The memo informs each participant of when they are expected to attend the class. It then goes on to give a brief description of the class, what the participant is expected to learn, and the level of computer expertise required for this class. The expertise is basically the ability to work with Windows 95 applications. In other words, participants are pre-screened on their computer skills before being placed in this class. Those that are new to computers are put through a different class to learn basic Windows-based applications skills.

Once a participant arrives in the class, they sign-in, pick up their training materials, and take a seat at a computer terminal. The instructor introduces herself then explains the objectives of the course. Each student shall learn how to:

- Understand the workings of a network browser and why it's important to your job
- Start the browser program Internet Explorer
- Enter a universal resource location (URL) addressing method used on the internet (i.e. www.avix.com)
- Use hyperlinks to move between web pages
- Use the home key to find the corporation's central switching point for its intranet
- Use the "Back" and "Forward" keys to maneuver between web pages
- Use the "Favorite" key to quickly locate favorite internet locations
- Open E-mail using the internet browser
- Print web pages

Comparing these objectives given to the class with the objectives for the course, you can see the direct correlation. However the objectives are presented to the participants in a slightly different manner. The actual practical application of the skills they are about to learn are highlighted. For example, you do not just say that they will learn how to use the Home key. Instead, point out that the home key has a purpose—namely how to find the central table of contents for documents within the corporate intranet. By keeping training practical and focused, you have a better chance of holding the interest of participants.

The instructor goes through the usual exercises to introduce all the participants in the class to each other. The actual instruction begins with a discussion of how a web browser works. This would proceed along the lines of the discussion presented in Chapter 1 of this book. The instructor would want to explain how the internet works, IP addressing, and the internal operation of web pages. This would be just enough information to make people aware of roughly how a web browser functions.

Now the hands-on portion of the class would begin. The instructor would have the participants turn to their computers and launch Internet Explorer by double-clicking its icon on the desktop. The instructional material would also point out other ways of launching the application—one from the start button and the other by clicking on an HTML file. In this way the students are made aware that there is more than one way to launch Internet Explorer (see Figure 12–1).

Now the discussion would turn to what makes up a URL. The different levels of a domain name are illustrated using the company's internet address. For illustration purposes let's assume that address looks like this: www.avix.com.

The participants would enter this URL and see the home page of the company appear on their screens. They would think that they are making their first steps into the internet. They do not need to know that a DNS service on your intranet made this possible and the internet was not even involved (see Figure 12–2).

This would be followed with a humorous and a serious list of other URLs for the participants to try. They can try as many as possible within the few minutes given to this exercise. This gives each participant a "feel" for how URLs work while typically generating amusing stories for the class. Humor is a good tool for remembering things, if it is not overused.

Figure 12-1. Different Methods of Launching Internet Explorer

Figure 12–2. Using URLs

Figure 12–3. Using the Back and Forward Keys

Illustrations such as Figure 12–2 help to guide the participants on where a URL is entered. This is both helpful in the class and later in practice. If a participant forgets where the URL is entered, they only need to flip open their training booklet to the section called "Entering URLs" to see the illustration again.

The training material is written with action-oriented titles and short sections. This makes it a handy reference for later when some of the skills may have been forgotten.

Now the discussion turns to hyperlinks. When the screens of the participants' computers are filled with the home page of the company, they can immediately locate and click on a linked portion of the page. This allows them to see how links work. To supplement this, they move into learning the "Back" and "Forward" keys (see Figure 12–3).

By flowing through the logical sequence of browser usage you keep the participants on track. You also demonstrate how different parts of the browser program work together.

Other parts of the training material are set up to clearly show how to go through a sequence of steps to reach a goal. In this case the function of the "Favorites" key is explained. The instructor points out that when you find a web page of particular importance you can bookmark it for later retrieval. The instructional sequence looks like this:

How to Bookmark a Favorite Web Page

When browsing the company intranet, or the internet, you may find a web page that is particularly helpful to your job. You can place a bookmark on this page so that you can return to it anytime in the future. The procedure is as follows:

  1. First go to the page you wish to bookmark in your browser.

2. Click on the "Favorites" button.

3. Select the "Add to Favorites" option.

4. When the dialog box appears, enter the name for the bookmark. Then click OK.

Now this page has been bookmarked. Whenever you wish to see this page again, open "favorites" in the selection menu and click on the name of the bookmark. Remember, we have a strict internet policy that restricts web browsing to business related matters. Therefore you are not allowed to bookmark pages that are not related to your job.

Now let's try finding a page on the company intranet and bookmark it.

1. Press the "home" button. Work down the table of contents of documents at the company and find the corporate intranet usage policy.

2. Click on this link. When the page appears, click on "Favorites" and mark this page.

3. Now enter a new URL (www.competitor.org). Once this page is in place, open your Favorites list and click the intranet policy bookmark. You should be transported back to the bookmarked page.

This simple, step-by-step method of explaining how the "favorite" button works and then conducting a hands-on exercise reinforces the learning of this new skill. True, the skill is minor, but by pointing out the practical application of this skill in the everyday use of a browser, the participants see why it is important to know this function of the browser.

The class would use these same techniques to learn how to open their E-mail through the browser. To make this relevant the instructor would have the participants open an E-mail that says:

"The information you need on unsolicited faxes is located at www.stopfax.com"

The instructor knows that these particular participants are constantly bombarded by market scam faxes. This message will peak their interest. They then learn to click on the link in the message to have the browser take them to this site, while they are still working on E-mail. Not only is the site interesting but they have seen one of the powerful functions of Internet Explorer demonstrated—the ability to put hyperlinks into E-mail.

The class ends with people learning to print the page on unsolicited faxes. They have learned new skills and helpful information they can use to eliminate an immediate problem in their job life. In other words, their attention was caught early in the class and held throughout. This is the mark of a good training package. People leave the course feeling they have learned something worthwhile. A well-planned method of evaluation at the end of the course will confirm the initial success of the training.

Further References

A demonstration of several online training seminars is available at www.isogroup.iserv.net

Internet Search Strings

Several sites are available for the discussion of web-based training. Try searching using one of the following terms:

"Web based training"

"Instructional Design"

"Long distance learning"

"Internet based training"

Chapter 13

Day-to-Day Operations, Procedures, Maintenance, and Monitoring

As an effective IS manager, you have to be able to demonstrate the existence and effectiveness of your management system. To be able to demonstrate your system, you need documentation. Most of this documentation will be written procedures and work instructions. You will also need job descriptions, quality records, policies, and a host of other documents.

During the first half of this book, you've read that proper procedures and work instructions make the day-to-day operation, maintenance, and monitoring of your internet technology much easier. With proper instructions people know what to do, when to do it, and what results are expected. Well written instructions are easy to use and understand. They encourage employees to follow procedures because they set the easiest path to completing a job successfully.

This chapter explores how many of these documents can be developed concurrently to save time and money while also creating more effective documentation. Specifically, we will look at the process of job and task analysis in the creation of procedures, work instructions, job descriptions, skills lists, and training material.

What is Job and Task Analysis?

The creation of a product or the performance of a service is seen as a single system consisting of a series of related processes. For each process, you will need a written procedure. Within each process will be a series of tasks to perform. Tasks performed by an individual can be grouped together as a work instruction. To give structure to the process of creating procedures, work instructions, and other documents, we will use the techniques of job and task analysis.

Job analysis and task analysis are two separate techniques that share many similar traits. Job analysis looks at the components of a specific job. Task analysis looks at a particular process and its component tasks. We will consider them as one activity in this discussion. Whether job or task analysis is conducted, they both break down the process being examined into its smallest components so they can be classified, organized, and clarified. We shall see how this is done in the following examples.

A process will usually involve many people and require them to write a procedure. In this chapter, we will examine the process and identify the steps necessary to complete the process. Likewise, we will look at an individual's job and identify the steps needed to complete the task at hand. Then this information will be supplemented with data about how the steps are to be completed, what to do when a step cannot be completed successfully, safety considerations, the skills required, and other similar information. The result will be a database of information about the job or process under study. By using this database, the IS manager will be able to create many of the documents an efficient IS department requires.

There are many approaches advocated for job and task analysis. In fact, there are many different schools of thought on how to perform job or task analysis. It is beyond the scope of this book to explore each of them. Instead, the general approach described here combines some of the methods. This approach will be adequate for creating the documentation needed for proper operation of your internet technology. However, if you wish to explore these techniques in greater depth, you should consult the literature for job and task analysis and seek the advice of an outside authority on this topic.

Figure 13–1 shows how job and task analysis can create a database of information that can be used to create a wide variety of documents. Note that there are two tracks of document development. The first is the creation of procedures and work instructions from the newly created database; the second track uses the same database to create job descriptions, skill requirements, competency checks, and training material.

How to Perform Job and Task Analysis

A simple approach to writing procedures is a process that involves the creation of a flowchart. The flowchart is a map of the process under study. From this map, a procedure is created. For creating procedures and work instructions under a deadline, this approach works just fine. However, if you have the time

Figure 13-1. Document Flow from Job/Task Analysis

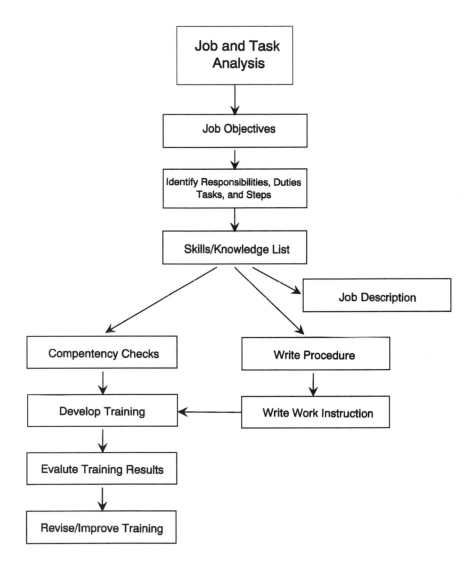

or if you wish to write several documents concurrently, then job and task analysis is recommended.

Let's begin by looking at a single process using both methods. This comparison will show that each method has its particular advantages. Flowcharting is faster, but job and task analysis is more effective. At the same time, the two methods can be easily combined so that the flowchart helps a job and task analysis team better understand the process involved.

Let's look at the process of making data backups. A computer technician has a regular schedule for backing up data from the web servers. Each day a daily backup is performed and the data copied to a streaming tape. Each Friday evening a complete backup is made of all of the files on the system. These tapes are stored in a protected area after they have been tested for accuracy. Once a month a practice restore session is held to confirm that the backup system will work properly in an emergency. Figure 13–2 shows a portion of the flowchart for the technician's tasks.

Each stage diagrammed on the flowchart is translated into a procedural step. As with policy statements, we follow a specific format. Basic identifica-

Figure 13–2. Flowchart of Backup Process

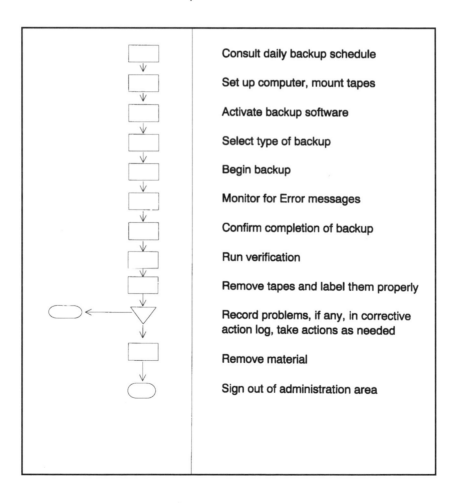

Consult daily backup schedule

Set up computer, mount tapes

Activate backup software

Select type of backup

Begin backup

Monitor for Error messages

Confirm completion of backup

Run verification

Remove tapes and label them properly

Record problems, if any, in corrective action log, take actions as needed

Remove material

Sign out of administration area

tion is made, revision dates noted, a signature of authorization obtained, and pages numbered. The steps within a procedure are also numbered to portray the level of involvement within the document. Let's look at the procedure for data backups.

Standard Operating Procedure 13-002

Data Backup of Web Servers and Network

Issued: 12/13/97 Revision: B (3/4/98)

Approval: J.C. Miller   Page 1 of 2

13.1—Purpose

To ensure the complete, accurate, and timely backup of web site and network files so that complete recovery from data disasters is always possible.

13.2—Scope

This procedure is for any web site within the company, whether for intranet or internet presentation.

13.3—Responsibilities

The Information Systems Manager will ultimately be responsible for the success of this procedure. The computer technicians shall be assigned the task of completing scheduled backups. The IS Manager will make these assignments.

13.4—Procedure

13.4.1—The technician consults the daily backup schedule and secures the proper tapes to be used.

13.4.2—Using the network command computer located in the Network Administrator's office, the technician activates the appropriate backup software in background mode.

13.4.3—Tapes are placed into the tape drives of each affected web server for the daily backups. A series of gigabyte tapes are placed into the tape drive of the network command computer to perform the once-a-week network backup.

13.4.4—Backup routines are now activated.

13.4.5—The technician should watch for error messages. Any error should be recorded in the backup log and, if necessary, corrective action taken.

13.4.6—Failure during backup requires the filling out of a corrective action form and investigation of the problem. If the problem cannot be determined and corrected within 30 minutes, the shift supervisor should be notified. At the discretion of the shift supervisor, the network administrator can also be notified.

13.4.7—Successful backups are marked and taken to the secure document vault in Building 58.

13.4.8—Once a month the daily backups and the weekly network backup tapes are taken to the test computer in Building 32. A full restoration is attempted and results noted. Restoration has to be 100% successful.

13.5—Reference forms

Colorado Backup Software manual

Iomega manuals

3M tape care and use guide

Backup log

Corrective action forms and log

As you can see, we create a basic procedure with criteria of workmanship included. This should be signed and dated as a controlled document to meet the requirements of ISO 9000. However, the procedure so far only looks at the backup process. Surely, the technician has other duties. A job description must be created that includes the skills, knowledge, and experience needed for backups. Eventually, some sort of training materials will be needed to help a new person learn to be a computer technician.

To do this effectively, you will need to form a good database of information about the job of computer technician. If you use this information to intelligently combine documents, the day-to-day operation of the company will become easier and more efficient.

Gaining Knowledge through Job and Task Analysis

Job and task analysis is a more structured approach to examining operations such as the process of making backups. This is accomplished by systematically breaking down a situation into its components. The following four levels of descending complexity are used.

1. Job Objective

2. Responsibilities
3. Duties
4. Tasks (with the steps taken to accomplish the task)

A job objective is the overall, general description of the job or process. In our example, it might look something like this:

"Job Title: Computer Technician
Job Objective: The computer technician is responsible for the set-up, operation, and routine maintenance of personal computers and the network. In addition, the technician is expected to meet internal requirements for computer operations and do so in an effective and efficient way."

A job responsibility is a broad description of related job duties. Job duties are a common collection of tasks the operator must perform. Tasks are the most basic units of work. Tasks are a collection of steps with a tangible output. Typically, a task is independent from other steps in the process. Therefore, we could break down our data backup example into these respective categories. Let's begin with the job responsibilities of a computer technician performing backups.

"Job Responsibilities:
    1.0 Preparation
    2.0 Running Software/Hardware Configuration
    3.0 Inspection
    4.0 Maintenance
    5.0 Paperwork
    6.0 Housekeeping"

Now let's take these responsibilities and list the duties for each one.

1.0 Preparation
    1.1 Reviews instructions
    1.2 Checks schedule
    1.3 Obtains proper blank tapes or previously used tapes

2.0 Running Software/Hardware Configuration
    2.1 Run server backups from central network machine

2.2 Switch tapes when necessary

3.0 Inspection
    3.1 Watch for error messages
    3.2 Test for accuracy of backup
    3.3.Take corrective actions when needed

4.0 Maintenance
    4.1 Monitor the process
    4.2 Check time to complete against expected times
    4.3 Keep track of tapes and label them appropriately
    4.4 Check storage conditions

5.0 Paperwork
    5.1 Backup report
    5.2 Time card
    5.3 Reaction logs

6.0 Housekeeping
    6.1 Keep area clean
    6.2 Check fire extinguisher
    6.3 Properly store tapes and other media

This type of information is obtained by directly observing the process, talking to experts, examining the quality plan and production plans, consulting the existing procedures and policies, interviewing the operator and supervisor, reading the operating manual for the software, and doing time/motion studies. Some human resource people go so far as to use surveys given to all employees in an area to establish norms.

At a minimum, you should observe the process, talk to the employees, and study the existing documentation. In addition, you may want to hold a meeting with the people responsible for planning and carrying out the backup process. In our example, this might include the technicians, the network administrator, the immediate supervisor, and a quality control representative familiar with the requirements for this process. Your findings can be presented to employees for evaluation of completeness and accuracy. The feedback from this group can be used to refine your list of responsibilities and duties.

While you have your team assembled, it is time to break each of the duties down into its constituent tasks. We recommend the use of index cards passed out to the assembled team. Each team member can jot down the tasks for each duty they are most familiar with. These can be posted under each duty on a bulletin board. Flipcharts, computer software, and other methods are also acceptable.

The team can freely arrange the tasks cards and discuss the addition or subtraction of tasks. Remember, a task should be stated as the minimal component of a duty and it should be independent. When describing the tasks, try to use a noun/verb format. To see how this looks, let's examine the tasks listed for one duty—the inspection of the process.

Responsibility: Inspection
    Duty: Watch for Error Messages
        Task: Monitor operating system level messages
        Task: Review the backup software's error log
        Task: Watch the monitor for run-time errors

Task statements should be brief and to the point. However, the task statements should not be so simple as to be obvious, such as "get tape." You should state only what the operator must do to complete the duty. These should be observable behaviors of the operator. As we shall see later, this information on tasks will be key to creating our array of documents.

Once the first list of tasks is developed, you will need to discuss the results in detail to obtain a final and complete list. Typically, you will break down the tasks into their constituent steps. A step is a single action that leads toward completion of a task. For example, the task of drilling holes into the pages of a new manual can be broken down into the steps of mounting a set of pages, locating a drilling site, actually drilling, and the repositioning of the pages. By breaking tasks down into the specific steps taken by an operator, you can open up your discussion of a task. Analyze the task by breaking it down into the following considerations:

1. Materials, tools, or equipment needed
2. Criteria of workmanship
3. Special conditions
4. Safety considerations
5. Reaction plan

The criteria of workmanship is a description of the successful completion of the standards for a task, or in other words, how the technician knows that the task is successfully completed. Special conditions are a description of any particular circumstances that affect how the task is performed. Typically, these are environmental or process based conditions. A reaction plan is the steps an operator should take if something other than success occurs during the task. As always, safety during the task should be discussed and noted.

These five considerations will give you greater insight into how a task is performed. At the same time, you can define the skills and knowledge needed to perform the tasks. This is highly recommended for critical tasks. It's also useful for situations where temporary employees are used or there is a high turnover in operators. The list of skills and knowledge will give you the ability to quickly locate a qualified operator, while the detailed list of steps to take will make training faster and easier.

While you are discussing the tasks, you may find that you need to add or combine duties or responsibilities for greater clarity. Feel free to do this so that you end up with a list of responsibilities, duties, and tasks that are well organized and make sense for the job or process involved.

Your final list of tasks is used to create the database of information on this particular job. In our example, we looked at a computer technician. You will want to build up a considerable amount of information about this one job. You will then see how information on the skills and level of knowledge for this job are revealed. In our example, it is quickly becoming obvious that the ability to accurately follow written instructions about software is a critical skill for this job.

When you have completed your list of tasks and the conditions under which they are performed, be sure to show them to people familiar with the job. You want to confirm the accuracy and completeness of your work. In most cases, these people will want to make changes and you will want the final documents to accurately reflect the realities of the job.

Writing Procedures or Work Instructions

Now that you have collected all of this information, it is time to put it to work. The first job will be to create the procedure or work instruction. In the example of the computer technician, you now have more than enough information to create your work instructions for particular stages of the backup process. In fact, you could even take the procedure above, created by using just a flowchart, and add in your additional information to make a detailed document that is both procedure and work instruction. This technique is highly recommended for small companies where just one or two people carry out the procedure.

For each step in the process, use the specific tasks you have identified. The information on safety, conditions, criteria of workmanship, reaction plans, and equipment needed are now noted.

Example: Work instruction created from job/task analysis

Work Instruction 13-05—Test of Backup Tapes

Parts Involved—Test computer, tape drive, software for backups, hard disk utilities

General Safety Considerations—Normal electrical safety precautions should be observed. Operator should be familiar with the firefighting equipment in this area.

Task 1. Obtain materials

Step 1: Sign out materials for processing.

Standard: Computer technician goes to secure tape storage area and signs out the second most recent copies of the daily backup and the weekly network backup tapes. Each tape should be clearly identified and labeled.

Step 2: Obtain software guides.

Standard: The software manuals for the backup software should be checked out of the IS department and taken with the tapes to the testing area. These should not be the controlled copies of the manuals. Instead, the backup copies of the manuals should be used.

Task 2. Preparation of Work Area

Step 1: Log on to the test computer using the "TestRun" account name and your password.

Step 2: Click on the backup program group.

Step 3: Place first test tape (the daily backup from two days ago) into the tape drive.

Standard: The technician should have the operations manual for the software at hand. Tape dates on labels should match those reported by the software.

Task 3. Restore data

Step 1: Using Windows Explorer, erase all files from the D:/ partition of the drive.

Step 2: Double click the "restore" option from the Zip Tools.

Step 3: Monitor restoration of data. Note any problems reported by the software. If restoration is not successful, try again. If still not restored, notify your supervisor and start filling out the corrective action report.

Standard: Daily backup tapes should restore all data accurately within a one-hour time frame.

Task 4. Test the Data

Step 1: Open the "file" menu item on the restore program and select "compare." You will need to specify that the tape be compared to the D:/ drive.

Step 2: Note any problems reported. Submit this report to your supervisor for signature.

Reaction Plan: Any problems involving corruption of the data should be noted in the reaction plan log. The root cause of the problem must be found and other backup tapes checked to determine the extent of the problem.

Step 3: Run all applications that were backed up. Using Windows Explorer, find the applications within each sub-directory and double click these to confirm that they are indeed active. Obtain from your supervisor a list of sample data files to call up. These should all load successfully.

The rest of the work instruction is expanded into the following responsibilities and duties. As you can see, the act of restoration and testing has been divided into its own grouping above. The standards, reaction plans, and special conditions have been added to the work instruction. The end of the work instruction might include the following information:

Further Duties:

4.0 Inspection

4.1 Five other backup tapes are selected from the previous month of backups and checked for the accuracy of labeling.

4.2 The results of this test are recorded on the control chart.

4.3 If any tape fails the restoration tests, the operator contacts the supervisor, segregates the affected lot of tapes, and documents the incident on the backup log.

5.0 Completion and Paperwork

5.1 Once a set of tapes passes the tests, the results are noted in the backup log.

5.2 Each completed tape must be returned to the secure storage area as quickly as possible after the tests are completed.

5.3 Control charts and logs should also be kept up to date with accurate information.

5.4 A daily time card has to be kept up to date and turned in once a week.

6.0 Maintenance

6.1 The tape drive heads should be cleaned at least once every quarter.

6.2 The current version of the backup and testing software should be checked for appropriateness once a year.

6.3 PC Tools should be run each week to clean and defragment the test hard drive.

7.0 Housekeeping

7.1 The work area should always be kept swept and clear of obstacles by the operator.

7.2 The fire extinguisher should be visually examined each week to assure that it has the proper charge.

7.3 Loose equipment, media, and unclaimed software not in use should be placed in the storage cabinet.

Although this document is much larger than usually necessary, it is easy to use and it contains much useful information. This creates several advantages.

The first advantage is that an unfamiliar operator can read through this work instruction and obtain a lot of information on what to do and when to do it. This helps in the training of replacements or with the use of temporary employees. Second, an experienced operator only needs to scan the tasks as a checklist to ensure that the process is proceeding as planned. Reference to the step level is only needed when an unusual circumstance occurs or when learning a new job.

These first two advantages also create the third advantage—the relief of supervisors. Most supervisors will tell you that the majority of their time is spent "firefighting." That is, their days are spent telling people what to do and solving problems as they arise. The use of detailed work instructions means that the employees can take more responsibility for initially correcting problems and for making process decisions. This frees up the supervisors' time for more important activities, such as organizing continuous improvement.

However, if you would prefer to use short work instructions, this too can be accomplished using our original database. Every job will have common elements. For example, most factory jobs will have safety rules, control charts, process logs, reaction plans and the like. These can be separated from the work instructions and posted as job aids at the work site.

The important point to remember is to create a documentation system that is easy to use and appropriate for your industrial situation. There are actually many ways to meet all of your documentation needs, including an intranet. You should spend some time and imagination planning your system and estimating the lowest cost solution to your needs.

Another advantage of the information gained from job and task analysis is the ability to create documents beyond the work instruction.

Creating a Job Description, List of Skills, Competency Checks, and Training Programs

Let's begin with a job description. Element 4.18 of ISO 9001 says that you need to document the skills, knowledge, and experience for each job that affects quality. The job and task analysis produced just such information. A job description is a good way to organize this information.

According to element 4.18, you need to document the knowledge, skill, and education requirements for each job within your plant. This is also the core information reported in a job description. A good job description will also include an outline of job responsibilities, pay range, levels of competency, and other relevant information. Naturally, many people may work under a single job description, so you should not need to create many job descriptions.

The data for completing a job description can be drawn from many sources, but the information generated in our previous job and task analysis can give you much of the data you will need. To write a job description for a technician, begin by listing the responsibilities of the job. These can be quickly fleshed out using the information gathered for the job and task.

To this you can add a list of skills, knowledge, and education required for the job. Knowledge is a person's awareness of how to perform a task or the way something works. Education can serve as a partial or full replacement for some knowledge requirements. A skill is something the person can demonstrate.

The next step in creating a job description is to incorporate the skills and knowledge required for the job that were already listed on the job and task analysis form.

Now you have to make a series of decisions to complete this part of the job description. You have to decide what levels of education will count as partial or full substitution for each of your items in the skill and knowledge lists. For example, does a high school diploma demonstrate that a person can read and write effectively? Does it mean that they can work with fractions? It should. If it does, then you will modify your knowledge and skill items to reflect these alternative ways to qualify for the job.

The resulting statements may look like the following:

"Candidate must have demonstrated ability to work with basic computer applications. Also must have the ability to correctly set up computer peripherals. Or, a candidate must hold a valid and current MSCE (Microsoft Certified Engineer) card."

The MSCE training would substitute for the need to demonstrate many of the application skills. Therefore, what you are trying to achieve is the shortest possible list that covers all of the skills, knowledge, or education needed to qualify for a particular job. It looks like a difficult process with many decisions, but you will find that if you have detailed tasks lists and a couple of job experts available, this will make the process much easier.

When you add this mixture of skills, knowledge, and education, along with any other relevant information, you end up with a full job description.

As always, your final job description should be examined by someone familiar with the job to assure completeness and accuracy. Because IS managers tend to work outside of the human resources department, you should also share your description with them. They should be able to spot violations of regulations affecting job descriptions, such as the need to add "right-to-know" items to your lists.

You can use the information we have already gathered to form the competency checks that will be used to confirm that a person has the ability to perform the assigned tasks. To develop competency checks, you need to identify the performance objectives for the job. For a skill requirement, a checklist could be used as the candidate demonstrates the ability to work with the software and computers. Other possibilities include the use of case studies, role-playing, simulations, form filling, and other such methods. Knowledge requirements can be checked using essays, multiple choice tests, case studies, fill in the blank tests, or oral examinations.

The important thing to keep in mind is that a specific level of competency is set for each qualification. These levels should accurately reflect the level of skill or knowledge needed for each job. Thus, from the initial job and task analysis, you are able to create work instructions, job descriptions, lists of skills and knowledge, and competency checks.

Developing Training Materials

This extensive collection of information for one particular job can be used to create training materials. For the computer technician, you have identified and sequenced the critical tasks of his job; you know the skills and knowledge required for this job; and, you have a set of performance objectives that have to be met. Taken together, this information leads straight to the type of training to develop for people who want to learn to be technicians.

This is accomplished by using the information already gathered to develop an instructional outline. Skill and knowledge requirements can be translated into a series of instructional modules. For example, a technician needs to learn the following topics:

1. Basic reading skills
2. Using Windows NT workstation
3. Report writing
4. Working with fractions
5. Business communications
6. Statistical process control
7. Safety procedures

There are many paths you can take from this point. One method is to sit down and look at the requirements for groups of jobs, for example, all of the IS related jobs. Look for common training needs across all of these jobs. You might discover that the following are required in most IS jobs.

- Team problem-solving
- Safety procedures
- Basic Windows NT workstation
- Simple math, reading, and writing skill improvement
- Use of the Netscape Browser v.4

This could form a core curriculum for your IS staff. In other words, anyone entering an IS job would be required to take training in these subject areas or demonstrate competency in these areas.

The main point here is that you are not training in the dark. You are now armed with tasks lists, skills/knowledge requirements, competency checks, and job objectives. This type of information is very helpful in developing training material to fit your needs. Your primary need is to assure that the right people with the right abilities are doing their assigned jobs.

Secondary to this is your ability to conform the training needs we outlined in the previous chapter. Because you have lists of training needs for all jobs, and a way to check current competency, you can create a training schedule for the next several years. People entering a job for the first time, or being transferred, will now have a list of training classes to attend and skills to master before they are fully qualified. Workers who are deficient go on to the training schedule for the courses that will bring them into conformance. At the same time, you will be able to better estimate what your training needs are to continually assure the abilities of your employees.

The reason for going through this much analysis for just one job was to make a point. This demonstrates that job and task analysis is one method that can not only help you create work instructions and procedures; it can also create a flow of documents to help you meet your needs for training, job descriptions, competency checks, management of personnel, and a host of other needs. It is not the only way to accomplish this, but it seems to be one of the more efficient paths to a better quality system.

Analyzing just one type of job, computer technician, illustrates the power and scope of information and documents that can be developed from job and task analysis. These same principles would apply to any job title, from president to receptionist. If you wish to use the information gathered for meeting training requirements to benefit your company in other ways, then the procedures outlined above are recommended.

As a word of caution, you must keep the analysis up to date. In other words, as processes and jobs change, so too must the database of information. It is recommended that the people working in the affected area be active participants in the original creation of your database. Then as the process or job changes, these same people can help update the database of information. The result is an active, useful, up-to-date system of documentation, and employees who feel very involved with their jobs.

At the same time, avoid the urge to create lengthy and detailed documents. Work instructions in particular should be kept short and to the point. Whenever possible, job aids, such as defect charts, reference diagrams, and the like should be used to keep the instructions simple to read and easy to use for the technician.

To learn more about job and task analysis, you can seek the guidance of an expert or enroll in a seminar on this topic—or both, if you are going to implement this technology seriously.

Storing Documentation on the Intranet

Another aspect of the day-to-day maintenance of internet technology involves the storage of the documentation used to support your system. Above, we discussed the creation of procedures and work instructions. Earlier in the book, we talked about corporate internet policies.

The question then arises, where should this information be stored, and how can you make it readily available to the system's users? If your company is running an intranet, the answer is simple. Store this documentation on the intranet.

Let's take the example of procedures. Procedures describe how each system operates. Therefore, you could have any number of people within your corporation interested in looking at a procedure. For the sake of illustration, we'll start with several people who, at different times, need to review the purchasing procedure. We will assume that these people normally do not read through purchasing related procedures. How do they quickly find the procedure they seek?

The answer to this question lies in the way you structure the storage of documents on your intranet. The best way to do this is to establish a central administration point where all users can access the same subdirectory or folder. That folder is called "procedures." Within the folder are subdirectories for each department. Procedures related to those departments are stored in the appropriate subdirectories.

Because you are encouraging your employees to use browser software, you would create a table of contents page as the home page for this common administration point. A person wishing to find the purchasing procedure for computer equipment has two different ways of locating it.

1. They can go to the table of contents page for procedures using their web browser and look down the list until they find the procedure they wish to examine. They click on this procedure and it is brought up instantly on their web server.

2. They can engage a search engine on your intranet and look for the term "Purchasing Procedure." Clicking on results list will bring up the procedure they wish to examine.

Therefore, your subdirectory structure will look something like this:

```
C:\
  C:\Procedures
    C:\Procedures\Finance
    C:\Procedures\Purchasing
    C:\Procedures\Manufacturing
    C:\Procedures\Sales
```

Keeping the Web Site Alive and Productive

Chapter 15 to the end of the book discusses the topic of maintaining and expanding your internet presence. Everything covered up until this point has focused on establishing an internet connection and presence for your company. The value of that connection and presence can be lost at the web site if it is not kept alive and productive.

Much of the planning discussion early in this book focused on the uses for your internet connection. Once you have implemented your web site you then constantly monitor its use for effectiveness. The effectiveness can be established in any of several ways. You can interview users of the site, send surveys, keep hit counts, and use other common tools.

This provides the feedback information you need to find troubled web sites. Keeping web sites alive and productive means keeping a motivated crew actively maintaining the sites. Users of the internet expect rapid response of information. For example, if a person is looking for the newest price on your product today, or a new product is announced, they expect the information to be posted immediately on your web site. Any lag in time represents disappointment of potential customers.

It is very important that you keep each team responsible for its part in the web site constantly at work on the material in the web pages, updating the information. The better you are at this task, the more valuable your web site becomes either on the internet or within your intranet.

Using In-House Technicians

Most companies expect computer oriented technicians to provide much of the content for their internet presence. As we shall see in later chapters, there is another source of content which can supplement the work of in-house technicians.

Your technical staff represents a limited resource. This resource must be used wisely in support of your Internet system. As you have probably learned by going through these exercises, a certain amount of overhead is necessary to maintain web sites and other internet presence. Therefore, you must plan carefully which technicians will be deployed within your internet system.

This will be especially critical for any sort of help desk that you have set up for users. You will quickly discover that people who are new to using the internet or an intranet experience many problems in the beginning. Therefore you need to staff the help desk to be ready to respond to the multiple questions that will emerge as you introduce the intranet to your company.

At the same time, you need to keep repair technicians handy. As you increase the number of people accessing the internet connection from within your company, problems are bound to happen. Browser software might fail, servers might go down, access and permissions may be set incorrectly, and a host of other potential problems related to the early phase of introduction can occur.

To keep employee interest high in using internet technology, you must be ready to rapidly respond to problems as they occur. This is best done by forming a small, rapid response repair team that's always on hand. This team is sent to the most critical problem being presented each day. For example, if a server is failing to correctly connect users to the internet, the connection must be fixed. It would give this problem priority over a single user having problems with a monitor.

Methods of Problem Prevention

Two concepts are introduced in this section which will make the day-to-day maintenance job much easier. The first concept is called problem detection and elimination, and the second concept is called prevention. A problem that is prevented is much more valuable to a company then the correction of an existing problem. It is easier to prevent a problem than it is to correct a problem once it occurs, and much less costly.

There are corrective actions that are used to fix problems once they are detected, but right now we want to focus on methods that can be used to prevent problems. The basic approach is to have management review your entire system continuously. That means that each the network administrator keeps logs of problems that have been encountered. Corrective action reports are filed by technical people for any problem encountered. The entire system is audited at least once a year.

The information that is gathered about the problems ongoing within your system gives management an important clue on the potential for a problem to occur. Take the example of users reporting failure of their browsers with certain web pages. Management may choose to investigate these problems more deeply because they seem to form a pattern. They can discover, by reading the logs and reports, that all of these failures occurred when the web browser was attempting to use a web page with a database link.

The technicians at the same time, might use various methods to get the browser to interface with the affected pages. However, if the problem tends to re-occur, management identifies this as a high potential area for future problems. Instead of encouraging more on-site fixes, the entire system is re-examined. Future problems are prevented by upgrading all browsers in the corporation and setting new guidelines for database connections to web pages. The initial investment is higher than just fixing a few problems, but prevents the problem from re-occurring in the future.

Corrective Actions and Preventive Actions

Whether using corrective actions or preventive actions, it is important that the IS manager works with a team. When examining problems, the potential of a problem to affect quality, cost, functionality, performance, dependability, safety, and customer satisfaction should be evaluated. This information is gathered from the reports generated from the logs that your system creates and from the expertise of your technical staff. In this way you have information that allows you to list and rank problems from the most critical to the most trivial.

In the case of preventive action, such ranking allows you to identify the largest problems with the highest potential to occur. These are the ones on which to focus your preventive actions. Even though you identify many potential problems, you attack only those that are most critical and those that you have the resources to address.

The method of attacking a problem follows the following steps:

1. *Assignment of responsibility*—You need to assign a particular person to a particular problem. Even though a team may be addressing the problem, one person is actually held responsible.

2. *Evaluation of the problem*—Next, you need to know exactly how important the problem is, with a rough estimate of costs to get this fixed. The normal economic calculations are made to decide the best course of action, whether to settle the whole problem now or to address portions of it over time.

3. *Search for possible causes*—The team now uses various problem solving methods to try to find the root cause of the problem.

4. *Analysis of the problem*—The team needs to identify the root cause and all of the different parts of the system it affects. This could include procedures, related processes, operations, records, servicing, and customer complaints. In other words, you establish the scope and the effect of the root cause. This also helps you to later establish how you will measure what corrective actions have been most effective.

5. *Elimination of root cause*—Steps are taken to illuminate the root cause of the problem and all related causes. The root cause should be attacked in a way that assures that re-occurrence is eliminated.

6. *Process changes*—It may be necessary to add additional monitoring and control procedures at the point of the problem occurrence. This will both confirm the effectiveness of your fix and hopefully alert you to any return of the problem.

7. *Permanent changes to the system*—In almost all cases you'll discover that management level changes are necessary to permanently eliminate the root cause. As our previous example showed, management needed to upgrade all browsers.

There is a wide variety of problem solving tools available to help you identify root causes, investigate the extent of a problem, and confirm the elimination of a problem. It is beyond the scope of this book to discuss all of these in detail. Some of these techniques include the following:

- Check lists
- Autopsy of failed equipment
- Pareto analysis
- Brainstorming
- Story boards
- Affinity diagrams
- Force field analysis
- Fish bone (cause and effect) charts
- Process capability analysis
- Simulations
- Correlation
- Designed experiments

- Interelationships diagrams
- Nominal group techniques
- Statistical process control
- Journals, logs, record analysis
- Ranking
- Quality function deployment

Two of the techniques will be emphasized here: brainstorming and statistical process control.

Brainstorming is a method of getting a team of people to express as many thoughts and ideas about a situation as possible. Typically the team leader goes around the room asking each person to contribute a thought on a particular topic. These are written down for the group to save. This process of sharing thoughts tends to generate additional analysis and thinking about the situation. The results of such a technique is the creation of a lot of information the group can use to start making decisions on how to correct or prevent the problem. It is very common to find that no one person has the correct idea on how to solve a problem. Instead, it takes the synthesis of the group to bring out root causes and effective solutions.

Statistical process control is very similar to the monitoring charts created by your computer software. For example, usage charts generated by Novell NetWare or by the Windows NT operating system, show the fluctuation in the use of system resources. What statistical process control does is allow you to calculate the average amount of usage and the range of normal variation.

This creates additional boundary limits on your charts called "control limits." When an event sends the chart over a control limit, you can be confident that this is statistically significant. In other words, it doesn't just look like a problem—you can be fairly confident it *is* a problem. This allows you to react to real problems and ignore false alarms. We discuss this technique more extensively in the coming chapters.

Web Site Reporting

You can monitor your web sites by first looking at how information about your internet technology is generated. To begin at the simplest level, let's look at the types of reports that can be generated about a particular web site.

People who have been using the internet regularly are familiar with hit counts. These are the number of times a request has been received for a particular web page. A single user requesting a particular page generates one hit count. If that same user returns to the page several times, then several hits are generated.

This result is a common problem for monitoring a web site. It is very easy to get information about how many times the page was requested. It is much more difficult to firmly establish how many people are visiting a web site. The counts are valuable to the IS manager because they show the volume of IP traffic being used by one site. The number of people accessing the site is more valuable to sales and marketing.

You can also monitor the amount of data being requested from or sent to a particular web site. This gives you a good picture of the data flow in and out of a particular site. All of the web sites on a single server can be added together to get the total data flow picture. When this total begins to approach the capability limits of an internet connection, you know you will have problems.

Another web site report is the number of times requests for information failed to be delivered. This can occur for any of several reasons. Noise on the connection, IP addressing problems, and corruption of data within a packet are all common causes. You can establish a certain level of tolerance for errors in the attempt to send packets. For example, you may set a tolerance level of five percent of all packets. By monitoring the error rate, you can see how well your system performs against your expectations.

Example: Setting up Microsoft's IIS to monitor activity

Windows NT and the Microsoft Internet Information Server both come equipped with software to monitor some of the variables just described. You can also obtain third party software for counting the number of hits to a web site or other relevant information.

What follows is a brief description of how to set up the monitoring software that comes with Microsoft's Internet Information Server. Specifically, you'll want to use the performance monitor under the administration tools for the Internet Information Server. This software allows you to create visual charts, written reports, and alerts, for the performance of your web server.

The software works by tracking objects. Each object has counters to track specific events. Objects you can include:

- Browsers
- Memory cache
- FTP server activity
- http service

- System memory
- Network resources
- Hard disks
- The microprocessor
- Remote access services
- TCP/IP

The overall health and operation of the server can also be monitored, and the software provides you with a wide range of other characteristics that can be monitored. Therefore, you must choose carefully those characteristics which are most important in evaluating the success of your system.

The following is only a representative list of what can be monitored. There is a greater number of performance characteristics than shown here:

- Bytes received per second
- Bytes sent per second
- CGI requests
- Connection attempts
- Total number of current users connected
- Number of files received
- Number of files sent
- Number of Get requests
- Login attempts
- Maximum number of connections to http service
- Not Found errors
- Post requests
- Cache flushes
- Directory listings
- Average amount of a synchronous I/O per minute
- Total of synchronous I/O requests rejected

As you can see, the capability of the software is high. To set up a chart to monitor some of these characteristics, take the following steps. Let's assume you want to monitor the number of bytes being sent and received from a particular service, such as http.

1. Click the "Start" key on the Window NT operating screen, select "Programs, Administration Tools (Common)," and then "Performance Monitor."

2. Click "File" and then "New Chart." This sets up a new monitoring chart.

3. Click "Edit" from the command menu, then "Add to Chart" to start the chart creation process.

4. In the window that pops open, first select the service you wish to monitor. In our example we would open the scrolling menu of objects and select the HTTP service. Now open the scrolling menu for counters and select the bytes received, sent, and total options (see Figure 13–3).

Figure 13-3. Scrolling Menu for Counters

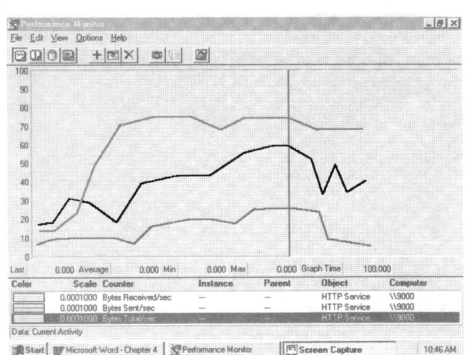

For each counter selected, be sure to designate the color to be used on the chart. Then click the "Add" button for each selection. When finished, click "Done" and the new chart appears. You can also set this software up to regularly produce reports or to alert you when problems occur.

Further References

Information Systems Policies and Procedures Manual, by George Jenkins, Prentice-Hall, 1997.

Information Technology Audit Handbook, by Doug Dayton, Prentice-Hall, 1997.

Building and Managing the Corporate Intranet, by Ronald L. Wagner and Eric Engelmann, McGraw-Hill, 1997.

Web Sites

The CIO magazine site at www.cio.com is an excellent source of daily management advice.

Internet Search Terms

"Management" + "Intranet"

"IT Administration"

phase three
Running the Network

Chapter 14
The Internet and the Law

The internet is business. Business brings with it rules, regulations and (eventually) taxes. As an IS manager, it is no longer enough to conquer an everchanging technical landscape; you are also going to be expected to manage an everchanging regulatory landscape as well. While you may spend hours contemplating rotational backup schedules, UPS protection for your servers, and this week's list of patches and upgrades for your system, most IS managers have had little if any training in the mundane and sometimes seemingly arbitrary area of law. Ever increasingly, this complacency can cost your company time and money; it can even cost you your career.

You don't have to become an attorney to be an IS manager. You do need to develop a sensitivity to some of the issues that come up in IS operations that have legal ramifications, and develop a strategy for dealing with them. Not every legal issue can be addressed in a single chapter, nor can every variation in facts be accounted for. You still need to use your company's resources, such as a legal department or human resources department, as soon as you recognize a problem developing. The first step to avoiding serious problems is to recognize that you *have* a problem early enough to allow remedial action.

Understanding Contract Basics

Purchasing equipment, licensing software, securing internet access; all of these activities involve reaching agreement with people you may or may not know. This is the key point to contracts: they are *agreements*. I strongly recommend written agreements, even when they are not required. Some agreements must be in writing to be enforceable. Most often agreements fall apart

321

because the involved people never discussed the difficult or sensitive issues fully, and so never reached true agreement. If you can't agree on a written statement of expectations now, when everyone is relaxed and friendly, how will you resolve it later when money and egos are on the line?

Many people take extreme positions in contracts, either insisting on the other side giving up everything, or giving away the entire deal to avoid conflict. The more balanced a contract, the more likely both sides will be to live up to its terms, and to benefit thereby. Strive for a "win-win" arrangement, but when in doubt, remember whose interest you are representing (if necessary, look at the company name on your paycheck to clarify this point).

Negotiation Tips

Often you will be presented with a preprinted agreement to sign. You will need to read it before signing. In fact, it's always a safe procedure to have any contract you sign reviewed by your legal department before you sign it. Reading the contract, and asking questions, will be disconcerting for the other party to the agreement; be prepared for some initial resistance to answering your questions. Don't be surprised if the person providing the agreement has never read it.

Here's the number one tip for negotiating a contract: When presented with a standard, pre-printed contract, it's okay to strike out sections, write in new ones, and generally change anything that you don't like, so long as the other party agrees to the changes. The legality of a document is not based on neatness. If this really bothers you, retype the agreement with your changes included, and ask the other party to sign your version. Otherwise, have both parties initial the changes, and be sure each of you has a copy of the completed agreement, as signed, for future reference.

Important Terms in Your Agreement

What, exactly, is being purchased?

If you're purchasing hardware, be sure to include exact model numbers, and any unique, required software. Is installation included, or extra? Who installs, and when? What service, support or training is involved? What are you responsible for doing, and when? Try to develop a roadmap, with a timetable, of the sequence of events that will lead up to you having what you want; that's what you are paying money for, after all.

With software, you most likely get only a license to use the software. What is a license, exactly? It is written permission to use the software under precisely defined conditions and circumstances. That's what all that language is that you routinely click through without reading during installation of the software. If you read through a couple of these (on a day when you are well-rested and not prone to nodding off), you may be shocked at how little you are actually getting for your money.

If you are having custom software written (and here I am including the wide range of custom work, from Java programming to design of your web pages by someone outside your company), you should get *everything,* including the source code for programming and the copyright which attaches automatically to any original work, including text, graphics and sound (copyright issues are discussed in more detail later in this chapter). Just remember that your programmer and designer can only give you what they already own. If they "borrow" work of others and include it in the work they do for you, you may find that you have purchased a lawsuit along with the custom work. With all custom work, your company legal department should provide, or review, the contract for such work, to avoid a wide range of "big cost" problems.

Consultants will be a constant part of your work life, although this role is often blurred with that of salesperson. Who is doing the work, in reality? The near-genius you are shown during the early discussions, or the college student with a six-week internship at the consultant's company? Ability and experience are the two things consultants sell: Look carefully at each, and specify who will be doing the work for you. How is the consultant's fee to be determined? A straight hourly rate, without limits, is an invitation to problems and hard feelings. Try to set milestones, specifying when work is to be completed at each stage of a project, and the maximum time (or cost) of each part of the project. If you can specify the right to terminate at the end of each section of the project, you will have a highly motivated consultant throughout your project.

Support agreements are your way of outsourcing the maintenance and problem-solving headaches of some or all of your system. You don't want someone there to share your pain; you want them to assume your pain, so you can deal with other things. Again, it is important to know exactly who is going to be providing your support, how quickly they will respond, and how soon they will have the problem resolved. No one will guarantee that every possible problem will be fixed in four hours' time, but they should at least tell you when the work will commence, and what they will do if the problem isn't solved relatively quickly. Be specific; if you are paying for four-hour response time, they should also be willing to escalate the problem, at your request, if the problem isn't resolved within a business day of the initial call, for example. Your best hope for consistently good support is a staggered payment schedule, quarterly or even monthly, if you can arrange that, and the right to cancel the support agreement on thirty days' written notice.

How long is this agreement in effect?

This is a fast-moving industry with generally falling prices. For most agreements, you want them to continue long enough to provide some stability in your otherwise chaotic workday, but not so long that you lose all influence over your providers, who will quickly focus their attention on new prospects once you sign on the dotted line. Unless there is good reason to deviate, I seldom sign a contract for more than one years' term.

Watch for automatic renewal provisions, particularly if there is a long lead time in order to cancel a contract, and especially if the other party can increase your cost unilaterally. Just this year, I was presented with a contract that required written notice to cancel sixty days before the anniversary date of the agreement. The vendor could increase the price of the service with thirty days notice *at any point during the term of the agreement*. This was an international company, by the way, not a small local outfit. We were able to negotiate on this point (allowing us to cancel within 30 days of any price increase), but how many others just signed the agreement without reading it? These types of provisions aren't intended to abuse customers (very few companies will continue in business if they do this), but can be enforced if you have agreed to them. Why tempt fate by leaving these provisions in your contract?

Sometimes you will be offered a discount for signing a longer-term agreement. Telephone lines are often priced this way, with both a lower long-term rate and waived installation fees if three or more years' contract is signed. Some of these make sense; look at the dollars saved, compared to the likelihood that you will no longer need the service in the future, and make your decision accordingly. If you are guaranteed lower rates offered during the term of the contract, the decision gets easier. As always, if discounts or lower rates aren't offered, don't be shy about asking for them. Three years is required in my area to get installation costs of a T-1 line waived. As of today I am comfortable that I will be using this T-1 for the next three years. I am reluctant to go longer. I pity the managers who are still living with ten-year telephone service contracts, watching prices fall all around them.

What if things don't go as planned?

Everyone hates to think about this, but the irony is, those who discuss the possibility of problems up front seem less likely to experience problems—possibly because it's no longer an unresolved conflict, just an alternative procedure.

Warranties are your first line of defense. Can you return the defective product for replacement or refund, and if so, how long do you have to discover the problem? For custom services, how do you measure success? Again, if you agree on what it is you expect at the end of the work, there's less room for debate than if you *assume* that your concept of success matches that of the other party. For example, can you agree on what is meant by "reliable computer access"?

Whenever possible, leave yourself an "out" in a contract. The right to terminate the agreement on thirty days' written notice, without need to show a defect or substandard performance, is your ultimate defense against a neglectful vendor. Used with discretion, such a provision encourages a vendor to continuously review your satisfaction level. Used to excess, it will cause vendors to avoid you as a high maintenance, possibly nonprofitable client. If a vendor is making a sizable investment in materials or people in order to service you, they won't agree to such a provision easily; be flexible, and recognize their needs as well as your own. If other clients of the vendor benefit from those investments, you can be a little more aggressive on this point.

Terms of payment

This is often the most interesting portion of an agreement to discuss. Vendors want as much money up front as they can get. Purchasers don't want to pay anything until the last possible minute, ideally after all goods or services have been provided and found to be as represented. Compromise is generally required. As an IS manager, your job is to protect the interests of your company, not subsidize the other person or company. You should strive to relate the amount of money paid to the material or services received at any given payment date. In a business transaction, money talks. So long as you are retaining a sizeable amount of money, the vendors and consultants you are dealing with are highly motivated to keep you satisfied.

Warranties and guarantees

It is not unreasonable to expect a product to work as represented, despite the comments you will hear from vendors when a failure occurs. The challenge, surprisingly, is determining whether or not what you received is what you purchased. Take the example of a PC that occasionally "crashes." If I reboot twice a day, I'm having a good day. I have users who are totally frustrated if they crash twice a week. I think the software we use is working; they think the software we use is defective. Who is right?

Hardware generally comes with well-defined representations providing for repair or replacement during the first weeks or months of ownership. This is also an area where there is a well-developed body of law to guide the resolution of these problems. A thirty-day "no-questions-asked" return option is your best guarantee of a working product, so long as you have time to install and adequately test the product in that timeframe. After that time, you will want to know how long the hardware is automatically covered by the manufacturer, and whether the labor to repair or replace a unit is included (a disk drive, for example, may include a replacement drive and installation, but it's up to you to do a restore of the data on the disk drive).

Software is unlikely to burst into flames or otherwise fail dramatically; most disputes over the question of whether it's working turn on performance, which can be dependent on outside factors such as the hardware you are running it on, or the amount of traffic on the internet during business hours. Computers and other hardware also contain operating systems and hardwired code, so performance issues can also show up in a hardware context as well. Your best guarantee of successful acquisition, from a performance perspective, is a set of easily measured standards which the provider will agree to in writing as part of the purchase contract. These can often be quite simple, but nonetheless, will create panic in most vendors. Give them time to test the measures you propose, and keep the standards generous enough to allow for normal variation in performance based on load. Above all, it must be measured easily and automatically. A pie chart showing less-than-promised performance leaves little room for debate.

Consulting services are extremely difficult to measure; focus on specifying the person who will perform the work, when the work will be completed, and a couple of simple but meaningful measures of success. Whenever possible, put the test in terms of a business function. For example, if your web site supports a telephone sales system, you know that screens must come up within a few seconds' time during the business day, or your customers will get impatient and unhappy. Put the consultant in the telephone sales department for as long as necessary, then demand that the system meet the required response times. You pay a consultant to get results, not to reward sincerity of effort.

Services, such as domain name hosting, are becoming more amenable to objective measurement of service provided. Ask what measures of performance they are willing to guarantee, then if they meet your needs, include them in the contract explicity. Identify them in the contract generally, and attach original materials or sample reports. Include discussions about when service may be interrupted, not just how often. Two hours' downtime during the day is a major failure; for a company dependent on the service around the clock, two hours in the middle of the night can be just as disastrous.

Most contracts will have a provision that excuses nonperformance due to events outside the control of either party (wars, strikes, floods, and so forth). Within reason, these are acceptable. The test should be whether the listed events are either under the control of one of the parties, or can be anticipated and avoided in other ways. If a tornado rips through your area, telephone lines may be down for several days, and there isn't much anyone can do to prevent this. Occasional brief power outages are predictable, on the other hand, and an unwillingness to install a reasonably-sized uninterruptible power supply wouldn't seem to me to be an excuse for nonperformance.

The final important point I'd like to make is that, despite everything said about the importance of contract provisions above, there are rights and obligations which arise despite the language of the contract. A clear contract will help you avoid disputes, but once a dispute comes up, check with an attorney *immediately.* There are actions that can or should be taken to minimize damages, and there are minimum obligations that cannot be waived, even if written into a contract.

Non-negotiable Agreements

Not all agreements are negotiable. You are unlikely to negotiate a special deal with Microsoft if you are only buying a dozen licenses for Windows 95. In this situation, read the terms of the agreement, and act accordingly. If you simply cannot live within the terms of the agreement, look for an alternative. I am amazed at how often people rely on "fervent hope" in these situations. Hoping you won't get caught violating an agreement is totally unrealistic: When the violation comes to light, everyone, including your coworkers and supervisors, will be totally comfortable blaming you for the violation. This is how jobs are lost.

Not all agrements must be signed to be valid, either. If you use a software package when the license specifically states that to do so constitutes agreement with the terms; when you load the software and click "Yes" to understanding and agreeing to abide by the terms of the agreement; when you use the software daily until that fateful knock on your door by an aggrieved vendor, the claim that "I didn't sign anything" isn't going to carry weight. Your actions, as well as your signature, can bind you to the terms of an agreement.

Modification of an Agreement

Generally if you have a signed written agreement, and want to change it after it has been signed, you will need another one in writing to make the modification. Many people don't bother with this formality, and this can come back to haunt them. Typically, over time, the contract gets modified in practice, and in certain circumstances the courts will recognize these modifications. Your goal, however, is to avoid court, and the costs and bad publicity which can go with a lawsuit. In practice, you should review your ongoing contracts at least annually, and if there has been a significant change in performance from that described in the contract, modify the agreement to reflect this. This is yet another reason to keep your contracts short—it forces you to review and revise them regularly.

What about an agreement you couldn't negotiate in the first place? Can it be changed unilaterally by the other side? The easy, but misleading answer is "No." Once you have an agreement, both sides are equally bound by the terms. However, particularly with software, an upgrade, or a later-purchased license for the same product, may have different provisions. Each transaction is generally going to be a new deal, and you will be as bound by your actions as you were when you first purchased the product.

Here's an example of how you can get in trouble if you aren't alert. Suppose you purchase a web page editing tool, which allows you to also install it on your webmaster employee's home computer, so long as both computers are not being used at the same time. (Reasons to avoid loading office software on an employee's home computer are discussed below.) Six months later, you purchase an upgrade for this software, and automatically put the upgrade on your employee's home computer as well. Unfortunately for you, the company licensing the software has either been sold or has changed their licensing policy, and the new license *does not* permit the home installation without purchasing a separate license for that purpose.

Even if you limit the upgrade to the office copy only, you have to be careful about the fact that the upgrade may modify the terms of the original contract, and your use of the upgrade at the office may ratify that change. Now, perhaps, even the older version at home, which hasn't been upgraded, may have been made illegal by the terms of the upgrade.

Now your employee leaves, and continues to use the old version of software at home, as part of his or her new job. It's quite possible that, even under the terms of the original license agreement, there is a violation, as you now have two separate people using the software, possibly at the same time.

Note that none of these scenarios involves someone knowingly making an unauthorized copy of the software for a friend or coworker, yet each may lead to a violation of the license agreement. These are the subtle issues that should be addressed by your company attorney *before* they are turned into legal disputes. Your job is to spot the potential problem; ideally, you will get written directions on such issues from your supervisor or attorney.

These scenarios illustrate the reasons I am reluctant to install business software on an employee's home computer. At a minimum, if you must do this, have your employee sign an agreement to remove the software and destroy any backup copies upon terminating employment with you. Also, all employees should agree not to provide copies to others.

If your company sanctions, or even requires, you to violate contracts or license agreements, look for another job. You are not excused from violation of the law just because someone told you to do it. Also, as a practical matter, there may not be any documentation that you were told to violate the law, leaving full responsibility on you.

Understanding Copyright Issues

When you buy a copyrighted work, such as software, a music recording, or a book of cartoons, typically you are only acquiring a license to personally use and enjoy that work. You may own the disk, or the CD, or the paper, but you have only limited rights in the material contained on those physical objects.

Because of the ease of copying brought about by photocopiers, disk drives, and even CD burners, you are probably surrounded by examples of copyright violations every day at the office. This familiarity breeds a contempt of copyright laws in others; you will not have that luxury. That a comic strip photocopied and posted around the office may not lead to a lawsuit is more a matter of economics than law; the same strip, copied and posted to your web site (and of course indexed for ease of locating), is much more likely to lead to an actual complaint and possible lawsuit.

Generally, work produced by employees of your company or organization in the normal course of their employment will belong to the company (your attorneys should have addressed this, where relevant, in the company's employment agreement). The moment a document is written or a drawing made, the creator or his or her employer has a copyright in the material produced. Whoever owns the copyright may do whatever they please with it. To enforce your copyright against others, you simply have to establish that you produced the work (a simple copyright filing), and that it has been copied by someone else without your permission. That is also all it takes for others to be in a position to sue you if *you* copy *their* protected work.

Copyrights last for various periods of time, depending on when the material was first created, and the nature of the material, but for practical purposes, think of it as "a very long time" (50 to 100 years or more is possible). Copyright is fairly weak protection for creative work (you can express the same ideas in different ways without violating copyright—look at the thousands of romance novels circulating, each with its own copyright notice), which partly explains why copyrights last so long. Old, historic work may no longer have copyright protection (but assume the copyright exists until it can be determined otherwise).

Your web site is basically a form of publication of materials and information, so you will routinely be dealing with works of others which are, or may be, copyrighted and therefore protected from unauthorized use by you. How do you avoid copyright violation? The easiest method is to get written permission for your intended use from the author or holder of the copyright. The exact use may have to be detailed, and a price for that use determined, but such agreements happen all the time in the publishing business.

What if the object of your desire doesn't contain a copyright notice (the traditional © or copyright with a date of first publication)? The work may well be protected even without this notice, or the notice may have been removed from the item by an intervening party. You cannot rely on a lack of copyright notice to protect you if you copy without permission.

There is an exception in the copyright law which may allow you to copy parts of an otherwise protected work. The classic example of this is a book review, where the author of the review quotes passages from the book being reviewed. This is another case where the safe route is to get written permission from the author for the quoted material. But, if the copied materials represent just a small part of the entire work, and if you have added significant value to the work (the review text around the quoted material, in my example), then you probably won't have a problem. This is a judgement call, best reviewed by company attorneys, or avoided in the first place by not using the material in question.

You generally can use information provided by governmental units as well. Here you must be cautious when the material comes through a third person: If it has been organized or presented in a unique way, the third person may not have protection on the contents, but may have protection for the formatting or organization of the information. When creating a web site containing material produced outside of your company, it is wise to have it reviewed initially, and periodically thereafter, by an attorney who can spot and eliminate potential violations of copyright law.

Trademarks and Service Marks

Many companies have names, slogans or images closely associated with the products or services they produce, which are jealously protected. Even trivial use of these images or phrases may dilute the value to the company, which is why they may be willing to litigate what you may consider a trivial violation. For a while, this was a hot area of contention in the assignment of domain names on the internet; people would reserve a common commercial name in the hopes that the company would purchase the name from them for big dollars. Nowadays, it is more likely that you would find yourself fighting a legal action rather than making a financial killing.

While this is a diminishing problem, it is wise to keep this in mind when searching for a domain name. Just because the name is not currently registered to another company or individual, doesn't mean you can use it if it is a registered mark. Using your company name, if it is registered, is safe. Using your own name may not be allowed, even if you really *are* Ronald McDonald. If you are moving from being a small local company to publishing internationally (which is what you are doing on the internet), be sure to talk with an intellectual property attorney if there is any chance that your intended name may infringe on another company's marks.

Confidentiality and Noncompetition Agreements and Trade Secrets

Copyright law is intended to encourage the publishing of new and unique works by providing some level of control by the author or owner of the work after the information becomes public. Another way to protect work is to keep it a secret. Sometimes, you are better served by keeping something secret (the classic example being the formula for Coca Cola). The information you are protecting might be the source code for software, a new product specification, or a business plan. Before hiring an employee, a company may require them to sign a confidentiality agreement, agreeing not to reveal to competitors any secrets they learn in the course of their employment. Employers may also have them sign a noncompetition agreement, preventing them from working in the same field for someone else. These are often limited in time or geographic area.

So, here you have a new employee or consultant, providing wonderful work for you which you publish on your internet site. Then, seemingly out of the blue, the competition comes along and entangles you in an employment dispute, or charges you with publishing secret information provided by their former employee to you. And all you were doing is managing the web site!

This is another example of your role in spotting potential problems before they become actual problems. As gatekeeper of the window that allows the whole world to look in on your company and its practices, you will find yourself in the center of problems seemingly unrelated to your primary job description. To protect yourself, as well as your company, you should insist that your company address the trade secret and non-compete issues in their employment agreements. When you see unbelivable amounts of "new" material being produced in impossibly short times, don't turn a blind eye to the possibility of copied (or stolen) materials being provided.

Creating Effective Internet Use Policies

Policies serve two purposes: First, they help reduce the potential legal liability of your company due to the improper actions of an individual, should a legal action be brought against the company. More importantly, they can provide users with guidelines that will allow them to avoid problems in the first place. Avoidance is always less expensive than corrective action. As manager of your internet site (which may including outgoing services, as well as publishing services), you may be expected to develop these policies, explain them to management, and have them implemented.

It's normally not convenient, or even feasible, to establish all of your policies at once. Neither is it practical to develop a policy from scratch. You are best served by collecting policies from others, then with their permission adapting them to your own particular needs. In my career, I have had to develop several policies, which I have had subjected to legal review before implementing. Following are some of the more important areas where policies can benefit you.

Internet usage

It's often a challenge to be both the champion of internet usage, and the person developing the sometimes restrictive policies on its use. The important point is to think like a business owner, and not like a home user of the internet. These are two totally different environments, and not surprisingly, the business environment is likely to be more restrictive than your personal use of this resource.

I like a policy that sets out its reason for existing up front. It's hard to anticipate every possible situation that may arise in the course of work, but if you are clear about your purpose, you will have a much easier time applying the policy to specific behavior. Be direct: The company is providing internet access to assist employees with performing their work functions. Any other use, unless specifically allowed under the policy, most likely will be restricted or prohibited.

Within that framework, you can provide some additional benefits to the employees of the company. For example, you may allow "reasonable" use of the company's internet connection before 8 a.m. and after 5 p.m., and on weekends, if that is outside of normal business hours. Bandwidth is always limited, and if put in that context, most people will be reasonable in their use. This will cover the situations where parents are researching for a child's school paper, for example, or an employee is shopping for a new car.

On the other hand, you clearly don't want illegal activities to be conducted through your company's system. Expressions of belief or philosophy that are not related to and approved by the business should never be expressed online through the company's internet connection. An employee shouldn't be allowed to run a sideline business on the company's computer system or through the company's internet connection, lest the company be found equally liable for the actions of this unrelated business. Materials which may reasonably offend other employees, possibly leading to a harassment suit, should not be permitted to be viewed or downloaded at any time.

Other areas will depend on the nature of your business. I don't like users downloading executable programs because they are generally lax about checking for viruses before running their downloads, and sometimes the programs are so large, and shared so widely, that it begins to interfere with operations. Data streaming services may be an issue because of the bandwidth consumed. The issue of network performance (as opposed to legal issues) can always be addressed later, when and if it becomes a problem.

Publishing a photodirectory of your company is a common first use of a web server. Both internally and externally, such publishing, with contact numbers, E-mail addresses and other related information can improve communication for your company. The risk, however, is that too much information will be published, and may be used by questionable individuals to stalk or otherwise harass employees of your office. Be sensitive to this possible misuse of your directory, and allow employees to omit photos, home addresses and phone numbers, and other nonessential information from your directory.

E-mail usage

Internal E-mail requires use policies as much as internet E-mail; often all E-mail use is, or can be, covered by a single policy. If you have an existing network

E-mail policy, you are best served by expanding on it, rather than trying to maintain separate policies on internal and external E-mail.

One big area with E-mail has little to do with actual content: This is the area of confidentiality. Many users develop a perception of their E-mail as being private to them. In the right circumstances, you may find that going into a user's E-mail, however justifiable from a business perspective, will raise issues of violation of privacy. E-mail policy should make clear to all employees that E-mail exists for the benefit of the business, and that others may from time to time find it necessary or convenient to go into an employee's E-mail and review the messages and attachments in their mailbox or trash area. You will have days when critical information has been E-mailed to an employee who is unexpectedly out ill, for example, and in the course of looking for that E-mail, you may learn more than you want to about the activities of a coworker. Employees getting E-mailed job offers will be offended, perhaps, when they return and find you were in their E-mail; an employee organizing the unionization of your office will be seeking legal recourse. A clear policy will at least reduce the likelihood of a legal issue arising out of a seemingly simple business issue.

The same policy should give express permission to appropriate personnel to examine E-mail messages where harassment or threats against others are alleged. This is another area where human resources and legal counsel should be involved, and you should receive direction from authorized individuals before playing detective. You should also limit your reporting on your findings to the person who authorized your review of E-mail; do not under any circumstances discuss it with friends or family, unless you wish to become involved in a defamation action in court.

Some businesses exchange confidential information over the internet. The ease of E-mailing, or forwarding E-mail, makes it far too easy to send sensitive information without sufficient forethought of the possible consequences. Fax cover sheets routinely contain confidentiality provisions requiring unintended recipients to destroy the information and/or notify the sender of the error; the same should be true with your E-mail, which can also end up going to unintended recipients.

If nonemployees are involved, they too should be advised of the potential risk of unintended disclosure, and their permission secured to use the internet. For highly sensitive information, particularly that which has independent pecuniary value, either use encryption, or find another way to deliver the message.

This last point bears repeating: If it's highly confidential, don't send it by E-mail. In practice I've had more problems caused by erroneous use of E-mail than by nefarious lurkers grabbing messages en route. E-mail address books are often searched alphabetically by last name, and the first "hit" is the one chosen as the recipient (even worse is the case where internal and external addresses are in the same list). I have myself, more than once, fired off a quick "inside" response to a forwarded message, only to find that I had responded to the originator of the forwarded message, and not the forwarding party (oops!).

Policy should also indicate when, and if, autoresponders on your E-mail system should be used. An autoresponse programmed into E-mail can notify an entire Listserv of your whereabouts and activities as quickly as it responds to internal E-mail. If you are on a critical mission for your company, telling everyone the details of your trip by autoresponder may inform your competition as well.

Another problem with autoresponders concerns their willingness to respond to all received messages, no matter the content. Your autoresponse may trigger an acknowledgement from a hosting site that the autoresponse was received. This triggers another autoresponse, which triggers another acknowledgement. I have returned to the office on a Monday only to find several thousand autoresponse-generated messages in my mailbox, usually because someone on a listserv has been autoresponding all weekend to the distributed messages (including their autoresponses). E-mail systems have collapsed under such loads; irate listserv members who need to clear out their overloaded E-mail boxes might well resort to the same legal remedies as currently exist for autodialing fax machines which don't "give up" after a few attempts to dial (what turns out to be) a voice number. Your E-mail system should suppress such response wars before they begin.

Upload/download capabilities

If you are running a web host, you may be liable for materials improperly uploaded to your site, if you had reason to know that copyright violations were occurring. Webmasters are, and will continue to be, a favorite target of legislation aimed at controlling illegal copying. Sometimes these laws are stricken down, but our goal is not to become a test case. If individuals can upload to a public location where others can download those materials, you are going to have problems. In most cases you can avoid this setup by having separate upload and download areas; someone who can review the material uploaded has the responsibility to move it to the download area if appropriate.

If you do need to allow the direct exchange of information between individuals, keep this part of the site private. This can typically be done by restricting access to known individuals, and through the use of passwords. It's arguable whether or not you should be reviewing the materials passing through your site, but if you do find improper materials on your site, remove them immediately. The offending poster of the information should be either strongly warned against further improper postings, or immediately removed at once from the group. Take the matter to your human resources department if the offender is an employee. The exact procedure should be a part of your internet use policy.

Backup policies

As already noted, backing up your critical data is a required activity on your web server. What is often missed completely is the legal implications of this practice. Information stored on backup tape or disk is information in the possession of your company, which must be provided when properly requested in any court proceeding, even if this represents hundreds of tapes or thousands of diskettes, or represents several man-years of labor to restore the information to a human-readable format. If you no longer have the hardware and software necessary to retrieve that information, it will be with great difficulty that you convince a judge to excuse you from complying with the request to produce. If it's not retrievable, then why have you been keeping it?

In setting backup policy, keep just enough backup information to allow you to restore your system in the event of a major hardware failure. Do you really need more than three complete backup copies? Is it really necessary to archive information from five years ago, or is that just the default setting for the backup software? Can you even restore individual E-mail messages, and if not, does it make any sense to keep backups of messages over one week old? Is everything worth backing up, or can you skip over public chat areas where the topic du jour is last night's baseball scores? These are critical questions to ask when setting up any backup policy. Your goal is not to hide information; it is to avoid the time and expense of proving what is, or is not, on old tapes.

If you are archiving information from your web site, be sure that you have a good reason for doing so. If there is good reason, then be sure you maintain the hardware and software necessary to access that information. When the technology becomes obsolete, either destroy the backup information, or migrate it to a newer, supportable method of archiving. Throwing out tapes is not enough; be sure to erase them, or destroy them totally to prevent their preservation or resurrection.

Also beware of "unintended" archiving. Companies sometimes sell old equipment to employees or outsiders. How many of your machines leave the premises with the disk contents intact? How often have you simply deleted the software or confidential information, ignoring the commonly available utilities and even built-in capabilities to "undelete" those files? At a minimum, reformat your disk drives before selling equipment (in a way that won't permit easy "unformatting." If there is any question of sensitive information or possible misuse, then destroy the disk drives.

A final note on backups and their destruction. Be sure to check with your legal department before starting a destruction policy, and make provision for them to notify you when there is a legal constraint on destruction of backups. When there is a lawsuit in progress, or sometimes even threatened, destroying backup tapes may be viewed as destroying evidence. This is a serious charge, and not one you want to be in the position of defending against. A standing policy of destroying tapes on a schedule, with written notification required when a legal action would forbid such destruction, is essential.

Sales on the Internet

As the internet continues to develop as a place to do business, there will be more calls to tax internet transactions. Some sites may already collect sales tax, although it is not often clear which governmental entities that money is to be paid to. Many more sites do not currently collect sales taxes. In theory, the purchaser is responsible for the payment of those taxes, while the merchant is viewed as the convenient collector of the tax. Before selling on the internet, it is critical that the sales tax, and any other relevant taxes to your business, be considered by your legal counsel. This is a rapidly changing area, so stay alert to articles, discussions and changes to the law in this area.

Further References

The law and the internet is such a dynamic subject I recommend that you keep up to date on the issues by searching for an internet legal site that best matches your needs. Try searching the following terms:

"Internet" + "Law" OR "Legal"

"Business OR Administration" + "Law OR Legal"

Chapter 15
Auditing the Internet or Intranet System

An audit is a systematic and independent examination of your system to determine whether activities comply with planned goals and objectives and whether the system is implemented effectively. The purpose of this chapter is to teach you how to audit your internet system.

At several points in the implementation process, you need to look over your entire system and make sure that it is working effectively. By auditing, you examine the conformance and effectiveness of your system and report your findings back to management. The key word to remember is "effective." The audit will not be restricted to a conformance audit. Instead, your auditors will also look at how well the system is working and whether it can be improved.

It is never too early in your implementation process to begin conducting internal audits. To conduct these audits, you will need policies, procedures, and work instructions in place. In addition, you need to select and train your auditors with great care to obtain the maximum benefits. By efficiently training an internal audit group, you can save thousands of dollars in consultation fees and have an effective tool for continuous improvement.

Understanding the Audit Cycle

The process of auditing follows a well-established structure. In general, the following steps are taken during every audit, whether it is internal or external.

1. Receipt of a mandate
2. Preparation

3. Notification/negotiation
4. Opening meeting
5. Collection of evidence of conformance/effectiveness
6. Closing meeting
7. Written report
8. Corrective actions
9. Follow-up until closure

An internal audit is performed for your whole system at least annually. Areas of special attention are audited more frequently by an internal audit team.

Receipt of a mandate

An official act by management is required to initiate an audit. For an internal audit, it can be as simple as issuing a memo from the internet steering committee requesting that an audit take place. Such a mandate has to identify the person responsible for coordinating and leading the audit. It should also state the scope and purpose of the audit. The scope of an audit will describe the areas to be checked and the standards to be applied.

Preparation

In general, the person receiving this mandate will be the IS manager. The IS manager can then assign a lead auditor from the IS department or another department. In smaller organizations, the IS manager also serves as the lead auditor. Either way, the lead auditor bears the brunt of the work assignment for an internal audit.

The lead auditor must begin by further defining the scope of the audit. The areas to be checked have to be matched up with a timetable. The people to be interviewed, the goals and objectives of the system to be checked, and the evidence that needs to be gathered are all listed as part of an overall audit plan. This requires the lead auditor to review organizational charts, policies, procedures, and other information to determine how much auditing will be required to find the level of conformance and effectiveness in your internet system. If the internet system seems inadequate at this point, the lead auditor has to report back to management that an audit is not possible until a working system is in place.

Let's look at a specific example. Let's assume that the lead auditor has been told to audit the document control system within his company's intranet. The objective of the preparation phase is to create an audit plan.

The lead auditor would read through the requirements for document control, look for an official company policy on this subject, and review the procedures related to document control. If satisfied that a system seems to be in place, the auditor would then look at the people responsible for control, and determine which documents should be controlled. From this information, the auditor would form an audit plan that would describe who will be doing the audit, what they will do when, and in what location.

Specifically, the auditor would detail the audit scope and objectives, identify the significant people in the process, list requirements, list the audit team members, lay out a schedule for the audit, identify the areas to be checked, assure confidentiality, and state the distribution list for the final report. All of these items taken together constitute the audit plan.

The audit plan for the document control system might look like this:

The scope and purpose of this audit is to assure that the document control process at Megalith Corporation conforms to the requirements of ISO 9001, element 4.5 and Corporate Policy number 27. Therefore, we propose the following actions for the audit to assure conformance and evaluate effectiveness of document control.

1. The managers of the information systems and quality assurance departments have the responsibility of the document control system. Their respective administrative assistants are responsible for the distribution of documents under this system.

2. All documents and computer records related to the design, purchasing, production, inspection, and the quality system in particular will be sampled and audited for conformance to the document control procedure. Areas to be checked will include record storage, all management offices, work stations, purchasing, quality assurance labs, and repair stations.

3. The lead auditor will be Ralph Metz, assisted by Judy Market. The opening meeting will be held at 8:00 a.m. on Monday, November 8th in Conference Room B. The closing meeting will be at the same location at 4:00 p.m. on the 8th.

4. The following schedule is proposed:

8:15—9:00	Interview key managers of document control system
9:00—10:30	Examine records within the intranet
10:30—11:30	Examine written records
11:30—12:30	Lunch
12:30—2:30	Examine work station areas
2:30—3:30	Examine server areas
3:30—4:00	Prepare findings

> 5. All information gathered will be held in strictest confidence. The final written report will be distributed to members of the internet steering committee and the managers of information systems and quality assurance."

Such an audit plan would be submitted for approval to managers being audited. Time schedules have to be coordinated so that meetings with key people do take place and that an effective audit is conducted.

Finally, the lead auditor selects the audit team members. Typically, a small company has an audit team of one or two. Large corporations have been known to use as many as five or more people for an audit team. Either way, you should use the minimal number of people for an effective audit.

This selected team meets to go over the audit plan and to draw up their working documents. If there have been previous audits, the team would review the past reports to see which weak areas need the most attention. Particular members of the audit team are assigned specific areas to examine and tasks to perform. The lead auditor makes these assignments.

The individual members of the audit team draw up checklists for their assignments. These will be used later to gather evidence of conformance. The lead auditor reviews these checklists and other supporting documents to make sure the team is ready for the audit.

Notification/negotiation

Once key managers have agreed to the proposed audit plan and the audit team has made its preparations, notification takes place. For an internal audit, a simple memo can serve as the notification. It would be sent to all people and departments targeted by the audit. It would tell them who is coming to audit, the purpose of the audit, and the time period for their part of the audit. In other words, it is a short summary of the formal audit plan.

Once notified, usually at least a week in advance, it is up to anyone who has scheduling or other conflicts to call the audit team to negotiate changes to the audit plan.

Opening meeting

The actual audit begins with a very short opening meeting. At this meeting, the lead auditor explains the purpose and scope of the audit, as well as the proposed schedule. Top managers from the affected areas should be in this meeting, as well as all of the network administrators. This is the time to quickly summarize the purpose of the audit again to assure that all involved managers are fully informed.

Collection of evidence

The bulk of any audit is the collection of objective evidence and interview data. Objective evidence is gathered by examining and copying documents, observing activities, and testing system components. Coupled with this is the interviewing of managers and participants in the system under examination. Usually, the items to be checked are part of a checklist.

For example, one item on the checklist might be:

> Sample six listings from the Master List of controlled documents. Confirm that these documents have the correct sharing settings and are only located in the specified subdirectories. Report any copy, either physical or electronic, discovered during the audit.

This is just one of many such points to cover during an audit. You would also list the questions to ask both managers and system users. The idea is to keep the audit within its scope and to cover the areas of interest in a systematic manner.

However, it is sometimes necessary for an auditor to follow a "hunch." The auditor can expand the investigation to follow this lead. That is why the training of an internal auditor is so important. It is very difficult to stick to the objectives of an audit and follow such leads. A good auditor has to know how far to check without becoming vindictive, and thus, no longer an independent, unbiased party.

While the evidence is being collected, the auditors will document all that they see, hear, smell, and feel about a particular system. These observations are recorded on the checklists and other related documents, and then reported to the lead auditor. It is the lead auditor, working with the team, who creates findings for each element of a system under examination. A finding in a registration audit is stated as conformance, nonconformance, or concern. The audit team has the freedom to describe strengths and weaknesses in detail. The objective is to provide enough information that an effective action plan can follow from the final written report. All findings must be fully supported by documented observations.

Closing meeting

At the end of an audit, the lead auditor meets with the other team members to collate the evidence and reach specific findings. A quick summary of the results are prepared for oral presentation during the closing meeting.

The closing meeting should include the key managers from the targeted areas and any other interested parties. At least one member of senior management should be present. The lead auditor provides a quick review of the purpose of the audit and the overall findings. Then specific nonconformances, concerns, and strengths are highlighted. The lead auditor promises to prepare a written report and asks for questions.

Next the lead auditor queries each affected manager on how long it will take to perform any necessary corrective actions. This tentative information is used later to prepare a formal plan of corrective action. Therefore, minutes should be taken at this meeting. Most closing meetings take less than one hour.

Written report

The lead auditor prepares a written report that states the findings of the audit team and the supporting evidence. This report must be signed and dated by the lead auditor and then distributed to all parties on the distribution list. As IS manager, your name should be on the top of the list.

The report is submitted as soon as possible. At least one member of senior management should be on the distribution list, especially if senior management created the original mandate for the audit.

Corrective actions

Management should react to an audit report with a specific plan of corrective action. This should be broken into two parts. The first part should be the assignment of specific tasks to particular managers. These managers should respond in writing as the corrective actions are completed.

For the second part, management should be looking at their overall system and exploring the possibility of updating or changing existing procedures to increase the effectiveness of the system. In addition, the cost efficiency of procedures should be examined as well. It is also suggested that management keep an eye on changing market or economic situations, or changing internal strategies, to assess the need for change within the existing internet system. Often technology can catch up to and pass an existing problem.

The timetable for corrective actions should be compiled by management and submitted back to the lead auditor for follow-up tracking and closure of the audit.

The completed corrective action plan is reviewed by management and submitted to the lead auditor. The lead auditor puts the corrective action plan in the audit file and schedules follow-up for each action item.

Follow-up until closure

All corrective actions taken must be documented. A simple memo reporting a successful corrective action, or a directive issued to change a procedure, are adequate evidence of management involvement. The reporting of the completion of a corrective action step is sent to the lead auditor, who, in turn, marks on the corrective action plan that the step has been completed. Each action item should have an expected date of completion. As the dates pass, the auditor notifies the responsible manager in writing and requests a response. Every item on the corrective action plan must be completed before the lead auditor is allowed to sign and close the audit file.

It is up to the discretion of the lead auditor as to whether to confirm the effectiveness of a corrective action with a second audit of the particular area involved. The lead auditor should not sign off a corrective action step until it is shown that the action taken was completely effective. If a corrective action is not completed and requests for completion are ignored, the lead auditor should report this to top management and request a re-audit.

Writing an Internal Audit Policy

When you write your policy for internal audits, you should be familiar with ISO 10011. This is the international standard on how to audit management systems. It can provide you with guidelines on how to audit, how to select auditors, and how to prepare audit reports.

Let's begin with the concept of independence. The auditors you use have to be independent of the functions under examination. In other words, the IS manager at Avix is not a suitable auditor of the internet system she created. The range of suitable auditors is narrow for this particular situation. The other IS technicians or possibly an engineer with internet technology experience would be candidates.

You have to note in your policy that all audit activities are reported directly to management. Taken together with the objective of using audits to improve a system, not punish people, you get something like this:

> It is Avix Manufacturing's policy to audit its information systems and internet technology at least annually. This internal audit is conducted by trained and independent auditors who confirm the conformance of our internet technology systems to planned goals and objectives. The primary aim of such auditing is to discover opportunities for improvement.

As you can see, the purpose of auditing is explained and the door is left open to use either internal personnel or consultants to do the auditing. The message of continuous improvement is repeated here as it was on earlier policies. The people experiencing an audit have to feel comfortable with the process. Also, note how the goals and objectives you established in earlier chapters are now used to confirm that the system you planned is the system you have.

Writing the Audit Procedures

A good internal audit system depends on a well written procedure for auditing. By basing your procedures on ISO 9000, ISO 10011, and other accepted practices, you will give both structure and conformity to your system. The key elements of the audit activity to keep in mind are:

1. Management's creation of the mandate to audit.
2. Preparation of an audit plan.
3. Assignment of people to the audit team.
4. Creation of audit documents and check sheets.
5. Opening meeting to explain scope and nature of the audit.
6. Collection of observable evidence of compliance and effectiveness.
7. Closing meeting and summary of findings.
8. Submission of a written report to management.
9. Corrective actions.

By combining these pieces of information, and with some training in auditing, you can create a simple, yet comprehensive system of internal audits. For maximum efficiency, this audit system can be used for other audit needs. Financial, supplier, and process audits can all use this same system.

The procedure must require the set up of an audit schedule, and you must stick to this schedule. Critical elements of your system should be checked more often than annually. Your written procedure for internal audits should be modeled on the preceding audit cycle.

Developing Work Instructions

While there are potentially many work instructions for auditing, most important will be the instructions for the creation of an audit report and the documentation and tracking of corrective action. Remember, the purpose of an audit is to open an opportunity for your company to improve. Therefore, a formal written report is required to document these opportunities and to demand action.

This report should contain the following:

1. The scope of the audit being conducted.
2. Review of the audit plan.
3. List of auditors and the people interviewed during the audit.
4. List of nonconformances with supporting evidence.
5. Summary of observations to highlight the strengths and weaknesses of the internet system.
6. Summary of the current conformance to planned goals and objectives.
7. Distribution list.
8. Attached corrective action requests.

Once the audit report is submitted, it is up to the management of your company to create a corrective action plan that names specific managers as responsible for each suggested action. The lead auditor should be given a copy of this plan. Using it, the lead auditor will create a log to track the completion of each corrective action. The audit file cannot be signed and closed out until all corrective actions have been taken.

In addition to an audit plan, auditors also work with checklists, sampling plans, mandates with specific instructions, and a defined scope of their responsibilities (see Figure 15–1). All of these can be seen as work instructions for the auditor. Therefore, these should be written documents that are considered "controlled" under your document control system.

All work instructions for internal auditors should include instructions on who receives the output being generated. In most cases, a clear path toward upper management must be defined. In turn, management must generate written responses that are acted on and recorded. In most cases, the IS manager will be the primary responder from upper management.

The call for an audit, the audit report, handwritten notes, minutes of management meetings, corrective action plans, and confirmation of corrective actions should be filed together in a case file. Each audit is treated as separate project.

Once your policy, procedures, and work instructions are in place, you are ready to train your auditing team.

Selecting an Auditor

ISO 10011-2 lists the specific characteristics a person must possess to be an auditor. Remember, a fully qualified auditor should have no power. The role of an auditor is to examine a system and report back to management. A person perceived to have the power to discipline people will inhibit the accurate

Figure 15-1. Examples of work instructions and forms for internal audits

Work Instruction #IT-24   Internal Audit Paperwork   (Also see procedure QA-3)

1.0 General

Existing policies (CP 4.17) and procedures (QA-3 and CP-2) require annual internal audits of the internet system against corporate plans and any other quality system standards or requirements in place. Such audits will have as deliverable items audit reports and corrective action notices.

2.0 Audit Report

2.1 It is the responsibility of the audit team leader to gather all audit findings and report them in a written summary to management.

2.2 Form # 223-D "Report Form" will be used for the purpose of reporting audit results.

2.3 The audit team leader fills in the names of the audit team, the people that were interviewed, the scope of the audit, the date, and the distribution list for the final report.

2.4 In the space provided for comments, the audit team leader will write out a list of nonconformances and concerns discovered during the audit. These will be supported with a summary of the evidence obtained to make these conclusions. Both strengths and weaknesses of the system should be reported. After each finding, the audit team leader should estimate the company's ability to correct the situation.

2.5 The report will be signed by the audit team leader and submitted to the information systems manager for approval of content and accuracy.

2.6 The information systems manager and audit team leader will present the final report to the management steering committee no later than ten days after the conclusion of an audit. The steering committee will then take corrective actions as needed.

3.0 Corrective Actions

3.1 When nonconformances are noted on a final report, the audit team leader will complete a form #323-C "Corrective Action Report (CAR)" for each nonconformance. These will accompany the final report to the management steering committee.

3.2 The management steering committee will then assign specific department managers the role of taking the corrective actions they feel are necessary. CARs can be rejected by the steering committee, but the reason has to be noted in the meeting minutes.

3.3 The audit team leader will note the CARs in the corrective action logbook and the names of the managers responsible for taking actions. The audit team leader will also note the projected date of completion.

3.4 Each responsible manager will respond in writing as to whether the corrective action was completed successfully. The audit team leader will note this by closing out entries in the corrective action log. Date of completion should be noted.

02/07/94   Revision 2.1.1   Approved by:

Form 223-D REPORT FORM for the IF/THEN Company		
Date:	Team Members:	Guests/Interviewees:
Facility:		
Filed by:		
Scope:		
General Comments:		

General Comments:

(use additional sheets as needed)

Detailed Report:

(use additional sheets as needed)

Distribution List:

Report Approved by: _____ Date: _____

| Revision 1.5.0 | 11/19/93 "c:\wp\report.frm" | Approved by: |

Form 23/B	Internal Audit Corrective Action Log			
Date reported:	Person responsible:	Corrective action suggested:	To be completed by:	Date completed:
02/07/94	J. Hooper	CAR #23 - write work instruction for presses	04/01/94	03/15/94
03/11/94	D. Facto	CAR #24 - implement control of back up records	05/01/94	

collection of information that is vital for management to make competitive decisions. Following are attributes to look for when selecting an auditor:

1. The first attribute of a good auditor is training in the formal approach to management audits. This includes training in methods of interviewing, observing, documenting, and reporting.

2. The auditor has to be able to plan, coordinate, communicate, and potentially lead a team of auditors.

3. The level of education should be post-secondary school. In other words, auditors tend to be drawn from the college educated or from people eligible for college education. The level of experience is more critical. ISO 10011-2 spells out that auditors should have at least four years of experience in the business they are auditing.

4. The standard also recommends that the auditor candidate observe and participate in at least four audits. It is assumed that such a person would be under supervision of an experienced auditor.

These, of course, are guidelines for auditors seeking registration. They can also be used internally to establish your own qualifications for auditors; however, you should use common sense to establish your own internal qualifications.

At the same time, you must never lose sight of the matching of personalities. One of the key characteristics to look for in an auditor is personality. For example, a dominant person might not fit in well with passive management teams. In contrast, a good-humored, sensitive individual can put interviewees quickly at ease and increase the efficiency of an audit.

Therefore, ISO 10011-2 addresses this issue as well. It says that a good auditor will possess the following characteristics:

1. Be open minded, objective, mature, analytical in nature, realistic, tenacious, and be capable of seeing the "big picture" in a given situation.
2. Be able to collect and evaluate objective evidence without prejudice.
3. Stay true to the purpose and scope of an audit.
4. Be able to change how people are treated to maintain the objectives of the audit.
5. Be immune to distractions.
6. Be dedicated to the task at hand.
7. Cope with stress well.
8. Be able to defend conclusions that are drawn from the audit.

Experienced auditors can testify to the importance of these characteristics. An average auditor will be subjected to non-cooperative people, lack of sleep, wide ranges of personalities, countless distractions, guides that try to direct attention away from weak areas of the system, and the unexpected. Through it all, the auditor must keep a cool head and collect the needed information. Diplomacy, imagination, and tenacity are critical characteristics.

Finally, a good auditor will be fluent in the language or languages in use within a company. The existence of bilingual work forces around the world make this a point of growing importance. You may not think that this is important if all of your workers speak the same language as management. But, experience has shown that an auditor that can speak the dialect and slang of the users will win quick respect of the workers.

At the same time, you may find that auditors might have to know Java, Perl, or HTML to talk intelligently with the web page design staff. This would be a parallel case of needing to know more than one "language."

How to interview auditors

To select a good auditor, it is highly recommended that you form a small panel. Such a panel should be made up of the IS manager, a senior management representative, a human resources representative, and at least one experienced auditor. Preferably, the experienced auditor should be the designated lead auditor. It is best when the lead auditor can have a strong say in picking the team members.

Naturally, you would have established levels of education, training, and experience. This would sort out some good choices for candidates, or establish potential candidates that may need additional training and/or experience. The panel should examine the resumes and personnel records of this pool of candidates with an eye on the management capabilities of the individuals under examination. That is, the panel should look at the person's ability to carry out audits on managers and conduct other management audit activities.

Face to face interviews with finalists will help establish who works well under pressure and how well they adapt to rapidly changing situations. This is not to imply that the finalists should be interrogated for hours. Instead, a simple set of prepared questions with a few example situations is adequate.

To maintain the competency of your selected auditors, you should take the following steps.

1. Ensure that the auditors are kept up to date with the current configuration of your internet system.
2. Require regular training in new audit methods. Usually every year you should determine whether additional training of the auditors is required.
3. Perform an evaluation review of each auditor at least once every three years. The record of performance, comments from the lead auditor, and a review by a panel similar to the one described above are recommended.

The best way to train the auditors

There are several schools of thought on how to train people to become auditors. One group suggests that a two- to three-day internal auditor's course is adequate to bring people up to speed. Another group thinks that auditors should be trained as part of a college education or work experience.

As usual, no single approach is entirely correct for every company. The best first step is to look at your situation. What are your internal needs? How much experience do potential auditors already have? Do you have a corporate image or level of professionalism to maintain? How much auditing do you need to do? How large is your company and does it have multiple sites?

Begin by looking at the size of your organization. If you are a 50-employee job shop, perhaps only one person needs to be trained as an auditor. If you are a corporation with many sites, like Megalith, then perhaps a trained audit team is necessary. A medium size manufacturing firm, like Avix, usually uses between two and five auditors.

Next, you have to consider the experience of the people nominated to be auditors and the level of professionalism you wish to project. A nationally known corporation may want all auditors certified after attending the week-long lead auditor course. At the same time, a small manufacturing firm may feel that a two-day course on internal auditing given to experienced management system auditors is adequate.

A strongly recommended step is that the level of experience and training required for a qualified auditor be documented as part of your audit procedure. You can add to this your test of independence. In this way, you will have clearly demonstrated that your auditors are appropriate for the job. This could include a description of the communication and leadership skills an auditor must possess to be effective.

A Checklist for Auditing Your Internet System

To further assist you in the auditing process, you may want to use the sample checklist provided below. This can be used as is, or you can modify it to your particular situation. An important point here is to notice that a systematic approach is being used. Also, the conformance of your existing system is being checked against the plans developed earlier in this book.

Audit checklist

Procedures, policies, work instructions
1. List the policies related to the internet system.
2. List the procedures related to your internet system.
3. List the work instructions related to your internet system.
4. For each of the items listed, produce a master list of people who have access. If the documentation is on an intranet, obtain a list of who has read-and-write access to these documents. Sample at least 12 of the users that have access to these documents and confirm that controlled copies are present, or that they have read or write permission on the intranet.
5. Interview the managers of each affected department and confirm that they are aware of the policies and procedures that apply to their area.

6. Select six users at random and ask them what the internet usage policy says.

7. The procedure for data backup calls for system-wide backup at least once a week. Pull the backup log and confirm that the schedule has been met.

8. The policy on passwords says that each user should change passwords at least once every thirty days. Examine the passwords log file and confirm that this is occurring.

9. The security policy says that passwords should not be kept near a computer or posted at an obvious location. Examine work spaces for the presence of easily obtained passwords or terminals logged on with no one present.

10. Work instructions to the users indicate that all data files should be clearly labeled. Examine a random sample of 50 such files to confirm this is being done.

11. Ask each systems administrator for analysis of the current accounts being used within their part of the system. This should match the criteria set forth in policies and procedures.

System layout

1. Obtain a map of the internet system within your company. Physically examine the existing system against the map. Note any discrepancies.

2. Check the make and model of each computer against what is listed on the map.

3. Run the system diagnostics program to confirm the following on each server and workstation:

   - RAM memory
   - Hard drive size
   - Remaining hard drive space available
   - Network interface card
   - Video system
   - Backup system available

4. Check all hubs and cables for clear identification.

Software

1. Obtain a list of current software that should be loaded on servers and the corresponding licensing agreements. Confirm that these are in place and the agreements are being followed.

2. List any additional software that is discovered on the servers.

3. Obtain a list of current software that should be loaded on workstations and the corresponding licensing agreements. Confirm that these are in place and agreements are being followed.

4. List any additional software that is discovered on the workstations.

5. Check the version number of all software and list these. Note a version out of range with other copies of the software.

Internet connections

1. Review the ISP contract. Confirm that all obligations are being met.

2. Confirm the location and type of internet connections at your company.

3. Confirm the communications equipment hooked at your end of the lines. Note any new equipment not noted on the systems map.

4. Review the cost of the internet connections versus other options.

5. Run communication checks on each of the lines and note the results.

Web sites

1. Browse each of the internal and external web sites of your company. Confirm that they meet the corporate image requirements of your company.

2. Check the revision date for each web site and report any that are more than six months old.

3. Checked authorization logs against pages in use. Report any discrepancies.

Personnel

1. Check the education, training, and experience level of each internet technician. Do they meet minimum requirements?

2. Is the help desk adequately staffed?

3. Does technical support respond to user requests within one working day?

4. Have critical personnel undergone security reviews?

As you can see from the checklist, many of the items are drawn from goals and objectives set for the company. Another large part of the checklist is the confirmation that employees are carrying out the policies and procedures.

Basically an auditor is sampling to determine that the system is being implemented consistently. Such sampling can involve a handful of selected sites, people, or documents. To be more valid statistically, you can randomly select your targets using established sampling plans. These can be found in most books on statistics or quality control.

Further References

Management Audits, by Allan J. Sayle, ASQ Quality Press, 1988.

ISO 10011, available from ASQ, Milwaukee, Wisconsin, (800) 248-1946.

Information Technology Audit Handbook, by Doug Dayton, Prentice Hall, 1997.

Web Search Terms

"Internal Audits"

"Management Audit"

"IT + Audit"

Web Sites

The Information Systems Audit and Control Association can be viewed at www.isaca.org.

Chapter 16
Marketing
the Internet Site

Now that you have created web pages, you have what is called "internet presence." Unfortunately, on the internet you have presence along with millions of other groups, organizations, businesses and individuals. You need to distinguish your presence so that customers, suppliers, and other interested parties can find and use your sites. That means you have to promote your internet presence to others. For intranets and internet connections, this includes promoting your presence to the employees of your company. This is the most important of all your promotions because, as we shall see in the next chapter, you will need the cooperation of internal personnel to keep your internet system successful.

Promoting Your Web Pages Internally

Because promoting your web page internally has a high priority, we begin our discussion there. First, you must determine the purpose of your intranet or internet connection. Let's review the primary mission of our four example companies.

1. Dickerson County School System—Their internet presence is being used to promote communications between parents, teachers, students, and other interested parties.

2. Avix Manufacturing—Their intranet is focused on promoting E-mail communications and sharing documents while their internet connection is there to serve customers.

3. The Law Firm—Their intranet will be used for training while they later plan to install an internet connection to help communications with clients and attorneys in the field.

4. Megalith—They want their web presence used for as many possible applications as can be conceived.

For your own company you'll need to distinguish the overall objective of your internet presence. Then you need to discuss how internal personnel will support that mission. You'll also want to know how the internet connection to your intranet can supplement that task.

Take the example of the Dickerson County School System. They want parents, teachers, and students to contribute to the web site. This can be done through a discussion area they have established. But that brings up the obvious problem: How do you encourage these people to contribute?

The school system will have to take several steps to encourage parents, teachers, and students not only to visit the web site, but to contribute. Part of that process will be the removal of the fear of the internet. Therefore, the school system has planned a series of public seminars. Some of these teach parents and students how to use the internet to supplement educational objectives. This would include topics such as how to filter out sites you do not want children to see. There would also be a review of proper usage of the web site. Added to this would be a demonstration of how parents and students can properly contribute to the discussion group.

Next, the school district would have seminars just for teachers to show them how to encourage their students to use the web site to look up homework assignments, view schedules of upcoming events, and use the web site's helpful links that give students information for their homework. Not only will this help to educate the teachers on how use the web site, but it will encourage students to also participate as part of their normal school activities.

Avix Manufacturing will be heavily dependent on sales personnel updating and maintaining their catalog of available parts and components. This catalog is what is posted to their internet web site. The cooperation of these people will then be critical to their overall mission.

To foster cooperation among these people, Avix management will address this group of people specifically. Job descriptions, evaluations, and reward mechanisms will be placed into the system to encourage participation. Regular checks by upper management will show the people involved that their jobs are critical to the success of the web site. At the same time, feedback about the success of the web site will be freely shared with these people.

The Law Firm will have an easier time encouraging people to use their intranet. As part of orientation for any new employee, they will take at least two courses over the intranet. These courses follow a regular face-to-face seminar of how to use the Law Firm intranet. Schedules of court dates, pending lawsuits, current situations with various clients, and other critical information will be posted on the intranet. All of the employees of the Law Firm will be reminded that the use of the intranet is critical to the success of their job.

For Megalith Corp. there is the need for wide scale, upper management support in promotions of all web sites. The job here is more difficult because Megalith will have several different types of web sites internally and on the internet. Our discussion below can illustrate how a company like Megalith can use many different forms of web sites that would be directly beneficial to the employees. By making the web sites beneficial and by training the employees on how to gain access, you take the first steps in encouraging internal personnel to use the company's web presence.

Good Ideas for Web Site Components for Internal Personnel

Before we talk about any other aspect of web design, keep this rule in mind—simple is best. Although multimedia pages have their place, most businesses only need to present information in a form that is quick and easy to read. This means black type on a white background and one or two logos. In most cases, your customers want to get the information and move on.

Likewise, you need to set just the right level of interactivity so that you freely encourage people to respond to your information. This is true for both internal and external users of a web site.

To encourage employees of your company to use the intranet, it is highly recommended that you place into your web pages features and capabilities that are directly beneficial to them. This helps increase the use of your web sites. Let's look at a few ideas that can be used to encourage participation.

Company profile page   This is a web site page that describes the size, scope, and purpose of your company. For publicly owned companies these pages are used to report the profitability the company had on share prices. As you can imagine, employees whose retirement accounts are tied to such performance would be very interested in looking at this page.

Company policies   Posting company policies on an intranet helps employees quickly locate information on how they should respond to different situations.

Company procedures   As discussed earlier, placing company procedures on an intranet means you don't have to distribute large binders of documents that are difficult to search. Instead, the employee can quickly locate a procedure by going to the table of contents. Or, they can use the search feature.

Search engine   The search engine is a small programming application embedded in a web page. It has the capability of indexing many other web pages. It allows employees to enter a term to search for, and have the search engine retrieve all related documents. For example, a lawyer at the Law Firm could enter the phrase " executive privilege" and have the intranet bring back all related documents including ongoing cases using this argument. We will talk about search engines on the internet later in this chapter.

Tips, tricks, and techniques   Because internet technology tends to be so dynamic, users of the system always like to learn about shortcuts and other little tricks used to make their jobs easier. By having the users post their discoveries into a central area, you encourage the formation of user groups within your company. Not only do the employees benefit by learning better ways to use the internet technology, but you are also encouraging the same employees to use the internet technology more often.

Company directory   Having the company directory posted on the intranet allows you to do something a printed directory cannot—include ever-changing images. A published table of contents with listed names of all employees in the company is one approach. By clicking on a name you would bring up an entire page of information about the employee with updated titles and credits, and a picture of the person. This can be invaluable when you are being assigned to a team and you wish to research who it is you'll be dealing with. However, this must be done with caution. You do not want to include personal information, home phone numbers, or any type of information which could be used by another employee for harassment purposes.

Meeting room schedule   A common problem in most companies with multiple meeting rooms is keeping the schedule for those rooms coordinated. By posting the schedule on an intranet page, everyone in the company can quickly determine whether a room is available for a meeting. Reservations can be posted to the web page to hold your preferred time slots.

Meeting agendas   Thanks to the miracle of hyperlinks, a person can look up the meeting schedule, collect meeting materials, read background reports, schedule themselves for the meeting, and print out the agenda. This eliminates the need to circulate memoranda and other material that can be lost. At the same time, it gives employees lots of access to the information they need to know.

Contests Money is always a good motivating factor. If your company normally has some sort of contest every year, try posting it to the intranet. Encourage people to register for, say a free vacation, on the intranet. Then hold the drawing live over the intranet with E-mail being sent to the lucky winners.

Surveys When management wants to know the employees' opinions on a particular topic, they can always post a survey form for anonymous feedback. Take the example of a company trying to decide whether they should offer a new benefits package. The survey form can be posted along with relevant information about the new package. Then each employee can submit a vote.

Job listings It is very easy to replace the job listing bulletin board with a web page on your intranet. Employees looking for new jobs within the company can consult this page from the privacy of their own desks.

List of Links Once people become familiar with the technology within the internet, they tend to enjoy sites that have a list of links for common topics. Take the example of the Dickerson County School System. Part of their web sites might be a list of links related to freedom of speech for students. Students interested in this topic can then quickly link to dozens of other internet sites to expand their knowledge.

These are just a few examples of the types of components you can add to your web site to make it more attractive to your own employees. Keep in mind that in the next chapter we're going to talk about your need to recruit and coordinate employees to provide content for your web site. If you start with employees who are enthusiastic users of your system, the job is much easier.

Promoting Your Web Site to the Outside World

Never forget this rule: Web sites are not independent of your normal methods of promoting your company. In fact, you want to integrate the web site into your normal promotional methods. Think of how many television ads you see that include the web site address for a company. The most promising aspect of this type of promotion is WebTV and eventually being able to "click-through" to a web site during its advertisement.

Your web site address should also be included on all normal business communications, such as letters, advertisements, catalogs, quotes, and the like. Before you launch the external promotion of your web sites you have to keep one thing in mind: Not only do people have to be able to find your sites, but the content of the site must be so valuable that they linger and come back again.

Therefore, you need to do a few simple steps before you start arranging your external promotion effort.

1. You should thoroughly test your web site to make sure that all information is correct and that links are active and accurate.
2. All web pages should include information on how people can contact you by other means, such as telephone numbers, fax numbers, E-mail address, and so on.
3. The security of your online ordering system should be thoroughly checked.
4. All web pages should be visually attractive.
5. You should browse your web pages using at least three different browsing programs to ensure that content is preserved.

The domain name

As part of the effort of setting up and testing your web site, strong consideration should be given to your domain name. The selection of a short and meaningful domain name can make a considerable difference in your promotional efforts. If the name is too long, users will have a hard time entering it accurately. Any misspellings or capitalization mistakes will result in landing at the wrong site or getting an "object not found" error message.

For example, an organization called the Bird Lovers Guild should not use the following domain name:

www.Birdloversguild.org

The name is too long to clearly see the organization's name. In addition, a person confused could leave a letter out of this address and land at the wrong site. Normally that is not much of a problem except that adult content sites like to use the misspellings of popular sites to glean unintentional visitors. A much better name would be either,

www.blg.org or,
www.bird.org

These names are short and to the point. This is assuming that the organization can obtain these domain names. Internic may have already assigned these names. But take a moment and think about the average bird lover looking for information on the internet. They may not know about search engines but they do know every type of bird in the world. This makes this organization typically a target for initial inquiries by potential new members. As we shall see, you do not rely on clever domain names alone to promote your site. The clever name only helps to make it memorable to potential customers.

Three of our four example companies have obvious domain names they should attempt to acquire.

www.avix.com
www.lawfirm.com
www.megalith.com

However, the Dickerson County School System will have a more difficult time coming up with the appropriate domain name. Chances are the name Dickerson has already been taken as a domain name of the internet. Therefore they can take advantage of the web hosting service they are using. For example, if they were using the web hosting service at 9000.net the domain name of their site could be,

www.Dickerson.9000.net

The site 9000.net is a top-level domain name. This allows this particular web host to assign any name they want below the top-level domain. The name Dickerson is less likely to have been used within a single domain.

Finally, you should consider multiple domain names where appropriate. For example, a car company could have a domain name for itself and one for each make of car. In that way, several domain names are on the web, each able to draw customers into the company's web pages. For example, the company domain name may be,

www.lexus.com

but the information on specific cars is located at:

www.LS400.com
www.ES300.com

www.GS300.com
www.RX300.com

and so on. In this way, a customer has many more chances of finding the company's information regardless of the search pattern being used.

Discovery exercise: Test your domain name

Try this test with a colleague or friend who is not very familiar with using the internet. Tell your friend that your company has a web site, and give name of your company. Do not reveal the exact web address. Challenge this person to find your web site. Measure how long it takes this person to discover where your company has its web site.

This exercise will quickly demonstrate how well placed your web site address is on the internet. For example, if I asked most internet users to find the web site for International Business Machines, most would correctly guess it would be at www.ibm.com. Some people would resort to popular search engines on the internet to look up your company. If they are unable to guess the web address or find it on one of the popular search engines then you know you have a considerable promotion job ahead of you. Your goal is to make your company's web address either immediately obvious to any user of the internet or "findable" within any commonly used search engine.

Using Internet Search Engines

One of the first steps to be taken when your web site is ready to be promoted is to contact the popular search engines on the internet. Before we talk about what you do to promote your site on a search engine, we should discuss how these applications work. Popular search engines include:

AltaVista	www.altavista.digital.com
Yahoo	www.yahoo.com
HotBot	www.hotbot.com
Excite	www.excite.com

There are actually hundreds of search engines on the internet. These are just a small sample of the most popular search engines. There are two basic functions a search engine performs to list a web site. The first one is to use a program called a webcrawler. This is a robot that explores the internet looking for links to web pages that are not already in the search engine's database.

These robot programs tend to run continuously searching out new web sites. They read your web site and index the information contained within. The database then attempts to correctly identify what your web pages are all about.

A second approach is the offering of a free service to list your web page on their database. To take advantage of this service you have to log on to the root search engine and describe your web page in detail. We will show you how to do this a little later on. The important point here is that the database of the search engine needs to be given critical keywords to use to help it correctly classify your site. You can leave that to chance or you can take aggressive steps to make sure that your listing is correct and that you land on the top of any list.

This last point is particularly important. Try searching Yahoo for an obscure topic like ISO 9000 and watch hundreds of hits come back. It takes a long time to search through these. Being on top of the list means that more people will click your site.

Steps to take to ensure you are listed properly on a search engine

Different search engines work differently. AltaVista will index the words on your web pages. This makes it a more comprehensive search engine. However, the price you pay is that most searches bring back thousands of hits. In contrast, Yahoo is a categorized list. Searches are more topical, and list hits are shorter. In either case, no one search engine has the entire internet listed, nor do all users go to one search engine. Therefore, you need to list your web site on multiple search engines and internet directories to be effective.

There are a number of internet services that will list your web page free to hundreds of search engines and directories. These include,

> www.net-promote.com
> www.register-it.com
> www.stpt.com
> www.webpromote.com
> www.CentralRegistry.com

To use these services you fill out a series of responses to questions about your web site, its address, and how it should be listed. This is then sent to the most popular search engines and directories listings. The cost for doing this ranges from free up to a few hundred dollars. The methods are fairly effective. However, going to each site and manually entering the information is more likely to generate the results you desire.

In addition, you cannot assume that all search engines were successfully informed about your site. Therefore to do a proper internet promotion, you must begin by listing the search engines and directories where you want your company name to be found. Using this list, you enter information about your web site and then conduct follow-up tests to see how and where your site comes up in the results.

Manually enter your site information   Let's take the example of Yahoo. Once you reach the main page at Yahoo, you must determine where your site should be listed. Yahoo allows up to two categories to have your site listed. We will use the example of Avix Manufacturing. They produce parts for the automotive industry. Therefore it would be in their interest to be listed under categories that potential customers would be searching. Avix must think like a customer.

After careful consideration, Avix decides that the best two categories for their company's web site are:

Business and Economy:Companies:Automotive:Manufacturers
Business and Economy:Companies:Manufacturing:Metal and Metal Stampings

The IS manager at Avix would click down through the Yahoo pages until reaching one of these category listings. At the bottom of the page is a small icon marked "Add URL." When this is clicked a series of questions appear. The IS manager will fill out information about the name of the web site, contact information, keywords that describe the site, and other relevant information. Once the series of forms are filled out the site is submitted to Yahoo for listing. Typically it takes over two weeks for your listing to appear on Yahoo.

Use good keywords   Critical to the success of a listing for your web page is the use of the proper keywords. The keywords will be used by indexing programs within the search engine. Therefore you must choose your keywords carefully. Take the example of the Law Firm.

For any law firm there are going to be some obvious keywords that would be used. Most search engines have a limit of 25 or fewer keywords. Therefore you would first brainstorm and make a long list of keywords and then reduce the list to the most important. For example, your list may begin with the obvious choices:

Law
Legal
attorneys
law firm

And so on. To this would be added other forms and types of key-words. For example, the firm may wish to list the type of legal cases they handle.

Civil
Divorce
Patent
Wills
Estate
Trust
Living-will

To determine the best keywords to use, you must once again think like a customer. Use any information you have about how customers normally find you *without* the internet. For example, people might use the Yellow Pages to find an attorney. Or, they rely on word-of-mouth recommendations. Or, they rely on references from professional organizations. Once you determine this, you now know the key information they are looking for. Thus, for example, the Law Firm may discover that most people don't start out searching specifically for an attorney. They may discover that most clients are businesses looking for someone who can help them solve problems. Therefore the final keywords contained a few interesting listings:

Negotiations
problem solving
conflict resolution
disputes

It is this form of clever thinking that makes ordinary web sites into extraordinary web sites. By finding the hook that brings in the customers, you increase your traffic exponentially and make the web site both profitable and beneficial.

Use meta tags The next step is to prepare your web site to be searched by the search engines. A little-known fact about web pages is the way that meta tags are used. Meta tags are not seen by people browsing your site. Instead they contain information about your site that is not shown on the browser. However the search engines do read the meta tags. Meta tags used to be used to give a title and description to web pages. Today their main use is to help search engines determine the type of site you are presenting.

The web site for a commercial enterprise should be developed with extensive use of meta tags. If you came up with 50 keywords you wanted to use, but the search engine only allows you to list 25, then meta tags are one answer to the problem. You can place the first 25 keywords into the form you fill out at the search engine. Then the next 25 keywords are implanted into your web page using meta tags. In that way, the search engine ends up reading all 50 keywords. Chapter 10 discusses how to set up meta tags in HTML code.

Track your success   Just because you were able to fill out forms to get listed on a search engine doesn't mean that you are now listed. Some of the lesser used search engines will list you within a day. More popular engines like AltaVista and Yahoo can take weeks. Thus, you need to monitor the success of your listing attempts.

The procedure is simple. You start with your list of search engines where you want to be listed. The more sites used, the more likely potential customers will find you. You go to each of these sites to make the listing and bookmark the search page. Once a week someone is assigned the job of testing the listing. For example, the Law Firm is relying heavily on the term "conflict resolution." Therefore, the test person enters the search term:

"conflict resolution"

The resulting hit list is then displayed. Your objective is to get your web page on the first page of listings and as high on the list as possible. The first page of hits is printed and submitted to you for evaluation. Critical search engines are targeted for special attention.

For example, the Law Firm may discover that conflict resolution on Yahoo invokes a short list of several categories. The original location chosen was under a "Legal" category. However, the first category listed is for Health:Psychology. You would then resubmit your URL listing for this first category. Your presence now moves to the top of the page. Most people will click the first few listings for a search result. The unusual presence of a legal recourse to conflicts in a psychology listing will be noticed.

Follow-ups to support your web listings

Once the web site is listed you cannot sit back and wait for people to come to your site. Now you have to become proactive in driving people toward your site. Remember, a web site is just one more form of contact your business has with the outside world.

Put the web address on all communications The web address should be part of all other forms of communication used by your business. It should be part of business cards, letterhead, brochures, catalogs, mailings, and any other form of business communication you now conduct.

Run an internet advertisement Advertising on the internet is a controversial subject for some companies. However, for cases where a company wants a lot of volume reaching its site, placing a "click-through" banner advertisement on one of the search engines can result in many more people looking at your site.

Still, you need to have a web page that will then keep the new visitors at your site as long as possible so that they take an interest in your services and products. You would not want to link an advertisement to a page with links to other sites or you will probably get most people passing right through your site to other destinations.

Take the example of a management consulting group. They may choose to place an advertisement on the web site of a popular management association. To do this type of advertising you need to first check critical information such as the number of hits the association receives each month and how many users typically click on the banner ads to reach other sites.

Run conventional advertisements with the web address In the print advertising and broadcast marketing done by your company, be sure to include your web site address. This is where the importance of a good domain name really counts. Think about the situation where you are listening to a radio advertisement for used Macintosh computers from the 1980s. Being a big collector of these, you take interest. At the end of the commercial the announcer says, "Be sure to see our list of available computers at www.edprint.demon. co.uk/se/index.html." Are you likely to remember this?

Now, if the announcer says, "See our list of products at OldMacs.com," won't you be more likely to remember this?

Conventions There are two ways to work the use of conventions. One is to have your booth at a convention running a computer showing your web site. Attendees are encouraged to browse, and everyone passing by gets a standard convention token gift with your web address in large letters.

The other direction is to broadcast your convention over the internet. Several professional organizations now broadcast their opening speeches over the internet with well placed link advertisements. Other organizations have posted the papers presented at their site and will sell you advertising space. For an organization like the Dickerson County School System, they can form a page of links to these sites related to controversies in education. By advertising the presence of such a page, more people are drawn into the web site.

Banner ads on other sites   We are including this idea to discourage you from using it. Banner ads are frequently cited as a good way to advertise for free. This is true, but banner ads are not recommended for larger businesses.

The way the ads work is that you agree to place someone's banner on your page if they place your banner on their page. Banners are then rotated and exchanged. The problem for business is that you are promoting someone else on your page and you have lost control of who will be displaying your banner. Neither of these situations is very beneficial.

Links from other sites   A better idea is to request sites related to your own to include links back to your web page. For example, the Law Firm could politely ask several well placed legal referral pages to list their link. A link on a popular web site can draw in thousands of new browsers.

Contests   Money is always a nice motivational device when used properly. A company like Megalith could run a contest to give away cars and vacations for a lucky few people that have used their online ordering system. With tens of thousands of people who use the system, the word would spread rapidly to others.

Listings in catalogs, directories, and press releases   You are not the only organization that writes about your business. Catalogs and directories printed by third parties contain information about your company. Including your web address and E-mail address for inquiries is always a good idea.

Take the example of Avix. A standard catalog of manufactured goods in the United States could be used by thousands of companies to find new suppliers. By listing web addresses along with the usual company description, Avix can not only distinguish itself from competitors but make new customers aware of another way of instantly getting information.

Managed mailing lists   An interesting feature of the internet is the use of managed mailing lists, such as Listserv. Listserv is an automated mailing list program. People subscribe to a mailing list on a particular topic. Anyone can enter comments on the topic and they are E-mailed to the entire list.

If you check carefully with the person responsible for keeping the list, you might be able to make brief announcements of new products or services you offer. For example, a mailing list on manufacturing excellence may allow

Avix to post a brief message that they have developed a new problem-solving method. A link to the Avix page could be included in the message.

A better approach is to be the list master. Start your own mailing list on a topic where your company is considered expert. For example, the Law Firm might start a mailing list discussion on the application of copyright claims across national borders. This could bring in thousands of interested parties that would then be dependent on the Law Firm for information.

However, if you take this route be aware that someone will have to spend considerable time moderating the list. Also you need to follow the strict guidelines of the internet if this evolves into a newsgroup. To learn how to start a mailing list or news group, look up these terms on any search engine:

Listserve
Majordomo
UseNet

On-line magazines Finally, there are a number of online magazine on particular topics. One or more of these might involve the type of business you conduct. By advertising on these sites or being an active contributor to their content, you encourage visitation by people already interested in the type of information your site will have.

Components to Put on External Web Pages to Promote their Use

The idea here is to create a web site that people want to use time and again. For example, a web site with constantly updated information of great importance to your target audience will be very successful. Look at the multimillion hits a day on the Jet Propulsion Laboratory's page whenever a Mars mission is in the news.

You want to generate a smaller but similar effect for your own company. In the case of Avix, they will have their catalog online. In that way regular customers can browse the catalog and place orders anytime day or night. The Dickerson County School System will be posting homework assignments on their web pages. In this way parents can log in after they get home from work to double check what work their children need to complete that night.

What to add to a web page is limited only by your imagination. However, you should limit your material to the smallest set that meets your mission goals. As we said earlier, a cluttered page is a useless page. Following are just some of the components you can consider for your company's page.

Search engines

You have two different choices here and both make sense for most sites. The major search engine sites on the internet will allow you to download code to place a link to their searching capabilities. Thus, you can make a web page that is tailored to helping people use your site to find information on a particular set of topics anywhere on the internet.

For example, people visiting the Dickerson site are already interested in their children's education. If you develop a page that gives clear instructions on how parents can search for current topics related to education, such as home schooling or charter academies, then you are providing a valuable service. Instead of going to the large search engines and searching over and over again for what they need, your page provides a better set of instructions on how to find what they need. Then you encourage the use of a bookmark to come back to the site. People quickly favor this site.

The other approach for sites with discussion groups and other lengthy sets of data is to plant your own search engine for your site. Popular web design programs will create a search page for your entire site. This allows people who are interested in education to visit, say, the Dickerson site and then look for information related to "taxes." All messages, announcements, and links at the Dickerson site related to taxation and education will be listed. By examining the list and clicking on interesting articles the visitor quickly finds the needed information. All intranets should have a search page.

Discussion groups

Nothing draws in visitors like a good discussion group. One that really impressed me a few years ago was the discussion group at the Pentax site. Here was a camera company sponsoring an unmoderated discussion of their product. People discussed openly the strengths and weaknesses of the Pentax cameras.

It brought in thousands of people to participate and many times more of people like myself trying to determine which camera to buy. I used the comments in the discussion group to help me make the decision. If you think about this, Pentax put very few resources into a massive marketing device that ran itself. How else could an individual find dozens of people in one place who used one particular model of camera and were able to discuss their experiences?

Company profile page

All business sites have to have a company profile page. People using the internet are naturally suspicious due to the large number of scams occurring on the internet. Therefore, a good move is to reassure your audience by explaining who you are, what your business does, where you are located, and the like. Public companies often put today's stock quote for their common shares on their web page.

Information request form

Interactivity is something many people enjoy about the internet. The internet is also one way to offer 24 hours a day service to potential customers. An information request form is a nonthreatening way to encourage visitors to ask questions. However, you must back up such forms with a system that responds as quickly as possible with valuable information.

Quote form

If you sell a product or a service, be ready to quote prices. A quoting form can be used in situations where a company's price might depend on several variables. Take the example of office furniture sales. The final price depends on the number of pieces being bought, destination, model year of the pieces, and several other factors. By getting this information from your customer up front you can respond quickly with a quote. Again you have to have the system in place to respond quickly with needed information. We strongly recommend that you point out in the response that this is the maximum price. If the customer wishes, a sales representative can call them to discuss possible discounts. In this way you never discourage a potential customer.

Internet-only special on products or services

People have taken the time to visit your site, so reward them. If you sell products or services, then offer a special deal or discount if they place an order through your internet site. Computer equipment sales sites often use this tactic. When you are searching for a new computer you find sites where there is a "weekly special." This encourages first time visitors to linger at the site and consider a different system at a potentially more profitable price.

Free downloads of data and graphics

I was recently given a 1989 Macintosh SE computer. Here was a machine that was considered way-obsolete. However, I found several sites on the internet that would provide free downloads of games, utilities, and applications for this machine. The most interesting one was at Apple Computer, the original manufacturer. They would give me System 7 for free. Free and thorough support of a computer product after more than eleven years is remarkable. It is also a valuable service that keeps the second and third owners of these machines coming back. As these owners come back through the Apple site, they see information about the newest line of Apple products.

Links page

Search engines are nice, but some internet users prefer to find a page of links related to the same topic. For example, if your company makes the engines for high power model rockets, a link page to all known model rocket sites on the web would be very valuable to your customers. You encourage visitors to bookmark the site as a handy reference tool while your company always leads the page with a brief ad for your own product.

Updates by E-mail

Alert your customers to changes, upgrades, or special offers. Web pages can contain a brief form that lets people sign up for regular updates by E-mail. Be sure that the first E-mail is sent immediately thanking them for signing up, giving instructions on how to stop the service, and explaining what type of information to expect.

Database

The advantage of a database on a computer is its rapid ability to find information or to create reports. The greatest disadvantage used to be the difficulty of making the database available to a large number of people. The internet changed all of that. The Library of Congress can now be searched by anyone in the world with an internet account.

Likewise, if your company has a valuable database of information it can be converted into a powerful tool of competition. In fact, using your internet technology can be a competitive weapon. One company offered to place all of the hospital records in a town of one million on a single, searchable database available through a web page.

Using firewalls and other security measures, the data was restricted to approved medical personnel only. However, all medical personnel in this city could now reach any patient's medical records from any computer site in town. This service was leased from the existing resources of the company. Thus, a new service was invented within the company using the left over capabilities of their internet service.

Guestbook

Whether to use a guestbook to have people log into your site is a tricky decision. On one hand it gives you the name and E-mail address of visitors, but it also discourages a lot of people from staying at your site. Therefore, when you use a guestbook be sure to explain its purpose and what you intend to do with the information provided. For example, it can always be made an option. People visiting the Megalith site might find an optional guest book with the following explanation:

> If you are interested in receiving early information on the release of our next version of our award winning SkipThis software, please register below. This information is kept confidential and will not be used for promotional programs or sold to other marketing concerns.

Definition of terms

If you think about the practice of law, it is filled with obscure terminology. Therefore, the Law Firm may choose to have a layman's definition page to explain fundamental legal terms. In this way potential customers are using this page to answer many simple questions before they contact the Law Firm. This saves time for the staff.

Table of contents

All business web sites with more than a few web pages should have a table of contents. This facilitates the rapid navigation of the site. Intranets should always have a central table of contents.

Clear paths of navigation with no dead ends

One of the most frustrating characteristics of badly designed web sites is that they often have poor navigation or dead ends. Many of the current software producer sites suffer from this problem. With hundreds of products, technical support, and other services, it can take a trip through a dozen pages to find a needed item.

All web pages should give the viewer the following options:

- Next page
- Previous page
- Home page
- Table of contents
- Links to the most popular pages
- Link back to the beginning of a segment of pages

In this way, you keep a visitor from getting lost. If the site is really large, then also use search engines, indexes, or break the site up into product-specific sites at different addresses.

Product descriptions

People want information from the internet. You should provide a thorough description of your product or service. For products, you can include a picture, but the description should be complete without the presence of the picture. For a service you should provide an example of its application or a recent customer's testimony.

The idea here is to make the nature and use of the product or service clear to the person reading through your web site. A good strategy is to also give the viewer a chance to order this product at the end of the description. The Amazon.com site does this very well and should be consulted for other related approaches.

Press releases/Press stories about your company

Even though you may be selling a product, don't forget to reprint the press coverage you have gotten for the product or about your company. These serve to assure potential customers that you are a serious company that will be in business for a long time.

Secure order area

Piracy of credit card information and other sensitive data is a major issue on the internet. When taking orders be sure to use a secure site (HTTPS). Then explain to your web site customers that this order taking point is secure. Also provide them with the option of printing an order form and faxing or mailing in the order. Although a little slower, it gives the customer choices for personal security.

Survey form

An organization like the Dickerson County School System can use a survey form as a marketing tool. By gathering parent and student opinions on concepts such as year-round schools, the district is fulfilling its charter of seeking continuous improvement of its services. This also provides the users of the web site a voice in community affairs.

Chat room

The Law Firm, for example, could bring in the nation's best known divorce attorney to answer questions in a chat room set up on a national internet service. Advertised heavily in both internet and legal publications, this novel activity can be a powerful marketing tool. Follow-up E-mails and questions would be sent to the Law Firm, whose name is used repeatedly during the chat session.

Broadcast/Audio files/Video files

One of the great discoveries my associates and I made about the internet is that it can expose "old" products to a new audience. We once produced an audiotape on constructive problem-solving. Several thousand copies were eventually sold and the market dried up. However, when we converted it to a downloadable audio file on the internet, suddenly thousands of new people came to listen. This drew many new people to our site.

The broadcasting of audio and video clips over the internet can work well as a promotional device, but it must be used with caution. It takes a very fast modem at the user's end to have the quality needed for the experience to be acceptable. It can require that users download a plug-in for the browser and these don't always work on all computers.

Upcoming events

Finally, it never hurts to be the official community bulletin board for a particular topic. The announcement of upcoming events is another area where many people are drawn on the internet. Because these types of sites have to be checked on a regular basis, it helps to build a regular client base for your site.

Case Study: ASR's Web Site

The following is a true story that illustrates how a small company with a minimal amount of web space can create a large impact. This is the story of one of my clients, the American Systems Registrar (ASR).

ASR is a very small company of less than a dozen people. What they do is register companies to international standards, such as ISO 9000. This is a small but very competitive field in business. Companies pay a registrar to audit their facilities against these standards. If they are found to be in conformance, a certificate of registration is issued and the company receives a minimum of one surveillance audit per year for the life of the certificate.

In many cases companies tend to select one registrar and stick with them. Large companies, like Underwriter's Laboratories and Lloyds of London, offer these services. Therefore, a small registrar like ASR has to compete against powerful companies for a limited market.

ASR designed their web site correctly by first designing their marketing strategy before they even considered whether to have a web site. In this way, they had a well formed idea of how to compete. They examined the registration field very closely and talked to many of the registered companies. This type of marketing research revealed several flaws in the system that could be exploited.

ASR took advantage of two of these opportunities. The first was the issue of price. Registration services cost money. For a 250-person manufacturer seeking ISO 9001 registration, the average first-year cost was around $11,000. However, it was quickly discovered that few registrars openly discussed prices or would print quotes to the public. Instead, pricing was broken down into a long and confusing list of items that may or may not apply to a specific company.

The second issue was the quality of service being rendered. At the time I took them on as a client, there were many stories circulating about "drive-by audits" where audit teams didn't seem to be performing fully to professional standards.

Taken together, these two items gave ASR two marketing opportunities. It was quickly decided that pointing out the quality flaws in the existing system was to speak negatively. A negative image tends to hurt the messenger as much as the intended targets. Therefore, all promotional material was couched in positive terms emphasizing the focus on high-quality service using only the best auditors.

Next, it was decided that pricing should be open and readily available to potential customers. This would include spelling out all terms and conditions in advance of any contract. Any company could call ASR and get a same-day quote on registration services.

Making the web page

Now it came time to make a web site for ASR. The management of the company was skeptical of the benefits of internet presence. A quick check of the internet search engines turned up several interesting facts:

- About half of all registration companies in North America have web pages.
- None of the competing web pages go beyond a description of the company and its services.
- No one mentions pricing.
- When searching on Yahoo for ISO registrars the banner ad that normally appears at the top of the results page shows an ad for a registrar.

Some further phone calls revealed that the banner ad on Yahoo was about to be vacated for three months. The web page development team used this information to convince the owners and managers of ASR that they had a rare opportunity to create a distinctive and useful web page for registration services while seizing a valuable internet advertisement location.

The proposed page was very simple (see Figure 16–1). The home page was a description of ASR emphasizing the quality of its audit staff. The top of the home page was the navigation bar. Instead of terms like "index," "next page," or other vague references, it presented links with hard hitting, direct language. This included phrases that spoke directly to the visitors such as,

"I need a quote"
"What about price?"
"The benefits of registration"

Figure 16–1. ASR Home Page Design

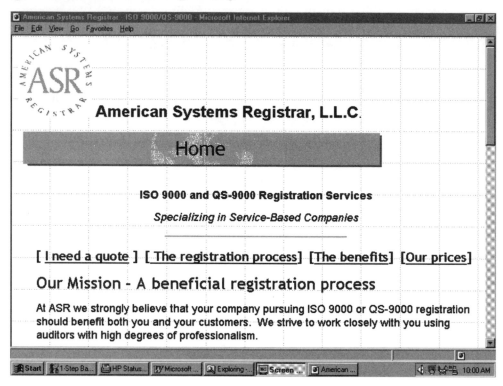

The "benefits of registration" page explained how a company can profit from registration. This included a lead-in quote explaining that "ASR is there to take the anxiety out of the process."

The price page published actual quotes given to real companies (see Figure 16–2). The names of the companies were not used, but a description of their size, type of product, and other company information were listed. This was a major distinction from the competition. For the first time, potential customers had a place where they could confidentially look at pricing information.

To follow up on that advantage the quote page had a profile sheet anybody could fill out and submit to ASR (see Figure 16–3). At the bottom of the form was the "Submit for a Quote" button. Clicking this sent the information directly to a person waiting at ASR. After a process to verify that the quote request seemed valid, the person would prepare a quote, contract, and cover letter that was faxed directly to the interested party. Average response time was less than four hours. All quotes received by 2:00 were processed and sent back

Figure 16-2. ASR Price Quote Page

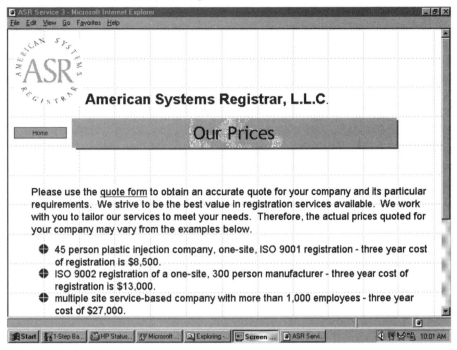

Figure 16-3. ASR Request for Quote Form

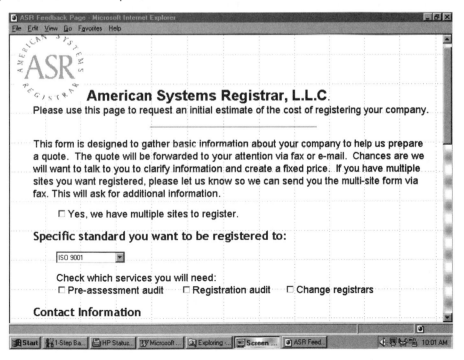

the same business day. Competitors were known to take up to several weeks to respond to such requests.

Results of the web page

The most difficult part of designing the web site was convincing ASR to spend the $2400 it took to secure the Yahoo banner ad for three months. Calls to Yahoo revealed that this banner had gotten the previous registrar an average of 1000 "click throughs" a month. ASR created a banner ad that essentially said, "For a free, no-obligation registration quote, click here."

Several thousand people clicked the ad during the three months. The ASR listing was manually placed on 25 search engines and maintained to keep ASR near the top of the hits list. This resulted in an average of two quotes a day just from the internet.

ASR originally expected to do two quotes a week during their first year of operation. That would have been roughly 100 quotes with between 20 to 25 signed contracts. Instead, the web page brought in an annual rate of 500 quotes. Clearly, the web site was successful.

Further study of web page statistics showed that thousands of people per week were hitting the site. The price page was showing the most hits even though it was one level down from the home page. That means that many other sites were linking to this particular page. This was another indication that ASR had guessed correctly that customers wanted better access to pricing information.

Today ASR has changed, expanded, and upgraded its marketing strategy. The success of its web site during its first six months of operation made the company successful much earlier than anyone expected. The lesson learned here is that the right few elements in a web page using traditional marketing techniques and strategies is just one more opportunity for your company to succeed.

Further References

The best place to get further information about how to position and use a web site is the internet itself. There is a sizable population of people that have had to perform these tasks before and that want to share their experiences.

Otherwise, you may want to read through:
> *Guerilla web Strategies: How to Promote and Market Your Web Site,* by Vince Gelormine, The Corialis Group, 1996.

Internet search terms
> "Web Site Promotion"
>
> "internet Marketing"
>
> "Listserve"
>
> "Search Engines"

Interesting web sites
> www.amazingsites.com
>
> www.geocities.com/~ericsum/spam/index.html
>
> www.deadlock.com/promote
>
> www.samizdat.com/public.html
>
> www.northernwebs.com/set/
>
> www.best.com/~mentorms/e_othpro.htm
>
> www.sitepromoter.com
>
> www.wilsonweb.com/webmarket
>
> www.tka.co.uk/magic/promote.htm
>
> www.pagebooster.com

You may also want to visit the marketing department at Brigham Young University:
> marketing.byu.edu

Chapter 17
Finding and Developing Sources of Content

Web sites live, eat, and breathe *content*. It is the information on a web page that makes it successful. Your job as IS manager is to find the people who can create content, form them into a team, and set up a system whereby only excellent quality material reaches your web sites.

That means you need a good document control procedure, a system of approving what gets placed on a web site, and a regular review of all sites to ensure that all information is accurate and up-to-date. This will be the second critical battle for your internet system that you must win. (The first was the battle to get full management commitment to your system.)

In this situation, you are fighting to keep IS personnel from becoming responsible for creating the content of the web sites. An internet system works best when responsibilities are decentralized. Although you do want the IS department to be responsible for implementing and maintaining the internet system, you want other departments to work on the *content* presented through internet technology. Most important of all, you want the people closest to the information to create the related content.

As an illustration, think about Avix Manufacturing. They wish to place a catalog of their products on the internet. The IS technicians could set up the web page and the database link. Then they could feed the database the information on different products as updates are issued from engineering and sales.

The problem is that the data will be at least several days old before it finally reaches the internet. At the same time, the IS people are not totally familiar with the product. They might make simple mistakes in descriptions that they would not notice. They would also not know about the best ways to describe various features or the needs of the customers.

Instead, the sales and engineering departments should be responsible for the contents of the database. IS would set up the initial web page and database links, but after that, the sales and engineering people would send updates directly to the database upon release. They would also notice small mistakes in information and correct these as detected. In addition, because they are close to the customers, they would understand the best way to portray changes or new products. In short, the people with the expertise should stick to the responsibilities they can handle best.

Structuring Your Existing Databases of Information

Whether you are developing an intranet or an internet presence, you have to confront the issue of existing information. Companies are repositories for databases of information. This includes examples such as:

- Customer databases
- Spreadsheets
- Policies, procedures, and work instructions
- Specifications
- Order forms
- Reports
- Memos
- Catalogs

A complete list would be hundreds of items long. Your primary problem is that much of this information will somehow have to be integrated into your internet technology to be presented to a target audience. Therefore, you must make a concerted effort to structure this information so it can be presented through a web site.

There are many different approaches that can be used to translate information into a new form of presentation. We will look at two popular models which usually apply to any internet system.

The "drill down" model for intranets and the internet

The first of these models is called "drill down." In this method, you present an initial piece of information that the viewer can then click on to break the data down into more detailed facts. Take the example of an annual report about the company. One of the data items being presented on the web page is the fact that the company made 11% profit this year. A curious viewer can click on the 11% figure and be presented with a spreadsheet that breaks down the cash flow for the company for the previous 12 months. Clicking on a category for the profits from services will bring up a list of services the company offers, and how much money was made from each service.

The viewer is "drilling down" through three layers of information. This model applies well to internet technology because it follows the form and function of hyperlinks. It allows you to present very simple and easy to understand information on your initial web pages. Further viewing will show more detailed information or further explanations of the facts by clicking on the affected area and being presented with more information. Clicking again will lead them to other definitions, explanations, and illustrations.

Thus, you can design web sites where the complexity of the site is determined by the viewer. Viewers who want quick, simple information merely read through the first page or two of your site. If more information is needed, the viewer can keep clicking on hyperlinks.

The challenge here is to structure existing data so it can be drilled successfully. The annual report example sounds very easy to set up. In most cases, it is not. What you'll find is that the spreadsheet on cash flow for the company is controlled by the financial department. A list of services offered by the company can only be obtained by contacting several departments. The actual profitability of each service is disputed by both finance and administration. The annual report is controlled by the administrative secretarial staff.

Your job as IS manager is to get these different political divisions to openly share their information. You will also need to put that information into a common format that is compatible to the internet services. This translation and linking activity will likely have to be done by your staff because the affected departments will say that they are too busy for this demanding task. As we shall see, the real answer is to use a format within the company that also complements the internet system without the need for translation activities.

The "value-added" model of information

At the same time that you are designing the type of data to be presented on the internet and how this information will be organized, you should worry about the value of the information being presented. Value-added means that the movement of information from your existing repositories to the internet/intranet increases the value of the data. Increased value can be obtained through any of the following:

- Lower costs
- Higher quality of information
- Greater accessibility of information
- Better productivity
- Market position improvement

Information costs money to create, store, distribute, and destroy. The management of data can be improved with intranet or internet based storage and distribution. Take the case of standard operating procedures. In the past these were printed in large books which were then distributed to all employees. These books cost money to print, distribute, and update. With an intranet, the same documents can be made available to all employees at very little cost. Updating the same information can be handled with ease from a central administration point. Document control becomes very easy. The value here is lower cost and greater access.

In one example, illustrated later in this chapter, Megalith is going to make investment information about the company available on the internet. This will increase their market position. Another example is the placement of production schedules and feedback forms on the Avix intranet. This will result in productivity gains and higher quality information for the general workforce. Thus, in these examples, the value of the information is improved by placing it on an intranet or a web page on the internet.

Validating Data
on Your Web Site

Another critical issue to consider when placing information onto web sites and other internet services is "validation." Validation is the process whereby you confirm that the content on your web site is what you intended and that it will meet the needs of your audience.

For proper validation, you need to develop a system for the way in which information is proposed for posting to a web site, reviewed, tested, approved, and placed. This system is described below in greater detail. The important part to remember is that you need to make sure your usage of information is valid.

In addition, you must confirm that the information has been verified. Is the spelling correct? Was the grammar checked? Were all records or facts successfully transferred to the web site?

Document Management

As mentioned several times in this book, you need some form of document control as part of your internet system. Document control principles are equally important for internet content. Configuration management techniques and software can be used to ensure that the proper version of information is placed, that all known copies of the data are tracked, and that the right people are receiving the data at the right place and at the right time.

To accomplish this, you will need the following items in your document control system for internet content.

1. A review process must be in place to ensure that the information is timely and adequate for the intended application prior to its placement on your internet system.

2. A master list should be kept that tracks all pieces of information (forms, records, databases, etc.) on the internet system.

3. All web pages should include a date of creation and the date of the most recent update.

4. The IS manager should appoint someone to audit the system to ensure that the people who need the information are able to access it.

5. Invalid or obsolete documents must be removed from the internet system immediately.

6. Updates to documents posted on the internet or intranet should be approved before being carried out.

Measures such as these ensure that the information being presented by your internet system is accurate and up-to-date. Later we will examine how to make the same information easy to understand by your audience.

Validation of a database on the internet

Let's take a specific example of using the internet technology to create a new repository for information. Suppose your corporation already keeps the following databases on its mainframes and on the local area network servers:

- List of customers (sales department)
- Account balances of customers (accounting)
- Shipment status (warehouse and distribution)
- Incoming products (purchasing)

The customer service representatives have always wanted a single point of access to this information. In the past, they have used a terminal emulation program on their computers to bring up the various databases to answer questions from the customers.

Under the new internet system you are developing, your company is using Microsoft Access to create tables of select information from each database into a single database that will be linked to a web page. The public portion of the web page will allow customers to ask for their current shipment status and outstanding balance. The internal portion of the page will allow customer service representatives to perform several important tasks, such as confirming a customer's account, order, money paid, status of shipment, and other bits of information.

Validation for this type of system would consist of designed processes that would confirm the validity of the data being reported to the customer service representatives. This would include:

1. Audits to ensure that the data format, record lengths, and character types of the original database and the web-page linked database are the same.
2. Systems to ensure that data being entered into the existing databases are accurate and timely. For example, are you using spreadsheets with confirmation rules and filters to help keep the information being entered accurate?
3. Testing of the retrieval and reporting functions of the web page.
4. Training on the use of the new database using sample sets of data.
5. Someone put into the position of making sure that the database operations stay synchronized with the web page.

This last point is particularly important. If one of the original databases changes its record format or adds a new field, its impact on the web page must be carefully examined and tested. Any effects on the web page must be corrected.

Dealing with legacy information

Next comes the issue of legacy information. In most cases the company will have existing databases that are made available to the intended audience in an alternative form. Take the simple example of the corporate phone book. A company may have previously printed a ten-page phone book listing the extensions of all employees.

Every time a few new people were hired, the book had to be reprinted and redistributed to the entire staff along with instructions to dispose of the previous book. It is easy to see that putting the same document on an intranet would save a lot of paper and trouble. The problem is that not all employees use the intranet. Therefore, some people would still need the book while others could always use the computer.

The solution would be some form of compromise. Each department may keep a book or two for those who want to look up an extension manually. Otherwise, anyone could also use the intranet for the same purpose. Most people would quickly discover that the choice on which to use will come down to whether a book or computer is closer.

Basically, you will have one of three situations involving legacy information:

1. The legacy information remains with no change to distribution method. Internet technology is not used.

2. The legacy information system stays in place and continues to be used, but an internet technology method of access and storage is implemented.

3. Internet technology supersedes the original application. The legacy method is phased out and the internet method takes over.

Forming a Content Team

The process of forming a team to handle the creation and placement of information for your web sites will be done in a fashion very similar to what we described for the implementation team. This includes:

- A procedure for how proposed internet information becomes web site content
- A clear path of getting content approved
- Quality control measures
- A team leader
- Close coordination of activities
- Assuring that everyone has the proper resources to do their job
- Accounting for differences in personalities

Unlike the implementation team, the first step for a content team is to be presented with a procedure for how content is created, approved, and placed on web sites.

A specific example will help you to understand how all of this works in practice. Let's assume that Megalith is interested in having a web site designed to meet the needs of current and potential investors in the corporation. The IS department will appoint a systems administrator to set up the web server, internet connections, and other related items. The investor relations department and the legal department will be charged with providing content.

The IS manager and the PR director are working together to launch this project. Their first decision is how much authority to give to a team from investor relations and legal. It is decided that the team will be given a considerable amount of authority. Specifically, they will create the procedures they will follow and retain almost full control of the web site.

Setting up a procedure

The IS manager and PR director meet with the managers of the legal and investor relations departments. The four decide on a system for creating and approving web site content. As part of that system they decide on the software tools to be used. In this case they decide to use Office 97. They could have used any number of combinations, such Lotus Notes and Net Objects Fusion, to create content and stay coordinated.

1. Proposed materials are drafted using Microsoft Word 97. A template will be created to control content and heading style formats.
2. E-mail is used to make assignments and ask for follow-up and progress reports. Proposed web content is sent to the legal department for review, and then on to investor relations.
3. Once both departments agree on the value and accuracy of the information, it is formatted in FrontPage 98 and sent to the managers of investor relations and legal for final approval.
3. Once approved, it is sent to the person assigned with editing the web site for placement.
4. Monitoring methods are begun with regular reports on the success of the site sent to the managers of IS, legal, investor relations, and public relations.

The formal procedure for this system will be drafted by the team.

Picking the team

The people involved in this process are the managers and whoever else will be needed to create content. At this point, the Megalith managers should select the people who will be allowed to work on web content in the two departments. In our example they select four people from investor relations and two from legal who will be assigned to this team.

These people will have to go through training on how to use the collaboration features of Office 97 and how information gets published to a web page at Megalith. Once familiar with the methods of the corporation, the team needs to pick its leader. This is the person who will keep the system on track and running smoothly.

One of the interesting characteristics of a content team is that they rarely meet face to face. One of the few times they would meet as a group would be to discuss how the system should run or how to make it work better. Otherwise, as we will see, they will spend their team time passing documents from one person to another.

The final team is,

Patty Moyer—legal secretary
Frank Terms—attorney
Iva Mercedes—investment expert
Phil Orders—stock strategist and team leader
Dan Grayrock—investment counselor
Sally Laydoun—technical writer

Putting the procedure into writing

This team will be responsible for the day-to-day creation of content. Therefore, they need to write a standard operating procedure for content creation. Like any procedure, it would describe who does what, when it happens, in which sequence, and with what type of software or equipment. Part of this procedure will specify the exact points of approval before the process can proceed.

The team drafts an initial procedure as a group. This is done in Microsoft Word and sent out via E-mail to the appropriate managers for comment. Further comments from the team are also collected by Phil Orders, the team leader. The revision feature of Word allows the document to be worked on by several people at the same time. Each person's suggested changes and edits are highlighted in a different color.

The final procedure looked like this:

Standard Operating Procedure 34-001

Creation and Approval of Web Content for Investor Relations Page

34.1 Purpose

To create a consistent, high quality approach in producing and placing information about investment activities related to Megalith on its web sites.

34.2 Scope

This procedure applies to any investment information placed on the web page for Megalith investors or potential investors.

34.3 Responsibilities

The investor relations manager is ultimately responsible for ensuring that this procedure is fully implemented, followed, and audited.

34.4 Procedure

34.4.1 When any Megalith employee has an idea about content for the investors' web page, an E-mail should be sent to the manager of investor relations. The idea should include a description of content, its value to investors, and how it relates to existing information.

34.4.2 If the idea is felt to have merit by the manager of investor relations, then an E-mail is sent to all content team members attaching the idea for comment. Team members will use the Yes/No/Maybe feature of Outlook E-mail to vote on whether to pursue this idea.

34.4.3 Approved ideas will be assigned to a particular person in investor relations to work with the person(s) originating the idea to expand it into a working draft. Microsoft Word 97 will be used to create this working draft. The template file "invest.top" will be used to set the format of the document.

34.4.4 The working draft is circulated via E-mail to the content team members for review and comment. These are collected and reviewed by the person assigned to create the draft. The legal department team members will comment on any possible legal problems.

34.4.5 Comments and suggestions are used to create the final draft of the document. This is sent to the managers of investor relations and legal for approval. Once approved, the document is sent to the technical writer in investor relations for translation from Word format to FrontPage HTML. The resulting web page(s) are posted in the test site E://FrontPageWebs/Test. The content team reviews this page using the following quality assurance tests:

- Spelling accuracy (must be 100%)
- Grammar (correct to the New York Times standard)
- Accuracy of information (must be 100%)
- Test any links
- Checklist of items on any corporate web page (look-and-feel standard)

34.4.6 Once approved by managers from legal, investor relations, and the originating department, the page is posted to the investment web site by the content team leader.

34.4.7 New web pages are then browsed using Lynx, Internet Explorer, Opera, and Navigator.

34.5 Auditing

The content value and accuracy of information are audited once a month as part of the total site audit.

34.6 Related Documents

14-002 Document Control

12-101 Policies on Investor Relations Communications

44-009 Audit Procedures (General)

14-015 Quality Control of Web Sites

This is a simplified version of an actual procedure. Please note that we have excluded any discussion of what happens if a draft is rejected at any point in this process. This was excluded to promote clarity. In your own company you would want to take into account the size and mission of your content teams. This is a relatively small team working near one another. The more distant the team and the more complex the task, the greater the need for very clear instructions with coordinated calendars.

Testing the procedure

It is one thing to have created a procedure; it is quite another to have it work well. As discussed earlier, I encourage the use of "best practices." Once a procedure is written and placed in the field, the people using the procedure should be encouraged to come up with better ways to achieve the same goals.

For example, the Megalith content team could test the procedure by developing a few web pages for the new investment site. The experiences of the team could be recorded in a discussion area of their own intranet page.

From this type of information sharing they may learn that not all the teeth in this corporate gear mesh easily.

Publishing to a Web Site

Now the team must decide on the actual tone and content of the investors' web site. The mission is clear. They need to create an easy to use, friendly, and unique web site for current and potential investors. They will also have to move carefully because investment information is a regulated activity.

Early in the process the team studies the needs of investors as well as other investment sites. They quickly find one aspect of their web site they wish to exploit. They want to create an E-mail alert service for anyone who takes the time to sign up on the web page. This service will send copies of any Megalith press releases directly to the E-mail accounts of interested parties.

Investors like to get early information on any company where their money is invested. This helps them to move rapidly before the positive or negative aspect of the news hits the markets. The team originally thought a unique feature would be to release such information about four hours ahead of the formal release to the press. Unfortunately, the legal department quickly pointed out that this might be interpreted as "insider trading." Therefore, the E-mail service would be timed to synchronize with the formal press release.

Controlling the Quality of Content

As stated in the previous chapter, it is the quality of the content of your company's web site that keeps people coming back and makes the site profitable. The IS manager plays a direct role in assuring the quality of content for web pages. This begins with the internet usage policy and includes the "look-and-feel" policy for web pages.

In the case of our example, the content team for the investment page would now plan the actual content of the web page. They would begin by examining the type of information that is already being provided to the public. This includes,

- Stock prospectus
- Copies of SEC filings
- Annual reports
- Press releases

- Announcements of stock buy-backs by management
- Announcements of new stock issues

Obviously, each of these items could be links on the home page of the site leading to a separate page for each topic. The advantage to the public is that this information would be immediately available. Traditionally, it would be mailed to interested parties.

It next occurs to the team that a couple of new features can be added to the investment page to make it unique and valuable. This includes:

1. *A current stock price quote for common and preferred shares.* This would be displayed in the upper corner of the home page with a 90-day trend chart next to each price. In this way, current investors and prospective investors can quickly obtain price information the moment they arrive at the home page.

2. *E-mail news service.* This is the service mentioned above where people who register with the site can receive press releases and other stock news as soon as it is released to the public.

3. *Online trading of shares.* The legal representatives on the team point out that with proper security commission permission, the company can post information about people buying and selling their shares of stock. The company already has a program where individuals can buy shares of Megalith directly from the company. The forms to do this are also duplicated on the web site. At the same time, a discussion group is set up for the posting of buy and sell offers by individuals.

Now we enter the dangerous part about creating web sites: the point where a team has developed an interesting and involved concept of the web site. What usually happens at this point is that most of the work of creating the site lands on one person's desk.

The proper approach is to have a strong and well-trained team leader that makes it clear that ideas will be assigned to specific team members. Furthermore, the leader needs to develop a shared vision of the final site. This is easier to accomplish with collaboration-capable software. For example, some software allows a nonfunctioning mock up of the proposed web site to be drafted and then posted to all group members.

Next, communication between the people involved has to be strongly encouraged and closely coordinated. This is also easier when the team leader posts the target objectives and milestones on the intranet. In addition, all E-mail traffic about the project is automatically copied to the project leader. In that way the leader can actively monitor developments and only intercede where really necessary.

Here is an example of an actual exchange on a group project for a web page.

> *"Rick, I have the outline for the page on past press releases but I can't get the template file to work with it in Word"—Carol*

> *"Carol, try opening the Tools command and selecting the template file."—Rick*

> *"Worked. I have attached a rough draft of what I have created for an interesting table of contents. Items are organized by either date of release, topic, or product involved."—Carol*

> *"Looks good but a little busy. Try breaking it into two pages where the first page is a choice of which of the three types of groupings the viewer wants to search."—Rick*

> *"Speaking of searching, where will the search engine go for the press releases?"—Leader*

> *"What search engine?"—Carol and Rick*

As you can see, the team members are going back and forth checking each step in the development of their respective pages. The obvious question is, why don't they just meet once a week for an hour to discuss all of this? The answer comes from the fact that the three people involved were in separate buildings miles apart. Time, distance, and other responsibilities make it far easier to just communicate by E-mail. Each person can respond when possible. Anyone can respond from home, in the field, or at a different building. The important thing is that communications keep flowing.

Also, the E-mail trail documents who did what and when it happened. In this way the team leader can watch for someone falling behind and shift resources to resolve the problem before it threatens the entire project.

How to measure content quality

The first step in making quality page contents is to have a clear idea of what you are trying to accomplish. A high-quality page is not the web site with the most graphics or fancy features. Instead, it is the page that accomplishes its mission the fastest. These characteristics can be measured.

Returning to our example of the investment page, the primary mission of the page is to deliver timely and accurate information to current and future investors. "Timely" is defined as meaning that the same information being sent by other means (e.g., press releases, news conferences, interviews, postings, filings, etc.) reaches the web page at the same moment of release.

The accuracy of the information means that it both matches the information being sent by other means and that it is free of errors. If an error is found in a press release being prepared for simultaneous transmission over the internet, assuring high quality would involve not just re-posting the correct version on the web page, but also being able to alert other agents of the company to correct the mistake before any information reaches the public.

Finally, the investor relations people would have to test to ensure that the information was communicated clearly enough for the target audience to understand its meaning. There are hundreds of books available that talk about the proper way to write for clear communication at the level of your audience. Therefore, your first step is to determine who the audience is for your web page. You will need to answer the following questions:

1. Who makes up your intended audience?
2. What is their reading level?
3. Do they require other supplemental means of receiving the message such as audio or video?
4. Where are your audience members located?
5. What type of browser do they use?
6. How can you measure their understanding of your message?

A different example: The ISO 9000 support group

The ISO 9000/QS-9000 Support Group is an international organization formed to assist companies seeking registration to international standards for management systems. When they used the questions above, they ran into several surprises.

First, they surveyed their current membership. All members receive a printed newsletter. They quickly discovered that fewer than half of the members had internet accounts. They also discovered that one-third of the members lived in developing nations. The best browsers most of these people could used was text-only. Reading levels varied widely and several languages could be involved.

The approach for the web page was changed to almost all text with some audio files. This allowed a wide range of browsers to be used. Next, the contents of the critical pages of the site were reproduced in audio form, and distributed to all members on audio cassettes so that even non-internet users got the same information.

Problems and solutions for Megalith's team

This type of analysis for the Megalith content team resulted in the discovery of some large problems. The most obvious was the posting of current stock prices, active forms management, and other planned features that required the use of CGI code and Java scripts. Unfortunately, a large segment of the target audience would most likely not have browsers compatible with these features.

The target audience had been seen as middle-class and upper middle-class investors from around the world that tend to have their own home-based computers. In addition, the audience was seen as well educated and likely to speak either English, French, or Spanish.

This led to several additions to the design for the web site. Now each page notified the viewer that it was best to have version 3.0 of Netscape Navigator or Internet Explorer to view the contents of the site. As an alternative, a more text-based version of the same pages was available through a single link. Next, an online translation of each page was also available.

In this way, it was easier for the audience to find and read the information. The next question is whether the information was being presented in a form that invited exploration and understanding. Too many web page designers assume that the viewer is reading the whole page.

To discover how well a web page is designed, it should be tested on a sample of your audience or a similar group. In the case of Megalith, the content team attends one of the stockholders' meetings and brings a computer loaded with a mock-up of the intended site. This is shown in the lobby outside the meeting to any passing person the team can round up.

Along with the mock-up of the intended page are two other web sites in completely different formats. The people used to test the sites are asked which ones they prefer to use and why. Each person is given several minutes to explore each web site. The idea here is to hide the fact that only one site is being considered. Instead, the team hunts for responses about the target site and how well the people understand what is being presented.

If they find that one of the other sites is being preferred and well-understood, then that approach to the final design of their site should be used.

Organizing the Flow of Content

After all of the planning, testing, and preparing, it is time to actually create the content of the web site. In a situation like the one we have been examining at Megalith, this will result in a strong flow of documents toward the site. This flow has to be carefully controlled to ensure that no one is overwhelmed with work demands and that each page is coordinated to mesh well with the other pages. The overall objective is to create a series of web pages that look like they belong together.

Again, the software being used will help in this effort. The presence of an intranet is also very helpful. This allows the timely posting of information and the tracking of documents. This is accomplished more easily if you take the following five steps.

1. Establish a central point for draft documents.   On the local area network you will want to establish subdirectories or folders for draft documents on various topics. One approach is to use the word "Draft" for the primary subdirectory and the topic names for the secondary subdirectories. This would create a structure that might look like this:

```
C:\
  \Draft
    \Draft\Policy
    \Draft\Procedures
    \Draft\Instructions
    \Draft\Reports
    \Draft\Forms
    \Draft\Graphics
```

You are limited only by your imagination. Draft documents would first be sent to a manager for initial approval before being posted to one of the draft subdirectories. These subdirectories would be given read permissions for those reviewing the document and read/write permissions for those working on the document. Groupware packages like Lotus Notes and Office 97 can be used to keep multiple authors organized.

2. Establish a central point for approved documents.   Once documents are located in the draft area, a document control method has to track their age and presence. Once a draft document has reached its final form, ready for your internet presentation, it is moved to a central subdirectory. In this case it might be called "Final" with subdirectories named again by topic. The important thing is that the document is moved, not copied. You do not want to leave obsolete documents behind to clog up subdirectories.

3. Use a private test site before final posting of content to your public web site.   Finally, the approved documents are converted into HTML and other internet compatible formats. These finished documents can still be stored in the Final area with .htm extensions. This then becomes your test area for pages about to be presented to the internet.

Using a series of browsers, the pages are viewed to ensure that all elements are displayed, loading times are acceptable, obvious mistakes are corrected, and that the intentions of the page are being met. The tests can be conducted over your local area network, but we strongly recommend that a test web site be set up hidden from the public.

This is accomplished by setting up a different domain name for this purpose or, more practically, by creating a subdirectory on your web site that has no links to your public pages. For example, at Avix this might be the web address:

www.avix.com/test

By dialing to this hidden test area with existing internet accounts, you see the pages the way your audience is likely to see the pages. Just be sure to restrict access to this site with password protection.

4. Use the collaboration features of available software.
Groupware has become good enough to coordinate projects such as the creation of web content by multiple authors. However, other forms of internet technology and non-internet technology can be used to coordinate your efforts. Here are a few examples:

Lotus Notes is an obvious choice because of its ability to have several different people post notes to a common document for a central authority to review. Office 97 works well with the revision features of Word and the E-mail capabilities of Outlook when combined with Exchange.

Internet chat rooms, mail lists, and web page discussion groups can all be used to coordinate schedules. Netscape and others offer calendar servers designed to coordinate groups of calendars and a master project calendar.

Less thought of, but still effective, is to use videoconferencing to help distant groups discuss common problems. Better still is to combine your options. For example, you can post the initial draft of a document for downloading on a private area of your web pages. Videoconferencing groups can then examine and modify the document while discussing the overall mission. Whiteboard software can also be used for multiple sites to mark up the same document. At the same time, private voting on which revisions to use are done over E-mail using anonymous accounts.

5. Publish HTML code to a web page design package, not directly to a web site.   This is a piece of advice you won't find in most books on making web pages. This advice comes from experience. Software packages like PageMaker, Word, WordPerfect, Excel, and other "non-internet" programs have options to publish to HTML format.

On the surface this sounds like a shortcut. You draft a document in Word and translate it into HTML code ready for the internet. In practice you will find that you want to add features like graphics, photos, forms, buttons, and the like. These can be problematic if your software doesn't have the flexibility of a full-blown web page design package.

Take the example of Microsoft's FrontPage 98. You can load in text and graphics from other software, like Word, WordPerfect and Excel. FrontPage allows you to add formatting information, forms, buttons, scrolling menus, and other enhancements directly to the page. Then you can either look at the page the way it will appear on a browser, or switch to the actual HTML code.

This type of flexibility makes it much easier to work with a web page. Therefore, translate your draft documents created in other packages by first loading them into a dedicated web page design program and saving it in HTML format.

Summary

Your internet system's survival will depend on the content of your web pages. This is why you fight a battle to ensure that the responsibility for the creation of content is disseminated across your company. In that way, the volume of content can continuously flow to your sites to keep your information fresh, accurate, and attractive. This brings in the visitors and encourages repeated use of your sites.

Further References

Paul Strasser's book, *The Politics of Information*, is an interesting discussion of how information is handled within organizations.

Converting Content for Web-Publishing: Time Saving Tools and Techniques, by Janice Warner, New Riders Publishing, 1996.

Internet Search Terms

Webmaster

"Document Control"

"Team Dynamics"

"Information Control" + "Dissemination"

"Web page creation" + "how to"

"Videoconferencing"

"Browser capability"

"HTML"

"page design and layout"

"page creation"

Interesting Web Sites

alt.html

alt.html.webedit

comp.infosystems.www.authoring.html

and the web page:

www.gooddocuments.com

Chapter 18
Measuring the Success of an Internet Site

By this point you should have made your internet connection and created web pages for the internet or your company's intranet. The file servers you use should have come with various packages that can generate statistics about your web sites. Your central problem will not be the generation of statistics. We will soon explain how that is done. Instead, the central problem is how to use the statistics effectively.

A Primer on Statistical Process Control

Before discussing how to set up statistical reports on the performance of your web sites, internet connections, and local area network, we need to digress for a moment. What follows is a very short course on statistics. Our emphasis will be on one particular form of statistical methods used in industry called Statistical Process Control, or SPC for short.

Discovery exercise: The mystery of the daily hit report

Most web servers can generate a report on the number of times a user "hits" a particular web page. Let's assume that your company has set up a daily hit count report for the company's home page. On a normal day around 300 people visit the site. However, one week you see the following pattern:

Monday	300
Tuesday	500
Wednesday	325
Thursday	155
Friday	300

Monday, Wednesday, and Friday seem pretty normal. But what about the other two days? Is the Tuesday count high enough that you suspect something unusual happened? Did something happen on Thursday out of the ordinary?

The correct answer is "I don't know." Without the use of a tool like SPC you do not know how much variation has to take place in the daily numbers before a significant event is being detected. Let's see how we can use SPC to make the job of monitoring your internet technology a lot easier by giving you guidelines on when to react to a situation and when to relax because what you are seeing is likely a random event.

Inside SPC

The objective of using SPC is to achieve continuous improvement. You accomplish this by monitoring your situation, counting the problems, and then eliminating each problem. The resulting count of problems should drop until it is zero.

Another way to look at SPC is to think of the initials as standing for "Stable, Predictable, and Capable." In managing internet technologies, this idea can be expanded as follows:

Stable   You need a process occurring that is stable over time, as in free of unexpected swings in your data. In the case of web page hits, you would get a fairly steady number of hits per day.

Predictable   The variation in the numbers stays the same. We shall shortly see how variation is measured. At the same time the average, trend, or pattern should remain predictable.

Capable   The level of performance you see in your system meets the planned design levels. If you are failing to meet your internet communication needs, forget about SPC and attack the larger problem of capability.

Once you have this type of situation, you can now strive for statistical control of your processes and systems. Statistical control means that you have defined "normal variation" of your process so well that any real problem that arises will be detected.

Think of normal variation as the background noise in your system. Characteristics that you will measure, such as page hits, percent of system resources used, number of error messages sent, and the like, will vary from random causes. By knowing this level of "normal" variation, you can establish limits that will indicate when the process has changed. These are called "control limits."

Second, you need to establish whether you are dealing with a steady average, trend, or pattern. The total count during a period of time or the average for a period can be plotted over time to form one of these three patterns.

1. *Steady Average.* The timeline of data is flat. Statistics such as the number of hits a page receives each week would tend to be a flat line over time for an established site.

2. *Trend.* In many internet situations you will see that counts are rising or falling over time. This is a trend. Trend measurement and analysis is a book in and of itself. We will look at a couple of examples later to see how to handle this type of situation.

3. *Pattern.* The number of users attached to your web sites rises and falls during the days and over the week. The level of usage rises after 8:00 a.m., peaks at two, and falls after 6:00 p.m. This is a rising and falling pattern repeated every workday.

By plotting out the timeline of data, you establish what is expected. By knowing what variations to expect, you can put control limits around the timelines. Putting these two ideas together creates what is called a "control chart." One more idea is added to complete the picture. Once a control limit is breached, a reaction plan can be invoked to correct or exploit the situation. The next monitoring period will indicate whether your actions worked.

An example of SPC in action

The first step in using an SPC system is to select the critical characteristics you want to monitor. For example, one of the characteristics that Megalith wants to measure for its corporate web sites is the number of 404 Error messages issued during a 24-hour period. The 404 Error is issued when a browser is unable to find a requested object. If the web site is designed correctly, then all links should lead somewhere, and the 404 message is only transmitted when the user manually requests something incorrectly, such as misspelling the site's name.

The objective of monitoring the 404 error count is to drive it down to as close to zero as possible. Megalith would begin by getting daily counts over a period of time. The best way to do this is to gather at least 25 and up to 100 counts in a row. This will establish the baseline.

In this example, the timeline is flat because the hit count is steady and the number of 404 errors is fairly steady with no trend up or down. Looking at a sample of 25 counts we find the following.

25	26	25	27	21
23	25	24	26	22
25	25	28	20	24
26	24	25	27	22
25	25	23	24	22

If we plot these points on a timeline we get the chart in Figure 18–1.

If you look at the data you can start to see that the average daily count is near 24. To find out, you would calculate a simple average. You add together all of the numbers and divide by the number of numbers.

Average = total of all numbers ÷ number of numbers

The total of all of these numbers is 609. There are twenty-five numbers. Therefore,

Average = 609 ÷ 25 = 24.36

We can now draw a straight line across our chart at 24.36. This is the average number of 404 errors we can expect each day. Obviously the actual daily counts will be a whole number somewhere near 24. The question now becomes, How far can a count drift from this average before we know that there is a problem?

To find the answer, we need some way of calculating the variation we can expect around this average. We will skip the statistical theory behind this

Figure 18-1. Megalith Timeline Chart

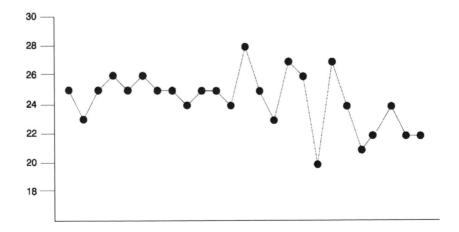

and just say that three standard deviations on each side of an average will mark out where over 99% of the variation should occur in our count.

There are interesting formulas for calculating a single standard deviation. These can be found in textbooks on statistics. Some pocket calculators can estimate these. However, the best approach is to use one of your electronic spreadsheets. Chances are you will be able to transfer reports generated by your web servers directly to spreadsheets for statistical analysis. Most modern spreadsheets have a standard deviation calculation function.

Doing this with our data reveals a single standard deviation of about 1.93. Multiply this by three and you get the range of variation on one side of an average. In our case we would multiply 1.93 by three.

Control Limits = ± (3 x 1.93) = ± 5.79 or,

Upper Control Limit (UCL) = 24.36 + (3 x 1.93) = 30.15
Lower Control Limit (LCL) = 24.36 – (3 x 1.93) = 18.57

Plotting this onto our control chart involves adding and then subtracting the 5.79 from our average of 24.36. That means that the upper control limit would be at 30.15 and the lower control limit would be at 18.57. Figure 18–2 shows what this control chart would now look like.

When we see a 404 error count of 31 or higher, we strongly suspect that the problem has gotten worse. This is the time to take corrective action. A

Figure 18-2. Revised Control Chart

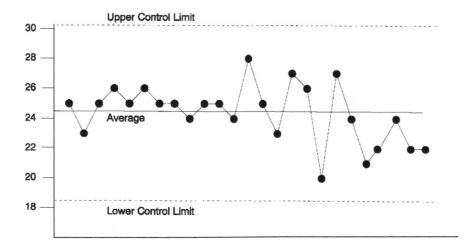

reaction plan is invoked and the problem worked on until the readings fall back toward the average, indicating that the problem has passed.

Here is the beauty of SPC—if we start taking actions as IS professionals to reduce the 404 problem and watch our control chart when readings fall toward and below 18, we know that we have significantly improved our internet system. The guesswork is gone. We have a direct measure of problems occurring and the success of system improvements. Changes beyond the control limits represent statistically significant changes to the process.

A few more rules to follow when using a control chart

Each day you collect information from your internet system. This is plotted onto different control charts. As points exceed control limits, you take action. Problems are addressed as they are detected and improvements, when discovered, are exploited.

However, there are several other things that can show up on a control chart. You may notice seven points on the chart trending up or down. This indicates that a problem is sneaking up on you. It seems natural that one of the next few points will probably exceed a control limit. Again, you react until the situation is corrected.

Another possibility is that two points out of three fall dangerously close to a control limit. Again you would react to that situation. In a similar fashion, you may find that the timeline of data suddenly shifts its average position. The points are all within control limits, but you are no longer getting one-half of the data points on each side of your average. This indicates that something has altered the average performance of what you are monitoring.

By examining the patterns being created on a control chart, you get strong clues as to the cause. One of the interesting characteristics of a control chart is that it detects identifiable causes of changes in average or variation. This allows you to react to the first problem, instead of waiting until several problems combine to bring your system down.

The reaction plan is a method of documenting what happened and what it took to correct the situation. In the early stages of using SPC, your reaction plan tells the person responsible for monitoring to circle the problem point(s) of data, log what steps were taken to find and correct the problem, and what finally worked.

After several months of keeping records such as these, you begin to build up a history of what problems occur and what solutions work. These logs can be posted to your intranet so that all systems administrators can see what others are discovering about your system. As we will see in the final chapter, troubleshooting will depend on this type of information for faster reaction times and more effective corrections. Eventually the same information is used to prevent the problems.

Now that we have seen how SPC works, we can examine what tools are available to monitor a web site, file server, or other piece of internet technology. For proper site management, software that monitors your intranet/internet site should be used in conjunction with SPC; neither is complete without the other. Putting these two tools together results in a dynamic monitoring program that can be directed toward continuous improvement of your system.

How Do You Know If Your Web Sites Are a "Success"?

Remember way back in the first few chapters of this book where you listed the mission, goals, and objectives of your internet technology? This is now used to formulate what constitutes a "successful" internet system. Once you know this, you can establish the exact characteristics to monitor, set up software to do the monitoring and reporting, and then use SPC and other techniques to improve the system.

In Chapter 2 we talked about several ways internet technology could benefit your company. They were:

- Increased access to data
- Increased communication with suppliers, subcontractors, vendors, and clients
- Reduction of travel time and expenses through the use of virtual teams
- Development of new methods of problem solving
- Increased market share
- Exposure to new marketplace
- Increased speed in handling of paperwork
- Increased research capability
- Increased speed at which internal personnel can access important information
- Flexible and adjustable training available 24 hours a day

The following example was presented in Chapter 2 to show how to justify a web site. The benefits of the internet technology for this limited application were reduced costs, higher availability of training, and consistency of training.

> Example: Currently each employee of our company is required to attend a two-hour training session on basic safety techniques in the factory. The cost of the instructor and materials averages $250 per participant. Our goal of making training available on the corporate intranet includes the objective of placing the safety training on the intranet. Part of the orientation for all new employees will be to participate in this training using the computers at their desks. The cost per participant for a one-year period of time is calculated to be $60 using the intranet method. For each participant the savings will be approximately $190. With an average of 100 employees per year needing this training, the total savings will be $19,000. The cost of the file server and related software to support the training system is approximately $5,000. We can look at a return on our investment of roughly $14,000.

Measuring the success of this projection and the final intranet site is fairly straightforward. First you would calculate the actual costs to set up the training site. This would be compared to the original estimate and reported to management.

Now you have to develop a list of the critical characteristics to measure to determine if the site was indeed successful. The following goals were laid out for this project:

- 24-hour access to training
- Lower cost per trained individual
- Higher quality of training
- Consistency of training
- Training available at each desktop

The first job is to sort out the goals that apply directly to the internet system. The cost per trained individual would be an accounting problem. The quality and consistency of the training would be issues for the human resources and quality assurance departments to work out. This leaves you with access and availability.

These two goals have to be defined by characteristics that can be directly measured using your monitoring software. Accessibility is defined as the training site being operational 24 hours a day. Availability means that any qualified user can reach the site. This can be broken down into the following measurements:

1. The number of minutes a day the site is down or otherwise not accessible. Target: 0 minutes.
2. The number of people connected to the site at any one time. Target: no more than twenty.
3. The average time to serve a web page to a browser. Target: no more than five seconds longer than an unhindered response.
4. No 404, 302, or 500 errors.
5. Confirmation on a monthly basis that all sites are open to the training area. Target: no reports from auditors or users of access denied by local area network.

To supplement this information and to help management to see the activity levels on the site, the number of hits, gets, and posts will be monitored. The resource activity logs will also be summarized. Changes to the training site and corrective actions taken on the site will be noted.

By carefully setting up the types of characteristics to measure, you establish what to monitor and what is important to your system. Too many IS managers today just collect as many statistics as possible, collate them, and then file the report. This is not the path to continuous improvement. Your efforts must focus on specific targets without neglecting something that could cause damage to your system because no one was watching a critical area.

Setting Up Software To Monitor Your Internet Technology

Several packages are available to help you monitor web sites, servers, hub activities, internet connections, and other pieces of the internet system. Each presents you with an extensive list of factors you can monitor and usually several ways to chart the data. The better ones offer alarm services to notify you immediately when something happens that you should know.

Some examples of the available software

Windows NT comes with monitoring software for both your local area network resources and the internet Information Service. Other operating systems also have similar programs. Novell Netware has reporting services. Unix programs are available to watch over the operating system.

Web serving software such as FastTrack and Enterprise Server from Netscape come with software for monitoring your site and generating reports. This includes programs that can analyze the event logs kept by the servers (appropriately called "Analyze"). This allows you to set up reports to look for patterns or problems (see Figure 18–3).

Third-party programs are also available to monitor your equipment, software, and internet connections. Programs like wwwstat can look at web page activities using Perl script. IIStats is used to examine the activities of the Microsoft IIS package. GetStats and MkStats are third-party log analysis tools. Statbot is a package that allows the users to generate their own statistics report.

A search of the internet will uncover hundreds of monitoring and reporting programs. Some work alone, while others are part of a larger administration package. The software you use will depend on your needs, the design of your system, and the mandates from management for reports.

A partial list of factors you can monitor

Once you have decided to use the software that came with your servers, routers, networks, and other hardware, or to purchase additional software, a

Figure 18-3. Fast Track and Enterprise Server

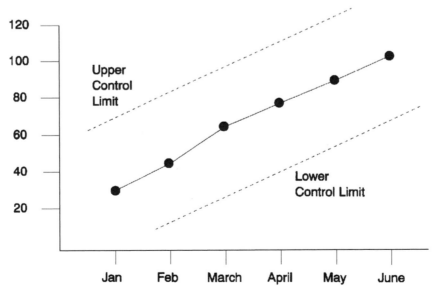

second major decision is required. Now you have to choose which points in your system you are going to monitor and what characteristics to measure.

Products like Microsoft's BackOffice and Novell's Netware come with the capability of monitoring the status of the local area network equipment. Not only can you monitor the health of the routers, hubs, back-up power supplies, and other components of a network, you can even sample user machines.

Therefore, part of your monitoring plan for the network will involve a chart or list of the points that are going to be monitored. At each of these points you should have a list of the characteristics being measured. The same is true for the plan to monitor your internet services and web sites.

Again, the web sites and internet services to be monitored are listed. For each point monitored you need to choose the appropriate characteristics to measure. What follows is a partial list of some of the possibilities:

- Total hits on a site
- Total visits to a site
- 302 code (a user was redirected from an obsolete site to a current site)
- 304 code (a page was taken from cache, not served from the web server)
- 404 code (a web item was not found when requested)
- 500 code (server error)
- Number of unique URLs requested by users
- Source host of the clients
- Amount of memory transmitted to clients
- Amount of memory received by server
- Total usage by month, week, day, hour, minute, or second
- Maximum throughput generated by server
- List of most frequently accessed pages
- List of most frequently downloaded files
- E-mail volumes
- Number of security violations
- Number of URL requests refused

As you can quickly see, you will be faced with a large number of choices for many different software packages. Which one to choose comes down to a question of what it is you want to learn.

Take the example of a company that is concerned that visitors to their web site have as few hassles as possible. The number of 404 and 500 codes generated would be of extreme interest. Likewise, the number of people visiting the site and the total hit count might be of interest.

Discovery exercise: Which site is most effective?

All of this discussion leads us to the central question of this chapter—how effective is our web site?

To learn how to determine this we need to engage in a brief exercise. Take a look at the average usage figures for two different but very real web sites:

Name:	ASR	ISO 9000 Support Group
URL:	asr.9000.net	isogroup.iserv.net
Hits per month:	3,000	56,000
Visits per month:	1,000	13,000

Which site is more effective?

The answer is not obvious. To demonstrate, let's look at the nature of the two sites. The ASR site is a registration service for companies seeking ISO 9000 certification. The site is free to access but services cost from about $3,000 and up. The ISO 9000 Support Group assists companies seeking registration to prepare them for registration by companies like ASR. The first half of their site is free, but a restricted area is open only to members. Membership is $249 a year and includes several non-internet services.

Thus, we have two similar services in the same field. Thirteen times more people visit the support group. The support group generates an average of over four page hits per visit. The ASR site gets just three hits on an average visit. So which site is more effective?

The answer is the ASR site. You see, the lesson here is that hit and visit counts are really not that important. The *mission* of the site is paramount. Too many IS managers get lost in hit counts. The mission of these sites is to sell services. The ASR site generates an average of 60 requests for quotes per month. The support group only generates about 12. The amount of business revenue per order is higher at ASR and the number of orders is higher, even though the hit count is a small fraction of the support group's!

The moral of this story is simple: You can have a million hits on a web site every day and still lose money for your company. In the end, you need to look at the real effect of the web site.

Methods for Measuring the Popularity of a Web Site

When we talk about the effectiveness, efficiency, and popularity of a web site, we are talking about the three most likely characteristics to matter to your management.

Effectiveness If usage of the web site generates a large percentage of orders, requests for information, and other actions from the target audience, these are measures of effectiveness. An effective site accomplishes its goals and objectives to a level where it is profitable to a company. For example, having a majority of parents and students use the Dickerson County School System site at least once a week indicates an effective site. Customers value the site and your organization benefits.

Some of the ways to measure effectiveness include:

- Repeat visitors
- Orders taken
- Questions submitted
- Technical support answers downloaded
- Files downloaded
- Services delivered
- Percentage of participants who complete a class

Efficiency This is defined as the delivery of the web site to the public at the lowest possible cost that maintains the level of quality you established. Cheaper, faster, and better ways to deliver your web-based information to your target audience increase the efficiency of a site. Ways to measure efficiency include:

- Annual cost of operation versus various measures of effectiveness
- Time taken to serve up the average page, file, etc.
- Number of simultaneous users that can be supported
- Dropping number of error codes related to delays, misrouting, and other impediments to efficiency
- Time from concept to delivery of ready web page
- Turnaround time for automated web page functions

- Turnaround time for answering requests from customers delivered over your internet system

Popularity   This is measured as a growing number of people using your site and an increasing number of repeat visitors. You want as many people as possible from your target audience to become dependent on your web-based information. Some of the ways to measure popularity include:

- Number of visitors versus repeat visitors
- Percent increase in site usage over a set period of time
- Number of file downloads per visitor
- Number of orders placed by the average visitor
- Number of new orders from a web site by new visitors
- Amount of press coverage of your sites
- Number of links to your site found on the internet
- Number of other sites listing your site as a "hot site" to visit

Naturally, you are making every effort possible to generate more popularity for your site. This will include actions such as press releases, convention displays, contests, direct mailing, web promotion, and the like. Your next question is, How effective are these methods in increasing your popularity?

Again, SPC can help us here. Let's assume that Avix starts monitoring the health of their web site featuring the catalog of products. The number of orders placed each 30-day weighted month are shown here.

Jan	30
Feb	44
Mar	62
Apr	77
May	88
June	105

If these orders are plotted out on a control chart, you will see a linear trend heading upward. Obviously the initial promotion efforts have worked and word of mouth is helping to double the number of orders and new customers every two months or so.

Avix decides that now would be good time to try a few more promotional campaigns. However, how will they know if these efforts are successful? The answer comes in the form of control limits.

Figure 18-4. Measuring Effects of Promotional Efforts

By calculating the amount of variation to expect in this count, they can establish when a new promotional method succeeds by driving the count through the upper control limit. In the same way, they can see when a promotional effort has petered out when the counts drift below the lower control limit. As a bonus, they can tell that a promotional effort had no effect when the count stays in statistical control (see Figure 18–4).

Other control charts can be used for effectiveness and efficiency measures to determine when new methods or equipment are working and when they have no real effect. Likewise, the control charts can be used to pursue continuous improvement.

For example, when the average time to deliver a 2 megabyte file drops from 3 minutes to 45 seconds, the average line on a chart can be readjusted down and a new effectiveness method tested. In this way the point of success keeps trending toward a final objective of perfection.

Hits versus visits and why neither is really helpful

We should take just a moment here to talk about hits and visits. A hit is recorded when a web resource is requested by a user. Unfortunately, if one of your web pages contains images, applets, and other objects, each could be recorded as a hit when the page is served. A visit or session is a count of one person visiting your site.

This is all very nice. A lot of people are curious about how many people are visiting their site and how many web objects they are requesting. If an average visitor requests a lot of objects, then your site is being used a lot. A site that shows visitors quickly leaving the site and making few requests indicates that your site's value might be low.

As we demonstrated above, the number of hits and visits are not by themselves very important. If your web page got just one visitor a day but that person ordered thousands of dollars of product, you might call your site a success. Therefore, the importance of hits and visits comes from combining this usage information with measures of effectiveness and efficiency.

Example statistics report for a web site

Let's see how this combining of statistics gives you the best picture on the level of success for your internet system. The following is an actual usage report for the 9000.net site the first few weeks it was in service. This information was used to correct undetected problems on the site and to judge the initial popularity of the site. The only marketing that had occurred at this point was a listing of the site on 25 search engines.

SimpleNet Statistics

Access Report for Sat Feb 14 1998 to Wed Apr 15 1998

Daily Totals for http://asr.9000.net/:

Date	Clients	Hits	Page Hits	KB Transmitted
Fri Mar 6 1998	1	12	7	42.46
Mon Mar 9 1998	1	12	7	42.46
Sun Mar 15 1998	3	16	9	53.97
Mon Mar 16 1998	5	38	18	110.02
Tue Mar 17 1998	1	11	6	34.72
Wed Mar 18 1998	2	16	8	52.48
Thu Mar 19 1998	4	16	11	66.93
Fri Mar 20 1998	10	99	57	338.02
Sat Mar 21 1998	29	158	73	458.25
Sun Mar 22 1998	10	64	31	201.62
Mon Mar 23 1998	30	158	72	467.67
Tue Mar 24 1998	26	189	98	597.66
Wed Mar 25 1998	25	159	72	486.67
Thu Mar 26 1998	30	143	62	386.87

Fri Mar 27 1998	28	125	60	396.93
Sat Mar 28 1998	13	69	33	224.92
Sun Mar 29 1998	9	38	17	112.96

Period Totals for http://asr.9000.net/:

Individual Clients	All Clients	Hits	Page Hits	KB Transmitted
555	576	3988	1916	12199.01

Daily Averages:

Clients	Hits	Page Hits	KB Transmitted
12	85	41	259.55

In this first part of the web site report we are trying to gauge the usage of this site. This report comes from the first few weeks the site was operational. You can see that the hit count increases steadily once the site is publicized. But notice how the hit count fades after only a few weeks. This indicates that the site needs more promotional efforts and sustained campaigns.

Next, we look at the ratio of clients (visits) to hits. The overall average is 12 clients a day with 85 hits. That is a ratio of seven page requests per client. This is an interesting statistic for this site considering that it only had four pages. Two of the pages have the option of requesting further information or a quote. The statistics show that the average person using the site is then interested in further information. The extra page hits are either coming from the visitor going back to look over previous pages, or from the serving of confirmation pages after information is requested. The conclusion here is that the site may not be popular (not a lot of traffic) but it is effective. Now let's continue to look down the report for more helpful information.

Top 5 Clients Accessing http://asr.9000.net/

73	Elara.Simplenet.Net
51	gr-max5-48.iserv.net
41	grand-rapids-252-13.iserv.net
40	grand-rapids-252-2.iserv.net
35	grand-rapids-252-52.iserv.net

Top 10 Files Accessed on http://asr.9000.net/

559	index.html
493	_themes/global/glohorsd.gif
490	_themes/global/glotextb.gif
490	_derived/index.htm_cmp_global000_bnr.gif
490	_borders/American_Systems_Registrar_Logo.gif
154	_derived/home_cmp_global000_gbtn.gif
118	_themes/global/globul1d.gif
102	Documents/_vti_bin/_vti_aut/author.exe
99	_vti_bin/_vti_aut/author.exe
96	prices.htm

Here we can see that someone coming from Simplenet is very interested in this site. We can also see that the next four sources of visitors are coming from the internal account for the registrar. This teaches you a very important lesson on web statistics—always filter out your own activities. What is being reflected here is the staff members of ASR checking out the new site.

The most requested files show another common problem with site statistics. The index page of the site is the obvious winner for hit counts. Following on its shirt tails are the logo and other graphic elements used on the page. Please note that the graphic elements were served less than the page where they are located. This happens when browsers don't make the request for graphic elements or cannot show graphic elements. If the gap between a page and its graphic elements is high, this tells you that your audience is using browsers that cannot see your entire page design or that they have "show images" switched off.

The "vti_bin" files are those used for the active elements of the web site. In this case, these are the listing of the author of the pages and revision dates that appear automatically on every page. This confirms that these automatic elements are working and that most users get to see the information.

Finally, the next real web page in the statistics list is tenth in frequency, the price list. As ASR expected, posting prices was revolutionary for their field and proved to be the first page people requested after the home page (index.html). The theory of the effectiveness of posting prices was demonstrated. Next, we can study the number and types of errors being generated.

Summary of HTTP Errors

64	404	Not Found
17	500	Internal Server Error

Requests Causing Errors

35	/Documents/
27	/robots.txt
25	/Documents/_vti_bin/shtml.exe/_vti_rpc
11	/_vti_bin/_vti_aut/author.exe
10	/Documents/_derived/nortbots.htm
8	/_vti_bin/shtml.exe/_vti_rpc
8	/Staff/_vti_bin/shtml.exe/_vti_rpc
5	/_themes/global/glohorsd.gif
4	/Documents/disc4_toc.htm
4	/Documents/_vti_bin/_vti_aut/author.exe

The report shows that in the first few weeks, 64 not found errors (404) were recorded. Given the low number of page hits recorded during the same time period, this indicates a possible problem. The ratio of 404 errors to total hits is 64 to 3,988 or about 1.6 percent. Anytime you have more than one percent of requests ending in a 404 error you should check your links.

The number of server errors was 17. Over a three-week period this is not too bad. Your objective is to get this number as close to zero as possible. The next step after seeing this figure would be to pull the event logs from your server and look up the causes of the 17 errors. If they are all minor and unseen by the users, then less priority would be given to this problem. However, failures that cause disruption in service should be addressed as soon as possible and prevented.

Evaluating Customer Feedback

Most web sites become fairly interactive with customers. Most sites will want to have an area where questions can be asked, issues discussed, or forms filled out. Even the act of placing the webmaster's internet E-mail address on the web page will generate customer feedback.

The best approach is to evaluate what type of feedback you would like to receive, and then design easy to use methods of obtaining that information. Take the example of Avix Manufacturing. They could include a customer inquiry page for general questions about their products. When potential customers look through their online catalog, each page has the "ask a question" option. If the bulk of these questions are along the lines of "what color do these come in?," Avix would learn that they need to add this information to their catalog to increase its effectiveness.

Intranets, like the one at the Law Firm, would also want customer feedback. One way of doing this is to have an "I am lost" option on each web page. Frustrated users of the intranet would be presented with a quick E-mail sending option that would be forwarded to a help desk person that is on duty. Within a minute or two the help desk person could give directions to the resource being sought. These requests would be logged so that the IS manager can upgrade the design of the intranet to avoid these types of problems.

Once obtained, you need to analyze the results to determine whether your site is being efficient and effective. The design and analysis of survey forms should be left to the professionals. They will have to work closely with your internet content team.

Increasing the Efficiency of Web Sites

Once established, a web site is a living document. It must be cared for, fed, and encouraged to grow stronger. We have looked at the issue of effectiveness; now we should discuss efficiency.

As mentioned before, efficiency is measured as the increase in capability of a site at the same or lower cost. Better software, hardware, and page design can all serve to increase the efficiency of a site. However, without good information on the current performance of your sites, you would be shooting in the dark by spending money on new technologies and techniques. Let's look at a specific example to see how efficiency is increased intelligently.

Example of a control chart for patterns of usage

Following is the actual usage report of the average number of users on a site for each hour of the day. Using this raw data we can create a control chart for a regular pattern and then begin to work toward more efficient use of the site. This will involve both filling in the ideal hours and spreading out usage at peak periods.

Hourly Averages:

Time	Hits	Percentage	KB Transmitted
Midnight to 1 am	1	1.4 %	3.92
1 am to 2 am	2	1.8 %	4.60
2 am to 3 am	2	2.3 %	6.81
3 am to 4 am	1	1.2 %	3.28
4 am to 5 am	1	1.2 %	2.94
5 am to 6 am	4	4.3 %	11.30
6 am to 7 am	4	5.1 %	13.92
7 am to 8 am	6	7.1 %	15.73
8 am to 9 am	8	9.1 %	25.77
9 am to 10 am	7	8.5 %	20.20
10 am to 11 am	6	7.4 %	19.09
11 am to 12 pm	7	8.6 %	23.58
12 pm to 1 pm	3	3.7 %	8.80
1 pm to 2 pm	6	7.3 %	17.54
2 pm to 3 pm	6	7.0 %	18.34
3 pm to 4 pm	3	3.0 %	7.98
4 pm to 5 pm	4	4.2 %	11.74
5 pm to 6 pm	3	3.7 %	9.84
6 pm to 7 pm	3	3.1 %	8.40
7 pm to 8 pm	2	2.0 %	4.74
8 pm to 9 pm	3	3.0 %	8.05
9 pm to 10 pm	2	1.8 %	5.08
10 pm to 11 pm	1	1.6 %	4.71
11 pm to Midnight	1	1.1 %	3.19

By plotting out these numbers across a 24-hour timeline we can quickly pick up patterns. The first observation comes from the raw numbers. This site is not getting a lot of hits. Eight hits in one hour can be handled by even the simplest system.

Next, we can see that the use of the site picks up around five o'clock in the morning, Eastern Standard time. It trails off at about three in the afternoon (see Figure 18–5).

This begins to tell you something about the audience. The first thing is that the majority of them are daytime workers accessing your site. This would imply that they have regular jobs and are accessing your sites from their company accounts. Next, they seem to be three hours ahead of you. This implies that Europe is the major user of the system.

This type of information helps you to identify the actual audience using the site. If the company had targeted North America and wanted heavy traffic around the clock, clearly this site is not meeting its goal. However, further investigation finds that Europeans come to look at the site, but it is the Americans around lunch time that place orders. Thus, a message has to be sent to the marketing staff to promote the site more strongly and to encourage usage at off-hours.

As IS manager you have to ask a larger question—did we overbuild the site? If the current internet connection is a 128K bps ISDN dedicated line, perhaps cutting it back to 64K bps or going to a dial-up access would better fit the light load. This would save the company money while maintaining an excellent access to internet based customers.

If the company expects the traffic on the site to pick up substantially, then the internet connection can be upgraded to meet demands. The problem is how to determine the right moment to change. Part one of setting up a way of knowing when more bandwidth is needed is to establish a hit count per hour when you feel the greater bandwidth should be activated. This can be calculated using the formulas presented in Chapter 9.

The second part of setting up a way to monitor the situation is to establish control limits on your timeline for usage. These will show the normal variation to expect for each hour. The average number of hits per hour are calculated and plotted. As you can see in Figure 18–5, this results in a stepped pattern.

Figure 18-5. The pattern of Hits per Hour over the Course of a Business Day

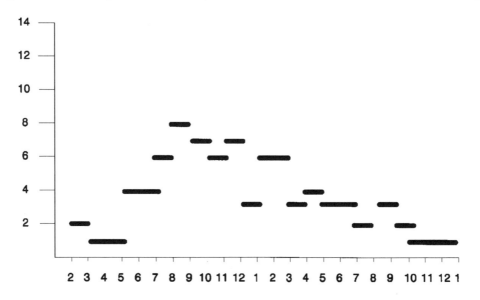

Figure 18-6. Using Standard Deviation to Calculate Control Limits

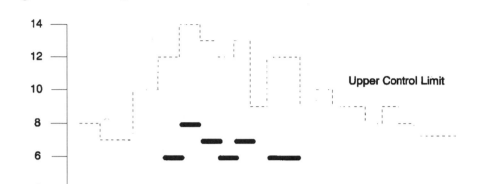

Using the standard deviation for counts within each hour, you can calculate the control limits. As Figure 18–6 shows, these follow the stepped pattern of each hour's average.

For example, if the following information were obtained for the period from noon to one o'clock each day:

Average = 9 hits
Standard Deviation = 2 hits

we can calculate the control limits for this one period of time.

Upper control limit = 9 hits + (3 x 2 hits) = 15 hits
Lower control limit = 9 hits - (3 x 2 hits) = 3 hits

As the overall volume of the hit counts increases, you would recalculate these figures for each hour. As you can imagine, a spreadsheet is particularly well suited to this task.

Now you have a way to know when the change in hit counts is real. When hit counts start exceeding control limits, you can be fairly sure that a change is taking place. If the count during peak times starts to exceed the upper control limits, then you know that peak traffic is increasing significantly. If it also exceeds the usage limit you set for bandwidth, it is time to upgrade your connection.

If the hit counts at the off-peak hours start to break control limits, you know that your efforts to encourage round-the-clock usage of the site are working. (No more arguments with other departments; just the facts.)

Avoiding Web Site Pitfalls in Efficiency

Perhaps the largest problem you face with increasing the efficiency of a site is getting carried away. Economics usually is a balancing act. Web site efficiency is a good example of the balance you try to achieve.

For example, you could offer to spend ten thousand dollars for a faster, better web server. The increase in throughput and bandwidth would be around 150% over your current capabilities. However, if your site is like the site described above with a handful of hits each hour, what is the point? True, you have increased bandwidth, but the cost is not recovered.

The second most threatening problem comes from fancy new technologies for the internet. A famous example is the use of streaming video. This is a great way to have live broadcast capabilities for your annual meeting or to deliver a training tape to all of your employees when they want to see it.

Unfortunately, streaming video is also a bandwidth monster. Not only does it require wide open bandwidth to work properly, but the slightest glitch in transmission causes a slight delay and a resulting stagger in the presentation. A sales pitch that skips and pauses will not impress. Video delivered at less than 30 frames a second has no place in business.

In short, the promises of a new technology must operate within the capabilities of your system. Otherwise, you sacrifice efficiency and effectiveness for the expansion of features.

This holds true for another common pitfall. Web page designers occasionally forget that they have to share bandwidth with other pages. This results in web pages packed with images, features, and interactive components. Each of these slows the serving of web pages. Pile on several dozen people trying to browse the same page and the efficiency of your site suffers. You will need to spend heavily on greater bandwidth. The proper solution is to minimalize your pages and avoid the problem.

Finally, there is the lack of interest in continuous improvement. If the IS manager and the management of the company do not pursue continuous improvement, then why should anyone else? This results in stagnant systems that stay the same even though opportunities for improvement are constantly presenting themselves.

Further References

Internet Search Terms
"Hypertext theory"

"Usage Statistics"

"Statistical Process Control"

Interesting Web Sites
usableweb.com (evaluates the usability of your sites)

www-survey.cc.gatech.edu (the Georgia Tech annual survey of World Wide Web usage)

www.umich.edu/~sgupta/hermes (study of consumer usage of the web)

www.domainstats.com

Chapter 19
Expanding
Your Internet System

This book has been dedicated to the idea of introducing an internet connection and its related technology to your company. I purposely stuck to simple technologies that can be implemented into most situations. This is the best way to start with the internet, small and well-tested. Eventually, you will want to expand your system and begin to integrate it into other systems. This chapter looks at what happens when you finish the implementation of internet technology and it is time to move on.

Setting Targets to Indicate Expansion

There might be a host of signals you receive as IS manager that indicates it is time to expand your internet technology. However, this assumes that you are monitoring for such signals. To set up a monitoring program for knowing when to expand your system, you start with the signals that are important to your company. Again, you turn to the goals and objectives you set for your internet system. When the majority of these are met and new needs are being expressed by your user community, it is time to expand.

Let's look at how this is done. The Megalith company set the following goal and objectives for a marketing web site:

Goal: Increase market position of Megalith's financial services

- Objective: Reach 1,000 inquiries on our financial services per week.
- Objective: Obtain a major corporate contract through the internet at least once a month.
- Objective: Respond to inquiries within 24 hours.

The financial promotion site has been operating for over a year now. The monitoring reports look at the number of inquiry forms filled out and the response time between receipt of request and the time the response was sent. The marketing department also produces a report on how major contracts are landed. This includes information on whether the internet site played an important part.

Once you establish the signals you are watching for, you incorporate these into your current monitoring activities. For example, the regular network usage reports will show you when more bandwidth is needed. At the same time, your annual audit of the entire system will eventually uncover the saturation of existing resources. One example: You might find that traffic is overwhelming the capacities of particular web servers.

Take, for example, the goal of generating 1,000 inquiries per week. Once a monitoring chart shows that the average is significantly above 1,000, the company must begin to decide if more capacity or other services are now needed. The decision for more capacity is fairly easy. If the internet connection, servers, and support staff can tolerate a greater flow of data, then the connection is widened.

The more difficult decision is whether to add more services or perform major modification on existing services. In our example the financial services group may find that internet traffic is overwhelming their staff. Temporary employees, more permanent employees, or shifting some of the load to other departments are obvious options. Less obvious is the expansion of the internet system into new areas and technologies to handle the increasing popularity of the system.

Other Technologies that Can Be Used with the Internet or with Intranets

One difficulty in adding on to your existing internet system comes from the fact that setting up the very basic systems described in this book probably proved to be a challenge. As I repeatedly mentioned in the beginning of this book, the act of implementing internet technology within a company is a process of carefully selecting the limited resources you have to achieve the maximum effect.

In the case of most major computer technologies, implementation tends to eat up most of your available time, money, and people. Without a carefully planned implementation that includes the dissemination of responsibilities to people outside of the IS department, you will find that your capacity to expand is greatly diminished. With this in mind, let's look at just a sampling of where you can go with internet technology once your system is in place and functioning correctly.

Discovery exercise: A simple question

What is the next "big thing" for the internet? Answer: No one knows. Look how fast search engines, the World Wide Web browsers, electronic trading of stocks, and other "hot" internet technologies appeared. It is very rare that anyone can predict what will happen next on the internet. The lesson here is that you should stay constantly prepared to review and evaluate new technologies and techniques as they come along. Getting into the next "hot technology" on the internet early means that you benefit early as well.

Faxing over the internet

Programs like Faxware and Internet Xchange for Fax give you a unique new service for your internet system. You can have documents sent to remote locations via the internet and directed to a local fax machine. For example, you can send a fax to London by having it directed to a cooperating location in London. It is delivered to a computer on the network with a fax modem. The document is then faxed locally to the phone number you are trying to reach. This saves you the cost of an overseas call. Another advantage of this type of software is that faxes coming into your company can be automatically routed to a recipient's computer. Using client software, the receiver can call up and review the fax. It can even be marked up and sent back through as a fax to the originator.

There are also a host of other technologies now on the market that allow your document systems (e.g., copiers, storage, faxes, etc.) to be incorporated into your local area network and intranet. This is all well and fine, but it requires a rigorous system of document control and usage policies.

For example, it would be easy for a person to send a document to a copier for printing over the network. A thousand copies later it might be discovered that the document has a major error. Document review, approval, and control would prevent this sort of disaster.

At the same time, you can imagine the fun of having a person forwarding incoming E-mail and faxes to the project office in another building the day after all messages from that machine were forwarded back to the original office. The result is an endless loop of faxes and E-mails flying through your system. Proper management and permissions with controls to eliminate looping will prevent this.

Push technology

Once touted as the next great step forward for the internet, "push" technology now faces a muddy future. The technology works by installing at a user's computer a client program that will request or receive information from a target site whenever the computer is idle, or during specifically scheduled times of the day.

One example of this is the constant acceptance of stock quotes during the day from an internet site to your computer. This can either scroll by at the bottom of the screen or be loaded into summary reports that are constantly updated. The user does nothing to get this information. It is literally "pushed" into the computer.

This has a lot of potential for companies. For example, you could load the client program on all of the computers in the Megalith corporation around the world. Then, twice a day, the machines accept company notices, the weekly newsletter, alerts, and other corporatewide communications. You could also send updates on policies this way. Because the internet is being used, the cost of distributing such information is very inexpensive.

At the same time Megalith could "push" information about new products and services, news alerts, and other regular company communications to their customers. If hundreds of companies are awaiting the newest product upgrade, they can be notified simultaneously.

This is all very powerful unless you forget that the average worker is already flooded with work and information. In other words, you want to push only the most critical information in very brief formats. People will quickly reject information that is not helpful or is too difficult to read. The time spent scanning the pushed information must be offset by benefits.

Video conferencing

This is one technology that has not yet reached its potential. To get the full benefits of being able to see the person you want to talk to, or to see several people in a simulated meeting, you need bandwidth. Therefore, video conferencing works best on local area networks and intranets.

To get full 30-frames-a-second, full-screen conferencing between distant offices, you will need a set of dedicated ISDN lines or a fractional T1. This is not cheap, but the results can be very beneficial. When the partners in the Law Firm want to meet to make a few decisions and vote on the next course for the company, there is no need to fly in the partners who live on the East Coast. Instead, they meet at the New York office and video conference with the Chicago office.

When design teams at three different suppliers want to spend a couple of days brainstorming the new product with your engineering team, they can do it using video conferencing to see each other and talk. An internet connection lets them post ideas, drawings, and documents for the group to review. Whiteboard software lets these documents be marked up. The result is teamwork without all of the travel expenses.

Online commerce

Anyone who can get a Visa, MasterCard, or American Express merchant account can open a shop on the internet. Several serious players in the world of money are trying to develop ways to use electronic cash on the internet. This would eventually allow you to collect immediate payment from visiting internet customers for your products and services.

Right now the most expedient way to conduct business on the internet is to use the same technology as any store. For example, you can use the HTTPS service to set up a secure location for credit card transactions. Encryption protects the credit card information. For people who don't trust the internet, you provide alternative routes for the payment information. This includes the option of faxing the information to your company or calling a sales representative directly.

The power of online commerce is being felt in several industries. I have a hard time finding a computer store in a retail location these days. Most of the ones I have dealt with in the past have found it much cheaper to have a computer assembly plant in a low rent area of town and to perform all commerce over telephones and the internet.

This year alone I have ordered cameras, computers, books, software, services, foods, antique appraisals, and photographs of the surface of Mars from the internet. I have also ordered the identical items in the past using a phone, fax, and credit card. The internet has only improved on an existing system.

The power of internet commerce lies in the fact that you can post catalogs and detailed information about your product for practically no cost. In the past, you had to limit the amount of information given about a product because of the cost of printing. This allows your customers to browse your information 24 hours a day, lets you update the information at any time, and take orders from anywhere in the world.

The most unique and underused aspect of internet commerce is that you can bring your distant customers together to discuss your product. For example, Pentax camera users can compare notes on new products and share tips and techniques. Minox subminiature camera owners can locate laboratories to process their film, fix their shutters, or sell their equipment. The value of the product increases because the customers are better informed. The customer is also empowered to make more knowledgeable decisions on products. Used properly, this can be a powerful addition to your internet presence.

Online transfer of funds

Most of the press on electronic cash focuses on consumers buying things on the internet. As shown above this is only a redundancy of existing technology. The more interesting and potentially powerful aspect of electronic cash for business is the ability to transfer funds outside of conventional wire transfer services.

Take the example of a company in Canada ordering products from a first-time supplier in Russia. The payment for the parts is sent to a neutral third party as electronic cash. The Russian company takes receipt of the amount but cannot translate it into hard cash until the Canadian firm provides the unlocking code. This comes after the shipment arrives and is carefully checked. The delays in transfers and releases of letters of credit are removed. The fees for this type of service are little or none.

It also raises the possibility of a corporation and its suppliers developing their own economy. By using an electronic version of cash they can transfer funds back and forth without regulation or fees. Naturally, once governments realize this, things will probably get interesting.

Virtual intranets

It is possible to set up intranets for wide area application using the internet as your backbone network. You can also set up virtual domain names under your company's top level domain name. This allows your company to have all of the capabilities of a web hosting service.

For a virtual intranet you would set up a domain name and then restrict access to the IP addresses of your branch offices. For example, if the top level domain name is avix.com, then you might set up sales.avix.com for the field sales force. In this way documents, E-mail, and database access can be used by any sales force member with a password into this domain.

Another application would be the granting of web sites to special sales representatives. For example, the makers of a luxury automobile might set up free web sites for their limited number of dealers at no charge. Content would be generated using corporate staff. This would put all of the dealer sites in one spot where a search engine, say for used cars, could be set up to access all of the sites. It would also preserve the look and feel qualities the corporation wants while giving each dealer a free marketing service.

Software distribution

For the producers of software the internet represents a great method of distribution. With 14.4K bps modems now seen as "slow," it is possible to efficiently download software to most internet users. Thus, a customer can look through your catalog, pick out the packages of interest, pay, and download the software.

This is also a great advantage for technical support. Take the case of a computer printer manufacturer. As customers buy their printers in a store, they find that they can use their internet accounts to download the print drivers for their particular computer. The customers get 24-hour access to what they need and you avoid phone calls and shipping fees.

Publication

One of the most powerful, yet unglamorous, aspects of the internet is that it gives anyone the chance to publish. Books, magazines, newsletters, bulletins, and the like can all be printed and distributed on the internet. The overhead costs are extremely low.

Take the example of a magazine with 40,000 readers and 64 pages of content each month. Printing, postage, and administration runs over $100,000 per month. At the same time, this same magazine will have about 24 to 30 pages of real content with the rest being advertisements or other "fillers." A couple of people can reproduce the same length of content and publish it on the internet for very little money.

This gives your company the capability of publishing works that normally are too unprofitable to print. Take the example of a white paper by a Megalith scientist explaining the extended applications of one of the company's products. Maybe a couple of hundred people would be interested in this subject. That small of a group would hardly be included in a large corporation's budget. Instead, it is posted for free on the internet and a small market is captured.

Intelligence gathering

The internet has a wide variety of competitive intelligence gathering capabilities: the use of agent programs to gather news articles about rival corporations and their employees; the ability to research publicly held companies; watching discussion groups and newsnet groups for comments on competing products or your own products. These are all examples of using the internet wisely for intelligence gathering.

However, such applications require careful coordination of resources, people, and schedules. You want to cast an effective net for information without tipping off the other companies about what you are doing.

At the same time, there is the possibility of launching internet attacks on competitors. Your security system should be set to repel attempts to invade your system. However, you must be aware of other types of threats that can be launched outside of your system. Take the example of a rival company E-mailing search engines saying that your company's site is no longer active or is listed too many times. This could result in your site being pushed down a results list.

Multi-user environments

The use of MUDs (Multi-User Domains) is an interesting technology. Multiple people can enter your web site and experience a common virtual reality. This ranges from interactive games to virtual shopping malls where each user actually can "look around" and pick up items for purchase.

Although an interesting idea, setting up a virtual environment for many users can be complex and very time consuming. You also have to have an audience interested in experiencing this type of technology. At the same time, each user usually needs just the right combination of software and hardware to get flawless access.

As you can see from the preceding discussion, the internet offers a lot of directions you can go after your basic connection is established. However, I have tried to highlight some of the shortfalls and other problems each of these example technologies might encompass. The idea is to warn you to proceed with caution.

When you expand your services, be sure to go through the same procedures described in this book. You need to examine your future and present needs. This includes a discussion with your marketing representatives on how the internet can better serve your company.

Incorporating Marketing Plans to Include Your Internet Site or Intranet

An early part of getting ready for expansion or changing of your internet system is to talk with the marketing people. Most internet connections are made to increase the presence of your company with the public. Once you have established that presence and gathered data for a while, it is time to ask some hard questions.

- How well has our current internet system supported our company's marketing strategy?
- How can we improve the relationship between existing market plans and the internet sites?
- What future marketing plans is the company pursuing?
- What role will the internet play in those plans?
- What technologies will we need to support our future plans?
- How well are the marketing people using the intranet to support their efforts?

From questions like these you learn more about how well the internet system meets expectations and what needs the company will have in the future. The company's marketing plans should include mentioning the web sites in all communications to the public, encouragement of web site users to request further information, and heavier dependency on the internet to send communications between marketing representatives.

Continuous Improvement and Other Strategies to Use

The next consideration is how your future plans will include continuous improvement. Although the focus of your efforts will be on expansion and change, you cannot lose sight of the need to keep improving the existing services. There have been too many companies that have introduced an exciting new service to their internet system only to find that the basic systems are breaking down from lack of attention. Therefore, any planning effort for expansion must begin with the allocation of enough resources to maintain the system and still pursue continuous improvement.

Another strategy to keep active is the further decentralization of your existing services and the decentralization of new services. If the production department wants an intranet that can also monitor machine conditions, the production schedule, and location of critical parts, then perhaps they should learn how to maintain the new service. Since they directly benefit from the new capability, they should be responsible for its effective operation.

Project management should be an established norm at your company by the time you finish implementing your internet system. The implementation should have taught everyone involved the importance of having an established system of coordinating tasks, schedules, and resources. The experience gained by the implementation should be preserved and shared with the people implementing your expansion.

Counterpoint: Some New Technologies Are Not Really Needed

Before we finally delve into the steps to take to implement new services, we should take a moment to point out that some exciting technologies are not really needed.

Discovery exercise:Another simple question

When was the last time you called an electronic bulletin board service? In 1995 my company ran a ten-line BBS for consulting companies on export regulations and standards. The number of users doubled every six months. By 1996 it was gone forever and replaced by a single internet web page.

The lesson here is that we had a substantial investment in the BBS, including a T1 line. Luckily we were renting the T1 and all of our computers were paid off. We were able to inexpensively convert to web pages and find new roles for our existing equipment. Think about what happened to the BBS companies that spent huge sums on new equipment and telecommunication lines just in time to see their user base desert to the internet.

When Do You Need to Expand?

The monitoring charts we discussed in the previous chapter and the regular auditing and testing of your system can be your indicators that it is time to expand or change. Some of the signals are obvious, such as more than 80% of your bandwidth being used during "average" hours with peak times exceeding your capabilities. Other signals include:

- Noticeable drop in the quality of service as the traffic flow increases
- Loss of efficiency within the system
- More complaints from users
- The rate of "lost E-mail" increases
- Server error count increases
- Local area network resources are almost entirely consumed by the intranet

- Management wants to see more effective marketing
- Staffing levels within the company increase
- Available disk space on servers decreases to low levels
- Delays are experienced when loading web pages
- Technical support reports a high number of "browsers crashing"

There are other indications, but it basically comes down to one of three situations:

1. Expansion of your company requires expansion of the internet system.
2. Increased competition with rivals forces expansion.
3. Management wants improvements in the system.

Whatever your reason is for expanding, you must do so by carefully planning to meet the needs of the audience and your customers. The audience is made up of the people who see your web sites, FTP sites, and so on. Your customers, in this case, are the people who will develop, run, and maintain your internet technology. This includes management.

Eight Steps to Take for Expansion

Following are the suggested steps to take when pursuing expansion of your internet services. You do not need to use this exact approach. Feel free to add and subtract from this list according to your situation.

Step 1: *Gather a list of needs from the customers.* Management, the content providers, and the users of the new technology should all be queried as to their particular needs. For example, the content producers may request particular software packages, timing around another large project, and other critical items. All of this information is gathered by the project manager.

Step 2: *Form a list of goals and objectives.* In a meeting with management and the people driving the implementation of a new internet service, you should list the goals and objectives for this project. These will later be used to establish the performance criteria for the new components of your system.

Step 3: *Research available resources.* You need to know whether the software and hardware exists, or whether it will have to be purchased. Purchased products should be evaluated and tested for appropriateness for this project. Then you have to determine whether enough people, time, and money exist to successfully implement.

Step 4: *Organize the implementation team, set the schedule.* Once a solid plan is established for what is needed, then the implementation team is selected. This team divides up the tasks to be performed and sets the schedule of completion for each objective.

Step 5: *Prototype if necessary.* For large scale expansions, the new technologies and equipment should be put through a prototype test. Take the example of a company integrating the function of copy machines into their intranet. This should be tested on a small scale to avoid large, costly problems.

Step 6: *Set quality criteria.* You need to establish the levels of quality expected from the new system. These are actively monitored, and documented as they are achieved.

Step 7: *Install and test.* The new software and hardware is installed and tested for success against the objectives set for the system.

Step 8: *Evaluate success.* At the end of implementation you evaluate the impact on the total system and the success level of both the total system and the new service. Again, you do not want to loose sight of the existing internet system. Expansions should have no negative impact on the existing system. Where possible, new services should enhance the existing system.

Dickerson County School System wants to expand services

For Dickerson, expansion comes naturally. The initial web site produces a slowly growing audience of parents and students. The staff is a little more hesitant to use the system. Therefore, the IS manager decides to put future emphasis in promotion into targeting the staff of the school system.

The original web site was based on a local internet service provider's server. The amount of traffic and the expected growth of the site brings up the question of whether it is time to move the web pages to the school system's own servers. A wide area network already links the various schools. The introduction of an intranet with the web site would promote staff usage.

However, the IS manager looks at the problem from an analytical approach. The monthly cost of renting the current site is $69. Expanding storage space and adding more services will increase this to $99. The cost of buying the software and hardware needed to install an internet web server that will also create an intranet is about $3,000. The dedicated internet connection would be $200 a month. Clearly, the web site can easily stay at the service provider's location.

Unfortunately, school systems don't always use logic and analysis to make decisions. One of the more aggressive teachers at the high school wrote up a grant proposal for buying the equipment for an intranet and web server. By the time the IS manager was informed of this, the entire School Board had endorsed the project. The cost of the internet connection would not be offset by the grant.

The IS manager now finds himself in a position that is not uncommon in most organizations; the decision has been made for him. This means that the IS manager must now formulate an implementation plan that he doesn't support. The end cost of operations will be twice the predicted cost of staying on the service provider's server. Also, the new equipment and intranet will have to be maintained by the IS manager because the grant didn't cover staffing requirements.

The prevention of this problem in your situation is to keep a political ear to the ground at all times. Also, you should insist that any proposal dealing with computer equipment or the internet should at least be copied to you for comment. Since that is not the case for this IS manager, he must make the best of the situation.

To do this, he will still follow the steps listed above. In this case, the IS manager would survey the needs of the school system, form an implementation team, and proceed with the project.

The Law Firm goes from intranet to internet

The Law Firm's intranet was successful for both training and document control. Soon the firm learned that it was effective to post court dates, pending cases, and other vital information to the intranet. The branch offices of the firm were connected over 128K bps ISDN lines.

The original intranet implementation team was now re-formed to create the expansion team. This team looked over the success of the original intranet. The strengths and shortcomings of the first system were examined. It was found that:

- Capacity needed to be expanded at some points
- 89% of office staff used the system

- 31% of help desk questions involved intranet access
- Information posting was timely and fairly trouble free
- Training had a series of issues to resolve

Looking back at their own objectives, the team decided that the data posting on the intranet was successful and could be left unchanged. Capacity issues seemed to be easy to address. However, the target of 95% of office staff using the system was not achieved, so more effort would be needed to promote the use of the technology. The level of help needed to support the system was lower than expected, so planning for future help support was trimmed back slightly.

The training issue took top priority. To begin with, it was discovered that about one in five people that used the intranet for learning a new topic already spent their entire day at a workstation. These people were simply tired of using computers for all of their work activities. These types of workers would be given traditional training as a means of improving their quality of worklife.

Next, it was suspected that some employees were taking the same training course several times. Each time, they registered as one of their coworkers. This was done so that the participant's coworkers could escape from doing time in training. The team had to rewrite the procedure on training so that a supervisor provided some form of verification that the proper employee took the training.

As for the capacity issue, it was soon discovered that the Detroit office quickly used up the ISDN line during peak hours. The IS manager and the internet implementation team decided on a different way to upgrade the connection. Instead of placing one or two more ISDN lines into service, they leased a full T-1 line on a metered rate from a local phone service company.

The 64K bps sections of the line were bundled into a single 384K bps data line and a dozen voice lines. At each end a channel bus was set up and the T-1 line split between the voice and data needs of the two offices. Now the intranet could be effectively utilized from Detroit while dedicated voice lines also connected the two offices. The result is a lower cost for phone calls and a data line charge rate lower than a dedicated 384K bps ISDN line.

Finally, the committee needed to ask themselves where the firm should go next with the overall system. Discussions with users, management, and current clients came to the following conclusions.

1. An internet presence was needed to offer basic legal advice world wide. If the firm was to survive and grow it needed to compete on a world scale. This would be part of the firm's other strategic goal of forming partners with firms in Europe, Asia, and South America.

2. Customers wanted the capability to access information about their cases at any time of the day or night. By setting up a restricted access area on the internet linked to a database of current activities, any client of the firm would be able to read the current status of their legal matters.

3. Attorneys in the field needed a way to access correspondence and other records from any location. The team discovered that the two most likely locations would either be in court or at home. The system they originally developed for home access through dial-back modems was expanded to more attorneys. The trickier part would be court access because of a lack of available, secure phone lines at the court buildings. Wireless access with heavy encryption technology would be tested.

In this situation, it is the users of the system who are driving its development. The original intranet was seen as one more tool for internal use. Now the users realize that it can be expanded into a competitive tool accessible to the world and also restricted to select audiences.

Avix Manufacturing explores electronic commerce

Avix Manufacturing discovers during the first months of using an internet-based catalog that it is extremely popular with customers. The engineers at various corporations can select the component they need and download the specifications sheet. This helps them to design new products without the delays of dealing directly with an Avix engineer. However, three basic services are quickly requested by the customers.

1. An engineer they can deal with through the internet.
2. The drawings for the parts in a format their CAD systems can use.
3. A way to deal with custom built or totally new parts.

At the same time the internal staff at Avix also makes some demands. They want the following capabilities:

1. To be able to invoice over the internet.
2. The collection of funds over the internet.
3. Documentation of all customer contacts including internet communications.

The IS manager must now form the expansion team and discuss these requirements. The idea is to find the minimal amount of hardware and software that will meet the needs of both customers and internal staff.

This is accomplished by brainstorming systems that can accommodate as many requirements as possible. The first step is to look for items on this list of needs that can be satisfied with existing systems. Take the example of having CAD system formatted drawings of all existing parts and components.

By having a common CAD drawing format, a customer's engineer can insert an Avix part straight into a new product in seconds. Hours of drawing and validating would not be necessary. The customer would benefit and Avix would have another marketing edge. The drawings could be accessed via an FTP file link in the catalog, along with the already existing specifications and further details files.

However, this requires Avix and its customers to settle on a common file format. Some customers are using AutoCAD and others are using proprietary CAD systems. The answer lies in the active surveying of customers for their preference. This can be done through mailings and by posting a feedback form on the Avix site. Users of the site can fill out their first three file format preferences for CAD drawings of the parts. In this way both existing and potential customers can have a say in the matter.

Avix would collect the information and make a determination. For example, they may find that most companies can deal with AutoCAD version 14 format drawings. If enough customers prefer a second type of CAD file, these could also be included in the FTP links.

Now comes the more difficult problem of meeting the remaining requirements. Clearly the customers and internal staff want a wider range of communications using the internet. The remaining five requirements involve communications between Avix and its customers. There has to be a system of free communication that can be documented.

The expansion team breaks down each of the requirements into the different ways it can be satisfied. For example, they considered the idea of making a specific engineer available for comment when a customer is working with a particular part. Obviously any system would involve dividing up the catalog among the engineers on staff at Avix. After that, the following systems are proposed:

- Clicking on a request for further information about a part also sends an E-mail to the affected engineer, who in turn replies with an E-mail asking if the customer needs further assistance.

- An option during ordering is an "I need engineering assistance" option. This notifies the affected engineers and an elected representative calls the customer to start the conversations.

- Customers needing engineering assistance are set up with a private account and access to a special subdirectory on the web site used specifically for communications between an Avix engineer and the customer.

This exercise is repeated for all of the remaining five requirements. The team now looks at the possibilities to see where one approach seems to meet the most requirements. It quickly becomes clear that the best solution to the multiple requirements is to have private accounts for specific customers.

When you control a web server, you have the capability of creating separate virtual directories for each customer. Each of these directories can be set up so that only the IP address of the customer and the affected Avix personnel can gain access. The directories are given the customer's name. For example,

www.avix.com/Ford
www.avix.com/Toyota
www.avix.com/Volkswagen

Inside each of these virtual directories are the services required by the affected audience.

For example, Avix wants to share data and messages with Toyota on a series of parts they regularly order. E-mail, a chat area, and an FTP site allow the engineers to exchange drawings, discuss changes, and place orders for parts. Orders can be secured by filling out the online order form which is custom designed to Toyota specifications. Invoicing of the amounts due from Toyota go out on a form that is E-mailed to the accounts receivable representative responsible for Avix.

All communications are logged and regular backups preserve the messages. E-mails are copied to a subdirectory which also copies the log files. This creates a common area for listing all communications between Avix and Toyota. At the same time, engineers taking phone calls or answering written communications with Toyota use a database to log the contact and response. This is linked to the web site's restricted area. The result is a database of all communications that can be retrieved and sorted.

Engineers at Avix may suddenly discover that Toyota is thinking of sending back some parts because they do not meet a specified stress test. Several engineers recall discussing this with Toyota and agreeing on a waiver for this requirement. By calling up the database and searching for all Toyota communications dealing with part 345EF involving stress questions, they can produce the needed documentation in seconds. This allows them to respond to Toyota very quickly, which in the automotive world can save contracts.

Megalith takes on the giants

When it comes to expansion plans, the unique environment of Megalith means that the company must play for keeps. The company is too large and high profile to settle for the ordinary in its systems. Therefore, the IS manager will lead a series of teams to study the future expansion of the Megalith system.

The original objective of the internet implementation was to coordinate the introduction of web sites and intranets throughout the corporation. Each systems administrator was responsible for his or her particular part of the system. Although successful in implementation, it quickly became obvious that Megalith had created several small presences on the internet instead of a single massive presence.

The corporate information page, the financial services page, and the order entry pages were all run by separate departments. Potential customers had several similar URLs to choose among on search engines. Take the example of a potential customer that needed several Megalith services. A search of the web discovered four distinct Megalith sites.

```
Megalith.com
Sales.megalith.com
investment.megalith.com
megalith.com/customer_service
```

Which of these best applied to the customers' needs? Not only couldn't Megalith answer this question, neither could the potential customer. Clearly, a single, central web site was called for.

However, marketing pointed out that without some sort of "hook" the central site could be overlooked. Therefore, Megalith decided that it needed something so obvious that customers would find the site whether they were looking for it or not. The problem then focused on what to develop that would meet this target.

The IS manager developed a single task force to find the answer. This team was made up of the key decision makers in the company. The IS staff supported this task force by providing information on what brought internet browsers to a specific site. This information would be used to generate ideas that could be explored and tested.

Obviously, some of the information also eliminated ideas. One of the top draws for a site is to offer "adult" material. This was way outside the scope of Megalith's marketing philosophy and rejected at the start. By eliminating the obvious and brainstorming new ideas from the surviving ideas, the task force could create something truly original.

A critical piece of information was obtained in the research by the task force. The audience using the Megalith sites was studied. It was quickly discovered that the customers likely to use a Megalith site were the executives of top companies from around the world. They were seeking out the consulting, financial services, and software products that Megalith produced to make their companies more competitive.

However, the critical piece of information that was discovered was that this audience was almost entirely made up of sports enthusiasts. Therefore, the Megalith team decided that the answers lay in a two-step approach. The company would find and buy out the largest sports coverage site on the internet. Then it would sponsor several key sporting events. On the sports coverage site and during competitions, the new central Megalith web site would be placed in a predominant position.

This type of expansion means that the IS manager will inherit the support staff of the sports site and also have the job of developing the new central site. This central site will link to the existing web sites offered by Megalith. The director of marketing will control URL placement. The director of finance and the lead attorney will handle acquisitions.

Summary

As form follows function in architecture, function follows operations on internet sites. The way your company does business will determine the general direction of your internet system. It will even do this against the tide of new technologies. For example, "push" technology may be your favorite new technology, but if customers are too busy to be "pushed," then another approach will succeed.

This marks the end of our discussion of how to implement an internet connection at your company. The next chapter deals with a separate issue, what to do when the system goes down. The main lesson to learn from the previous chapters is that you cannot be seduced by the software and hardware used by internet systems. They play a very minor role. Your job is to make an internet connection and the accompanying technology a success at your company. As we have seen, that involves defining "success" and then demonstrating that it was achieved.

The first system installed must work the first time and be found valuable by both internal staff and external customers. As we have seen in this chapter, when it is time to expand, expansion can only come on the heels of a successful system. A well-planned internet system allows expansion by having a community of users that demand more from the useful tools that are associated with the internet.

Further References

Creating Killer Web Sites, 2nd Edition, by David Seigel, Hayden Books, 1997.

Internet Search Terms

"Site Announcement" OR "promotion"

"Announcement Services"

"Internet FAX"

"Video conferencing"

Also see the web sites listed in Chapter 16.

Chapter 20
Troubleshooting
the Internet

Despite the best intentions of internet technologies, current operating systems, and modern computer hardware, systems will crash or experience problems on a regular basis. This is a reality you have to anticipate. The focus of this final chapter is on how to prevent these problems, how to react, how to know when to react, and yet still continuously improve your system.

What To Do When the Web Goes Down

Once again we should briefly review the differences between reaction, prevention, and improvement.

Reaction = when a problem forces you to take action.

Prevention = anticipating where a problem may occur and avoiding the situation.

Continuous Improvement = make a system work a little better each day.

In a perfect world you want all three of these activities working together under a single procedure. In the case of an internet system, that means you have a standard reaction plan to follow when a problem is detected. At the same time, you are proactively looking for trouble spots and eliminating as many as possible. The management level of your company also encourages everyone to look for ways to improve the system to make it more effective and efficient with a goal of reducing potential problems.

Let's look at some examples of these in action to see the environment you are trying to create. At the same time, you will see several of the mistakes IS managers currently make in controlling problems.

Let's begin with a discussion of what "detection" means. In many current internet systems and local area networks, problems are detected when the system crashes or when many users start reporting the same difficulty. This is known as the "detection by pain" method of determining you have a problem. This is the least effective method of detection.

A better plan is to take a proactive approach to detection. That is, look for the symptoms of a problem so that the problem can be detected before it takes full effect. For example, before a local area network crashes, several symptoms may occur, such as a slowing down of response times, multiple access errors on the command console, and the like. By watching for these you can try to head off the crash. A problem prevented is cheaper and easier to fix then a problem experienced.

The reaction plans

A good system has multiple levels of reaction plans. In the case of internet technology, one reaction plan is used within the IS department and another is used by other users of the system. Combined with a help desk or technical support center, you form three layers of defense between problems and real trouble.

A reaction plan lays out the steps to be taken in the event of a problem or a serious warning of a problem about to occur. At the IS Department level for internet systems, this would involve the monitoring systems for the servers, routers, hubs, internet connection, and internet related software. The reaction plan is broken down into the following components:

- Description of when to react
- Steps to take, people to notify
- What to document
- How to know that the situation has been corrected

The IS department reaction plan could list several different areas that are to be regularly monitored for signs of trouble. The actual document could be a single procedure, a work instruction for each situation, or a set of instructions at each internet workstation. Let's take the example of a fairly large company with several points in their internet system where monitoring is required.

The reaction plan at each web server may list the following conditions to monitor.

Reaction Plan—Web Servers

The IIS monitoring program is to be active at all times during normal operations. Signs of pending trouble include:

1. Resource usage on the tracking chart above 90%.
2. Message that a Windows NT or IIS service has shut down.
3. Error codes indicated by alarm tones from the server.

When these conditions are encountered take the following steps:

1. Open the server log on the desk and enter the date, time, and description of the problem.
2. For excess resource utilization, redirect IP addresses under 155.xxx.xxx.xx to the backup server. For loss of services, attempt a restart. If that doesn't work check the network connection point for a loose cable. Error codes should be referenced to the appropriate technical guide on the bookshelf above the desk and suggested corrections attempted.
3. Each attempt to correct the situation should be recorded in the server log along with the outcome (either successful or not).
4. If the problem cannot be corrected within 15 minutes—or if the system crashes—notify the systems administrator immediately.
5. Once a problem is corrected, indicate in the server log the steps taken and sign your name.

As you can see, the reaction plan is simple and direct. You tell the operator what to watch for, what to try, and when to call for help. All steps should be documented. This is done to help form future and better reaction plans. The more you record about what goes wrong and what tends to fix the problem, the better you can write your reaction plan.

At the same time, management should be studying these reaction plans and the error logs to determine root causes for the problems. Chronic problems usually indicate the need for management level corrections to the system. For example, a chronic occurrence of resource shortages may indicate that the company's web server needs more resource capability such as increased memory, wider bandwidth, and the like.

At the technical support and help desk level, the technical service people should be armed with a large database of information about what solutions exist for common problems. This area of your corrective action system should have a procedure to follow when people call in with problems.

Trivial or noncomputer problems should be re-routed to the appropriate location. Minor problems should be handled only when major problems are not being addressed. During crunch times at the help desk, you need to indicate to the people with minor problems that a solution will come shortly. Major and critical problems have to be handled immediately.

At the user's level, you can also post reaction plans. Back in the first chapters of this book, we indicated that the company's internet policy could be printed on a small card attached to each computer. On that card you should have enough space left over to print a short reaction plan the user can follow before calling for help.

For example,

> If the browser seems to freeze, check the lower left corner of the screen to see if the status bar is showing that a large graphic or other page element is loading. If so, just wait about a minute and the web page you want should appear.

> If the cursor arrow freezes, check the connection to the front of your machine from the mouse and then try Control, Alt, Delete then Cancel.

> For any other problems, write down the error message and codes, don't alter anything on the computer and call the help desk at extension 541.

As we see here, a few sentences cover the two most common problems reported for a system. Also shown are the fixes that usually work for these problems. Otherwise the user knows what to record and do before calling the help desk.

The reason you post short reaction plans with users is to keep your corrective action system from being constantly overwhelmed. The average manager thinks the job of management is planning, controlling, and implementing policies within a company. In reality most managers spend most of their days putting out "fires." Everyone seems to have a problem and they want the manager to take care of it.

A good manager teaches the staff to handle the small problems by themselves. This is possible by learning the right one or two things to try when a problem is encountered. In the case of an internet system, most problems encountered by users involve the network and the browser. By knowing the first couple of solutions to try, the user can typically solve around three-quarters of all problems without anyone else's help. This keeps a considerable load of minor problems or problems with simple solutions away from the help desk. The result is a more efficient system of corrective action.

Preventive actions

As discussed before in this and other chapters, preventive action is the concept of looking for where trouble *might* happen and eliminating the causes before the problem is experienced. We talked earlier about actively monitoring critical points of your internet system to try and anticipate a problem occurring. Statistical process control charts are good tools for this goal.

Another approach is for you to review the internet system for possible trouble spots. Reading through error logs, looking at documentation created by reaction plans, examining the activities of the help desk, auditing the procedures, and just talking to the people that run or use the system can provide valuable information. However, you will need a way to organize that information and find patterns that indicate weak spots in your system.

One way to do this is to have an "intelligent" database. Information can be entered on the different situations you examine. You make notes on common elements such as:

- Types of problems
- Effects of the problem
- Sources of the problem
- Root cause
- Software, hardware, department, and connection involved
- Time and day of problems

By generating different reports based on the sorting and scoring of each problem, you can start to see patterns. These patterns can reveal everything from clues to potential trouble spots to the solution to your problem.

For example, you may find that your internet connection seems to drop its transmission speed each Wednesday around three in the afternoon. Some investigation may reveal that the ISP is performing upgrades at that time. You can then contact the ISP and tell them to move their activity to a better time of the day.

A classic story of detecting a solution to a problem through this method involved the mystery of the router that would reset at what seemed to be random times. Careful examination of the unit found no faults in the hardware. Replacing the unit had no effect. Then the dates and times of the resets were plotted and showed no occurrence in winter, a lot in spring. The problem was seasonal.

It turned out that the router was located in a distant building high up above the ceiling panels. An alarm message was set for the next time a reset was encountered. When the alarm came, the IS manager ran to the site and discovered that a rain shower had just begun. A small leak in the roof caused water to drip on the power cord, run down to the power supply, and cause light arcing. The router detected the power fluctuations and would shut down to reset. The root cause was the leak in the roof. The leak was fixed and the router ran without problems.

Another approach is to use cause and effect charts. The chronic problem or related set of problems is placed on the right side of the chart. A large arrow leads up to the problem. Several branches come off of the arrow (see Figure 20–1). The theory behind this method is that one or more forces are occurring in your system to cause the problem. In other words, problems are not accidents; the system is somehow set up to cause the problem. Your job is to find the causes that divert your system from its objectives toward the effect (problem).

The major causes are hardware, software, people, management, environment, or measurement. That is:

- Hardware—which equipment or part of the equipment could be the cause.
- Software—which programs, applications, macros, or other software components might be at fault.
- People—could incorrect operation be at fault?
- Management—the procedure or work instruction is not correct or one management mandate interferes with another.
- Environment—heat, humidity, current flows, dust, lighting, radio interference, and so on.

Figure 20-1. Cause and Effect Chart

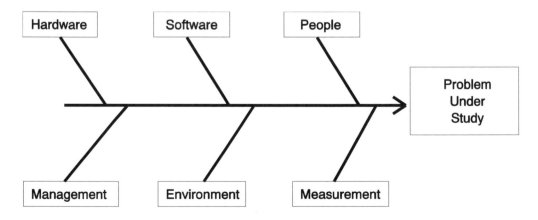

- Measurement—is the system for measuring the situation correct, are false error messages generated or errors going undetected?

All possibilities are listed by a team that is familiar with the problem. Once all of the possible causes are brainstormed, the group looks at existing information and provides their own knowledge to list the ten most likely causes. These are investigated. The ones that prove to be actual causes are eliminated through system changes, redesigns, or other methods. Eventually you eliminate the chronic problem using this proactive method.

Finally, you should have planned for redundancy and backup where you knew the critical services would be located on your system. If Avix is smart they will always have a backup web server with a copy of the company's catalog ready to take over if the first server goes down. The same would be true of the internet connection. In this way, even a massive problem with the internet system at Avix would go undetected by the internet customers.

However, as part of your corrective action system, when you discover chronic problems that are not easily eliminated, then you should, as a last resort, consider redundancy and backup systems. For example, you might discover that the local area network in your company crashes a couple of times a week, knocking out your web servers. The web server should then be replicated through disk-mirroring with a second, free-standing web server hooked to the same internet connection. When the LAN goes down, the backup server goes into action.

Also, you should have a regular system of preventive maintenance. The health of connections, hubs, routers, hard drives, modems, repeaters, and the like should be checked at regular intervals. Hard disks should be regularly defragged and checked for viruses. The continuity of electrical circuits over network lines should be checked. Software settings should be double checked. These and other preventive measures should be carried out to find problems before they become serious trouble and to keep all of your equipment and software in top form.

Another way of performing preventive maintenance is to have a record of the age of all of your equipment and the current version number of all software. In this way you can see that critical pieces of equipment are becoming "old" and might need preventive replacement or preventive upgrading.

Continuous improvement

Finally, you want to continuously improve the working portions of your system as well. If you dedicate all of your corrective action time to fixing problems, the problems will never end. However, if you dedicate some time to constantly improving your system you have a chance of making your job a little easier each day and watching the number of problems steadily decrease.

A considerable portion of this text discusses the importance of continuous improvement and offers suggestions on how to achieve this goal. For corrective action there should be in the related procedures suggestions on how the information being gathered about problems would also note opportunities for improvement. An example can demonstrate how this would work.

Take the reaction plan we listed above for the IS department. Notice how it focuses on when a problem is detected. All we need to do is to highlight when the operator should note that the system is working better than usual. Let's suppose that the resource utilization chart being created by the IIS monitoring program is in place and updated each minute. An operator is working on updating part of the computer's programming. As a precaution, the operator gives the router connected to the internet line more available memory and the ability to act as a partial proxy device. By chance, the operator notices that during the peak period of the day that resource utilization is down significantly.

A quick check of page hits and other usage data reveals that traffic to the site is as heavy as ever. However, the server is handling it without the usual problems. This is a significant improvement in the operation of the system. It should be documented and investigated as diligently as any serious problem would be investigated. What is being detected here is the opportunity for improvement. These should be reported and exploited. This is one path to continuous improvement.

Another path is to prototype and test new ways of delivering the same services. If you have a spare server, router, and test connection to the internet, you can experiment with new software and hardware combinations. Different settings for existing hardware and software can also be tested. Is it better to route IP packets at the ISP or once they reach your routers? How much cache or proxy service is needed for peak performance? These and a hundred other questions can be answered by using properly designed experiments.

Avoiding Micromanagement

One area for an IS manager to avoid is micromanagement. Most IS managers are former technicians, engineers, and other professionals who have had heavy hands-on involvement with computer systems. As such, it is difficult to break the habit of wanting to wade into the hardware or software whenever there is a problem.

Remember that you are a manager. Other people on your staff fix computer problems. Let them do their work. Your role is to ensure that they have the proper resources and time allotments to get the job done.

Someone else does phone work. If your former job involved the installation of phone systems, software, new hardware, or other items, it can be very difficult to convince the people that used to call you for help to call the new person in charge of this function. If you insist on watching your people work or constantly want status reports, you are sending a clear message that you do not trust their abilities or dedication to the task. Therefore, you need to practice the following actions:

- Assign a task to a staff member and don't check on progress more than once.
- Learn how to politely tell senior managers that someone else will be sent to load a new ribbon on their typewriter.
- Set aside specific times for your staff members to be able to discuss "issues" involving current projects.
- Make it clear to staff that getting the job done right the first time is a top priority.
- Be professional at all times.

You can be close to your staff and dedicated to helping them do their jobs more easily. However, you are not trying to be their friend. A clear line of command should exist with an equally clear open path of communication back from your staff. Getting involved with every project and wanting constant status reports is not only bad for staff morale, but a grand waste of your own time.

Creating and Using a "Book of Knowledge"

The question then arises as to how you keep people on target if you are not constantly checking their work. The answer comes from the experiences that are being logged everyday in error log books, reaction plan notes, memos to management, audit results, SPC charts, and other feedback mechanisms.

For every project you engage in, your team builds a considerable number of experiences. Some of these are pleasant and others are not so pleasant. Either way it represents knowledge. To develop a highly effective and continually improving staff, you need to use this knowledge. This can be done through two central mechanisms. Both can be used to respond better and faster to internet problems.

The Book of Knowledge

The first tool is called a book of knowledge. Project teams should keep a running journal of the problems and opportunities they encountered during the project. A good place to start is the project to implement an internet connection for your company. This running journal filled in by various team members builds a record of what problems were encountered and, more importantly, how they were solved.

At the end of the project, you have the team deliver a final report on what happened. In this report they summarize the journal and make suggestions on what they would do differently next time. Doing this creates several advantages for the future.

- New project teams working on similar projects can read the report and the journal to discover procedures they want to perform and pitfalls they want to avoid.
- Trouble-solving teams can look in the journal to find mistakes that may have been made.
- Other project teams can use the report to train new members of the team on what they can expect.
- Management can study the reports to see if many teams in the company seem to run into the same problems. If so, the management systems need adjustment.
- Training personnel can use real-life examples from the journals to highlight the importance of particular parts of technology or skills they are reviewing.

In short, you want living documents that are shared between teams so that all groups continue to learn more about ways of successfully carrying out projects. By proactively using such information, your teams become smarter each day. Even with new members joining and veterans leaving the teams, the teams continue to learn.

Best practices

Throughout this book we have seen the need to have policies, procedures, and work instructions. A good approach with these is to have employees think of these as "best practices." The current procedure for submitting Java applets, for example, can be thought of as the way things are done in your company. However, it should be noted that this is the current "best" way to submit applets for approval. If an employee or team discovers a better way of making submissions it should be considered by management.

If management agrees that the new way is better, faster, cheaper, or more closely integrated to other procedures, then the new way becomes the new "best practice." This leads to several benefits for your company:

- Operations continuously become more efficient and effective.
- Employees feel they are empowered to control their own jobs.
- Quality of work improves.
- The knowledge of all employees is being tapped.
- Management responsibilities are shared.
- People actually have a reason to read the procedures.

In short, this proactive approach is highly recommended. It also works well for developing better reaction plans and procedures for when the internet system goes down.

Finding Help Within the Company

The beginning pages of this book mentioned the current crisis in the lack of qualified people to fully manage computer systems. This leads to the question of where you can find qualified technical people to help keep the system running. The answer, in general, is you cannot find such people.

Instead, you need to locate people as close to your needs as possible and then train them up to the level of expertise you require. Quality computer people can be located coming out of reputable colleges, technical schools, other professions, and other companies. Here is a typical situation.

You need three more technicians that can keep the web and E-mail servers healthy. Unfortunately, that requires someone who knows Windows NT very well, the IIS extremely well, and can work around hardware problems. The difficulty is that anyone with this level of skill wants $60,000 a year or better. Your management will only allow one-half of this rate.

The answer is to contract three students just finishing two-year computer programs at the local community college. The agreement is that you will start them at $26,000 a year and provide them with intensive training to increase their skills. The second year they will make $34,000. After that they will be eligible for senior positions within your department at even higher wages. In essence, if they commit for three or four years of working with your company, you will give them a fair wage and a large set of highly prized skills.

The students should be bright enough to realize that the experience of working with an internet system and obtaining certification or being trained to specific software packages will enhance their value with your company as well as with other companies. In other words, experience and training can be as valuable as money.

Companies such as Novell and Microsoft offer certifications for specific software packages. By paying for the training and testing for such certification, you move the inexperienced students to a professional level. In essence, you are designing an apprentice program for your recruits.

Next, you need to build loyalty among the people you do find. If a spouse is sick and in the hospital, you should go and offer any help you can. You should recognize good work and birthdays. Perks, rewards, and other methods of motivation should be used abundantly to make it clear that your workers are valuable members of your team.

The situation to avoid is the one that occurred in the 1980s when the few people who could run both Computer Aided Design and Computer Aided Manufacturing software became a flock of migrating professionals. People with these skills were known to float from one company to another, following ever-increasing pay offers. Consequently, there was a flow of technical people through companies that resulted in a person with two years at a company being the senior person.

Locating Outside Help

As mentioned earlier in this book, it can be equally difficult to locate technical support vendors who are highly qualified, reliable, and able to work with your staff. However, there are other outside sources for help.

The Usenet and discussion groups on the internet provide plenty of information on specific internet topics. When you need to know how to refine your Unix system to best support web servers you go to the Unix web server support group on the internet. Here you can find the names of people that seem to know the technology well. By E-mail communicating with them, you can try to get their cooperation in helping you with specific problems at your company. This is a form of networking with professionals, except that you never see them and your meeting room is the size of the Earth.

A clever method of getting outside help for very little money is to set up or sponsor the local user group for the technology you are using. For example, your local area network may be based on Novell software and web servers. By setting up the local Novell users support group, you get many different experts in a room once a month to discuss the problems. Because you run the group, you set the agenda. The result is that you get your company's problems on the agenda.

Finally, there are sharing arangements that can be set up between companies. For example, two or three companies can band together to contract the full schedule of a particularly talented technician. The technician can come from a technical support company or be on staff with another company.

Megalith would probably engage in the practice of using roving troubleshooters. An individual or small team of highly trained people would move between corporate sites solving major problems. Positions on such teams are actively sought after by other personnel because their activities tend to get the attention of top management.

Keeping Senior Management Happy

Speaking of management, *problems* with the internet system will tend to be what management will notice. Unless you actively publicize to management the success of the system, while suppressing any problems, the overall impression created might be negative. A negative impression left with the people who determine your budget and future with the company is never a good idea.

Management should be kept constantly aware of the activities and benefits of the internet system. The best way to start the process of accomplishing this goal is to make management active participants in its implementation. Once a system is in place, the management team should be one of the first groups to attend training. Few things motivate people to use a new system like seeing the top bosses use it regularly.

Next, you need to keep your immediate boss fully informed on the internet system status. This does not mean a barrage of reports. Instead, you should sit down with your immediate manager and create a list of what items he or she wants to see. Then the key goals and objectives of interest to the rest of the management team should be discussed.

Once a short list of the really critical-to-management issues is determined, you need to establish how these will be monitored and reported. Let's look at an example of how this might be done. Working with your boss you determine that the following issues are of great interest to the management team:

- How many new clients were obtained through the internet?
- How many times was the web page down?

- What percentage of staff is trained to use the system?
- How many mistakes were made processing information through the internet system?
- How fast are we responding to customers?

Let's be a little more specific. Our example this time is an insurance company that uses their web site to take requests for insurance quotes. The information is processed by dividing it up among several people on the corporate intranet. The information is gathered by an account representative who calls the interested party within an hour of the submission of the request to give a firm quote.

The type of measurement information management wants to see includes:

1. The number of new clients each month for whom the internet was their first contact with the company. This is obtained by a note placed on the initial contact form indicating whether a new customer phoned the company, sent a fax, visited an agent, returned a mail solicitation, or used the web page.

2. The total number of minutes per month the web site was not operating. The target is zero.

3. The number of trained staffed members and percentage of total staff required to learn the system. This is reported by the training department. As a nice touch the IS manager then audits class participants one month after training to see how many now use the system regularly on their job.

4. The number of errors reported on internal responses to a quote request. These are counted by the account representative as the number of times a form had to be returned to the sender within the company for correction.

5. The time and date of the quote request is already imprinted on the E-mail message that delivers the information to the company. This is sent to a database file along with the time and date of the entry made by an account representative into the underwriting database on when a formal quote was presented. The difference between these two time periods will be averaged and a standard deviation calculated.

The best approach in this type of reporting situation is to keep it simple and easy to understand. In other words, try to use simple language and graphics. Below is an example report submitted to management by the IS manager.

Monthly Management Report on Status of Internet System

- Number of new clients from the web site: 1,243 (up 16% from last month).
- On July 1, 1998 at noon we had gone 43,565 minutes since our last downtime of the company web page.
- 93% of targeted staff people have taken internet technology training, 98% of these report that they use the system regularly one month after training. We are two weeks ahead on the training schedule.
- 42 errors were reported on internal forms, down 17 from last month but short of our target of zero.

Average response time to quote requests:

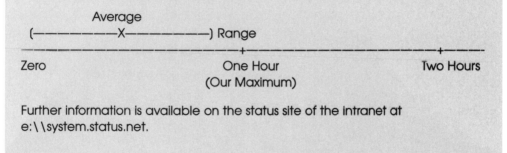

```
               Average
(——————————X——————————) Range
———————————————————————————+————————————————————————+————
Zero                    One Hour                   Two Hours
                      (Our Maximum)
```

Further information is available on the status site of the intranet at
e:\\system.status.net.

Notice the quick and easy way information is presented. Bar charts could have also been used to show the progress of these figures over the past several months. Trends or stagnation would be obvious. The note at the end about a site with a full status report means that this report could be delivered by E-mail and members of management could click through to the site. There they could further investigate the situation on their own. This saves you the need to meet with different managers to explain the numbers.

Providing Additional Training

The last step in introducing the internet to your company is to start your part of the process over again. Now you go back and begin to educate yourself on what is new and what is planned for the internet. In that way, when management comes back to ask for an expansion or incorporation of the internet connection you will be ready to start the implementation process again.

Further References

Always have available the extended technical reference material offered for your software and hardware. For example, a company running Microsoft based software would have books such as:

Microsoft Windows NT Technical Support Training, Microsoft Press.

Microsoft Internet Explorer 4 Technical Support Training, Microsoft Press.

Then there are third-party books on this subject, such as:

Delivering World Class Technical Support, by Lori Laub. John Wiley and Sons, 1996.

Help: The Art of Computer Technical Support, by Ralph Wilson. Addison-Wesley, 1991.

Internet Search Terms

"Technical Support"

"Help Desk"

"Problem-Solving"

Interesting Web Sites

www.helpstar.com (help desk software)

www.naw.org (national association of webmasters)

www.world-webmasters.org

Appendices

Appendix A
Glossary of Technical Terms and Acronyms

ActiveX   Microsoft created program code downloadable by your browser which runs in real time, much like Java applets.

analog   data represented as changes in voltage.

applet   very small Java programs.

Archie   a program used to locate files on the internet.

ASCII or American Standard Code for Information Interchange   a standard way of representing ordinary text as a stream of binary numbers.

ATM or Asynchronous Transfer Mode   a networking standard with greater bandwidth and audio/video capabilities built in.

bandwidth   the maximum speed by which data can be transmitted over a wire or wireless network connection.

bits and Bytes   a bit is the smallest piece of information used by a computer. A byte is made up of 8 bits. A Kilobyte is equivalent to 1024 bytes. A Megabyte is equivalent to 1024 Kilobytes. A Gigabyte is equivalent to 1024 Megabytes.

bookmark   a link set up in a browser to a particular web page or URL.

bridge   a network device that forms a connection between two separate networks and routes all communications regardless of destination (see **router**).

cache   an amount of memory used to store frequently used data. This speeds up the reading of data by holding frequently requested web pages or other information in fast memory.

digital   the use of binary numbers (0s and 1s) to represent data.

"dial-up" account   an internet connection where a phone line is being used to dial into an internet service provider or ISP.

DNS   (Domain Name Service). A program used to link domain names to particular IP addresses.

domain   a unique name that represents each computer on the internet (i.e. 9000.net).

E-mail   (electronic mail). A way to send messages electronically over networks.

encryption   the process of converting data into an unreadable code for everyone except the person with the key to decode the data.

file server   a computer set up to "serve" files to client computers on the network.

firewall   a security system where incoming and outgoing internet traffic is stopped, examined, and then distributed or turned away.

FTP   (File Transfer Protocol). A standardized method for moving files between computers on the internet.

gateway   a computer positioned between your network and the internet connection to control the flow of information into and out of your network to the internet.

Gopher   a computer application for the internet whose purpose is to locate, retrieve and record information from the internet. Developed at the University of Minnesota in 1991.

IEEE   (Institute of Electrical & Electronic Engineers). A source of many communication standards.

Internet Relay Chat   a program that enables many people to type messages to the group in real time.

InterNIC   a service establish to determine the domain names for the internet.

ISDN   (Integrated Services Digital Network). A fast digital phone line that can deliver computer communications, voice, fax, and other data transfers.

Independent Service Provider (ISP)   third-party supplier of internet services to the general public.

Host Computer   a computer that provides a particular service to a user.

HTML   (Hypertext Markup Language). Used to program the look of information presented on web pages.

hypertext   text that can have embedded links to other text, locations, or data sources.

HTTP   (Hypertext Transfer Protocol). Method of exchanging hypertext information over networks.

internet   a network of networks now existing worldwide.

intranet   the technologies and programs designed for the internet being applied in-house on a local area network.

internet domain names   see **domain**.

Internet newsgroups   discussion forums hosted on the internet.

ISP   see **independent service provider**.

JAVA   an interpreted, object-orientated program language with a syntax and structure similar to C++, designed specifically for the internet by Sun Microsystems

LAN   (Local Area Network). A group of computers, peripheral devices, shared printers, and shared directories and files that are linked together.

ListServ   A program that allows you to subscribe to a mailing list which distributes E-mail to the members of the list, typically on a particular subject.

MIME   (Multipurpose Internet Mail Extensions). A standard by which people can send each other E-mail messages that contain files, pictures, videos, sounds, or a host of other objects.

modem   A modulation/demodulation device that converts information from analog to digital and vice versa.

Network news transport protocol (NNTP)   allows your browser to work as internet newsgroups.

Newsgroups   see **internet newsgroups**.

ODBC   (Open Database Connectivity). This allows databases created in programs such as Excel, Oracle, Access, and the like to be linked to web pages.

packets   small bundles of digital information. The size and make up of packets is determined by the protocol being used (i.e. TCP/IP).

PERL   (Practical Extraction and Report Language). Its basic function is in the manipulation of files and text and in producing reports.

POP   (Post Office Protocol). A standard for exchanging E-mail between the internet and a personal computer.

PPP (Point-to-Point Protocol). A method of connecting to the internet over a modem while still using TCP/IP.

proxy server a computer that accesses the internet and gathers requested web pages into a cache memory.

push technology a method of sending information to a user of the internet without the user having to request the data.

router a physical device that is used to link to different networks by routing packets to the appropriate destination (also see **bridge**).

server see **file server**.

SLIP (Serial Line Internet Protocol). A method used to connect a personal computer to the internet using a modem and a connection by a telephone line.

SMTP (Simple Mail Transfer Protocol). A method used to transfer E-mail messages between computers and networks.

TCP/IP protocol IP stands for internet protocol. Transmission control protocol or TCP establishes communications between two computers on a network.

telnet part of the TCP/IP protocol allowing a user to logon to a computer from a remote location.

UNIX a multitasking operating system developed in 1969 and written in the C+ language. It exists in many forms and is probably the most widely used operating system on the internet.

URL (Uniform Resource Locator). A form of pointer that locates information on the internet.

web browser software programs that use the standards and protocols of the internet, especially the World Wide Web, to make it possible for any computer platform to connect with and utilize the internet.

web page An HTML document that contains information which can be seen on the Internet using a browser.

web server A computer with a capability to share files with other computers on a network is called a server. When files being shared are intended for internet content, via the World Wide Web, we call that computer a web server.

World Wide Web a collection of standards and protocols that allow for universal viewing and usage of information.

Y2K   Year 2000. A reference to the problems expected in operating systems and general software that did not account for a four-digit year dating system.

Further information on terminology can be obtained on the internet using the search term "internet term" or "definitions internet OR intranet."

A site dedicated to definitions is at http://www.users.bigpond.com/jenkos/

Example Request for Quote from a Real Network Build Situation

"We gratefully appreciate the contribution of this excellent example of a request for quote from Optimal Solutions, Incorporated, of Grand Rapids, Michigan. Their expertise in build-to-design concepts are well-noted. Readers should contact them directly at (616) 281-6040 or by E-mail at jeff@optimalinternet.com. Their web page is at www.optimalinternet.com."

Thornapple-Kellogg School Data Network System

Design Build

Contents

Public Notice of Request for Proposal

Thornapple Kellogg School is accepting Design/Build proposals from qualified contractors for the final phase of its computer network integration project. Proposals are due Thursday March 5, 1998 at 2:00 PM at the district business office. Bids will be opened and each project total will be read aloud according to the District's construction bid opening process. All bidders are required to submit itemized pricing on the supplied bid forms.

The district's current integrator is Optimal Solutions, Grandville, MI (616) 281-6040. The contact is Jeff Ingle. While the district is pleased with the efforts thus far of Optimal Solutions, District and State guidelines and laws require the district to competitively bid this project.

Bidder Qualifications

Qualified firms must include detailed documentation of their experience, mastery and local staff certifications within their proposals including:

- 3COM Certification in CoreBuilder 6000 (and under) Switching equipment
- 3COM NetBuilder Certification
- Compaq Service Authorization
- Apple Service Authorization
- SoftArc - FirstClass Internet/Intranet groupware "Gold Certification"
- Microsoft Certified Professional with proven Microsoft NT Server expertise
- Microsoft Internet Information Server proven expertise
- Prior K-12 School WAN Experience (3 districts minimum) in similar projects
- The district has a large amount of 3COM equipment. Alternate bidders must document and price the replacement of existing equipment in a manner that all server and/or electronic communications devices are cohesive within the total project implementation. Network management software shall manage all of the data communications system.

Summary of Work

This phase of the project is summarized as follows:

1. Wide Area Network Communications Materials and Integration.
2. Local Area Network Communications Materials and Integration.
3. Cohesive migration from Building-based LAN to District-based WAN.
4. Migration of building-based AppleTalk, IPX, and TCP/IP strategies to District-based Layer 3 Switched AppleTalk, and TCP/IP.
5. Training, on-site support, and telephone support for the system over the next two years (Minimum time for bidding purposes - 250 hours).
   - Windows NT 4.x File Server and IIS
   - 3COM (or bidder equivalent) Network Management and Device Configuration
   - Compaq ProLiant file servers and workstations (Deskpro & Presario)
   - Apple PowerMacintosh 5200 and above workstations
   - Apple PowerMacintosh 8500 File Server and AppleShare 5.x
   - SoftArc FirstClass Groupware Internet/Intranet software
   - Project Management

1 General Bid Conditions

This section outlines general conditions to be met in preparing and submitting a bid proposal.

1.1 *Bid Due Date and Place*

Proposals shall be received no later than 2:00 p.m., local time, March 5, 1998 at the Thornapple-Kellogg Administration Office, 3885 Bender Road. Middleville, MI 49333. Bids will be opened and read at that time.

1.2 *Exceptions and Partial Bids*

Bidder shall address each item in this package as specified. All required labor and equipment must be quoted. Any exception must be noted and explained. All bids must include the entire project. Partial bids will not be considered.

1.3 *Withdrawal of Bid*

Bidders may withdraw their bids at any time prior to opening time of bids and will not be assessed any penalties. Bids must be firm for a period of 60 days.

Summary of Needed Equipment

District Switch

1	Layer 3 Switch
2	Power Supplies
6	100BaseFX Full Duplexed Switch Ports
2	GB Ethernet SX Ports
1	Open Slot for Future Expansion

High School

File Servers

Upgrade 3 Compaq Proliant Servers with GB LX Ethernet Adapter

3   GB Ethernet SX - PCI Adapters

GB Ethernet Switch

1   12 Port GB Ethernet Switch

IDF Switching Equipment

23   Switch with:
       1 - GB SX Port
       Stacking with 2GB Backplane
       2 - 100BaseT Ports
       24 - Switched 10BaseT Ports
       SNMP Management

New Middle School

Move all currently installed and operating High School
Equipment to Middle School

McFall Elementary

MDF Switch

1   Add 100BaseFX Switch Module to owner provided
3 COM LinkSwitch 1000

West Elementary

MDF Switch

1   Add 100BaseFX Switch Module to owner provided
3 COM LinkSwitch 1000

Page Elementary

MDF Switch

1   Add 100BaseFX Switch Module to owner provided
3 COM LinkSwitch 1000

Administration
MDF Switch

1   Switch with:
       1 - 100BaseFX Full Duplexed Port
       2 - 100BaseT Ports
       12 - Switched 10BaseT Ports

Transportation

1   12 Port Hub with 1 10BaseFOIRL
connection to High School

Maintenance

1   12 Port Hub with 1 10BaseFOIRL
connection to High School

1.4   *Rights of Owner*

The Owner reserves the right to waive any formalities to bid, to reject any or all bids, or to accept the bid that is most favorable to the Owner. The Owner does not incur any responsibility for Bidder's costs in preparing the bid proposal.

1.5   *Accuracy of RFP Plans and Diagrams*

Any plans, diagrams, and other descriptive information included with this request are for the purposes of scope, identification, and scheduling only. Dimensions should not be scaled. The Bidder should not use quantities, elevations, measurements, and locations for bidding purposes without field verification.

1.6   *Subcontractors*

The Bidder must list all proposed subcontractors with contracts or purchase agreements in excess of $5,000.00. No single subcontract may exceed 25% of the Lump Sum Bid without written approval of the Owner. Proposed subcontractors must demonstrate qualifications to perform the specified work and must be bound to all contractual obligations to which the Contractor shall be bound. Subcontractors shall provide references to the Owner upon request.

1.7   *Labor Cost Structure*

Labor and management charges and fee structures shall be fixed for the project. The Contractor is required to submit a fixed labor cost structure for the entire project.

1.8   *Award of Contract*

The Contract shall be deemed awarded when a contractual agreement between the Owner and chosen Bidder has been signed by both parties.

1.9   *Questions*

For technical questions contact Kevin Briggs (616) 795-3394. For questions regarding bid procedures, contact Alice Jansma, Thornapple-Kellogg School, (616) 795-3313. Questions regarding this document must be submitted at least seven (7) days before the bid due date to allow written addenda to be issued.

1.10 Addenda

All written addenda become part of this Request for Proposal. Addenda will be mailed, delivered, or faxed to each person or firm attending the bid meeting and will be available for inspection. No addendum will be issued later than three (3) days prior to the bid due date. (Parties not attending the meeting may contact the district to receive bid documents and addenda.)

1.11 Warranty

Warranty on workmanship shall be at least two years from the date the Owner accepts the completed work. The Contractor shall replace such material or installation services if defective, provided notice is given by the Owner within the warranty period.

1.12 Submission Requirements

The proposal must be organized according to the bid forms included with this document. Proposals will be judged according to their conformance with the specified outline. Outside of bid proposal package must clearly indicate which systems are being bid.

1.13 Number of Copies

The Bidder shall provide 3 complete copies of the bid proposal labeled Master, Copy 2, and Copy 3 marked: "Thornapple-Kellogg Data Network Proposal"

1.14 Bid Security

A 5% Bid Bond is required. The bond must be in the form of a certified check or a bond executed by a surety company authorized by the State of Michigan. The amount of the bond shall be forfeited if the Contractor, after being awarded the bid, fails to enter into an appropriate contract with the Owner within (30) days.

1.15 Performance Bond and Payment Bond

Successful bidders, for work valued at $50,000 or more, will be required to secure Performance, Labor and Material Bonds issued for the full amount of the contract by a company licensed to do business in the state of Michigan and having an A.M. Best rating of A- or better. The cost of these bonds are to be included in the proposal amount.

1.16 Bid Proposal Guidelines

Submit bid proposals in a sealed envelope with the bid category clearly identified on the outside. Proposals should be organized in the following manner:

1.16.1	Bid Security	
1.16.2	Bidder's Signature Form	
	Use the form provided for the appropriate bid category:	
1.16.3	Cover Letter	
	Begin the proposal with a cover letter introducing yourself and your company.	
1.16.4	Executive Summary	
	Include a concise description of the proposed solution.	
1.16.5	Technical Summary	
	Document your plan for accomplishing the issues listed in section 3 (pages 10 & 11) of the request for proposal.	
1.16.6	Topology Drawing	
	Include a color-coded network layout of the proposed system	
	1.16.5.1	Each Building
	1.16.5.2	WAN Connections
1.16.7	Product Literature	
	Include literature for all proposed equipment. Clearly highlight portions of product literature intended for your proposal. Cross out information not part of this bid.	
1.16.8	Bidder Response Forms	
	Include the forms supplied in Appendix A. (Forms are also available on diskette in Microsoft Office 97 format.) Forms are identified by project in the header by the left margin. Fill out only those forms that pertain to the projects being bid.	

1.17 No Bid Situation

The Owner requests a brief cover letter from contractors who choose not to bid on the project. Receiving this letter will ensure that your company will remain on the district's bid list. Address a brief cover letter to:

Thornapple-Kellogg School
Data Network Proposal
3885 Bender Road
Middleville, MI   49333

1.18 Bid Evaluation

Bids will be evaluated and weighted according to the following criteria:

    1.18.1   Compliance with Proposal Requirements
- a) Bid Bond
- b) Proposal Format
- c) Thoroughness
- d) Bill of Material

    1.18.2   Experience
- a) Scale of Projects
- b) Institutional Experience
- c) References

    1.18.3   Equipment Quality & Design
- a) Architecture
- b) Performance
- c) Dependability
- d) Ease of Use
- e) Extensibility
- f) Cost

    1.18.4   Base Bid
- a) Support Fees
- b) Maintenance Costs

1.19 Shipping

F.O.B., Thornapple-Kellogg School

2   Definition of Work

2.1   Wide Area Network Communications Electronics

Contractor will provide workstation integration, training, and on-site support for the total computer communications system. This includes both pre-owned equipment and new equipment as proposed by each bidder. Single and mul-timode fiber-based WAN Links currently being installed link the districts' buildings as follows:

    2.1.1   High School
            The high school is the campus hub for the building-to-building network. The enclosed topology map indicates the dis-

tricts' currently owned equipment in addition to equipment needed.

a) Page Elementary (Remote Building)
b) West Elementary (Remote Building)
c) McFall Elementary (Remote Building)
d) New Middle School (Remote Building)
e) Transportation/Bus Garage (Remote Building)
f) Administration (Remote Building)

2.1.2   Old Middle School
The Old Middle School will be connected to the WAN as an IDF from McFall Elementary School.

2.2   Local Area Network Equipment

2.2.1   New Middle School
The new middle school will be ready for network electronics installation and workstation integration in conjunction with the construction schedule. The district is planning to move the equipment currently installed at the high school to this new facility.

Bidders should be aware and include in their proposals labor for moving and installing this owned equipment at the new middle school in conjunction with construction progress. It is anticipated that the building will be ready for the migration of this equipment in October 1998.

Configure port-based security to servers and printers for students and staff. Configure VLANs to prevent physical access to unauthorized devices. Allow building network administrators global access to district network resources.

2.2.2   Middle School Cabling
Optimal Solutions is currently preparing the low voltage data, telephone, and video cabling bid specifications for the new middle school. It is expected that the bid for this work will be made publicly available in April/May 1998. Optimal Solutions will not be bidding on the cabling project.

2.2.3   Existing High School
The high school plans to take advantage of the newly adopted 802.p and 802.q standards set forth recently by the IEEE. The district has determined that these new standards will help the ease of administration and security of the network with

the district's most sophisticated users. For this reason, it has been determined that the district will migrate the data communications equipment from the high school to the new middle school and install new equipment complying to the newly adopted 802.p and 802.q standards.

2.2.4 Elementary Schools
The elementary schools have existing LAN equipment, AppleShare file servers, and PowerMacintosh workstations. The three elementary schools require a high speed connection to the network core (high school).

Additionally, bidders are required to provide file server software upgrades to AppleShare 5.x (migrating from AppleShare 4.2.1). Each AppleShare 5.x server shall also provide DHCP services to Macintosh and Windows based workstations.

2.2.5 Transportation/Bus Garage
The transportation and bus garage will have less than 8 computers and printers connected to the network.

2.2.6 Administration Building
The administration building ownes 6-8 computers, 2-3 Network Printers, and one Novell Internetware (4.11) File Server. The district plans to migrate access of the RANDS financial management software to school administrators.

2.2.7 Existing Middle School
Future long range plans for the existing middle school facility are uncertain. The requirements are to connect the middle school to the WAN via McFall Elementary. Bidders should treat the existing middle school as an IDF off McFall's MDF.

3 Design Documentation Requirements

TK requires each bidder to submit a plan for migrating the existing building-based management LAN topology to the requested district based WAN topology. Bidders shall use the current and requested topology maps in preparing their proposals. Bidders electing to submit an alternate bid must include documentation and associated pricing for migrating to their solution.

Within their bid proposal Bidders shall document strategic descriptions and pricing for the following:

3.1 Network Topology

Include overall network topology drawing. Include segmentation plans.

3.2 Installation Plans

Include a strategy for installation.

3.3 Physical Segmentation Design

Switching and collision domain design within physical segmentation.

3.4 Logical Segmentation Design

Configuration of multiple VLANs with multi-protocol, Layer 3 routing.

3.5 IPX Routing

Configuration of IPX routing between VLANs. Integrate all IPX-based file servers. Configure SAP filtering to hide the Administrative server from educational users.

3.6 AppleTalk Routing

Configuration of AppleTalk routing and zone assignment between VLANs. Integrate all AppleTalk resources into routing processes. Configure AppleTalk filtering to hide Administrative resources from educational users.

3.7 IP Routing

Configuration private IP networks between VLANs and integration with existing proxy server (Windows NT) and Internet routers. Configure and integrate all IP-based file servers into IP routing processes. Configure dynamic addressing within each network.

3.8 File Server Security

Method to prevent student access to unauthorized File Servers.

3.9 Printing Security

Method to prevent student access to unauthorized printers in offices, labs, and other buildings (PowerMacintosh, Windows 95, Windows NT).

3.10 *Desktop Security*

Remote Access Validation and Security; remote workstation network access strategies.

3.11 *AppleShare Upgrades*

AppleShare 4.2.1 to AppleShare IP (5.x) upgrade at 3 elementary schools. Implementation of DHCP services.

3.12 *User Account Creation*

Strategy for creating the following user accounts on Windows NT servers:

3.12.1   Student Accounts at High School

3.12.2   Staff Accounts at High School

3.12.3   Staff Accounts at New Middle School

3.13 *FirstClass Mail Server Configuration*

SoftArc FirstClass Intranet groupware migration from LAN and modem gateway configuration to WAN configuration.

3.14 *Workstion Configuration Strategy*

3.14.1   Workstation configuration and printer access deployment of all office computer systems (45)

3.14.2   10 lab workstations at each elementary and middle school lab

3.14.3   10 lab stations in each of two high school labs, 5 teacher computers at each school.

3.14.4   Building and district level computer personnel will observe the processes so that they can complete the installation of the remaining systems.

3.15 *Network Management*

Network Management equipment, training plans, and remote Internet based administration strategy.

3.16 Remote Administration

Internet secure access for remote administration (equipment and services).

3.17 Schedule

Project Timeline and milestone identification.
>   3.18   Project Management Strategy

4   Migration of Systems

Bidders will notice in the existing topology drawing that each building has an independent network. The purpose of this section is to aid bidders in their preparation.

4.1   Table of Existing Systems

The following table shows the existing equipment at each building along with current protocol and network addressing configurations.

School	Server(s)	AppleTalk	IPX	TCP/IP	WAN Connection
High School	NT 4.0	None	Yes	Subnetted Class C from REMC 8 & Merit	To Administration
Administration	Internetware (4.11)	Yes	Yes	Subnetted Class C from REMC 8 & Merit	To High School
Page Elem.	AppleShare 4.2.1	Yes	No	No	None
West Elem.	AppleShare 4.2.1	Yes	No	No	None
McFall Elem.	AppleShare 4.2.1	Yes	No	No	None
Old Middle School	AppleShare 4.2.1	Yes	No	No	None
Maintenance & Bus Garage	None	None	None	None	None

4.2   Table of Requested Systems

The following table shows the new equipment proposed for each building along with targeted protocol and network addressing configurations.

School	Server(s)	Apple Talk	IPX	TCP/IP Addressing	WAN Connection
High School	NT 4.0 (Staff) NT 4.0 (Student) Intranet (FirstClass) Internet (MS IIS) NT 4.0 (MS & Elem. Staff)	Yes	Yes	Bidder Design	WAN Core
Administration	Internetware (4.11)	Yes	Yes	Bidder Design	To High School
Page Elem.	NT 4.0 (Staff) AppleShare 5.x (Student)	Yes	Yes	Bidder Design	To High School
West Elem.	NT 4.0 (Staff) AppleShare 5.x (Student)	Yes	Yes	Bidder Design	To High School
McFall Elem.	NT 4.0 (Staff) AppleShare 5.x (Student)	Yes	Yes	Bidder Design	To High School
New Middle School	NT 4.0 (Staff) AppleShare 5.x (Student)	Yes	Yes	Bidder Design	To High School
Maintenance & Bus Garage	None – Access HS Staff Server	No	Yes	Bidder Design	To High School

4.3 Student User Requirements

Below are the application and network access requirements for student users.

  4.3.1 High School

   a) Network Applications

   - Internet IP Address (TCP/IP through Microsoft ISS DNS Server)
   - Access to Windows '95 Start Menu through authenticated Network Login
   - NetScape Communicator
   - Microsoft Explorer
   - SoftArc FirstClass Intranet Client
   - Existing CD ROM Tower - Various Windows '95/NT CD ROMs

   b) Local Applications

   - Microsoft Office
   - Subject Area Curriculum Software as determined by PDC and BDC group level authority.

   c) Network Storage

   - Students will save and access documents and applications according to their server privileges.

4.3.2   New Middle School
a) Network Applications
- Internet (TCP/IP through Microsoft ISS DNS Server or AppleShare 5.x IP Server)
- NetScape Communicator
- Microsoft Explorer
- CD ROM Tower Access - Access to applications housed in currently owned Optical Access International CD ROM Towers connected to AppleShare File Servers.

b) Local Applications
- ClarisWorks
- Subject Area Curriculum Software as determined by building administrators (approximately 250 MB, 20 Applications)

c) Network Storage
- Students will save and access documents and applications according to their server privileges.

4.3.3   Elementary Schools
a) Network Applications
- Internet (TCP/IP through Microsoft ISS DNS Server or AppleShare 5.x IP Server)
- NetScape Communicator
- Microsoft Explorer
- CD ROM Tower Access - Access to applications housed in currently owned Optical Access International CD ROM Towers connected to AppleShare File Servers.

b) Local Applications
- ClarisWorks
- Subject Area Curriculum Software as determined by building administrators (approximately 250 MB, 20 Applications)

c) Network Storage
- Students will save and access documents and applications according to their server privileges.

4.4 *Staff User Requirements*

Staff shall have access to all student resources. Additionally, they shall have access to the staff resources as indicated in table 4.2.

5 Equipment Specifications

Listed below are the minimum specifications for each component of the data network system.

5.1 District MDF Switch (Network Core)

5.1.1   Layer 3 Switching at Wire Speed. 3.5m packets per second.

5.1.2   Supports Layer 3 Switching of AppleTalk, IPX, IP.

5.1.3   Supports 802.p and 802.q IEEE Standards.

5.1.4   Supports VLAN implementation of existing 3Com SuperStack II LinkSwitch 1000 series switches (or replaces this equipment).

5.1.5   Supports ATM OC/12, GB Ethernet SX, 100BaseFX Full Duplex.

5.1.6   Operates above 95 degrees Fahrenheit.

5.1.7   Dual - Load Balancing Power Supplies.

5.1.8   Managed by same manufacturer's network management software.

5.2 High School MDF GB Ethernet Switch

5.2.1   GB Ethernet Switch Supporting SX connections for server farm and IDF Switch uplinks.

5.2.2   Minimum 12 Switched GB Ethernet Ports.

5.2.3   Non-Blocking Backplane.

5.2.4   Supports GB Ethernet SX Uplink from District Layer 3 Switch.

5.2.5   Supports 802.p and 802.q IEEE Standards

5.2.6   Managed by the same manufacturer's network management software.

5.3 High School IDF Switches

5.3.1   GB Ethernet SX Uplink from MDF GB Switch.

5.3.2   24 Switched 10BaseT Ethernet ports.

5.3.3   Wire Speed Switching.

5.3.4   100BaseTX Switched Port.

5.3.5   Managed by the same manufacture's network management software.

5.4 *Elementary School Switch Upgrades*

5.4.1   Upgrade or replacement of 3COM SuperStack II LinkSwitch 1000.

5.4.2   Duplexed 100BaseFX Multimode Backbone connection to District Switch.

5.4.3   Managed by the same manufacturer's network management software.

5.5 *Hubs*

5.5.1   No additional hubs will be needed for this implementation. All high school connections shall be switched.

5.6 *Network Management*

5.6.1   Network Management Software must manage all proposed network communications equipment.

5.6.2   In addition to managing the product within the scope of this project, system must manage existing 3COM 3C509 ethernet adapters.

5.6.3   Network Management Software must operate under Windows NT or Windows 95 operating system.

5.6.4   Network Management Software must support remote administration through the internet setting off alerts at the integrator's location for alerts and failures.

School	Existing File Server	New Server Equipement Needed	Existing MDF Switch	New MDF Switch Needed	Existing IDF Switch	New IDF Switch Needed	Existing Hubs
High School	Student (NT) - Proliant 5000	GB LX PCI Card	Move to New Middle School - 1 - 3COM LS 3000 FX (5 Port)	1 - Layer 3 Switch	Move to New Middle School - 5 - 3COM LS 1000 (12 Port) with GB Ethernet SX	23 - 24 Port Switch with 24 10MB Ports, 2 - 100BaseT Ports, 1 GB Uplink to MDF, Config. to 2 GB Backplane with other switches in each IDF	Move to new Middle School
	CD ROM Tower	None		1 - 12 Port GB Switch			
	Staff Elem. & MS (NT) - Proliant 3000	GB LX PCI Card		1 - 12 port 10/100 Switch with GB Ethernet SX Uplink			
	Staff H.S. (NT) - Proliant 3000	GB LX PCI Card		1 - Network Management Workstation			
	FirstClass & Intranet (NT)	None		1 - Network Management Software			
McFall Elem	PowerMacintosh 8500 with AppleShare 4.2.1	Upgrade to AppleShare IP Server & DHCP	1 - 3COM LinkSwitch 1000	Full Duplex FX Module	None	None	8 - 3COM 12 Port FMS II
West Elem	PowerMacintosh 8500 with AppleShare 4.2.1	Upgrade to AppleShare IP Server & DHCP	1 - 3COM LinkSwitch 1000	Full Duplex FX Module	None	None	8 - 3COM 12 Port FMS II
Page Elem	PowerMacintosh 8500 with AppleShare 4.2.1	Upgrade to AppleShare IP Server & DHCP	1 - 3COM LinkSwitch 1000	Full Duplex FX Module	None	None	8 - 3COM 12 Port FMS II
New Middle School	PowerMacintosh 8500 with AppleShare 4.2.1	Upgrade to AppleShare IP Server & DHCP	1 - From High School	None	5 - From High School	None	20 - From High School
Admin	Admin - (NetWare 4.11) Proliant 1200	None	None	1 - 12 Port 10/100 Switch with 100BaseFX Duplexed Module	None	None	1 - 3COM 12 Port FMS II
Transportation	None	None	None	1 - 12 Port 10Base T Hub with Fiber Transceiver	None	None	None
Bus Garage	None	None	None	1 - 12 Port 10Base T Hub with Fiber Transceiver	None	None	None

Thornapple Kellogg Wide Area Network - Proposed by Optimal Solutions Inc.

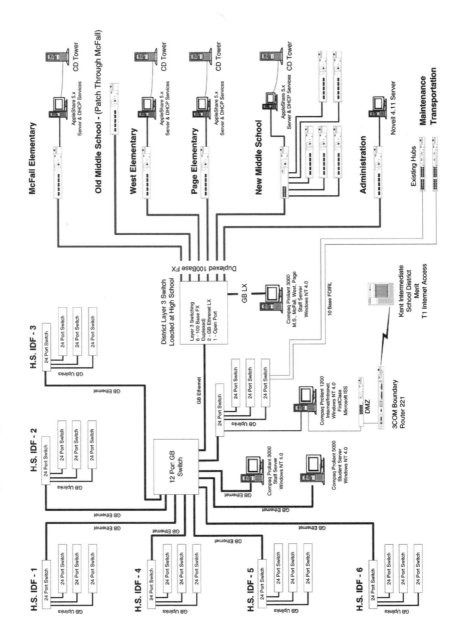

Appendix C
Key Internet Resource Sites

The Internet is a dynamic and changing world. It includes many helpful sites for further research into the topics covered in this book. Some of these sites will move, change, or vanish as time passes. The search terms at the end of each chapter can be used to find new sources of information. Otherwise, try out some of these sites, especially those that offer links to related information.

Hardware

Workstations:

IBM—www.ibm.com

Sun—www.usec.sun.com

Digital—www.workstation.digital.com

Compaq—www.compaq.com

HP—www.hp.com

Communication/Networks:

3Com—www.3com.com

Arescom—www.arescom.com

Bay Networks—www.baynetworks.com

Cisco Systems—cio.cisco.com

Novell—remote.novell.com

Xyplex—www.xyplex.com

Qualcomm—www.qualcomm.com

Software

Servers:

Apache—www.apache.org

Netscape—home.netscape.com/download

Linux—www.redhat.com

IIS—www.microsoft.com/iis

Internet Fax:

Xchange for Fax—www.ntxc.com/product/ixf.htm

Support Groups

Administration:

Webmaster—webbusiness.cio.com

Wilson Internet Services—www.wilsonweb.com/articles

Portland's Windows NT User Group—www.ntique.org

Advanced Practice Council—www.simnet.org/public/cofi/apc.html

Society for Information Management—www.simnet.org

Web Based Management—
www.mindspring.com/~jlindsay/webbased.htm

Training:

BPR OnLine Learning—www.prosci.com

New Tools for Teaching—ccat.sas.upenn.edu/jod/teachdemo

Computer College Silicon Valley—www.ccsv.com

First Train for the Internet—www.firsttrain.com

Key Point Software—www.keypoint.com

MentorNet—www.mentornet.com

Web Academy—www.webacademy.com

Security Issues:

Security Archives—
www.cs.purdue.edu/coast/archive/data/catagory_index.html

NIST Computer Security Clearinghouse—csrc.ncsl.nist.gov

Data Interchange Standard—www.disa.org

Info Systems Audit and Control Assoc.—www.isacany.org

Internet Security Policy—csrc.nist.gov/isptg

Control and Audit—www.arts.uwaterloo.ca/ACCT/CCAG

Virus Software—oracle.uvision.com/idx/SOFTWARE

Windows NT Security—www.isacany.org/ntdoc-1.htm

Technical Support

Purchasing:

Procurement Guide—www.mpt.go.jp/Procurement

DOE Acquisition Guide—www.pr.doe.gov/dear.html

Computer Manager Magazine—www.compumgr.com

Further Reading

Online Magazines:

CIO—www.cio.com

Electronic Software Publishing—www.elsop.com

IT Update—www.itworks.be/ITUpdate

Computer Weekly—www.computerweekly.co.uk

InfoWorld—www.infoworld.com

Information Week—techweb.cmp.com

OnLine Magazine—www.onlineinc.com

Budgets:

Cal Poly Intranet Budget—www.intranet.csupomona.edu/~intranet

Budget Intranet—www.wcmh.com/lantimes/96jun/606s047a.html
Policies:

Example Internet Policies—
gopher://riceinfo.rice.edu:1170/00/More/Acceptable/

Web Page Design:

Amazing Web Sites—www.amazingsites.com

Power Promotion—deadlock.com/promote

How to Promote—www.samizdat.com

Search Engines—northernwebs.com/set/

Secrets of Searching—www.best.com/~mentorms/e_measure.htm

Web Marketing Today—www.wilsonweb.com/webmarket

Web Promotion—www.tka.co.uk/magic/promote.htm

An Invitation to Form a Users' Group of IS Managers

As you probably realized by reading through this book, the largest problem facing IS managers today is a need for real management training and techniques in the IS department. Therefore, here is an invitation to visit our web site,

www.9000.net

Here, consultants and others will discuss the topics and issues affecting today's IS manager. We will also answer questions you may have after reading this book. The information gathered there will help update the contents of this book and to post further information on critical topics.

In the future, there may a moderated discussion group or mailing list just for IS managers. The web site will have details.

Index